International Debt Statistics 2016

International Debt Statistics 2016

WORLD BANK GROUP

1 2 3 4 18 17 16 15

ISBN (paper): 978-1-4648-0681-0
ISBN (electronic): 978-1-4648-0682-7
DOI: 10.1596/978-1-4648-0681-0
ISSN (paper): 2310-2667
ISSN (electronic): 2310-2675

Cover design: Jomo Tariku, World Bank Group
Cover image by Jomo Tariku, World Bank Group

Library of Congress Cataloging-in-Publication Data has been applied for

Table of Contents

Preface

This year's edition of *International Debt Statistics*, successor to *Global Development Finance* and *World Debt Tables*, and the fourth in the series, is designed to respond to user demand for timely, comprehensive data on trends in external debt in low- and middle-income countries. It also provides summary information on the external debt of high-income countries and public (domestic and external) debt for a select group of countries.

The World Bank's Debtor Reporting System (DRS), from which the aggregate and country tables presented in this report are drawn, was established in 1951. *World Debt Tables*, the first publication that included DRS external debt data, appeared in 1973 and gained increased attention during the debt crisis of the 1980s. Since then, the publication and data have undergone numerous revisions and iterations to address the challenges and demands posed by the global economic conditions.

Presentation and access to data have been refined to improve the user experience. The printed edition of *International Debt Statistics 2016* now provides a summary overview and a select set of indicators, while an expanded dataset is available online (datatopics.worldbank.org/debt/ids).

By providing comprehensive and timely data that reflects the latest additions and revisions, and by expanding the scope of the data available online, we aim to serve the needs of our users and to reach a wider audience. Improvements in data dissemination are matched with ongoing efforts to improve the quality and timeliness of data collection. In partnership with the major providers of debt data management systems to low- and middle-income countries, the Commonwealth Secretariat (COMSEC) and the United Nations Conference on Trade and Development (UNCTAD), we are working toward an established standard code and a set of system links that will enable countries to provide their DRS reports electronically in a seamless and automated data exchange process.

As these changes take place, we welcome your feedback and suggestions for further improvements at data@worldbank.org.

Haishan Fu
Director, Development Data Group

Acknowledgments

This volume was prepared by the Financial Data Team of the Development Data Group (DECDG), led by Evis Rucaj under the management of Neil Fantom, and comprising Parul Agarwal, Peter Bourke, Cynthia Nyanchama Nyakeri, Malvina Pollock, Rubena Sukaj, Sun Hwa Song, Rasiel Vellos, and Alagiriswamy Venkatesan, who worked closely with other teams in DECDG. The team was assisted by Elysee Kiti. The overview of current developments was prepared by Malvina Pollock, Evis Rucaj, and Rasiel Vellos in consultation with the staff of DECDG; country economists reviewed the data tables. The work was carried out under the direction of Haishan Fu. Valuable advice was provided by the Operations and Strategy unit of the Vice Presidency.

The production of this volume was managed by Azita Amjadi. The online database was prepared by Shelley Fu and William Prince. International Debt Statistics electronic products were prepared by a team led by Malarvizhi Veerappan under the supervision of Soong Sup Lee and comprising Prasanth Alluri, Rajesh Danda, Jean-Pierre Djomalieu, Ramgopal Erabelly, Shelley Fu, Ancy Kachappilly, Gytis Kanchas, Karthik Krishnamoorthy, Ugendran Machakkalai, Vilas Mandlekar, and Nacer Megherbi. The cover was designed by Jomo Tariku. Susan Graham, Jewel McFadden, and Nora Ridolfi from the Publishing and Knowledge Division of the World Bank coordinated the publication and dissemination of the book.

User Guide to Tables

International Debt Statistics 2016 focuses on financial flows, trends in external debt, and other major financial indicators for low-, middle-, and high-income countries. The report includes more than 200 time series indicators from 1970 to 2014 for most reporting countries. This edition of *International Debt Statistics* (IDS) has been reconfigured to offer a more condensed presentation of the principal indicators, along with additional tables showcasing Quarterly External Debt Statistics and Public Sector Debt.

Tables

Aggregate Tables

The aggregate tables are labeled by region name. Data are shown for all low- and middle-income countries and six regional groups (East Asia and Pacific, Europe and Central Asia, Latin America and the Caribbean, Middle East and North Africa, South Asia, and Sub-Saharan Africa).

Country Tables

Country tables are labeled by country name and ordered alphabetically. Data are shown for 120 low- and middle-income countries that report public and publicly guaranteed external debt to the World Bank's Debtor Reporting System (DRS). The tables also include key debt ratios and the composition of external debt stocks and flows for each country.

Each table shows a time series with the most recent six years, as well as 2000 and 2006 as companion years. Full time series data are available for all countries in the World Bank's Open Data website (http://data.worldbank.org/data-catalog/international-debt-statistics).

Statistics

The general cutoff date for countries to report data for this publication was end-September 2015. The economic aggregates presented in the tables are prepared for the convenience of users. Although debt ratios can give useful information about developments in a debt-servicing capacity, conclusions drawn from them will not be valid unless accompanied by careful economic evaluation.

The macroeconomic data provided are collected from national statistical organizations, which in some cases may be subject to a considerable margin of error. The usual care must be taken in interpreting the ratios, particularly for the most recent years, because figures may be preliminary and subject to revision.

Notes at the bottom of each country table summarize major events that have taken place in the country in recent years; describe the sources of information for short-term and private nonguaranteed external debt if the reports were not provided by the country; and highlight main issues in the data collection process. Unless otherwise specified, data on long-term public and publicly guaranteed external debt for 2014 are based on reports provided by the country.

More detailed information on data sources, methodology, and compilation is provided in the appendix at the back of this book.

Aggregate Measures for Income Groups and Regions

Aggregate measures for income groups and regions include the 120 low- and middle-income countries that report public and publicly guaranteed external debt to the World Bank's DRS, whenever data are available. The aggregate "All low- and middle-income countries" is the sum of data for 120 countries.

Classification of Countries

For operational and analytical purposes, the World Bank's main criterion for classifying countries is gross national income (GNI) per capita (calculated by the *World Bank Atlas* method). Every country is classified as low-income, middle-income, or high-income. Low- and middle-income countries are sometimes referred to as developing countries. The term is used for convenience; it is not intended to imply that all countries in the group are experiencing similar development or that other countries have reached a preferred or final stage of development. Because GNI per capita changes over time, the country composition of income groups may change from one edition of *International Debt Statistics* to the next. Once the classification is fixed for an edition, based on GNI per capita in the most recent year for which data are available, all historical data presented are based on the same country grouping.

Symbols

0 or 0.0 means zero or small enough that the number would round to zero at the displayed number of decimal places.

.. means that data are not available or that aggregates cannot be calculated because of missing data in the years shown.

$ indicates current U.S. dollars unless otherwise specified.

User Guide to IDS Online Tables

The extended version of country tables that were previously available in the *International Debt Statistics* print edition is now available online. Using an automated query process, these reference tables will be updated based on the revisions to the International Debt Statistics database.

Users can access all the online tables, download the PDF version of the publication, view the report as an eBook on ISSUU, as well as access the database and download the archived editions of the publication by going to http://data.worldbank.org/products/ids.

How to Access IDS Online Country Tables

To access the IDS online tables, visit http://datatopics.worldbank.org/debt/ids and select from "Country," "Region," or "Topic" options.

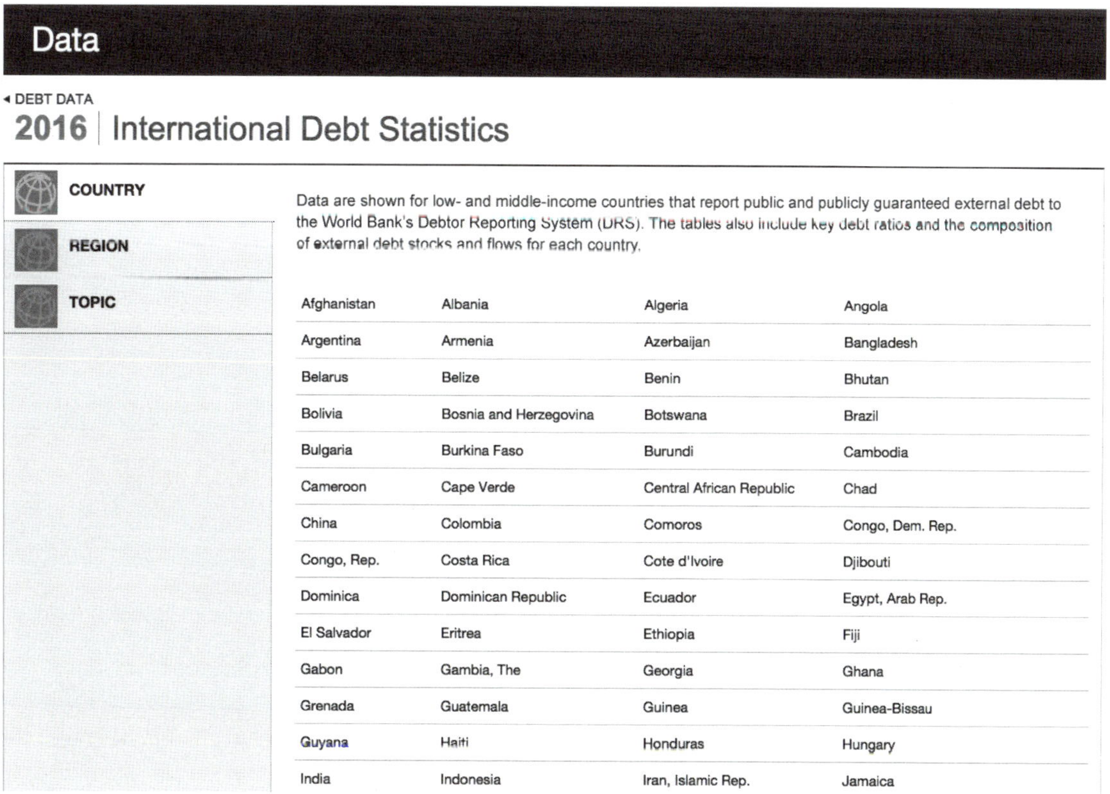
Data

◂ DEBT DATA

2016 | International Debt Statistics

COUNTRY

REGION

TOPIC

Data are shown for low- and middle-income countries that report public and publicly guaranteed external debt to the World Bank's Debtor Reporting System (DRS). The tables also include key debt ratios and the composition of external debt stocks and flows for each country.

Afghanistan	Albania	Algeria	Angola
Argentina	Armenia	Azerbaijan	Bangladesh
Belarus	Belize	Benin	Bhutan
Bolivia	Bosnia and Herzegovina	Botswana	Brazil
Bulgaria	Burkina Faso	Burundi	Cambodia
Cameroon	Cape Verde	Central African Republic	Chad
China	Colombia	Comoros	Congo, Dem. Rep.
Congo, Rep.	Costa Rica	Cote d'Ivoire	Djibouti
Dominica	Dominican Republic	Ecuador	Egypt, Arab Rep.
El Salvador	Eritrea	Ethiopia	Fiji
Gabon	Gambia, The	Georgia	Ghana
Grenada	Guatemala	Guinea	Guinea-Bissau
Guyana	Haiti	Honduras	Hungary
India	Indonesia	Iran, Islamic Rep.	Jamaica

To access a specific country table directly without going through the above landing page, use the URL http://datatopics.worldbank.org/debt/ids/ and the country code (for example, http://datatopics.worldbank.org/debt/ids/country/DZA to view the table for Algeria). Similarly, to view the regional table, click on the "Region" tab and select one of the listed regions (for example http://datatopics.worldbank.org/debt/ids/region/SAS to view the table for South Asia).

2016 | International Debt Statistics

Data > Data Topics > Debt Data > Country Tables > Algeria

$ millions, unless otherwise indicated	2009	2010	2011	2012	2013	2014
1. Summary external debt data						
External debt stocks	6,246.4	7,405.5	7,246.0	6,044.8	5,495.3	5,231.3
Long-term external debt	4,744.5	4,034.6	3,622.5	3,063.6	2,448.8	2,058.1
Public and publicly guaranteed	3,300.6	3,053.1	2,655.0	2,245.6	1,626.9	1,437.6
Private nonguaranteed	1,443.9	981.6	967.5	818.0	821.9	620.5
Use of IMF credit	198.1	1,878.4	1,845.2	1,839.5	1,841.5	1,845.2
Short-term external debt	1,303.7	1,492.5	1,778.2	1,141.6	1,205.0	1,328.0
of which Interest arrears on long-term	0.0	0.0	0.0	0.0	0.0	0.0
Official creditors	0.0	0.0	0.0	0.0	0.0	0.0
Private creditors	0.0	0.0	0.0	0.0	0.0	0.0
Memo: principal arrears on LDOD	0.0	0.0	0.0	0.0	0.0	0.0
Official creditors	0.0	0.0	0.0	0.0	0.0	0.0
Private creditors	0.0	0.0	0.0	0.0	0.0	0.0
External debt flows						
Disbursements	675.1	211.3	42.9	30.0	28.5	22.0
Long-term external debt	675.1	211.3	42.9	30.0	28.5	22.0
IMF purchases	0.0	0.0	0.0	0.0	0.0	0.0
Principal repayments	1,058.0	909.6	557.4	535.7	741.7	459.3
Long-term external debt	1,058.0	909.6	557.4	535.7	741.7	459.3
IMF repurchases	0.0	0.0	0.0	0.0	0.0	0.0
Net flows	171.2	-509.6	-228.8	-1,142.3	-649.8	-314.2
Long-term external debt	-382.8	-698.4	-514.5	-505.7	-713.2	-437.2
Short-term external debt	554.1	188.7	285.8	-636.6	63.4	123.0
Interest payments	193.7	145.7	118.8	103.6	123.1	73.0
Long-term external debt	161.2	123.5	94.9	80.2	103.1	50.7
IMF charges	1.6	4.3	5.9	2.0	0.5	2.4
Short-term external debt	30.8	17.9	18.0	21.4	19.4	19.9
Net transfers on external debt	-22.5	-655.4	-347.6	-1,245.9	-772.9	-387.3

Indicators

The indicator codes for each of the indicators online and in the publication are listed below. To view a specific indicator online, go to http://data.worldbank.org/indicator/ and add the indicator code at the end of the url; for example, to view a page for total debt stocks, this line should be in your browser: http://data.worldbank.org/indicator/DT.DOD.DECT.CD

1. SUMMARY EXTERNAL DEBT DATA

External debt stocks	DT.DOD.DECT.CD	**External debt flows**	
Long-term external debt	DT.DOD.DLXF.CD	**Disbursements**	DT.DIS.DLTF.CD
Public and publicly guaranteed	DT.DOD.DPPG.CD	Long-term external debt	DT.DIS.DLXF.CD
Private nonguaranteed	DT.DOD.DPNG.CD	IMF purchases	DT.DIS.DIMF.CD
Use of IMF credit	DT.DOD.DIMF.CD	**Principal repayments**	DT.AMT.DLTF.CD
Short-term debt	DT.DOD.DSTC.CD	Long-term external debt	DT.AMT.DLXF.CD
interest arrears on long-term	DT.IXA.DPPG.CD	IMF repurchases	DT.AMT.DIMF.CD
		Net flows	DT.NFL.DECT.CD
		Long-term external debt	DT.NFL.DLXF.CD
Memorandum items		Short-term external debt	DT.NFL.DSTC.CD
Principal arrears on long-term	DT.AXA.DPPG.CD	**Interest payments (INT)**	DT.INT.DECT.CD
Long-term public sector debt	DT.DOD.DPPG.CD	Long-term external debt	DT.INT.DLXF.CD
Long-term private sector debt	DT.DOD.PRVS.CD	IMF charges	DT.INT.DIMF.CD
Public & publicly guaranteed commitments	DT.COM.DPPG.CD	Short-term external debt	DT.INT.DSTC.CD

2. OTHER NON-DEBT RESOURCE FLOWS

Foreign direct investment (net equity inflows)	BX.KLT.DINV.CD.WD
Portfolio equity flows	BX.PEF.TOTL.CD.WD

3. CURRENCY COMPOSITION OF PUBLIC AND PUBLICLY GUARANTEED DEBT (%)

Euro	DT.CUR.EURO.ZS
Japanese yen	DT.CUR.JYEN.ZS
Pound sterling	DT.CUR.UKPS.ZS
Swiss franc	DT.CUR.SWFR.ZS
U.S. dollars	DT.CUR.USDL.ZS

4. AVERAGE TERMS OF NEW COMMITMENTS

Official creditors	
Interest (%)	DT.INR.OFFT
Maturity (years)	DT.MAT.OFFT
Grace period (years)	DT.GPA.OFFT
Private creditors	
Interest (%)	DT.INR.PRVT
Maturity (years)	DT.MAT.PRVT
Grace period (years)	DT.GPA.PRVT

5. MAJOR ECONOMIC AGGREGATES

Gross national income (GNI)	NY.GNP.MKTP.CD
Exports of goods, services, and primary income	BX.GSR.TOTL.CD
Personal transfers and compensation of employees	BX.TRF.PWKR.CD.DT
Imports of goods, services, and primary income	BM.GSR.TOTL.CD
Primary income on FDI (payments)	BX.KLT.DREM.CD.DT
International reserves	FI.RES.TOTL.CD

6. RATIOS

External debt stocks to exports (%)	DT.DOD.DECT.EX.ZS
External debt stocks to GNI (%)	DT.DOD.DECT.GN.ZS
Debt service to exports (%)	DOD.DECT.GN.ZS
Short-term to external debt stocks (%)	DT.DOD.DSTC.ZS
Multilateral to external debt stocks (%)	DT.DOD.MLAT.ZS
Reserves to external debt stocks (%)	FI.RES.TOTL.DT.ZS
Current account balance	BN.CAB.XOKA.CD
Reserves to imports (months)	FI.RES.TOTL.MO

7. LONG-TERM EXTERNAL DEBT

Debt outstanding and disbursed	DT.DOD.DLXF.CD	Interest payments	DT.INT.DLXF.CD
Public and publicly guaranteed	DT.DOD.DPPG.CD	**Public and publicly guaranteed**	DT.INT.DPPG.CD
Official creditors	DT.DOD.OFFT.CD	Official creditors	DT.INT.OFFT.CD
Multilateral	DT.DOD.MLAT.CD	Multilateral	DT.INT.MLAT.CD
of which: IBRD	DT.DOD.MIBR.CD	of which: IBRD	DT.INT.MIBR.CD
IDA	DT.DOD.MIDA.CD	IDA	DT.INT.MIDA.CD
Bilateral	DT.DOD.BLAT.CD	Bilateral	DT.INT.BLAT.CD
Private creditors	DT.DOD.PRVT.CD	Private creditors	DT.INT.PRVT.CD
of which: Bonds	DT.DOD.PBND.CD	of which: Bonds	DT.INT.PBND.CD
Commercial banks	DT.DOD.PCBK.CD	Commercial banks	DT.INT.PCBK.CD
Private nonguaranteed	DT.DOD.DPNG.CD	Private nonguaranteed	DT.INT.DPNG.CD
of which: Bonds	DT.DOD.PNGB.CD	of which: Bonds	DT.INT.PNGB.CD
Disbursements	DT.DIS.DLXF.CD	**Principal repayments**	DT.AMT.DLXF.CD
Public and publicly guaranteed	DT.DIS.DPPG.CD	Public and publicly guaranteed	DT.AMT.DPPG.CD
Official creditors	DT.DIS.OFFT.CD	Official creditors	DT.AMT.OFFT.CD
Multilateral	DT.DIS.MLAT.CD	Multilateral	DT.AMT.MLAT.CD
of which: IBRD	DT.DIS.MIBR.CD	of which: IBRD	DT.AMT.MIBR.CD
IDA	DT.DIS.MIDA.CD	IDA	DT.AMT.MIDA.CD
Bilateral	DT.DIS.BLAT.CD	Bilateral	DT.AMT.BLAT.CD
Private creditors	DT.DIS.PRVT.CD	Private creditors	DT.AMT.PRVT.CD
of which: Bonds	DT.DIS.PBND.CD	of which: Bonds	DT.AMT.PBND.CD
Commercial banks	DT.DIS.PCBK.CD	Commercial banks	DT.AMT.PCBK.CD
Private nonguaranteed	DT.DIS.DPNG.CD	**Private nonguaranteed**	DT.AMT.DPNG.CD
of which: Bonds	DT.DIS.PNGB.CD	of which: Bonds	DT.AMT.PNGB.CD

8. DEBT STOCK-FLOW RECONCILATION

Total change in external debt stocks	DT.DOD.DECT.CD.CG
Net flows on external debt	DT.NFL.DECT.CD

9. DEBT STOCK-FLOW RECONCILATION

Total amount rescheduled	DT.DXR.DPPG.CD
Total amount forgiven	DT.DFR.DPPG.CD
Debt buyback	DT.DSB.DPPG.CD

10. CONTRACTUAL OBLIGATIONS ON OUTSTANDING LONG-TERM EXTERNAL DEBT

Official creditors	
Principal	DT.AMT.OFFT.CD
Interest	DT.INT.OFFT.CD
Private creditors	
Principal	DT.AMT.PRVT.CD
Interest	DT.INT.PRVT.CD

How to Use the DataBank

DataBank (http://databank.worldbank.org) is an online web resource that provides simple and quick access to collections of time series data. It has advanced functions for selecting and displaying data, performing customized queries, downloading data, and creating charts and maps. Users can create dynamic, custom reports based on their selection of countries, indicators, and years. All these reports can be easily edited, shared, and embedded as widgets on websites or blogs. For more information, see http://databank.worldbank.org/help.

Actions

Click to share the table using either the embed code or the URL

Click to edit and revise the table in DataBank

Click to export all metadata to Excel

Click to export the table to Excel

Click to export the table and corresponding indicator metadata to PDF

Click to print the table and corresponding indicator metadata

Click to access the IDS Online Tables Help file

PART I
Overview

Introduction

International Debt Statistics 2016 presents data and analysis on the external debt of low- and middle-income countries for 2014, based on actual flows and debt-related transactions reported to the World Bank Debtor Reporting System (DRS) by 120 low- and middle-income countries. The *International Debt Statistics 2016* provides users with comprehensive stock and flow data on the external debt of individual low- and middle-income countries and for regional and analytical groupings and data on aggregate net capital flows (debt and equity) in 2014. In addition, *International Debt Statistics* (IDS) showcases other debt data collected and compiled by the World Bank. These include the high-frequency, quarterly data for high-income and low- and middle-income countries reported to the joint World Bank–International Monetary Fund (IMF) Quarterly External Debt Statistics (QEDS) and to the Public Sector Debt (PSD). The main messages from the 2014 data are:

(a) Net debt flows to low- and middle-income countries were $464 billion in 2014, a decrease of 18 percent from the comparable figure for 2013. The decline was driven down by a precipitous fall in net short-term debt flows that fell 60 percent to $72 billion ($188 billion in 2013).
(b) Net equity inflows, $668 billion, were 7 percent higher than the 2013 level propelled by a 4 percent increase in net foreign direct investment and robust portfolio equity flows, which were up 29 percent. Aggregate net financial flows totaled $1,132 billion, 5 percent lower than 2013, but stable when measured relative to low- and middle-income countries' gross national income (GNI) at 5 percent.
(c) External debt burdens in low- and middle-income countries remained moderate. The ratio of external debt to GNI averaged 22 percent in 2014, and the ratio of external debt to exports averaged 79 percent. International reserves stood at 114 percent of external debt stocks.
(d) Countries reporting to the QEDS and PSD confirm that external debt levels in high-income countries are, on average, much higher than those of low- and middle-income countries, but that government debt-to-GDP ratios moderated in 2014.

Trends in Debt Stocks and Flows, 2014

Debt stock accumulation slowed to 7 percent in 2014

Figure O.1 External Debt Stock of Low- and Middle-Income Countries, 2009–14

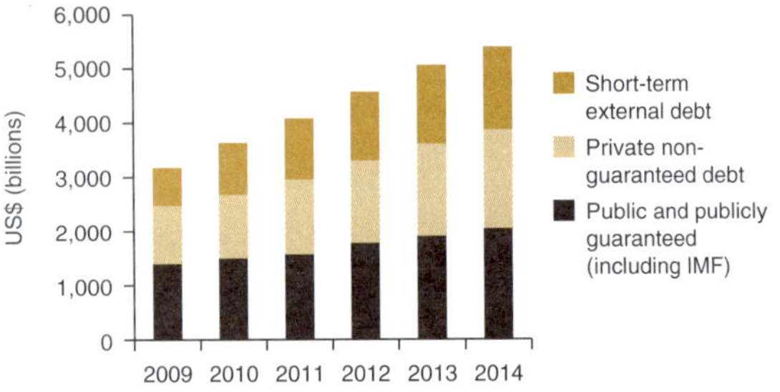

Source: World Bank Debtor Reporting System.

The total debt outstanding to low- and middle-income countries rose 7 percent in 2014, compared with an 11 percent increase recorded in 2013, and driven largely by the much slower rate of accumulation of short-term debt stocks. They rose only 5 percent compared with 15 percent in 2013. Public and publicly guaranteed debt and private non-guaranteed debt stocks increased at much the same pace, 9 percent and 7 percent, respectively. The combined stock of external debt of low- and middle-income countries rose from \$5.1 trillion in 2013 to \$5.4 trillion at the end of 2014. This reflects net debt inflows of \$464 billion, debt forgiveness, and the effect of year-on-year exchange-rate adjustments between local currencies and the U.S. dollar (approximately one-third of the debt of low- and middle-income countries is denominated in U.S. dollars). The stock of long-term debt at end 2014 was divided somewhat evenly between public and publicly guaranteed and private non-guaranteed debt. Short-term debt, as a share of total debt outstanding was 28 percent, unchanged from 2013.

Net debt flows fall 18 percent as short-term debt inflows contract sharply

Figure O.2 Net Debt Flows to Low- and Middle-Income Countries, 2009–14

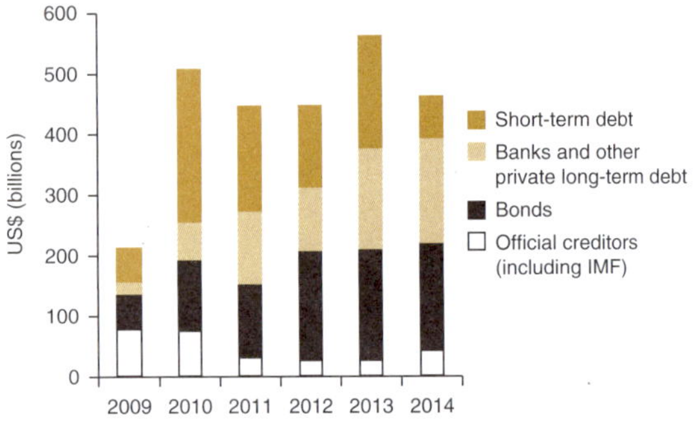

Source: World Bank Debtor Reporting System.

Net debt flows totaled \$464 billion in 2014, 18 percent lower than the comparable figure for 2013, driven almost entirely by a 62 percent drop in net short-term debt flows, which fell to \$72 billion (\$188 billion in 2013). Net debt inflows from official creditors (including the IMF) were \$44 billion, up over 50 percent from their 2013 level; but as a share of total net debt inflows, it remained small. Private creditors accounted for 91 percent of net debt inflows in 2014. Long-term debt inflows from private creditors held steady at \$349 billion, thanks to another record year for bond issuance and resilient commercial bank flows. Viewed from the borrower perspective, there was a noticeable change in the composition of debt inflows from private creditors in 2014. The sharp contraction in short-term inflows reduced their share of debt flows to 17 percent in 2014, from approximately 35 percent in 2013. With regard to long-term debt inflows, just over 50 percent went to non-guaranteed private sector borrowers in 2014 as compared with 62 percent in 2013.

External debt burdens remain moderate

Figure O.3 Key Debt Indicator Trends in Low- and Middle-Income Countries, 2000–14

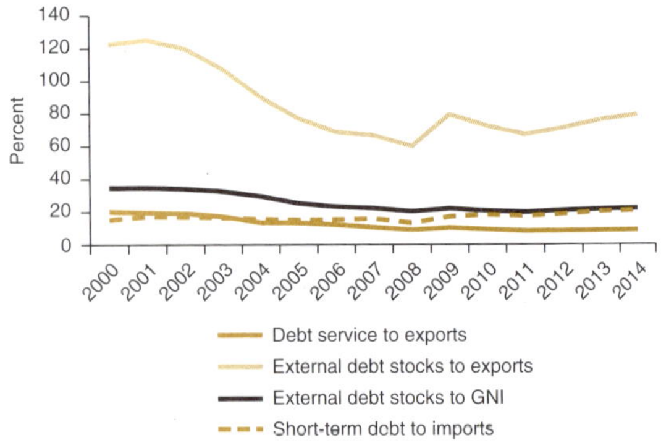

Sources: World Bank Debtor Reporting System and International Monetary Fund.

The majority of low- and middle-income countries have seen the ratio of outstanding external debt to GNI and to export earnings stay relatively steady: an average of 22 percent of GNI and 79 percent of export earnings at end 2014, broadly in line with 2013 and sharply below the comparable ratios for 2000 (35 percent and 123 percent, respectively). Risks associated with short-term debt (28 percent of external debt stocks) were mitigated by international reserves in excess of total external debt stocks, 114 percent at end 2014. There has been a significant improvement in external debt servicing capacity over the past decade as a consequence of increased export earnings, debt restructuring, and outright debt relief from official and private creditors, primarily in the context of the Heavily Indebted Poor Countries (HIPC) Initiative and the Multilateral Development Relief Initiative (MDRI). Additionally, an increasing number has been able to access international capital markets and secure attractive borrowing terms. The debt service-to-export ratio averaged 9 percent in 2014, a marginal increase over its 2013 level but less than half the 20 percent recorded in 2000.

Aggregate Financial Flows to Low- and Middle-Income Countries, 2014

Net financial flows fall 5 percent in 2014 and net short-term debt inflows plunge

Net financial flows, debt and equity combined, totaled $1,132 billion in 2014, 5 percent lower than 2013. The decline was driven by a precipitous fall in net short-term debt flows, which fell by over 60 percent in 2014 to $72 billion ($188 billion in 2013). Net equity flows rose to $668 billion, 7 percent higher than their 2013 level, propelled by a 4 percent increase in net foreign direct investment and robust portfolio equity inflows, up 29 percent above their 2013 level, to $93 billion. China was dominant, accounting for 51 percent of net equity flows to low- and middle-income countries in 2014 and for 42 percent of the contraction in net short-term debt inflows. Low- and middle-income countries, other than China, saw a slightly higher (6 percent) decline in net financial flows in 2014 to $706 billion, with net equity flows rising only 2 percent and net debt inflows down by 12 percent to $379 billion.

Figure O.4 Net Financial Flows, Debt and Equity, 2009–14

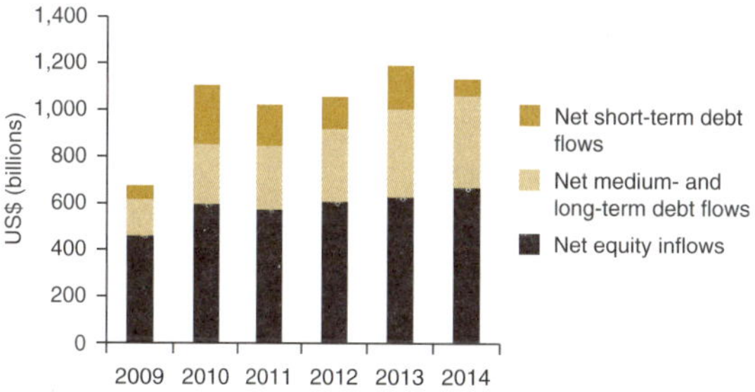

Sources: World Bank Debtor Reporting System, International Monetary Fund, and Bank for International Settlements.

Foreign direct investment was half of net financial flows but the recipient country picture is mixed

Foreign direct investment proved resilient, accounting for slightly over half of net financial inflows in 2014. This is consistent with UNCTAD's *World Investment Report 2015*,[1] which finds that low- and middle-income countries were the destination for more than half of global foreign direct investment in 2014. Investors continue to be attracted by improved business and regulatory environments, growth prospects, and buoyant and expanding domestic markets. The net inflow of foreign direct investment was $576 billion in 2014, 4 percent higher than the 2013 level ($555 billion) with half of these inflows directed at China. Elsewhere the picture was mixed. In Brazil, the second largest recipient of foreign direct investment after China, net inflows were up 38 percent in 2014. In contrast, in Mexico they fell back to their 2012 level, reflecting the one-off nature of the record $20 billion 2013 purchase of Grupo Modelo by AM-Bev Belgium. Countries in Sub-Saharan Africa recorded the sharpest contraction in net foreign direct investment inflows in 2014 (18 percent), while those in South Asia enjoyed the most rapid (17 percent) increase.

Figure O.5 Net Foreign Direct Investment Inflows to Major Recipients, 2013 and 2014

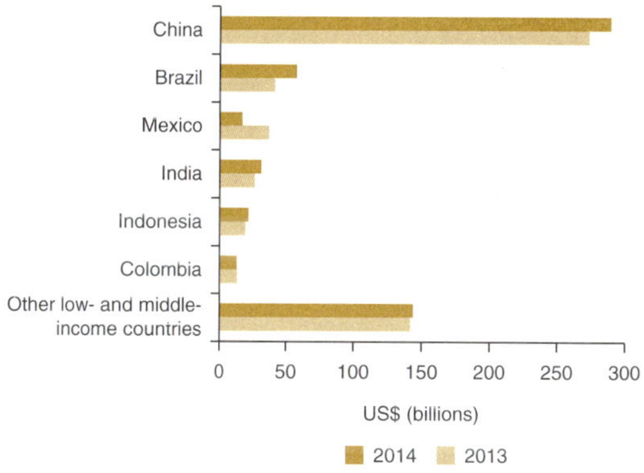

Source: International Monetary Fund.

Portfolio equity flows remain strong but highly concentrated in a small number of countries

Portfolio equity flows rebounded in 2014 to $93 billion, on a par with the 2012 level and up 29 percent over the comparable figure for 2013 ($72 billion). Investors sought emerging markets perceived as offering high returns, leading to some diversification in the destination of portfolio equity flows but, in general, they remained highly concentrated in only a handful of low- and middle-income countries. China was the destination of choice and absorbed 56 percent of portfolio equity flows in 2014, with Brazil and India each accounting for an additional 12 percent. Trends were diverse with China recording a 58 percent rise in net portfolio equity flows in 2014 to $52 billion; India a 40 percent ($12 billion) decline; and Brazil net inflows of $12 billion, unchanged from 2013. Portfolio equity flows were susceptible to political turmoil, as exemplified by strong outflows from Thailand and Ukraine. Concerns over economic prospects also led to a downturn in oil-exporting countries like Nigeria.

Figure O.6 Net Inflow of Portfolio Equity to Major Recipients, 2012–14

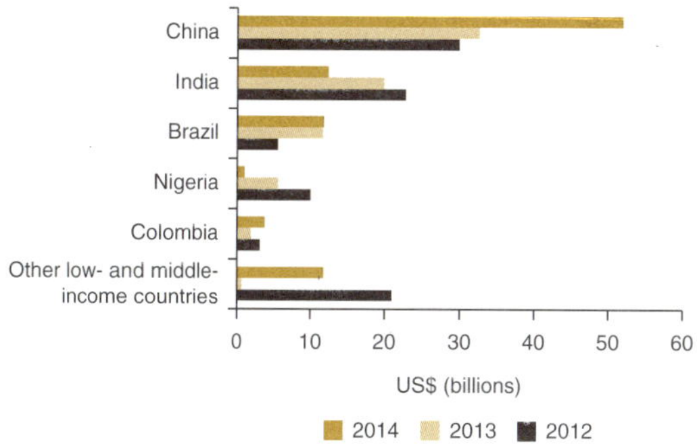

Source: International Monetary Fund.

1. UNCTAD (United Nations Conference on Trade and Development). 2015. *World Investment Report 2015: Reforming International Investment Governance*. New York and Geneva: UNCTAD.

Highlights

All Low- and Middle-Income Countries

Brazil and China command a major share of net debt inflows in 2014

Figure O.7 Net Debt Flows for Select Country Groups, 2013 and 2014

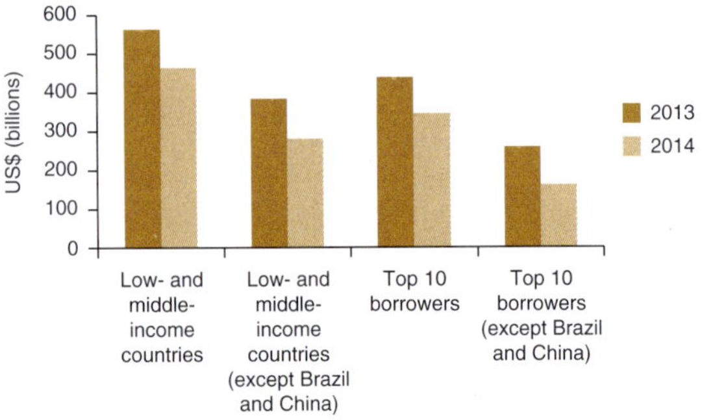

Source: World Bank Debtor Reporting System.

Forty percent of the combined net debt inflows to low- and middle-income countries in 2014 went to just two countries, Brazil and China. Together they received $183 billion but there was a sharp difference in the evolving trend. Net debt flows to China registered a 37 percent decline, whereas in Brazil the comparable flows soared to $98 billion, 120 percent higher than the 2013 level. For the top ten borrowers, measured on the basis of end 2014 external debt stocks, combined net debt inflows dropped 27 percent, although collectively the top ten commanded 74 percent of net debt flows to low- and middle-income countries in 2014. When Brazil and China are excluded, the decline in net debt flows to the remaining eight countries in the group in 2014 was an even steeper 37 percent, largely on account of the precipitous fall in net debt flows to Malaysia and Thailand. Low- and middle-income countries, excluding the top ten borrowers, saw net debt flows drop by only 5 percent in 2014. This was in large part attributable to a much lower level of volatility in short-term debt flows.

Across regions the composition of net debt inflows varies considerably

Figure O.8 Regional Composition of Net Debt Flows 2014

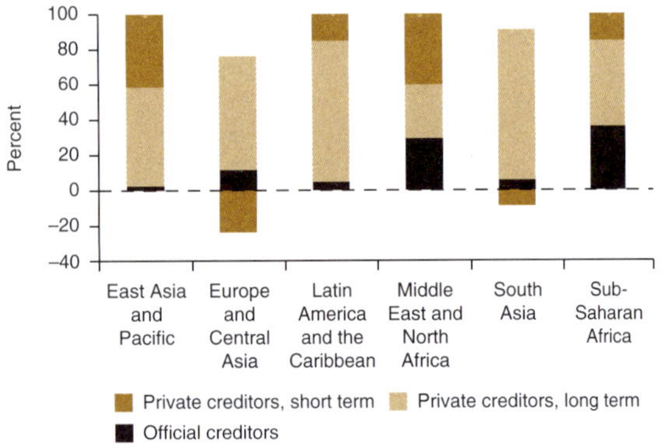

Source: World Bank Debtor Reporting System.

Debt flows to low- and middle-income countries comprise long-term flows from official creditors and long- and short-term flows from private creditors. In 2014 the composition of net debt flows was: official creditors 9 percent, private creditors (long-term) 75 percent, and (short-term) 15 percent. At the regional level, the composition varied considerably. Net inflows from official creditors constituted 36 percent of net debt inflows to Sub-Saharan Africa and 30 percent to countries in the Middle East and North Africa; in other regions the share was negligible. Private creditors accounted for 97 percent of net debt inflows to East Asia and Pacific and 95 percent to Latin America and the Caribbean. Short-term inflows accounted for over 40 percent of net debt inflows in East Asia and Pacific and the Middle East and North Africa regions, but only 15 percent in Latin America and the Caribbean. In contrast, the Europe and Central Asia and South Asia regions recorded an outflow of short-term debt in 2014.

Private sector external borrowing accounts for the greatest share of net debt flows

Figure O.9 Composition of Net External Debt Flows by Type of Borrower, 2009–14

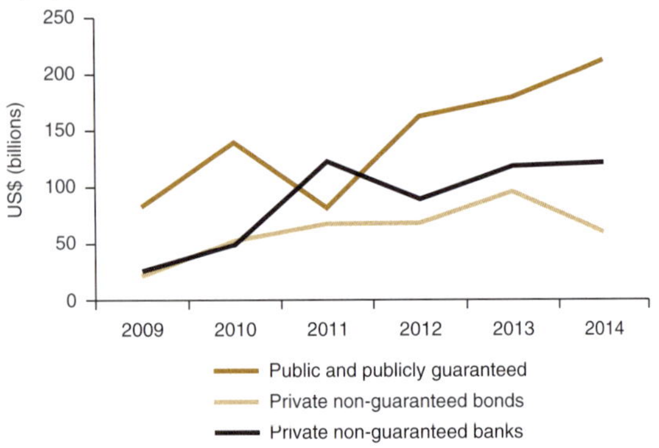

Source: World Bank Debtor Reporting System.

In recent years the external debt of low- and middle-income countries has become increasingly characterized by an important shift from public and publicly guaranteed debt to non-guaranteed debt of the private sector. Since 2009, over 50 percent of net long-term debt flows have gone to private sector borrowers not benefiting from any public guarantee, and as a result, at end 2014 they accounted for close to 50 percent of all outstanding long-term external debt of low- and middle-income countries. Paralleling this rise has been an evolution in the composition of these flows, with bond issuance by private sector entities constituting an increasingly important component: it averaged 44 percent of net long-term debt inflows to private sector entities in 2013–14 as compared to 35 percent in 2012. Net debt flows to private sector borrowers are heavily concentrated in countries in the East Asia and Pacific and Latin America and Caribbean regions, which accounted for 67 percent of these flows in 2014.

Bond issuance continues apace

Bond issuance remained an important source of external financing for many low- and middle-income countries, totaling $242 billion in 2014, up marginally from 2013. There was an important shift in borrower composition and in the regional distribution. Bond issuance by public sector borrowers rose 32 percent to $146 billion, equivalent to 60 percent of total bond issuance in 2014 (46 percent in 2013). A principal driver was the purchase of domestically issued bonds by non-residents, in particular in India, a 25 percent increase in issuance by borrowers in Latin America and the Caribbean, and a 29 percent rise in sovereign bonds in Sub-Saharan Africa, including debut sovereign issues by Ethiopia and Kenya. Bond issuance by corporate borrowers fell 25 percent, reflecting a sharp slowdown in issuance by corporations in Latin America and the Caribbean and Europe and Central Asia.

Figure O.10 Bond Issuance by Public and Private Sector Borrowers, 2013 and 2014

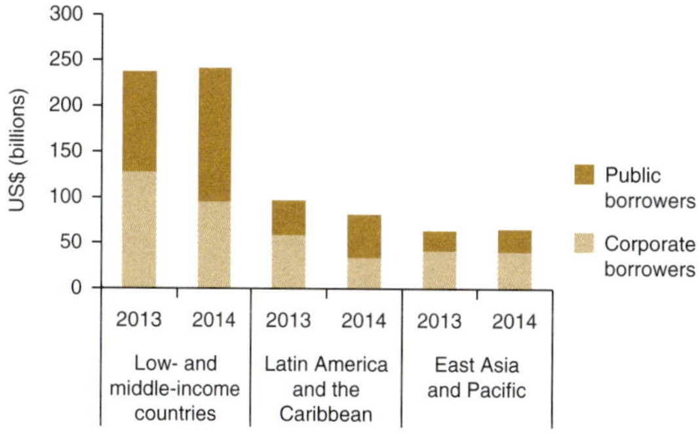

Source: World Bank Debtor Reporting System.

Inflows from multilateral creditors are more than double those of bilateral creditors in 2014

Net debt inflows from official creditors, excluding the IMF, fell by 4 percent in 2014 to $43 billion. This moderate decline masked a divergent trajectory in 2014 relative to 2013 for multilateral and bilateral inflows. The former rose by 29 percent in 2014 to $31 billion, while the latter fell by one-third, to $14 billion. The rebound in net inflows from multilateral creditors was driven by a 24 percent rise in those from the World Bank (IBRD and IDA). Net inflows from other multilateral institutions increased at a much slower pace, 5 percent in 2014. The principal beneficiaries of inflows from multilateral creditors were countries in Sub-Saharan Africa and South Asia: together they accounted for close to two-thirds of such flows in 2014. The sharp reversal of the upward trajectory in net inflows from bilateral creditors of recent years was in large part attributable to the sharp fall in those to the Arab Republic of Egypt. This decline reflects the exceptionally high level of the bilateral support the country received in 2013.

Figure O.11 Bilateral and Multilateral Net Debt Flows, 2007–14

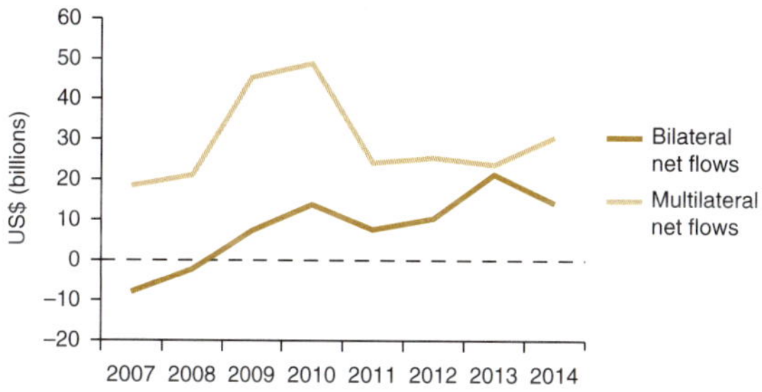

Source: World Bank Debtor Reporting System.

The World Bank dominates inflows from multilateral creditors

Gross disbursements by the World Bank (IBRD and IDA) rose to $29 billion, an increase of 13 percent over the comparable figure for 2013, and equivalent to 47 percent of gross disbursements from all multilateral institutions, excluding the IMF. Gross disbursements from other multilateral institutions dipped 2 percent in 2014. IBRD disbursements were concentrated in creditworthy countries in Latin America and the Caribbean, East Asia and Pacific, and Europe and Central Asia. Those disbursements from IDA, reserved for the world's poorest countries, were directed primarily at Sub-Saharan Africa and South Asia. These regions received 46 percent and 36 percent, respectively, of IDA disbursements (excluding IDA grants) in 2014. The World Bank, the most important source of multilateral financing, accounted for 63 percent of multilateral disbursements to Sub-Saharan Africa in 2014. The Inter-American Bank accounted for 40 percent of disbursements from multilateral creditors to countries in Latin America and the Caribbean in 2014, and the Asian Development Bank for 45 percent to East Asia and Pacific.

Figure O.12 Disbursements from IBRD and IDA, Regional Distribution, 2014

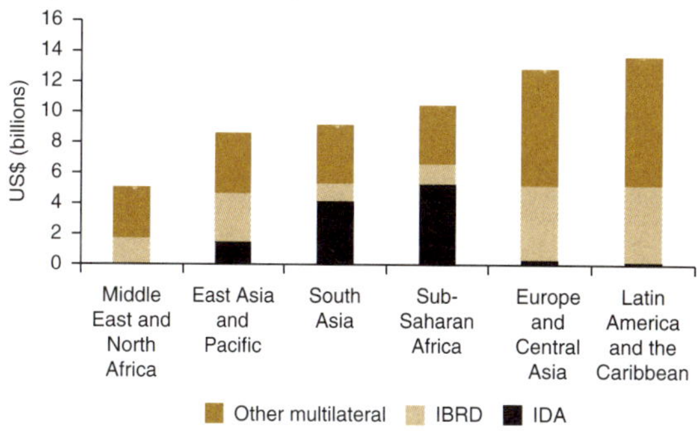

Source: World Bank Debtor Reporting System.

East Asia and Pacific

China drives the trend in net financial flows in the region

Figure O.13 Net Financial Flows, 2007–14

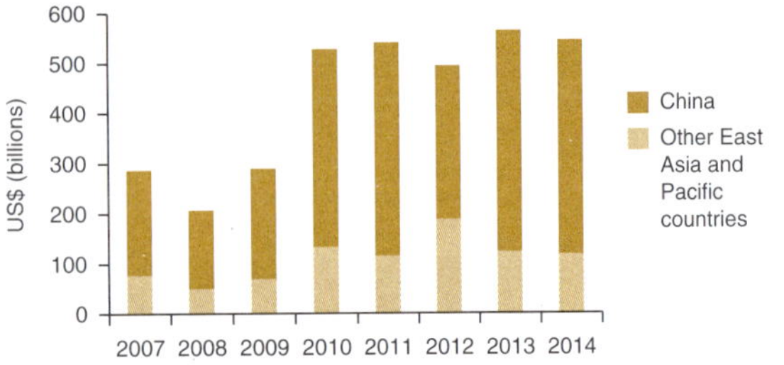

Source: World Bank Debtor Reporting System.

Net financial flows to the region fell moderately, 3 percent, in 2014 to $545 billion, and remained broadly unchanged relative to the region's gross national income (GNI) at 4 percent. But there was a marked shift in composition with net debt flows falling 31 percent from the 2013 level, to $145 billion—equivalent to a little over a quarter of net financial flows in 2014, down from close to 40 percent in 2013. In contrast, net equity flows rose 13 percent to $349 billion on the back of resilient net foreign direct investment and strong portfolio equity inflows; the latter jumped 76 percent in 2014 to $51 billion ($29 billion in 2013). China remained dominant, accounting for 76 percent of net financial inflows to the region in 2014, and driving the downturn in net debt flows; these plummeted to $85 billion, 37 percent below their 2013 level ($135 billion). Countries in the East Asia and Pacific region, excluding China, also saw only a moderate, 4 percent decline in net financial flows in 2014.

Net debt inflows to the region present a mixed picture in 2014

Figure O.14 Net Debt Flows, 2008–14

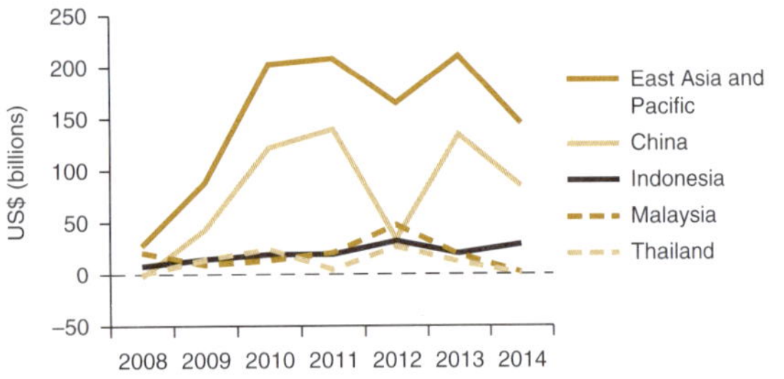

Source: World Bank Debtor Reporting System.

The downturn in net debt flows was driven by China, which accounted for 59 percent of net debt flows to the region in 2014 (64 percent in 2013) and where net debt inflows fell 36 percent in 2014 to $85 billion ($135 billion in 2013). In Malaysia and Thailand, net debt inflows plummeted to around 10 percent of their 2013 level on account of a sharp contraction in short-term debt flows. Other major borrowers, notably Indonesia and the Philippines, recorded increased net debt inflows in 2014. In Indonesia they rose 45 percent due to the combined effect of increased bond issuance by public sector borrowers and a 70 percent jump in long-term net inflows from commercial banks to private non-guaranteed borrowers. In the Philippines the driving force was a rapid surge in net long-term commercial bank flows to private sector borrowers. The same was true for Vietnam, which recorded a 10 percent increase in net debt inflows in 2013, and again in 2014, underpinned by a surge in net debt inflows to the private sector.

Private sector borrowers account for the largest share of external borrowing

Figure O.15 Gross Disbursements by Type of Borrower, 2009–14

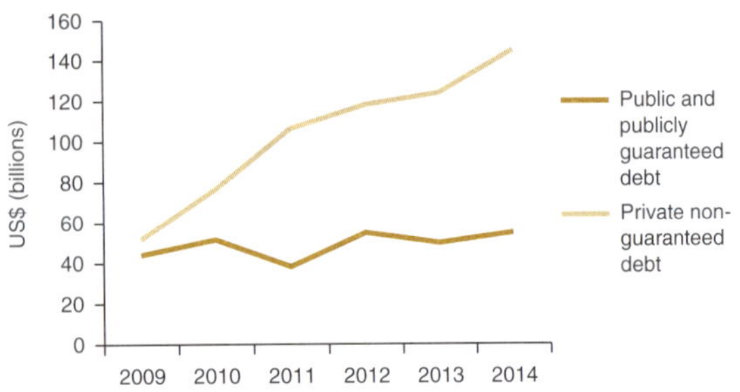

Source: World Bank Debtor Reporting System.

In 2009, disbursements of long-term debt to countries in East Asia and Pacific, excluding China, were almost equally divided between public and publicly guaranteed (51 percent) and private non-guaranteed (49 percent) borrowers. Since then, long-term debt inflows to private sectors across the region have been on a sharp upward trajectory and by 2014 accounted for almost 73 percent of disbursements of long-term debt. They were, however, highly concentrated in three countries, Indonesia, the Philippines, and Thailand, which together absorb around 80 percent of these inflows. Commercial bank and intra-company lending associated with foreign direct investment was an important catalyst of these increased flows, but access to international capital markets has also been an important factor. Bonds issued by corporations in the region was $46 billion in 2014, close to 35 percent of total long-term disbursements of private non guaranteed debt.

Europe and Central Asia

Net debt flows drop sharply in 2014 but equity flows remain stable

Net financial flows to the region fell 38 percent in 2014, to $84 billion ($135 billion in 2013). Debt flows were volatile, down 56 percent in 2014 to $41 billion—a marked turnaround from 2013 when comparable flows surged 80 percent, to $93 billion. In stark contrast, equity flows remained stable at $41 billion. Driving the downward trajectory for debt flows was the sharp contraction in short-term debt inflows to an outflow of $18 billion in 2014, a pronounced reversal from net inflows of $35 billion in 2013. Much of this shift was attributable to Turkey, where net short-debt flows plunged to $2 billion ($30 billion in 2013). There was a significant fall in overall net debt flows in 2014 to Kazakhstan, down $6 billion and, not surprisingly, Ukraine with an outflow of $11 billion, against an inflow of $7 billion in 2013. Inflows from official creditors to the region accounted for 22 percent of net debt inflows in 2014. They rose to $9 billion (an outflow of $9 billion in 2013), reflecting multilateral and bilateral support for Ukraine and much lower outflows to the IMF.

Figure O.16 Net Capital Flows, 2009–14

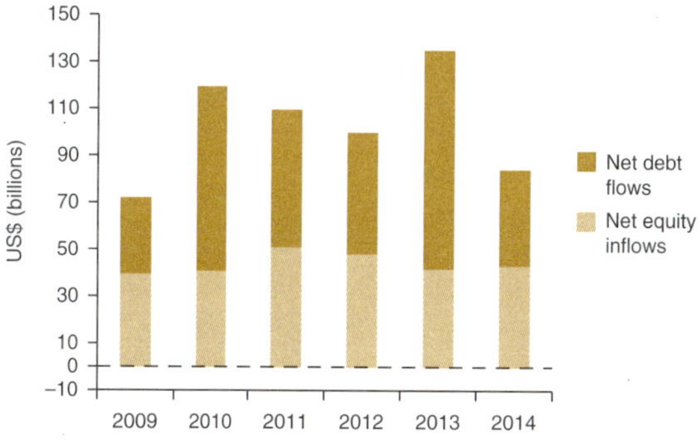

Source: World Bank Debtor Reporting System.

Private sector borrowing has accelerated sharply over the past three years

After being hard hit by the global economic crisis of 2008, private sectors across the region recovered strongly. In 2013 net long-term inflows to private entities, without public sector guarantee, climbed to $44 billion, surpassing comparable flows to public and publicly guaranteed borrowers ($31 billion) and accounting for 60 percent of net long-term debt flows to the region. The momentum slowed in 2014 when net long-term inflows to the private sector declined by 27 percent, compared with a 6 percent drop in those to public and publicly guaranteed borrowers, driven by a sharp contraction in flows to Ukraine, which turned negative, and a marked decline in those to Kazakhstan. In the past five years Kazakhstan and Turkey commanded around 80 percent of inflows to private sector entities in the region, but most Europea and Central Asia countries have recorded an increase in private non-guaranteed debt. The composition of net long-term debt inflows to private sector borrowers has evolved with bond issuance averaging one-third of these flows in 2013–14.

Figure O.17 Net Long-Term Debt Inflows by Type of Borrower, 2009–14

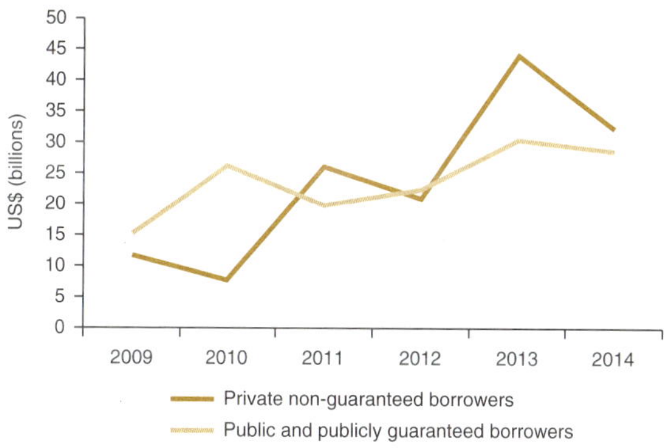

Source: World Bank Debtor Reporting System.

Equity inflows remain strong for the majority of countries in the region

Equity, as a share of net financial flows, rose significantly in 2014, and accounted for half of such flows, compared with a little over 30 percent in 2013. With the exception of Ukraine, where equity flows fell precipitously, most countries across the region attracted a rising volume of equity flows. The region as a whole, excluding Ukraine, was up 16 percent from the 2013 level to $43 billion, with Azerbaijan, Kazakhstan, Turkey, and Turkmenistan together accounting for 68 percent of foreign direct investment flows and 91 percent of portfolio equity flows in 2014. Net inflows of foreign direct investment to other countries in the region, excluding Ukraine, rose by a more moderate 3 percent. There was significant growth in some of the smaller countries in the region, notably Albania and Georgia, where foreign direct investment inflows were up 37 percent and 49 percent, respectively, in 2014, while those to the Former Yugoslavic Republic of Macedonia soared 94 percent, albeit from a relatively low base.

Figure O.18 Foreign Direct Investment Inflows, 2012–14

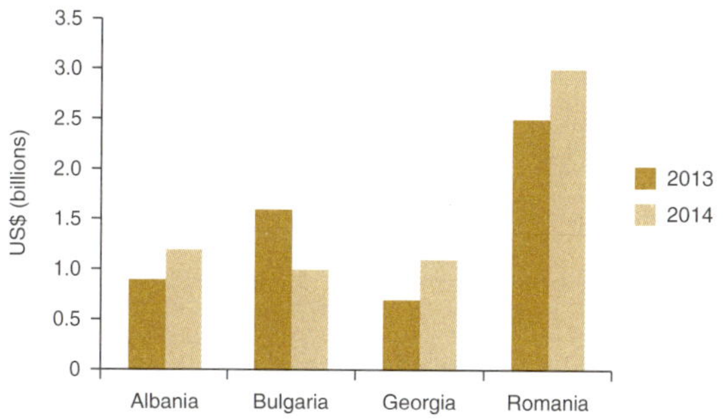

Source: World Bank Debtor Reporting System.

Latin America and the Caribbean

Long-term debt inflows from private creditors remain stable in 2014 but their composition shifts

Figure O.19 Composition of Net Debt Inflows, 2013 and 2014

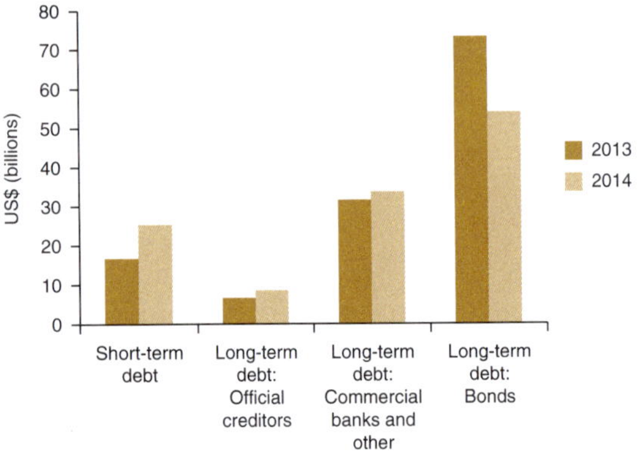

Source: World Bank Debtor Reporting System.

Net debt inflows rose moderately in 2014 to $168 billion ($161 billion in 2013) but were characterized by a marked change in composition. Short-term inflows rose 51 percent to $26 billion and accounted for 15 percent of net debt inflows to the region (10 percent in 2013). In aggregate the change in the level of long-term debt inflows from private creditors in 2014 was moderate, $168 billion compared with $161 billion in 2013, but shifts within this category of debt flows were more pronounced. Long-term net inflows from commercial banks rose 18 percent over their 2013 level, to $75 billion, while net inflows from bond issuance fell 26 percent in the same period, to $54 billion. A fall in bond issuance by private corporations was the main reason for the sharp, 66 percent drop in net inflows from bonds in 2014. New issues by these borrowers were down to around half those of the previous year. Official creditors accounted for only a modest, 5 percent share of net debt flows, although they rose 28 percent in 2014, to $8.7 billion

Net financial inflows to Mexico and Brazil display a very divergent trend in 2014

Figure O.20 Net Financial Flows to Brazil and Mexico by Type, 2012–14

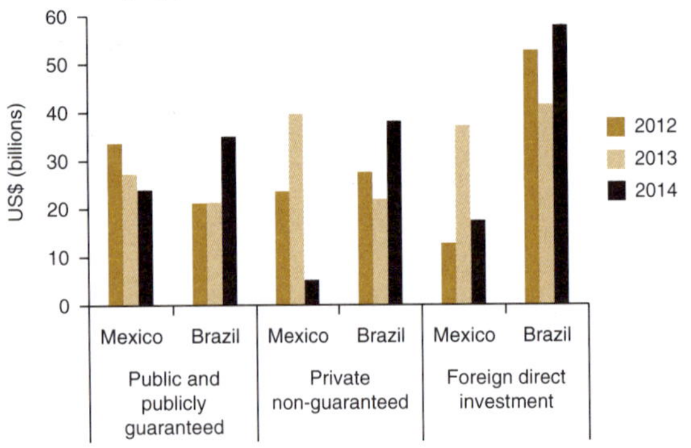

Source: World Bank Debtor Reporting System.

Net financial flows to Brazil and Mexico combined totaled $217 billion in 2014, equivalent to 73 percent of those to the region as a whole. However, there was wide disparity in trend and composition. Net financial flows to Brazil, $167 billion in 2014, were 71 percent higher than the 2013 level and more than triple the comparable 2014 flows to Mexico. This increase was the result of a significant rise in net debt inflows to both public and publicly guaranteed and non-guaranteed private sector borrowers, which rose by 63 percent and 73 percent, respectively, in 2014. In parallel, net foreign direct investment jumped 39 percent to $58 billion, making Brazil the second most important destination, after China, for foreign direct investment in low- and middle-income countries. In stark contrast, net financial flows to Mexico dropped by 41 percent in 2014, to $50 billion, due to an 87 percent fall in net debt flows to private sector borrowers and a 53 percent downturn in foreign direct investment.

Net debt inflows accelerate in other countries in Latin American and the Caribbean

Figure O.21 Net Financial Flows, Excluding Brazil and Mexico, 2010–14

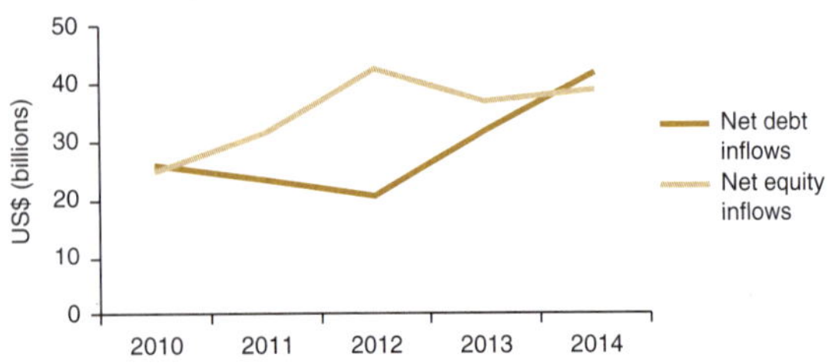

Source: World Bank Debtor Reporting System.

Since 2009, external debt stocks of countries in Latin America and the Caribbean, excluding Brazil and Mexico, have grown on average by 12 percent annually. At end 2014, their combined external debt outstanding totaled $357 billion, equivalent to 27 percent of the region as a whole ($1,347 billion). Net financial flows to this group (excluding Brazil and Mexico) rose 18 percent in 2014, with net debt inflows increasing by 32 percent, to $42 billion, and net equity inflows posting a more moderate 5 percent increase to $39 billion. The growing dominance of debt flows was attributable to several factors. Notably a 20 percent rise in bond issuance by public sector borrowers (mainly in Colombia, Ecuador, and Panama) in 2014 and an 18 percent increase in external borrowing by private sector entities. After peaking in 2012, the net inflow of foreign direct investment leveled off to $35 billion in 2014, with the Dominican Republic, Honduras, and Peru as the principal recipients.

Middle East and North Africa

Net financial flows fall due to a marked reduction in net long-term debt flows

Net financial flows to the region fell 28 percent in 2014, to $21.5 billion, primarily because of the sharp drop in net debt flows to $8 billion, half the 2013 level. Net equity inflows continued on a downward trajectory, falling by a further 5 percent in 2014 to $13.3 billion, with foreign direct investment flows down by 10 percent, while portfolio equity inflows turned positive for the first time since 2010. They rose to $0.6 billion, a marked turnaround from the net outflow of $0.3 billion recorded in 2013, largely accounted for by a re-emergence of net portfolio equity flows into Egypt. There was a moderate increase in foreign direct investment flows to Jordan, Lebanon, and Morocco in 2014; together they accounted for two-thirds of those to the region as a whole, but inflows to the Islamic Republic of Iran fell 30 percent, to $2.1 billion ($3 billion in 2013). The fall in net debt flows reflects the retrenchment by official, notably bilateral, creditors from an unusually high level in 2013, and a slowdown in bond issuance by sovereigns and other public sector borrowers.

Figure O.22 Net Financial Flows, 2009–14

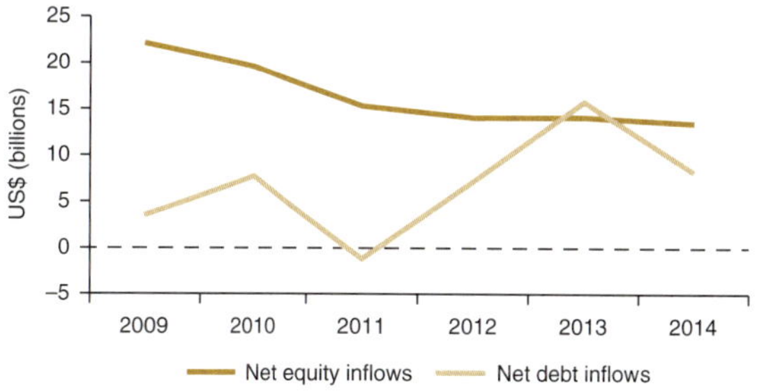

Source: World Bank Debtor Reporting System.

Net debt inflows to the region rise sharply but are heavily concentrated

Net debt flows declined in 2014 and there was a marked change in composition and destination. Net short-term debt inflows rose to $3.3 billion, a reversal of the net outflow of $0.6 billion in 2013, which served in part to offset the 70 percent fall in net long-term debt flows. These flows were heavily concentrated in Morocco, $2.3 billion, and Egypt, $0.5 billion. It was a similar story for long-term debt flows: net outflows of $3.5 billion from Egypt (as compared with inflows of $8.4 billion in 2013) dominated the regional trend. This reversal resulted from a sharp fall in net debt inflows from bilateral creditors, which fell back to their historic level following the large-scale budgetary support from bilateral lenders in the Gulf in 2013. Added to this was a $2.5 billion bullet payment on a short duration bond issued in 2013. Net long-term debt inflows to Jordan also fell in 2014 to $1.3 billion, less than half the 2013 level. In marked contrast, those to Morocco rose 30 percent to $4.5 billion.

Figure O.23 Net Debt Inflows by Country, 2012–14

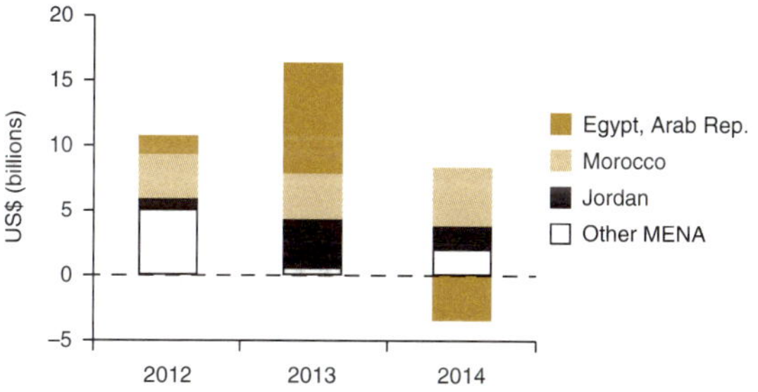

Source: World Bank Debtor Reporting System.

Debt-to-export ratios remain much lower than in other low- and middle-income countries

The ratio of external debt to exports and to GNI for the region averaged 55 percent and 15 percent, respectively, in 2014, broadly unchanged from 2013 and well below those for low- and middle-income countries: 79 percent of exports and 22 percent of GNI at end 2014. The debt service-to-exports ratio jumped to 5.5 percent in 2014 (4.9 percent in 2013) reflecting the 12 percent increase in debt service payments, mainly for Egypt. Nevertheless it remained well below the average of 8.9 percent for low- and middle-income countries. The region's favorable debt indicators result from the high share of equity in net financial flows in prior years, and robust export earnings over the past decade, although these fell back markedly in 2013–14. International reserves were equivalent to 146 percent of external debt stock at the end of 2014, but the regional aggregate was heavily influenced by Algeria, where international reserves, $179 billion, are high, and external debt stock is low, $5.5 billion, equivalent to only 8 percent of exports.

Figure O.24 Debt Ratios, 2013–14

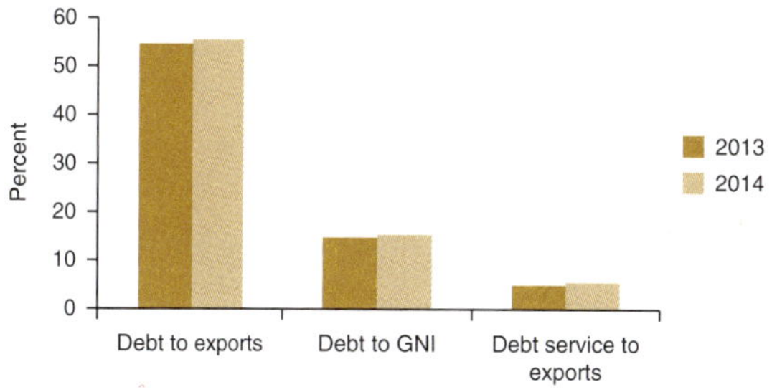

Source: World Bank Debtor Reporting System.

South Asia

India dominates the trend in net financial flows

Figure O.25 Net Financial Flows by Type, 2009–14

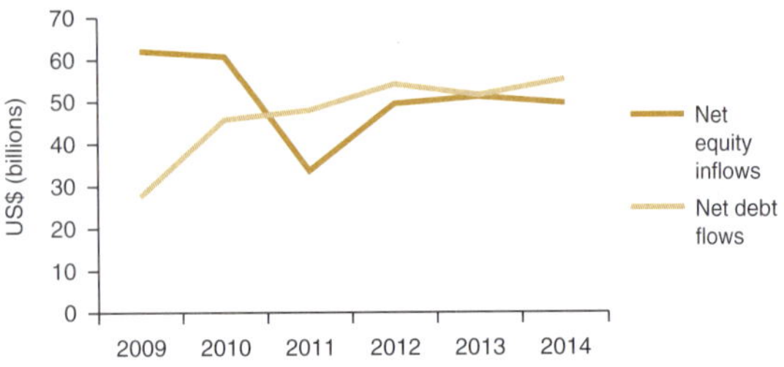

Source: World Bank Debtor Reporting System.

Net financial flows to the region rose marginally, 2 percent, in 2014 with the rise in net debt flows and foreign direct investment, 7 percent and 17 percent, respectively, largely offsetting the 33 percent fall in portfolio equity flows. The dominant factor was India, far and away the largest South Asian economy, which accounted for over 82 percent of net financial flows in the region in 2014. Private creditors accounted for the majority of debt flows, 93 percent in 2014, and again directed primarily at India. The 33 percent rise in long-term net debt from private creditors in 2014 to $57 billion was accompanied by an important change in composition. Whereas in 2013 the bulk of these inflows came from commercial banks, in 2014 they were mainly in the form of bonds. This was a consequence in part of the return to international bond markets by Pakistan and Sri Lanka in 2014 but, overwhelmingly, reflected the surge in the purchase of bonds issued in the Indian domestic market by non-residents.

Debt indicators vary widely across the region

Figure O.26 Debt Indicators for Selected Countries, 2014

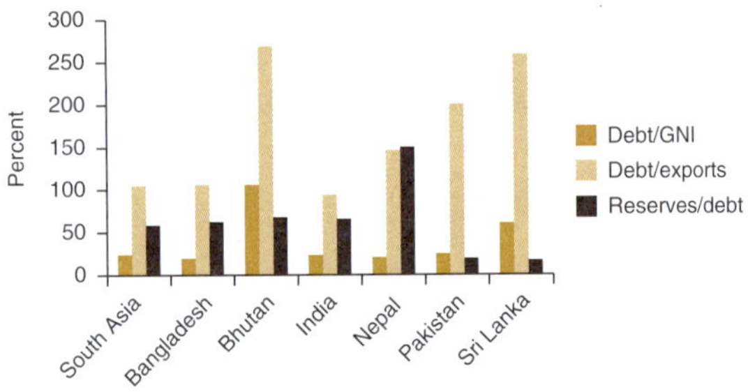

Source: World Bank Debtor Reporting System.

The ratio of external debt stock to GNI for the region, 24 percent in 2014, and the ratio of external debt stock to exports, 104 percent, were broadly in line with those of 2013. Additionally, and not surprisingly, these averages were determined by, and closely correlated with, India's debt ratios (23 percent to GNI and 93 percent to exports), given the weight of the Indian economy compared with that of its neighbors. Across the region, however, there was a wide disparity in ratios. The debt-to-export ratio ranged from a high of 268 percent and 258 percent for Bhutan and Sri Lanka, respectively, to a low of 105 percent for Bangladesh. Bhutan had the highest ratio of external debt to GNI, 105 percent, which contrasts with Bangladesh and Nepal, around 20 percent in both countries. Predictably, the ratio of international reserves to debt for the region, 59 percent, also mirrors that of India, 66 percent, given its regional dominance, but it masks a wide range from 150 percent for Nepal to 17 percent for Sri Lanka.

Net financial flows increase 24 percent, excluding India

Figure O.27 Net Financial Flows to Select Countries, 2013 and 2014

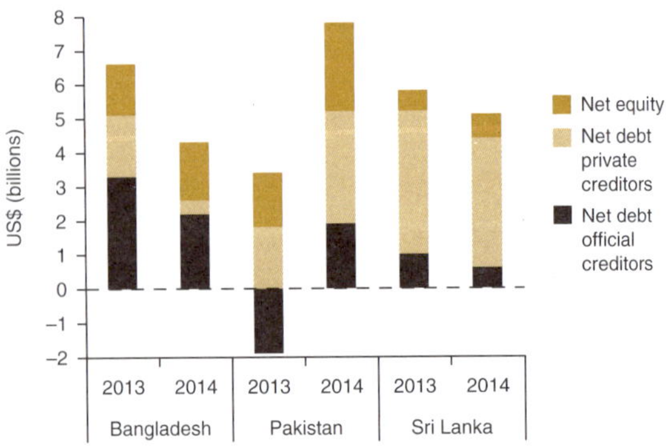

Source: World Bank Debtor Reporting System.

Net financial flows to South Asian countries, excluding India, rose 24 percent in 2014 to $18.5 billion, on account of a 23 percent increase in net debt flows and a 25 percent jump in net equity inflows, principally from portfolio equity that more than doubled. Net debt flows accounted for 71 percent of net financial flows to the group in 2014, similar to the share in 2013. Net debt flows to Pakistan jumped to $5.2 billion, from an outflow of $0.07 billion in 2013 (a consequence of the $3.6 billion repayment to the IMF). Contrasting this, Bangladesh saw net debt inflows drop to $2.6 billion, around half the 2013 level, due to a 33 percent fall in inflows from official creditors and a collapse in inflows to private sector borrowers. In Sri Lanka, net debt inflows fell 15 percent as a consequence of lower inflows to, and higher principal payments by, non-guaranteed private sector borrowers. The rise in net equity inflows was more broadly based but particularly strong in Pakistan, where they rose to $2.6 billion in 2014 ($1.6 billion in 2013), reflecting rising Chinese investment in large-scale infrastructure projects.

Sub-Saharan Africa

Net debt inflows offset the decline in net equity flows

Net financial flows to Sub-Saharan Africa rose 10 percent in 2014, to $78 billion, with a 20 percent drop in net equity flows, more than offset by a 48 percent rise in net debt flows. The decline in net equity flows was driven in large measure by the $3.9 billion outflow of foreign direct investment from Angola and much lower net inflows of portfolio equity to Nigeria. Net debt inflows rose to $47 billion ($31 billion in 2013) of which 64 percent were accounted for by private creditors. Around 26 percent of net debt flows to the region went to South Africa: its share of comparable debt flows in 2013 was 11 percent. Net financial inflows to the region, excluding South Africa, fell 3 percent in 2014 with a 23 percent rise in net debt inflows, to $34 billion ($28 billion in 2013), not enough to offset the 23 percent drop in net equity flows.

Figure O.28 Net Financial Flows, 2009–14

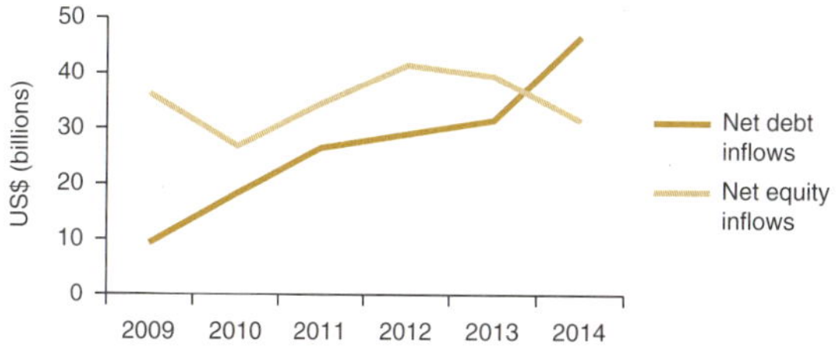

Source: World Bank Debtor Reporting System.

Long-term debt inflows rise 34 percent with private creditors dominant

External borrowing by countries in the region, excluding South Africa, has risen rapidly and been marked by a distinct change in borrowing patterns and creditor composition. Disbursements of long-term debt increased 34 percent in 2014 (to $54 billion), triple the comparable figures for other low- and middle-income countries, with private creditors accounting for 60 percent (50 percent in 2013). Disbursements from private creditors have also become more diversified. In 2010, all long-term private debt was attributable to banks and other private creditors, whereas in 2014, 27 percent was accounted for by bond issuance. Borrowing patterns have also changed with disbursements from private creditors now going primarily to non-guaranteed private-sector borrowers. Disbursements from official creditors (excluding the IMF) rose 30 percent between 2010 and 2013. The momentum continued in 2014 when they rose a further 8 percent to $21.5 billion. This increase was largely attributable to a 14 percent rise in disbursements by multilateral creditors, notably those from the World Bank. Disbursements from IDA, $5 billion in 2014, were unchanged from their 2013 level, but IDA remained by far the single largest multilateral creditor. China was again the continent's most important bilateral creditor.

Figure O.29 Disbursements to the Region, Excluding South Africa, 2007–14

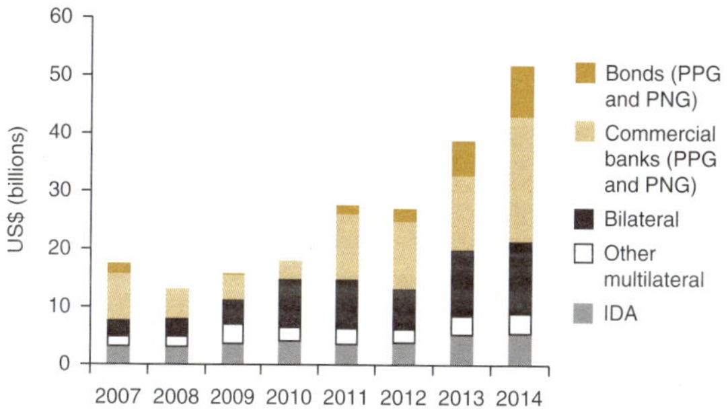

Source: World Bank Debtor Reporting System.
Notes: PNG = private non-guaranteed; PPG = public and publicly guaranteed.

Bond issuance booms

Historically, bond issuance in Sub-Saharan Africa was confined to South Africa, but following Ghana's debut issue in 2007, sovereign bond issuance by countries in the region, including those that benefited from HIPC and MDRI debt relief, has been a rapidly rising phenomenon. Benign global market conditions and the investor desire for higher returns have facilitated access to international capital markets. Sovereign borrowers, excluding South Africa, issued $6 billion in 2014, equivalent to 29 percent of disbursements from official creditors and 25 percent of foreign direct investment inflows. The debut sovereign bonds issued by Ethiopia ($1 billion) and Kenya ($2 billion) were massively over-subscribed, and the same applied for countries returning to the market, such as Ghana and Zambia. Proceeds of sovereign bonds are used to benchmark for future government and corporate bond markets issues, to manage the public debt portfolio, and for infrastructure financing. In Ethiopia, the 10-year, 6.625 percent Eurobond issued in December, 2014, is earmarked for development of sugarcane plantations, a hydropower dam, and amelioration and extension of the railway network.

Figure O.30 Bond Issuance in the Region, Excluding South Africa, 2007–14

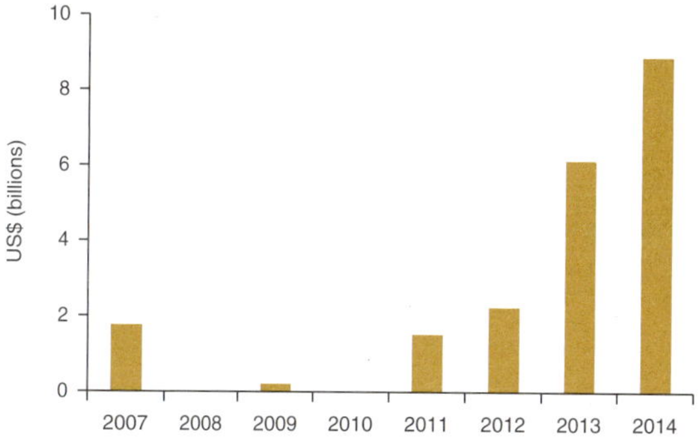

Source: World Bank Debtor Reporting System.

External debt stocks in high-income countries fell slightly in 2014

Figure O.31 High-Income Countries, External Debt Stock by sector, 2013 and 2014

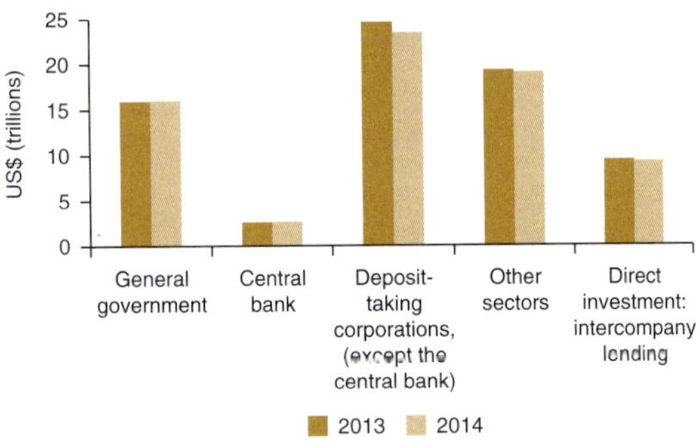

Source: World Bank Quarterly External Debt Statistics.

After five consecutive years of growth, the external debt stock of high-income countries reporting to the QEDS saw a marginal, 2 percent, decline in 2014 to $70.0 trillion at year-end. This was largely the result of a contraction in the external debt of the private sector, specifically a $1.1 trillion (5 percent) reduction in the external debt liabilities of commercial banks. The combined external debt stock of general governments, $15.9 trillion at end 2014, was largely unchanged from its year-end 2013 level, while obligations in respect of debt securities rose slightly, to $30.1 trillion. Although some countries, notably Australia, Belgium, Italy, Spain, and the United States, saw external obligations of the general government, measured in U.S. dollars, rise in 2014, this increase was offset by a reduction in comparable external debt stock in most European countries.

G-7 countries record divergent external debt trends in 2014

Table O.1 High-Income Countries, External Debt Stock, 2010–14
US$ trillions

	2010	2011	2012	2013	2014
Gross External Debt	64.045	66.985	69.657	71.437	69.987
of which,					
G7 Countries	*40.455*	*42.612*	*43.941*	*44.280*	*44.247*
Other high-income countries	*23.590*	*24.373*	*25.716*	*27.157*	*25.740*

Source: World Bank Debtor Reporting System.

The combined external debt stock of the Group of Seven (G7) countries stood at $44.2 trillion at end 2014, virtually unchanged from 2013, and equivalent to 63 percent of the external debt stock of all high-income countries reporting to QEDS. The aggregate masks disparate trends at the individual country level. Both Canada and the United States recorded an increase in external debt stock in 2014, 7 percent and 5 percent, respectively. In contrast, the other five countries in the group all saw external debt stock decline over the same period, with the most pronounced reduction recorded by Germany and Italy: both saw outstanding external debt fall 7 percent in 2014. In high-income countries, other than those in the G7, external debt stocks fell 5 percent in 2014, in U.S. dollar terms. Here again trends were divergent, but the key countries to reduce external debt in 2014 were Ireland, Luxembourg, Netherlands, the Russian Federation, and Spain. Taken together, they accounted for about 70 percent of the decline in external debt in non-G7 countries.

External debt-to-GDP ratios post a moderate improvement in 2014

Figure O.32 G7 Countries, External Debt to GDP Ratio, 2010–14

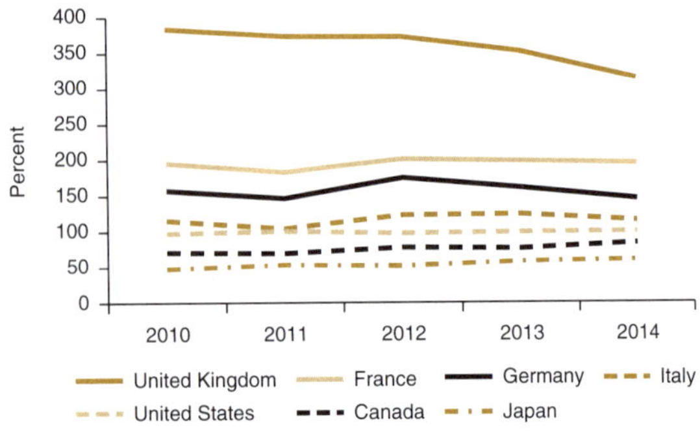

Source: World Bank Quarterly External Debt Statistics.

High-income countries reported a slight improvement in the external debt-to-GDP ratio in 2014, to 140 percent, from 145 percent in 2013. This resulted from the combined effect of growth in output and a reduction in external debt stock in many high-income countries. Among G-7 countries, Canada recorded the largest increase in the external debt-to-GDP ratio: it deteriorated from 76 percent in 2013 to 83 percent in 2014, while in Japan and in the United States, the ratio was broadly unchanged, 59 percent and 99 percent, respectively. The other countries in the group all saw the ratio improving in 2014. The reduction was most pronounced in Germany, where GDP growth and prudent fiscal policies served to bring the debt-to-GDP ratio down to 145 percent, from 161 percent at end 2013. The United Kingdom has by far the highest external debt-to-GDP ratio among G-7 countries, but there too the debt-to-GDP ratio stayed on its downward trajectory to 313 percent at end 2014.

Public Sector Debt

Government debt-to-GDP ratios in EU-15 countries continued to rise in 2014

Government debt levels in the EU-15 countries, measured in U.S. dollars, fell by an average of 7 percent in 2014, to $12.8 trillion ($13.6 trillion in 2013), but this decline was in part attributable to Euro–U.S. dollar exchange rate movements. While many countries in this group have reduced government debt in relation to GDP, for others it continued to rise. For EU-15 countries as a whole, the government debt-to-GDP ratio averaged 84.4 percent in 2014, as compared to 83.2 percent in 2013. Greece remains the most indebted country in the group. Despite concerted efforts by the authorities to tighten fiscal policies and implement structural economic reforms in 2014, the government debt-to-GDP ratio increased by a further 3 percentage points, to 181.4 percent, its highest level to date. Portugal and Italy had the second and third highest debt-to-GDP ratios among the EU-15 countries; 138 percent and 127 percent, respectively, at end 2014. In Ireland, the debt-to-GDP ratio fell by 10 percentage points in 2014 to 114 percent.

Figure O.33 Select EU-15 countries: Government Debt-to-GDP Ratio, 2010 and 2013–14

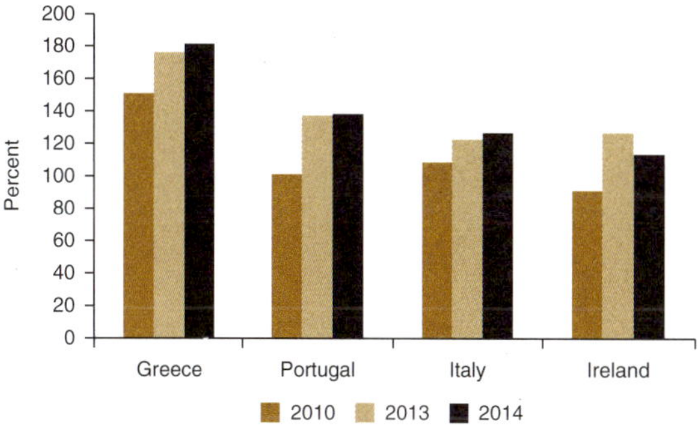

Source: World Bank Public Sector Debt Database.

Japan has by far the highest government debt-to-GDP ratio of OECD countries

Since the 2008 global financial crisis, government debt levels in many OECD countries have remained on a rising trajectory, despite concerted efforts at fiscal consolidation. However, government debt burdens vary significantly as evidenced by the debt-to-GDP ratio that ranged, in 2014, from as low as 7 percent for Estonia to as high as 206 percent for Japan, which relies primarily on the domestic bond market to raise the funds needed to finance the continuously rising costs of supporting its aging population. OECD countries outside the Euro Zone, with the second and third highest debt-to-GDP ratio, were the United States and the United Kingdom, 97 percent and 94 percent, respectively, at the end of 2014. Although ratios for the United Kingdom and the United States are similar, their debt profiles differ. Virtually all government debt of the United Kingdom is financed by the domestic creditors, whereas over one-third of government debt in the United States is owed to external creditors.

Figure O.34 OECD Countries: Government Debt-to-GDP Ratio, 2014

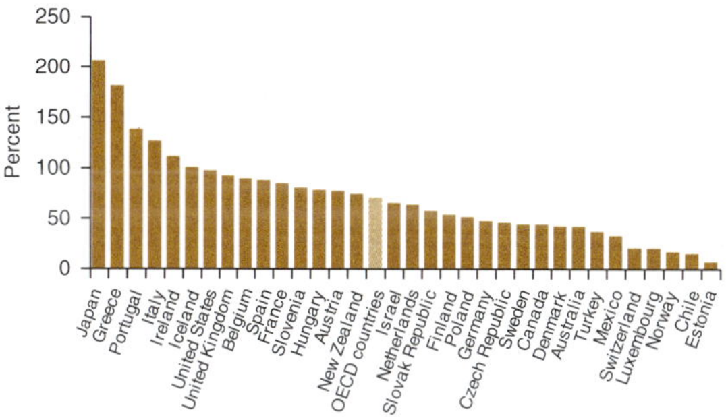

Source: World Bank Public Sector Debt Database.

Emerging market countries government debt levels and composition vary widely

In the aftermath of the 2008 global economic crisis, government debt, in relation to GDP, has been on a rising trend in some emerging market countries. In Brazil and Mexico, government debt-to-GDP ratios increased from 47.8 percent and 27.1 percent, respectively, in 2009 to 54.4 percent and 33.2 percent, respectively, in 2014. However, the composition of government debt in these countries is dissimilar. In Brazil, domestic debt constitutes around 97 percent of total government debt, and virtually all government bond issuance is in the domestic market. For Mexico, two-thirds of the government debt, is owed to external creditors with around 88 percent financed by government bonds. In contrast, China and India have seen the central government debt-to-GDP ratio improve in response to fiscal consolidation policies. At the end of 2014, it stood at 15.1 percent in China and 65.8 percent in India, as compared to 16.8 percent and 72.5 percent, respectively, in 2010.

Figure O.35 Government Debt-to-GDP Ratio for Select Emerging Markets, 2010 and 2014

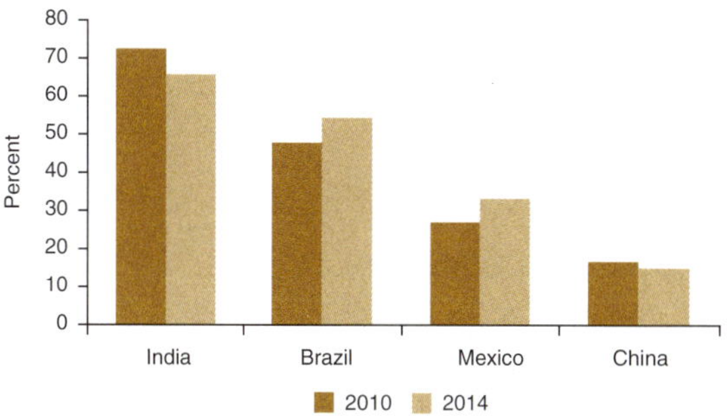

Source: World Bank Public Sector Debt Database.

PART II
Aggregate and Country Tables

ALL LOW- AND MIDDLE-INCOME COUNTRIES

(US$ billion, unless otherwise indicated)

	2000	2005	2009	2010	2011	2012	2013	2014
Summary external debt data								
External debt stocks	**1,743.3**	**2,090.8**	**3,174.9**	**3,630.8**	**4,078.6**	**4,564.2**	**5,056.1**	**5,391.5**
Long-term external debt	1,461.3	1,623.0	2,346.7	2,538.1	2,814.4	3,169.9	3,493.1	3,770.6
Public and publicly guaranteed	1,053.4	1,115.6	1,268.1	1,359.4	1,428.1	1,644.3	1,788.7	1,942.9
Official creditors	648.4	651.5	736.7	790.6	823.7	844.6	869.8	869.2
Use of IMF credit	53.4	50.9	128.9	138.7	138.7	130.4	112.6	97.0
Private creditors	405.0	464.0	531.4	568.8	604.5	799.7	918.8	1,073.7
of which: Bonds	224.2	312.3	386.6	418.6	461.6	627.6	701.3	807.4
Private nonguaranteed	407.9	507.5	1,078.6	1,178.8	1,386.3	1,525.6	1,704.4	1,827.7
of which: Bonds	81.0	115.1	187.6	231.1	255.7	287.8	352.6	395.1
Short-term external debt	228.6	416.8	699.2	954.0	1,125.5	1,264.0	1,450.4	1,523.8
interest arrears on long-term	27.2	17.7	15.3	16.0	12.4	14.5	13.2	14.9
Long-term external debt								
Disbursements	**199.2**	**304.5**	**433.1**	**565.4**	**621.2**	**674.8**	**805.0**	**846.5**
Public and publicly guaranteed	117.7	125.4	179.5	235.7	191.6	256.2	291.4	326.4
Official creditors	48.2	43.9	95.7	107.0	87.3	86.1	103.6	101.2
Private creditors	69.5	81.5	83.8	128.7	104.3	170.0	187.8	225.2
of which: Bonds	42.0	56.8	60.7	90.1	76.7	128.6	109.7	145.7
Private nonguaranteed	81.5	179.1	253.6	329.7	429.5	418.6	513.6	520.1
of which: Bonds	10.7	33.6	35.6	68.0	86.7	92.8	128.4	96.2
Principal repayments	**178.8**	**236.9**	**303.3**	**324.1**	**349.3**	**354.9**	**411.6**	**452.9**
Public and publicly guaranteed	92.1	116.3	96.6	96.1	110.0	93.8	112.3	113.9
Official creditors	43.1	48.2	42.8	44.0	55.2	50.0	58.2	56.1
Private creditors	49.0	68.2	53.9	52.2	54.8	43.9	54.1	57.8
of which: Bonds	16.5	39.4	25.5	26.5	24.8	17.4	23.3	29.6
Private nonguaranteed	86.8	120.6	206.7	227.9	239.3	261.0	299.2	339.0
of which: Bonds	13.2	15.6	14.4	15.3	19.1	24.6	32.4	36.5
Interest payments	**75.1**	**69.3**	**85.9**	**84.4**	**103.1**	**118.9**	**112.6**	**122.2**
Public and publicly guaranteed	50.0	51.2	44.3	43.4	47.5	72.0	55.8	58.5
Official creditors	22.4	20.3	15.7	14.6	15.4	17.1	16.2	15.9
Private creditors	27.6	30.9	28.6	28.8	32.1	54.9	39.6	42.6
of which: Bonds	16.0	25.1	23.4	24.6	27.8	50.2	34.5	36.6
Private nonguaranteed	25.1	18.0	41.6	41.0	55.5	46.9	56.8	63.8
of which: Bonds	6.4	6.3	10.2	11.5	16.8	12.4	18.1	23.3
Net financial flows								
Net inflows	144.8	400.7	674.6	1,105.2	1,020.6	1,054.8	1,190.4	1,132.3
Net debt inflows	2.2	97.7	213.9	508.7	447.5	447.9	563.5	463.9
Official creditors	-2.7	-37.3	79.4	76.4	32.6	27.7	27.6	43.8
of which: World Bank	7.4	4.1	18.1	22.9	6.8	12.5	14.0	17.3
of which: IMF	-7.9	-33.0	26.4	13.4	0.5	-8.4	-17.7	-1.3
Private creditors	4.9	135.0	134.5	432.3	414.9	420.1	535.8	420.1
Long-term	15.2	71.9	76.8	178.3	239.8	283.7	348.0	348.5
Bonds	23.0	35.3	56.4	116.4	119.5	179.4	182.4	175.8
Banks and other private	-7.8	36.5	20.4	61.9	120.2	104.3	165.6	172.7
Short-term	-10.3	63.1	57.8	254.0	175.1	136.4	187.8	71.6
Net equity inflows	142.6	303.0	460.7	596.4	573.1	607.0	626.9	668.4
Foreign direct investment	124.7	237.9	348.6	472.5	569.4	514.5	554.6	575.7
Portfolio equity	17.9	65.1	112.0	124.0	3.7	92.5	72.3	92.7
Major economic aggregates								
Gross national income (GNI)	5,033.0	8,266.7	14,376.7	17,607.7	20,612.5	21,799.7	23,169.9	24,271.5
Exports of goods, services & prim. income	1,423.4	2,720.3	4,009.9	5,033.2	6,083.5	6,430.2	6,642.2	6,813.5
Imports of goods, services & prim. income	1,517.6	2,789.0	4,122.6	5,271.3	6,485.6	6,810.3	7,140.4	7,278.2
Primary income on FDI	59.7	162.0	287.7	401.6	483.7	454.0	486.6	190.4
Personal transfers & comp. of employees	76.2	176.3	280.5	312.5	348.5	372.1	383.4	421.8
International reserves	529.8	1,667.7	4,165.5	4,843.3	5,325.1	5,586.6	6,109.9	6,120.1
Ratios								
External debt stocks to exports (%)	122.5	76.9	79.2	72.1	67.0	71.0	76.1	79.1
External debt stocks to GNI (%)	34.6	25.3	22.1	20.6	19.8	20.9	21.8	22.2
Debt service to exports (%)	20.0	13.3	10.1	9.0	8.2	8.3	8.5	8.9
Short-term to external debt stocks (%)	13.1	19.9	22.0	26.3	27.6	27.7	28.7	28.3
Multilateral to external debt stocks (%)	17.0	16.5	13.1	12.7	11.8	11.0	10.5	9.9
Reserves to external debt stocks (%)	30.4	79.8	131.2	133.4	130.6	122.4	120.8	113.5

EAST ASIA AND PACIFIC

(US$ billion, unless otherwise indicated)

	2000	2005	2009	2010	2011	2012	2013	2014
Summary external debt data								
External debt stocks	**497.4**	**641.5**	**938.7**	**1,105.7**	**1,314.8**	**1,514.4**	**1,684.5**	**1,816.6**
Long-term external debt	418.2	432.7	565.2	582.9	642.6	759.6	798.3	871.6
Public and publicly guaranteed	271.0	277.3	344.7	338.0	338.0	405.7	416.5	431.9
Official creditors	171.5	173.0	203.7	211.8	216.9	211.4	198.2	191.5
Use of IMF credit	17.8	10.0	20.8	20.5	20.4	20.3	20.3	19.0
Private creditors	99.5	104.4	140.9	126.2	121.1	194.3	218.4	240.3
of which: Bonds	35.8	64.9	104.9	87.9	92.4	171.0	187.9	203.0
Private nonguaranteed	147.2	155.4	220.5	244.9	304.6	353.8	381.8	439.7
of which: Bonds	36.7	36.2	41.0	49.4	65.1	88.0	109.0	141.8
Short-term external debt	61.4	198.9	352.7	502.3	651.8	734.5	865.9	926.0
interest arrears on long-term	5.3	1.1	1.3	1.4	1.4	1.2	1.1	0.9
Long-term external debt								
Disbursements	**42.2**	**78.3**	**96.2**	**128.4**	**144.8**	**173.3**	**173.8**	**200.0**
Public and publicly guaranteed	28.7	29.0	44.2	51.7	38.3	55.0	49.8	55.0
Official creditors	15.6	9.1	16.8	17.0	15.1	16.6	15.9	17.9
Private creditors	13.1	19.9	27.4	34.6	23.2	38.5	33.8	37.2
of which: Bonds	4.5	14.5	19.2	20.7	20.0	36.3	22.1	24.9
Private nonguaranteed	13.4	49.3	51.9	76.7	106.5	118.2	124.0	145.0
of which: Bonds	3.2	7.8	5.9	15.7	23.3	30.1	42.2	41.1
Principal repayments	**47.0**	**66.9**	**80.3**	**74.7**	**85.8**	**90.8**	**94.1**	**114.8**
Public and publicly guaranteed	22.8	24.4	25.5	25.1	29.7	23.8	20.7	30.1
Official creditors	10.2	10.8	12.9	12.9	15.0	14.7	15.8	14.1
Private creditors	12.5	13.6	12.6	12.2	14.7	9.1	4.9	16.0
of which: Bonds	1.2	4.3	5.3	5.1	5.7	1.6	0.4	11.2
Private nonguaranteed	24.2	42.5	54.8	49.7	56.1	67.0	73.4	84.7
of which: Bonds	6.6	4.3	3.9	2.7	4.1	3.0	9.2	8.5
Interest payments	**20.4**	**12.6**	**14.1**	**17.1**	**19.7**	**18.4**	**21.3**	**25.2**
Public and publicly guaranteed	12.9	8.5	9.4	9.6	10.3	11.3	11.0	11.1
Official creditors	7.2	4.0	4.0	3.7	3.9	4.7	3.9	3.6
Private creditors	5.7	4.5	5.4	5.9	6.4	6.6	7.1	7.5
of which: Bonds	2.3	3.1	4.4	4.9	5.4	5.7	6.5	7.0
Private nonguaranteed	7.5	4.1	4.7	7.5	9.4	7.1	10.3	14.1
of which: Bonds	2.6	1.6	1.7	1.7	4.1	3.5	5.2	7.2
Net financial flows								
Net inflows	37.3	189.2	290.4	528.4	541.5	495.1	564.8	545.3
Net debt inflows	-14.4	46.7	88.8	203.1	208.4	165.3	211.1	145.4
Official creditors	6.6	-3.2	4.1	4.2	0.0	1.8	0.0	3.7
of which: World Bank	1.8	-0.6	2.2	2.7	0.9	1.4	2.4	1.7
of which: IMF	1.2	-1.6	0.1	0.0	0.0	-0.1	-0.1	-0.1
Private creditors	-21.0	50.0	84.7	198.9	208.4	163.5	211.1	141.7
Long-term	-10.2	13.1	11.9	49.5	58.9	80.6	79.6	81.4
Bonds	0.0	13.7	15.8	28.7	33.5	61.8	54.7	46.3
Banks and other private	-10.2	-0.7	-3.9	20.8	25.3	18.8	24.8	35.2
Short-term	-10.8	36.9	72.8	149.5	149.5	82.9	131.5	60.3
Net equity inflows	51.8	142.4	201.6	325.4	333.0	329.8	353.7	399.9
Foreign direct investment	45.2	117.6	170.0	284.7	325.9	294.5	325.0	349.4
Portfolio equity	6.6	24.9	31.6	40.7	7.1	35.3	28.8	50.5
Major economic aggregates								
Gross national income (GNI)	1,695.8	3,049.0	6,407.9	7,741.3	9,389.7	10,526.2	11,568.2	12,434.8
Exports of goods, services & prim. income	636.1	1,296.8	2,014.7	2,603.0	3,106.4	3,368.5	3,580.2	3,755.1
Imports of goods, services & prim. income	606.3	1,195.1	1,767.1	2,393.1	2,988.1	3,196.6	3,441.3	3,575.0
Primary income on FDI	31.7	80.0	144.5	212.6	261.1	240.1	278.8	51.0
Personal transfers & comp. of employees	15.8	34.3	60.4	75.8	85.9	88.4	92.4	121.6
International reserves	275.5	1,003.8	2,779.4	3,315.6	3,708.8	3,871.9	4,344.3	4,352.2
Ratios								
External debt stocks to exports (%)	78.2	49.5	46.6	42.5	42.3	45.0	47.0	48.4
External debt stocks to GNI (%)	29.3	21.0	14.6	14.3	14.0	14.4	14.6	14.6
Debt service to exports (%)	11.4	6.6	4.9	4.7	4.4	4.3	3.3	3.8
Short-term to external debt stocks (%)	12.4	31.0	37.6	45.4	49.6	48.5	51.4	51.0
Multilateral to external debt stocks (%)	13.2	10.0	8.6	7.8	6.8	6.0	5.5	5.1
Reserves to external debt stocks (%)	55.4	156.5	296.1	299.9	282.1	255.7	257.9	239.6

EUROPE AND CENTRAL ASIA

(US$ billion, unless otherwise indicated)

	2000	2005	2009	2010	2011	2012	2013	2014
Summary external debt data								
External debt stocks	**203.3**	**357.9**	**777.7**	**837.1**	**873.9**	**926.4**	**1,030.6**	**1,024.0**
Long-term external debt	148.2	253.0	600.0	614.8	640.8	683.3	770.4	790.5
Public and publicly guaranteed	104.1	118.3	171.5	192.7	208.2	230.3	260.6	272.1
Official creditors	43.0	50.6	86.0	100.3	108.6	112.6	120.7	121.7
Use of IMF credit	15.2	24.6	45.3	53.5	52.4	44.3	28.5	17.9
Private creditors	61.1	67.7	85.5	92.4	99.6	117.7	139.9	150.4
of which: Bonds	29.6	35.3	52.7	61.2	70.4	89.0	113.7	129.5
Private nonguaranteed	44.1	134.7	428.5	422.1	432.6	453.0	509.7	518.4
of which: Bonds	1.9	12.7	34.1	32.9	28.1	33.5	49.7	53.5
Short-term external debt	39.9	80.3	132.5	168.7	180.6	198.7	231.7	215.6
interest arrears on long-term	4.0	0.9	1.5	2.2	0.6	2.4	0.9	3.2
Long-term external debt								
Disbursements	**34.1**	**90.8**	**140.4**	**166.3**	**167.1**	**161.2**	**215.8**	**176.1**
Public and publicly guaranteed	19.6	14.5	27.6	38.2	33.1	38.1	49.4	44.5
Official creditors	5.9	4.7	21.2	21.2	17.0	12.0	16.9	18.3
Private creditors	13.7	9.8	6.4	17.0	16.1	26.2	32.5	26.2
of which: Bonds	7.5	6.8	4.0	13.6	12.3	22.7	28.6	23.9
Private nonguaranteed	14.5	76.3	112.8	128.1	134.0	123.0	166.4	131.5
of which: Bonds	0.5	6.9	1.0	4.5	4.5	8.7	20.8	15.7
Principal repayments	**21.9**	**51.5**	**113.3**	**132.2**	**121.1**	**117.6**	**141.2**	**115.1**
Public and publicly guaranteed	10.3	15.0	12.3	11.9	13.3	15.6	18.9	15.9
Official creditors	4.4	4.9	4.6	4.9	7.3	8.4	9.7	7.8
Private creditors	5.9	10.2	7.7	7.0	6.0	7.2	9.2	8.1
of which: Bonds	1.9	6.4	3.6	3.9	2.3	3.5	4.2	3.9
Private nonguaranteed	11.6	36.4	101.1	120.3	107.8	102.0	122.3	99.2
of which: Bonds	0.1	1.2	3.5	3.4	5.5	4.6	6.2	4.6
Interest payments	**8.0**	**11.5**	**25.7**	**21.6**	**29.2**	**22.3**	**24.4**	**25.2**
Public and publicly guaranteed	5.5	6.7	7.5	6.9	7.9	8.7	9.2	10.3
Official creditors	1.7	1.7	2.2	1.9	2.4	2.6	2.3	2.5
Private creditors	3.8	5.0	5.3	5.0	5.5	6.2	6.9	7.7
of which: Bonds	2.1	3.3	3.8	3.8	4.4	5.0	5.9	6.9
Private nonguaranteed	2.4	4.8	18.3	14.7	21.3	13.6	15.2	15.0
of which: Bonds	0.1	1.0	2.5	2.2	2.2	1.8	2.1	3.1
Net financial flows								
Net inflows	28.1	90.7	72.3	119.6	109.7	100.1	135.3	84.4
Net debt inflows	21.1	52.5	32.6	78.6	58.5	51.8	93.3	41.1
Official creditors	3.9	-6.6	36.8	25.4	8.7	-4.4	-8.6	9.1
of which: World Bank	1.7	0.0	3.4	3.9	2.9	2.0	2.1	3.0
of which: IMF	2.4	-6.4	20.2	9.0	-1.0	-8.0	-15.8	-1.4
Private creditors	17.2	59.0	-4.2	53.2	49.8	56.2	101.9	32.0
Long-term	10.7	39.5	10.5	17.7	36.3	39.9	67.4	50.5
Bonds	5.9	6.1	-2.2	10.7	9.0	23.2	39.0	31.1
Banks and other private	4.7	33.4	12.7	7.0	27.2	16.7	28.4	19.4
Short-term	6.6	19.6	-14.7	35.5	13.6	16.3	34.5	-18.5
Net equity inflows	7.0	38.3	39.7	41.0	51.2	48.3	41.9	43.2
Foreign direct investment	6.3	31.6	36.6	37.1	51.7	41.5	38.8	40.4
Portfolio equity	0.7	6.6	3.0	4.0	-0.5	6.9	3.1	2.8
Major economic aggregates								
Gross national income (GNI)	425.4	881.7	1,301.2	1,485.0	1,655.1	1,692.9	1,821.0	1,766.3
Exports of goods, services & prim. income	130.2	290.5	432.5	503.5	636.0	665.3	676.5	670.9
Imports of goods, services & prim. income	154.6	345.7	491.9	583.5	741.3	753.0	781.1	735.9
Primary income on FDI	2.0	12.3	26.0	32.9	45.6	45.2	48.1	17.9
Personal transfers & comp. of employees	7.9	17.8	33.2	33.7	39.6	43.0	47.4	43.5
International reserves	35.0	119.4	217.6	238.6	242.0	255.2	268.3	242.2
Ratios								
External debt stocks to exports (%)	156.2	123.2	179.8	166.3	137.4	139.2	152.3	152.6
External debt stocks to GNI (%)	47.8	40.6	59.8	56.4	52.8	54.7	56.6	58.0
Debt service to exports (%)	26.6	26.2	33.2	32.0	25.0	23.2	27.9	22.8
Short-term to external debt stocks (%)	19.6	22.4	17.0	20.2	20.7	21.5	22.5	21.1
Multilateral to external debt stocks (%)	10.5	8.8	7.6	8.6	9.0	9.1	9.1	9.0
Reserves to external debt stocks (%)	17.2	33.4	28.0	28.5	27.7	27.5	26.0	23.6

LATIN AMERICA AND THE CARIBBEAN

(US$ billion, unless otherwise indicated)

	2000	2005	2009	2010	2011	2012	2013	2014
Summary external debt data								
External debt stocks	**524.4**	**517.4**	**677.2**	**827.2**	**948.5**	**1,068.7**	**1,204.6**	**1,346.8**
Long-term external debt	453.5	448.9	576.5	675.4	805.6	910.9	1,030.1	1,148.4
Public and publicly guaranteed	270.1	314.0	322.1	366.3	389.3	452.7	512.8	588.8
Official creditors	108.8	105.8	117.9	137.8	139.3	149.0	154.2	160.3
Use of IMF credit	5.0	3.0	15.8	16.6	16.8	16.7	16.5	14.9
Private creditors	161.3	208.2	204.2	228.5	249.9	303.6	358.5	428.4
of which: Bonds	131.4	172.0	169.9	190.0	210.0	249.0	273.2	305.4
Private nonguaranteed	183.4	135.0	254.4	309.1	416.4	458.3	517.4	559.6
of which: Bonds	38.7	55.5	87.0	126.0	137.7	142.4	170.5	176.9
Short-term external debt	65.9	65.5	85.0	135.2	126.1	141.1	158.0	183.5
interest arrears on long-term	1.6	1.1	0.8	0.8	0.8	0.8	0.8	0.8
Long-term external debt								
Disbursements	**89.3**	**81.1**	**126.4**	**175.3**	**205.2**	**219.2**	**253.1**	**241.6**
Public and publicly guaranteed	40.5	45.4	60.2	79.9	61.4	90.1	104.4	105.8
Official creditors	13.0	10.9	25.4	30.8	18.1	19.9	20.3	18.4
Private creditors	27.5	34.4	34.8	49.1	43.3	70.1	84.1	87.4
of which: Bonds	21.6	29.0	30.2	36.3	32.9	48.6	38.4	48.0
Private nonguaranteed	48.8	35.7	66.2	95.4	143.8	129.1	148.6	135.8
of which: Bonds	6.2	14.8	25.9	45.4	53.8	49.7	59.3	34.6
Principal repayments	**81.7**	**70.4**	**71.1**	**71.2**	**88.5**	**93.2**	**109.1**	**98.8**
Public and publicly guaranteed	33.1	37.3	30.7	33.1	36.6	25.1	38.0	24.7
Official creditors	14.0	13.6	10.9	11.2	15.5	9.8	13.5	9.7
Private creditors	19.1	23.7	19.8	21.9	21.1	15.3	24.5	15.1
of which: Bonds	12.0	17.1	12.1	14.6	11.9	7.5	10.4	9.5
Private nonguaranteed	48.6	33.1	40.4	38.1	51.9	68.1	71.0	74.0
of which: Bonds	6.5	9.7	5.2	5.6	6.6	11.8	13.9	19.0
Interest payments	**33.2**	**27.4**	**31.4**	**31.2**	**37.4**	**58.1**	**45.2**	**46.7**
Public and publicly guaranteed	19.5	20.2	17.7	17.2	19.0	40.1	22.9	23.5
Official creditors	6.3	4.4	3.9	3.7	3.9	4.0	4.1	3.8
Private creditors	13.3	15.8	13.8	13.5	15.2	36.2	18.8	19.7
of which: Bonds	10.4	14.5	12.2	12.3	13.9	34.7	16.8	17.0
Private nonguaranteed	13.7	7.2	13.7	14.1	18.3	18.0	22.2	23.2
of which: Bonds	3.3	3.3	5.3	6.6	9.0	5.8	9.6	11.5
Net financial flows								
Net inflows	54.4	49.0	151.9	279.2	213.6	265.1	287.7	299.1
Net debt inflows	-8.0	-12.2	52.6	155.8	107.7	140.9	160.7	167.8
Official creditors	-12.0	-26.5	14.9	20.9	2.9	10.0	6.6	8.1
of which: World Bank	1.6	0.0	6.0	8.3	-3.1	3.5	2.7	3.1
of which: IMF	-11.0	-23.8	0.4	1.3	0.2	-0.1	-0.2	-0.6
Private creditors	4.0	14.3	37.7	134.9	104.9	130.9	154.1	159.6
Long-term	8.5	13.4	40.8	84.6	114.1	115.8	137.2	134.1
Bonds	9.4	16.9	38.8	61.5	68.1	79.1	73.4	54.1
Banks and other private	-0.8	-3.5	2.0	23.2	45.9	36.7	63.8	80.0
Short-term	-4.5	0.9	-3.1	50.3	-9.2	15.0	16.9	25.5
Net equity inflows	62.4	61.2	99.3	123.4	105.8	124.2	127.0	131.3
Foreign direct investment	58.7	50.5	58.0	83.9	102.8	105.6	113.8	110.8
Portfolio equity	3.7	10.7	41.3	39.4	3.0	18.6	13.2	20.5
Major economic aggregates								
Gross national income (GNI)	1,582.7	2,118.3	3,104.3	3,966.4	4,574.1	4,478.0	4,569.8	4,571.1
Exports of goods, services & prim. income	337.2	487.7	610.8	770.7	941.1	970.9	980.7	982.0
Imports of goods, services & prim. income	407.3	540.5	710.1	907.2	1,101.2	1,136.4	1,193.0	1,221.5
Primary income on FDI	15.6	33.8	53.3	66.1	82.3	79.6	91.6	74.0
Personal transfers & comp. of employees	20.0	48.2	54.3	55.4	58.7	59.5	60.5	63.4
International reserves	97.7	176.9	434.6	521.2	618.9	678.3	695.8	720.6
Ratios								
External debt stocks to exports (%)	155.5	106.1	110.9	107.3	100.8	110.1	122.8	137.2
External debt stocks to GNI (%)	33.1	24.4	21.8	20.9	20.7	23.9	26.4	29.5
Debt service to exports (%)	39.2	26.2	17.1	13.8	13.8	16.1	16.4	15.6
Short-term to external debt stocks (%)	12.6	12.7	12.5	16.3	13.3	13.2	13.1	13.6
Multilateral to external debt stocks (%)	13.4	15.6	13.5	12.9	11.1	10.5	9.6	8.9
Reserves to external debt stocks (%)	18.6	34.2	64.2	63.0	65.3	63.5	57.8	53.5

MIDDLE EAST AND NORTH AFRICA

(US$ billion, unless otherwise indicated)

	2000	2005	2009	2010	2011	2012	2013	2014
Summary external debt data								
External debt stocks	**143.7**	**150.6**	**160.6**	**167.9**	**165.7**	**172.5**	**188.9**	**187.9**
Long-term external debt	116.3	122.2	119.5	121.8	120.5	130.4	146.5	141.3
Public and publicly guaranteed	112.3	115.4	112.6	114.0	112.5	121.3	136.6	131.8
Official creditors	88.1	77.7	78.3	78.1	78.5	82.4	90.2	84.9
Use of IMF credit	3.5	1.6	8.3	8.3	8.2	8.6	9.5	10.2
Private creditors	24.3	37.7	34.3	35.9	34.0	38.8	46.3	46.9
of which: Bonds	7.3	21.5	23.5	26.6	25.9	31.5	39.1	39.8
Private nonguaranteed	4.0	6.8	6.9	7.8	8.0	9.1	9.9	9.5
of which: Bonds	0.8	1.0	0.7	0.5	0.5	0.7	0.7	0.7
Short-term external debt	23.9	26.8	32.8	37.8	36.9	33.5	33.0	36.4
interest arrears on long-term	2.6	0.3	0.3	0.3	0.4	0.5	0.6	0.6
Long-term external debt								
Disbursements	**9.2**	**14.9**	**13.6**	**14.8**	**13.5**	**21.8**	**27.2**	**17.0**
Public and publicly guaranteed	7.9	13.0	12.0	13.5	12.0	18.9	23.8	14.5
Official creditors	3.4	5.5	8.2	7.2	7.6	10.4	13.8	7.9
Private creditors	4.5	7.5	3.9	6.2	4.5	8.5	10.0	6.6
of which: Bonds	2.0	4.1	2.9	5.5	4.0	8.3	9.5	4.9
Private nonguaranteed	1.3	1.9	1.6	1.4	1.5	2.9	3.5	2.4
of which: Bonds	0.1	0.5	0.2	0.0	0.0	0.5	0.0	0.0
Principal repayments	**10.6**	**14.2**	**13.2**	**12.2**	**14.0**	**11.6**	**11.9**	**13.7**
Public and publicly guaranteed	10.4	13.3	11.0	10.3	12.7	9.6	9.0	11.6
Official creditors	5.9	7.9	5.6	6.0	6.5	6.2	6.4	7.1
Private creditors	4.5	5.5	5.4	4.4	6.1	3.4	2.6	4.5
of which: Bonds	0.8	1.9	3.0	2.2	4.6	2.6	1.7	3.8
Private nonguaranteed	0.2	0.8	2.3	1.8	1.3	2.0	2.9	2.0
of which: Bonds	0.1	0.3	0.0	0.2	0.0	0.3	0.0	0.0
Interest payments	**4.9**	**4.7**	**4.4**	**4.3**	**4.2**	**4.0**	**4.2**	**4.2**
Public and publicly guaranteed	4.7	4.5	4.1	4.0	4.0	3.7	4.0	4.1
Official creditors	3.1	2.5	2.0	2.1	1.9	1.9	1.8	1.7
Private creditors	1.6	2.0	2.1	1.9	2.0	1.9	2.1	2.4
of which: Bonds	0.5	1.3	1.7	1.6	1.8	1.7	1.9	2.2
Private nonguaranteed	0.2	0.3	0.3	0.3	0.2	0.2	0.3	0.1
of which: Bonds	0.1	0.1	0.0	0.1	0.0	0.0	0.0	0.0
Net financial flows								
Net inflows	4.8	13.4	25.5	27.1	13.9	21.1	29.7	21.5
Net debt inflows	0.8	0.5	3.4	7.6	-1.3	7.1	15.7	8.1
Official creditors	-2.7	-3.1	2.5	1.3	1.0	4.7	8.3	2.4
of which: World Bank	-0.3	0.0	0.9	0.8	0.9	0.8	1.1	0.9
of which: IMF	-0.2	-0.7	-0.1	0.0	-0.1	0.5	0.9	1.5
Private creditors	3.5	3.7	1.0	6.3	-2.3	2.4	7.4	5.7
Long-term	1.1	3.1	-2.1	1.4	-1.5	6.0	8.0	2.5
Bonds	1.3	2.5	0.1	3.2	-0.6	5.8	7.8	1.1
Banks and other private	-0.2	0.6	-2.2	-1.8	-0.8	0.1	0.2	1.3
Short-term	2.4	0.6	3.1	4.9	-0.9	-3.6	-0.6	3.3
Net equity inflows	4.0	12.9	22.0	19.5	15.2	14.0	14.0	13.3
Foreign direct investment	3.7	10.5	20.8	17.5	15.9	15.3	14.3	12.8
Portfolio equity	0.3	2.4	1.2	2.0	-0.6	-1.3	-0.3	0.6
Major economic aggregates								
Gross national income (GNI)	364.8	543.9	917.8	1,073.0	1,306.5	1,325.9	1,289.6	1,228.6
Exports of goods, services & prim. income	119.3	206.9	314.7	328.8	382.7	412.6	346.7	339.1
Imports of goods, services & prim. income	110.5	206.7	341.3	362.2	400.9	419.1	404.9	408.6
Primary income on FDI	1.7	10.7	14.0	17.5	18.1	19.0	20.0	7.5
Personal transfers & comp. of employees	10.5	21.7	30.2	35.9	36.8	43.2	43.4	48.4
International reserves	44.0	138.2	280.5	298.5	274.6	279.2	289.7	273.6
Ratios								
External debt stocks to exports (%)	120.5	72.8	51.0	51.1	43.3	41.8	54.5	55.4
External debt stocks to GNI (%)	39.4	27.7	17.5	15.6	12.7	13.0	14.7	15.3
Debt service to exports (%)	14.2	10.2	5.8	5.2	4.9	4.0	4.9	5.5
Short-term to external debt stocks (%)	16.6	17.8	20.4	22.5	22.3	19.4	17.5	19.3
Multilateral to external debt stocks (%)	16.0	17.3	21.8	21.6	23.1	23.8	23.6	22.7
Reserves to external debt stocks (%)	30.6	91.8	174.6	177.7	165.8	161.9	153.3	145.6

SOUTH ASIA

(US$ billion, unless otherwise indicated)

	2000	2005	2009	2010	2011	2012	2013	2014
Summary external debt data								
External debt stocks	**162.4**	**189.9**	**364.8**	**411.3**	**463.9**	**530.2**	**572.6**	**613.4**
Long-term external debt	153.1	174.6	292.3	324.5	355.3	405.3	447.4	495.4
Public and publicly guaranteed	134.6	116.6	169.7	190.1	203.9	234.4	239.8	274.0
Official creditors	101.9	109.8	146.0	157.4	166.0	170.8	173.0	167.3
Use of IMF credit	3.2	3.7	18.7	20.3	20.3	18.8	16.0	14.6
Private creditors	32.7	6.8	23.7	32.7	37.9	63.6	66.8	106.7
of which: Bonds	10.9	2.5	12.7	18.3	21.1	29.1	28.2	61.9
Private nonguaranteed	18.5	58.0	122.6	134.3	151.4	170.9	207.6	221.4
of which: Bonds	1.6	6.5	16.2	13.5	11.1	8.1	8.4	7.0
Short-term external debt	6.1	11.6	53.8	66.5	88.4	106.2	109.2	103.4
interest arrears on long-term	0.1	0.0	0.0	0.1	0.2	0.2	0.1	0.3
Long-term external debt								
Disbursements	**14.0**	**24.5**	**35.3**	**54.7**	**52.1**	**63.1**	**85.6**	**148.0**
Public and publicly guaranteed	13.4	11.0	17.9	31.9	21.8	28.4	26.5	63.3
Official creditors	6.1	7.4	12.8	14.9	13.7	12.6	16.1	15.9
Private creditors	7.3	3.6	5.1	17.0	8.1	15.8	10.4	47.4
of which: Bonds	5.5	2.3	2.3	12.1	3.0	8.5	3.3	33.9
Private nonguaranteed	0.6	13.5	17.4	22.8	30.3	34.6	59.1	84.7
of which: Bonds	0.0	3.5	2.5	1.3	0.7	0.7	1.3	1.0
Principal repayments	**9.0**	**21.8**	**15.1**	**23.7**	**26.0**	**25.4**	**34.7**	**86.5**
Public and publicly guaranteed	8.3	14.5	8.7	8.9	10.2	10.1	14.8	18.7
Official creditors	5.1	4.5	5.4	6.0	7.1	6.9	7.9	11.6
Private creditors	3.3	10.0	3.3	2.8	3.0	3.2	6.9	7.2
of which: Bonds	0.1	8.6	1.1	0.7	0.2	0.5	4.2	0.2
Private nonguaranteed	0.7	7.3	6.4	14.9	15.8	15.3	19.9	67.7
of which: Bonds	0.0	0.1	1.8	2.5	2.8	3.7	1.1	2.3
Interest payments	**5.3**	**5.2**	**6.5**	**6.4**	**7.8**	**9.8**	**10.6**	**13.2**
Public and publicly guaranteed	4.4	4.0	2.7	2.7	2.7	3.3	3.1	3.7
Official creditors	2.3	1.9	2.1	2.0	2.1	2.5	2.2	2.1
Private creditors	2.1	2.0	0.5	0.7	0.6	0.8	1.0	1.6
of which: Bonds	0.2	1.8	0.3	0.2	0.3	0.4	0.5	0.7
Private nonguaranteed	0.9	1.3	3.8	3.7	5.1	6.5	7.5	9.4
of which: Bonds	0.2	0.2	0.3	0.5	0.9	0.5	0.5	0.4
Net financial flows								
Net inflows	10.6	27.4	89.3	106.2	81.3	103.2	102.3	104.4
Net debt inflows	3.8	4.3	27.4	45.6	47.8	53.9	51.3	55.0
Official creditors	0.8	2.9	10.9	10.8	6.6	4.1	5.5	3.8
of which: World Bank	1.0	2.3	2.4	3.3	2.0	0.9	0.7	2.4
of which: IMF	-0.3	0.0	3.6	2.0	0.0	-1.5	-2.8	-0.5
Private creditors	3.0	1.4	16.4	34.8	41.2	49.8	45.9	51.2
Long-term	3.9	-0.3	12.7	22.1	19.5	32.0	42.7	57.2
Bonds	5.4	-2.8	1.9	10.1	0.7	5.0	-0.6	32.4
Banks and other private	-1.5	2.6	10.9	12.0	18.8	27.0	43.3	24.8
Short-term	-0.9	1.7	3.7	12.7	21.7	17.8	3.2	-6.0
Net equity inflows	6.9	23.1	61.9	60.6	33.5	49.3	50.9	49.4
Foreign direct investment	4.4	10.7	37.8	30.8	37.8	25.9	30.4	35.7
Portfolio equity	2.5	12.4	24.2	29.8	-4.3	23.3	20.5	13.7
Major economic aggregates								
Gross national income (GNI)	624.7	1,053.0	1,710.8	2,083.9	2,281.4	2,293.0	2,354.5	2,605.6
Exports of goods, services & prim. income	88.8	202.2	330.1	429.3	538.4	535.7	565.6	588.4
Imports of goods, services & prim. income	117.6	260.5	440.6	577.9	715.6	752.9	741.4	754.2
Primary income on FDI	0.7	8.0	16.4	25.8	27.9	21.1	18.7	24.3
Personal transfers & comp. of employees	17.2	34.2	75.1	82.4	96.5	108.1	111.0	115.9
International reserves	43.3	149.5	298.8	315.4	310.6	310.8	318.9	358.9
Ratios								
External debt stocks to exports (%)	183.0	93.9	110.5	95.8	86.2	99.0	101.2	104.2
External debt stocks to GNI (%)	26.0	18.0	21.3	19.7	20.3	23.1	24.3	23.5
Debt service to exports (%)	17.2	13.8	6.9	7.3	6.6	7.4	9.0	17.5
Short-term to external debt stocks (%)	3.7	6.1	14.8	16.2	19.0	20.0	19.1	16.9
Multilateral to external debt stocks (%)	37.6	36.6	26.0	24.7	23.0	20.5	19.1	17.7
Reserves to external debt stocks (%)	26.7	78.7	81.9	76.7	67.0	58.6	55.7	58.5

SUB-SAHARAN AFRICA

(US$ billion, unless otherwise indicated)

	2000	2005	2009	2010	2011	2012	2013	2014
Summary external debt data								
External debt stocks	**212.1**	**233.4**	**255.7**	**281.6**	**311.9**	**352.0**	**375.0**	**402.8**
Long-term external debt	172.0	191.6	193.3	218.7	249.5	280.4	300.4	323.5
Public and publicly guaranteed	161.3	174.0	147.6	158.2	176.2	199.9	222.4	244.4
Official creditors	135.2	134.7	104.9	105.2	114.3	118.3	133.5	143.4
Use of IMF credit	8.7	8.1	20.0	19.5	20.7	21.6	21.9	20.4
Private creditors	26.1	39.3	42.7	53.1	61.9	81.6	88.9	101.0
of which: Bonds	9.1	16.0	22.9	34.7	41.7	58.0	59.1	67.9
Private nonguaranteed	10.7	17.6	45.8	60.5	73.3	80.5	78.0	79.0
of which: Bonds	1.4	3.2	8.5	8.8	13.1	15.0	14.4	15.2
Short-term external debt	31.4	33.7	42.4	43.4	41.6	50.0	52.6	59.0
interest arrears on long-term	13.5	14.2	11.4	11.2	9.0	9.4	9.8	9.1
Long-term external debt								
Disbursements	**10.4**	**15.0**	**21.2**	**25.8**	**38.5**	**36.3**	**49.5**	**63.9**
Public and publicly guaranteed	7.5	12.7	17.5	20.5	25.0	25.6	37.5	43.2
Official creditors	4.1	6.3	11.3	15.8	15.9	14.7	20.5	22.8
Private creditors	3.4	6.4	6.2	4.8	9.1	10.9	17.0	20.4
of which: Bonds	0.8	0.0	2.2	2.0	4.5	4.3	7.9	10.1
Private nonguaranteed	2.9	2.4	3.7	5.3	13.5	10.7	12.0	20.7
of which: Bonds	0.7	0.0	0.2	1.1	4.4	3.2	4.8	3.8
Principal repayments	**8.5**	**12.2**	**10.2**	**10.1**	**13.9**	**16.3**	**20.6**	**24.1**
Public and publicly guaranteed	7.2	11.8	8.5	6.9	7.6	9.6	10.8	12.9
Official creditors	3.4	6.6	3.3	3.0	3.8	4.0	4.9	5.9
Private creditors	3.7	5.2	5.2	3.9	3.9	5.7	6.0	7.0
of which: Bonds	0.5	1.1	0.3	0.0	0.1	1.8	2.4	1.1
Private nonguaranteed	1.4	0.4	1.7	3.2	6.3	6.6	9.7	11.3
of which: Bonds	0.0	0.0	0.0	0.8	0.0	1.3	2.1	2.1
Interest payments	**3.3**	**7.8**	**3.8**	**3.8**	**4.8**	**6.3**	**6.8**	**7.7**
Public and publicly guaranteed	2.9	7.4	3.0	3.0	3.6	4.8	5.5	5.8
Official creditors	1.8	5.9	1.5	1.1	1.2	1.6	1.9	2.2
Private creditors	1.1	1.5	1.5	1.9	2.4	3.2	3.6	3.6
of which: Bonds	0.6	0.9	1.1	1.7	2.1	2.7	2.8	2.8
Private nonguaranteed	0.4	0.4	0.8	0.8	1.2	1.5	1.3	1.9
of which: Bonds	0.0	0.2	0.4	0.5	0.7	0.8	0.7	1.1
Net financial flows								
Net inflows	9.6	31.0	45.2	44.7	60.6	70.2	70.6	77.7
Net debt inflows	-1.0	5.9	9.1	18.1	26.3	28.8	31.3	46.5
Official creditors	0.8	-0.7	10.2	13.9	13.4	11.5	15.9	16.7
of which: World Bank	1.5	2.4	3.1	4.0	3.2	3.9	5.0	6.2
of which: IMF	0.1	-0.4	2.2	1.2	1.4	0.9	0.2	-0.3
Private creditors	-1.8	6.6	-1.1	4.2	12.9	17.3	15.5	29.8
Long-term	1.2	3.1	3.0	2.9	12.5	9.3	13.3	22.8
Bonds	1.0	-1.1	2.1	2.3	8.7	4.4	8.1	10.8
Banks and other private	0.2	4.2	0.9	0.7	3.7	4.9	5.1	12.0
Short-term	-2.9	3.5	-4.1	1.2	0.4	7.9	2.2	7.1
Net equity inflows	10.6	25.1	36.1	26.6	34.3	41.3	39.3	31.2
Foreign direct investment	6.4	17.0	25.4	18.4	35.4	31.7	32.3	26.6
Portfolio equity	4.2	8.2	10.8	8.2	-1.1	9.6	7.0	4.5
Major economic aggregates								
Gross national income (GNI)	338.8	620.7	937.2	1,258.4	1,409.7	1,487.5	1,563.6	1,646.8
Exports of goods, services & prim. income	114.3	238.7	308.7	399.5	480.5	477.3	487.0	462.9
Imports of goods, services & prim. income	118.2	241.6	377.4	452.3	541.2	553.6	577.8	579.4
Primary income on FDI	8.0	17.2	33.6	46.7	48.6	49.0	29.5	15.7
Personal transfers & comp. of employees	4.8	20.1	27.2	29.3	30.9	29.9	28.7	29.0
International reserves	34.2	79.8	154.6	154.1	170.1	191.2	192.8	172.4
Ratios								
External debt stocks to exports (%)	185.5	97.8	82.8	70.5	64.9	73.7	77.0	87.0
External debt stocks to GNI (%)	62.6	37.6	27.3	22.4	22.1	23.7	24.0	24.5
Debt service to exports (%)	11.8	9.0	5.0	3.7	4.1	5.0	6.0	7.3
Short-term to external debt stocks (%)	14.8	14.4	16.6	15.4	13.3	14.2	14.0	14.6
Multilateral to external debt stocks (%)	25.7	31.0	21.4	20.8	20.1	18.8	19.7	19.2
Reserves to external debt stocks (%)	16.1	34.2	60.5	54.7	54.6	54.3	51.4	42.8

AFGHANISTAN

(US$ million, unless otherwise indicated)

	2000	2005	2009	2010	2011	2012	2013	2014
Summary external debt data								
External debt stocks	..	..	**2,470**	**2,423**	**2,627**	**2,709**	**2,577**	**2,555**
Long-term external debt	..	..	2,097	1,966	2,023	2,071	2,097	1,999
Short-term external debt	..	..	20	102	232	250	104	221
interest arrears on long-term	..	..	20	67	210	219	85	188
Use of IMF credit	..	..	353	355	373	388	376	335
Long-term external debt								
Debt outstanding and disbursed	..	..	**2,097**	**1,966**	**2,023**	**2,071**	**2,097**	**1,999**
Public and publicly guaranteed	..	..	2,097	1,966	2,023	2,071	2,097	1,999
Official creditors	..	..	2,097	1,966	2,023	2,071	2,097	1,999
Private creditors	..	..	0	0	0	0	0	0
of which: Bonds	..	..	0	0	0	0	0	0
Private nonguaranteed	..	..	..	..	..	..	..	..
of which: Bonds	..	..	..	..	..	..	..	..
Disbursements	..	..	**109**	**76**	**62**	**52**	**36**	**32**
Public and publicly guaranteed	..	..	109	76	62	52	36	32
Official creditors	..	..	109	76	62	52	36	32
Private creditors	..	..	0	0	0	0	0	0
of which: Bonds	..	..	0	0	0	0	0	0
Private nonguaranteed	..	..	..	..	..	..	..	..
of which: Bonds	..	..	..	..	..	..	..	..
Principal repayments	..	..	**3**	**1**	**1**	**1**	**4**	**8**
Public and publicly guaranteed	..	..	3	1	1	1	4	8
Official creditors	..	..	3	1	1	1	4	8
Private creditors	..	..	0	0	0	0	0	0
of which: Bonds	..	..	0	0	0	0	0	0
Private nonguaranteed	..	..	..	..	..	..	..	..
of which: Bonds	..	..	..	..	..	..	..	..
Interest payments	..	..	**7**	**7**	**9**	**8**	**8**	**9**
Public and publicly guaranteed	..	..	7	7	9	8	8	9
Official creditors	..	..	7	7	9	8	8	9
Private creditors	..	..	0	0	0	0	0	0
of which: Bonds	..	..	0	0	0	0	0	0
Private nonguaranteed	..	..	..	..	..	..	..	..
of which: Bonds	..	..	..	..	..	..	..	..
Net financial flows								
Net debt inflows	..	..	123	119	67	75	7	18
Official creditors (incl. IMF)	..	..	123	84	80	66	19	4
Private creditors	..	..	..	35	-13	9	-12	14
Long-term	..	..	..	..	..	..	..	..
Public and publicly guaranteed	..	..	..	..	..	..	..	..
Private nonguaranteed	..	..	..	..	..	..	..	..
Short-term	..	..	..	35	-13	9	-12	14
Net equity inflows								
Foreign direct investment	..	..	214	76	91	94	60	54
Portfolio equity	..	..	..	0	0	2	0	..
Major economic aggregates								
Gross national income (GNI)	..	..	12,541	15,999	18,013	20,638	20,452	20,951
Exports of goods, services & prim. income	..	..	2,546	3,920	4,300	4,238	4,221	..
Imports of goods, services & prim. income	..	..	4,467	6,840	8,204	11,885	11,576	..
Primary income on FDI	..	..	0	0	0	2	0	..
Personal transfers & comp. of employees	..	..	152	331	247	385	538	636
International reserves	..	..	3,501	4,174	5,268	5,983	6,442	6,681
Ratios								
External debt stocks to exports (%)	..	..	97.0	61.8	61.1	63.9	61.0	..
External debt stocks to GNI (%)	..	..	19.7	15.1	14.6	13.1	12.6	12.2
Debt service to exports (%)	..	..	0.4	0.3	0.3	0.3	0.6	..
Reserves to external debt stocks (%)	..	..	141.8	172.3	200.5	220.9	250.0	261.5

Notes:

Short-term debt is based on data from the BIS. Data include the effects of Paris Club debt restructuring agreements signed in 2010 and HIPC and MDRI debt relief.

ALBANIA

(US$ million, unless otherwise indicated)

	2000	2005	2009	2010	2011	2012	2013	2014
Summary external debt data								
External debt stocks	**1,122**	**2,101**	**4,310**	**5,201**	**6,228**	**7,157**	**8,430**	**8,000**
Long-term external debt	937	1,788	3,485	4,328	5,019	5,580	6,701	6,376
Short-term external debt	37	155	681	743	1,092	1,470	1,632	1,474
interest arrears on long-term	3	1	0	0	0	0	0	0
Use of IMF credit	148	158	144	129	117	107	97	151
Long-term external debt								
Debt outstanding and disbursed	**937**	**1,788**	**3,485**	**4,328**	**5,019**	**5,580**	**6,701**	**6,376**
Public and publicly guaranteed	921	1,375	2,602	3,043	3,287	3,552	3,759	3,671
Official creditors	895	1,343	2,129	2,171	2,309	2,538	2,691	2,749
Private creditors	26	32	472	872	977	1,015	1,068	922
of which: Bonds	0	0	82	477	556	567	593	522
Private nonguaranteed	16	413	884	1,285	1,732	2,027	2,943	2,705
of which: Bonds	..	..	..	..	..	..	..	..
Disbursements	**119**	**489**	**457**	**820**	**755**	**683**	**749**	**733**
Public and publicly guaranteed	119	119	291	631	418	336	258	448
Official creditors	119	119	256	198	274	315	249	433
Private creditors	0	0	34	433	144	21	9	15
of which: Bonds	0	0	0	398	101	0	0	0
Private nonguaranteed	..	370	167	189	336	347	491	285
of which: Bonds	..	..	..	..	..	..	..	..
Principal repayments	**9**	**41**	**112**	**127**	**143**	**160**	**200**	**231**
Public and publicly guaranteed	9	40	80	89	102	108	125	178
Official creditors	8	39	78	86	99	105	122	144
Private creditors	1	1	2	3	3	3	2	35
of which: Bonds	0	0	0	0	0	0	0	0
Private nonguaranteed	..	1	32	38	41	52	75	52
of which: Bonds	..	..	..	..	..	..	..	..
Interest payments	**8**	**25**	**58**	**47**	**85**	**84**	**80**	**93**
Public and publicly guaranteed	7	23	50	39	77	74	72	79
Official creditors	7	23	35	31	36	37	36	44
Private creditors	0	0	14	7	41	37	36	35
of which: Bonds	0	0	2	1	32	30	31	30
Private nonguaranteed	1	1	8	8	8	9	8	14
of which: Bonds	..	..	..	..	..	..	..	..
Net financial flows								
Net debt inflows	130	605	-134	744	948	891	701	406
Official creditors (incl. IMF)	122	83	168	99	163	200	116	352
Private creditors	7	522	-302	644	785	691	585	54
Long-term	-1	368	167	582	437	313	423	213
Public and publicly guaranteed	-1	-1	33	431	141	18	7	-20
Private nonguaranteed	..	369	134	151	295	295	416	232
Short-term	8	154	-469	63	349	378	162	-158
Net equity inflows								
Foreign direct investment	143	262	1,038	1,052	813	714	846	1,157
Portfolio equity	..	..	-4	7	23	18	2	1
Major economic aggregates								
Gross national income (GNI)	3,790	8,541	11,853	11,807	12,856	12,253	12,945	13,158
Exports of goods, services & prim. income	819	1,687	3,439	3,704	4,078	3,800	4,027	4,071
Imports of goods, services & prim. income	1,509	3,553	6,598	6,280	7,010	6,189	6,310	6,800
Primary income on FDI	0	2	448	381	140	169	29	271
Personal transfers & comp. of employees	598	1,290	1,318	1,156	1,126	1,027	1,094	1,142
International reserves	616	1,404	2,314	2,470	2,394	2,516	2,712	2,604
Ratios								
External debt stocks to exports (%)	137.0	124.5	125.3	140.4	152.7	188.3	209.3	196.5
External debt stocks to GNI (%)	29.6	24.6	36.4	44.0	48.4	58.4	65.1	60.8
Debt service to exports (%)	3.7	4.8	5.7	5.2	5.9	6.7	7.3	8.2
Reserves to external debt stocks (%)	54.9	66.8	53.7	47.5	38.4	35.2	32.2	32.6

Notes:

Long-term private nonguaranteed debt data for 2014 are World Bank staff estimates based on reports provided by the country.

ALGERIA

(US$ million, unless otherwise indicated)

	2000	2005	2009	2010	2011	2012	2013	2014
Summary external debt data								
External debt stocks	**25,477**	**17,092**	**7,405**	**7,246**	**6,045**	**5,495**	**5,231**	**5,453**
Long-term external debt	23,369	16,393	4,035	3,623	3,064	2,449	2,058	1,742
Short-term external debt	222	516	1,492	1,778	1,142	1,205	1,328	1,975
interest arrears on long-term	0	0	0	0	0	0	0	0
Use of IMF credit	1,886	184	1,878	1,845	1,840	1,842	1,845	1,736
Long-term external debt								
Debt outstanding and disbursed	**23,369**	**16,393**	**4,035**	**3,623**	**3,064**	**2,449**	**2,058**	**1,742**
Public and publicly guaranteed	23,369	15,527	3,053	2,655	2,246	1,627	1,438	1,112
Official creditors	17,518	12,500	2,092	1,889	1,643	1,198	1,117	882
Private creditors	5,851	3,027	961	766	603	429	321	230
of which: Bonds	0	0	0	0	0	0	0	0
Private nonguaranteed	..	866	982	968	818	822	620	630
of which: Bonds	..	..	..	..	..	..	..	..
Disbursements	**1,219**	**1,240**	**211**	**43**	**30**	**29**	**22**	**43**
Public and publicly guaranteed	1,219	777	88	41	30	28	22	4
Official creditors	799	446	86	40	26	28	22	4
Private creditors	420	331	2	1	4	0	0	0
of which: Bonds	0	0	0	0	0	0	0	0
Private nonguaranteed	..	463	123	2	0	0	..	39
of which: Bonds	..	..	..	..	..	..	..	..
Principal repayments	**2,721**	**4,448**	**910**	**557**	**536**	**742**	**459**	**234**
Public and publicly guaranteed	2,721	4,219	388	324	415	589	257	210
Official creditors	1,055	3,014	155	167	255	488	139	137
Private creditors	1,666	1,205	233	157	160	101	117	72
of which: Bonds	0	0	0	0	0	0	0	0
Private nonguaranteed	..	229	522	234	121	153	203	24
of which: Bonds	..	..	..	..	..	..	..	..
Interest payments	**1,552**	**889**	**124**	**95**	**80**	**103**	**51**	**37**
Public and publicly guaranteed	1,552	864	75	64	58	85	38	28
Official creditors	1,132	719	34	35	32	67	20	17
Private creditors	421	145	41	29	26	18	18	11
of which: Bonds	0	0	0	0	0	0	0	0
Private nonguaranteed	..	25	49	31	22	18	13	9
of which: Bonds	..	..	..	..	..	..	..	..
Net financial flows								
Net debt inflows	-1,568	-3,734	-510	-229	-1,142	-650	-314	456
Official creditors (incl. IMF)	-349	-3,180	-69	-127	-228	-460	-117	-133
Private creditors	-1,219	-555	-441	-101	-914	-190	-197	589
Long-term	-1,246	-640	-629	-387	-277	-253	-320	-58
Public and publicly guaranteed	-1,246	-874	-231	-155	-157	-101	-117	-72
Private nonguaranteed	..	234	-398	-232	-121	-152	-203	15
Short-term	27	85	189	286	-637	63	123	647
Net equity inflows								
Foreign direct investment	280	1,156	2,833	2,315	2,628	1,565	1,717	1,488
Portfolio equity	..	..	..	..	..	..	..	..
Major economic aggregates								
Gross national income (GNI)	52,080	98,611	135,997	160,996	197,183	202,016	206,268	209,782
Exports of goods, services & prim. income	..	50,268	52,892	65,259	80,950	79,280	71,788	66,710
Imports of goods, services & prim. income	..	31,155	55,112	55,615	65,957	70,150	73,703	79,430
Primary income on FDI	..	5,485	5,891	4,858	6,313	7,453	8,001	..
Personal transfers & comp. of employees	790	170	150	197	203	215	210	2,020
International reserves	12,024	56,303	149,041	162,614	182,822	191,297	194,712	179,618
Ratios								
External debt stocks to exports (%)	..	34.0	14.0	11.1	7.5	6.9	7.3	8.2
External debt stocks to GNI (%)	48.9	17.3	5.4	4.5	3.1	2.7	2.5	2.6
Debt service to exports (%)	..	11.9	2.0	1.0	0.8	1.1	0.7	0.4
Reserves to external debt stocks (%)	47.2	329.4	2,012.6	2,244.2	3,024.5	3,481.1	3,722.1	3,293.9

ANGOLA

(US$ million, unless otherwise indicated)

	2000	2005	2009	2010	2011	2012	2013	2014
Summary external debt data								
External debt stocks	**9,763**	**12,224**	**17,014**	**16,949**	**19,298**	**21,106**	**25,004**	**28,450**
Long-term external debt	8,085	9,518	13,635	15,466	17,525	19,203	23,349	27,373
Short-term external debt	1,323	2,316	2,593	181	168	164	176	162
interest arrears on long-term	874	577	85	68	62	58	70	58
Use of IMF credit	356	390	787	1,302	1,606	1,740	1,479	914
Long-term external debt								
Debt outstanding and disbursed	**8,085**	**9,518**	**13,635**	**15,466**	**17,525**	**19,203**	**23,349**	**27,373**
Public and publicly guaranteed	8,085	9,518	13,635	15,466	17,525	19,203	23,349	27,373
Official creditors	2,703	3,174	4,822	8,161	9,687	9,615	11,825	13,727
Private creditors	5,382	6,344	8,813	7,305	7,837	9,588	11,525	13,646
of which: Bonds	0	0	0	0	10	1,000	1,000	1,000
Private nonguaranteed	..	..	..	..	..	..	..	..
of which: Bonds	..	..	..	..	..	..	..	..
Disbursements	**1,045**	**3,676**	**3,543**	**3,951**	**4,793**	**5,215**	**7,825**	**10,140**
Public and publicly guaranteed	1,045	3,676	3,543	3,951	4,793	5,215	7,825	10,140
Official creditors	34	321	1,111	3,658	2,353	1,103	3,612	3,666
Private creditors	1,011	3,355	2,432	293	2,440	4,112	4,213	6,474
of which: Bonds	0	0	0	0	10	1,051	0	0
Private nonguaranteed	..	..	..	..	..	..	..	..
of which: Bonds	..	..	..	..	..	..	..	..
Principal repayments	**1,530**	**2,289**	**3,131**	**2,110**	**2,681**	**3,554**	**3,723**	**5,773**
Public and publicly guaranteed	1,530	2,289	3,131	2,110	2,681	3,554	3,723	5,773
Official creditors	268	505	310	283	820	1,164	1,380	1,649
Private creditors	1,262	1,784	2,821	1,827	1,862	2,390	2,344	4,124
of which: Bonds	0	0	0	0	0	61	0	0
Private nonguaranteed	..	..	..	..	..	..	..	..
of which: Bonds	..	..	..	..	..	..	..	..
Interest payments	**149**	**257**	**392**	**176**	**154**	**640**	**919**	**1,021**
Public and publicly guaranteed	149	257	392	176	154	640	919	1,021
Official creditors	36	61	143	114	79	321	414	444
Private creditors	113	195	250	63	75	319	505	576
of which: Bonds	0	0	0	0	0	1	47	70
Private nonguaranteed	..	..	..	..	..	..	..	..
of which: Bonds	..	..	..	..	..	..	..	..
Net financial flows								
Net debt inflows	-733	2,603	952	-29	2,421	1,791	3,840	3,865
Official creditors (incl. IMF)	-234	-185	1,155	3,900	1,849	70	1,970	1,516
Private creditors	-499	2,788	-203	-3,929	572	1,722	1,870	2,349
Long-term	-251	1,572	-390	-1,534	579	1,722	1,870	2,351
Public and publicly guaranteed	-251	1,572	-390	-1,534	579	1,722	1,870	2,351
Private nonguaranteed	..	..	..	..	..	..	..	..
Short-term	-248	1,216	187	-2,395	-7	0	0	-2
Net equity inflows								
Foreign direct investment	879	1,140	2,743	3,326	4,070	4,357	4,184	3,881
Portfolio equity	..	..	..	..	..	..	..	..
Major economic aggregates								
Gross national income (GNI)	7,449	24,230	68,299	73,946	93,056	103,175	112,275	118,860
Exports of goods, services & prim. income	8,222	24,312	41,582	51,586	68,252	72,133	70,381	68,014
Imports of goods, services & prim. income	7,454	19,201	48,784	43,642	53,805	56,518	59,909	60,750
Primary income on FDI	929	3,406	6,130	7,526	9,040	9,722	9,331	..
Personal transfers & comp. of employees	..	..	0	18	0	0	0	0
International reserves	1,198	3,197	13,664	19,749	28,786	33,415	32,780	28,130
Ratios								
External debt stocks to exports (%)	118.7	50.3	40.9	32.9	28.3	29.3	35.5	41.8
External debt stocks to GNI (%)	131.1	50.5	24.9	22.9	20.7	20.5	22.3	23.9
Debt service to exports (%)	20.9	10.8	8.5	4.5	4.2	5.8	7.0	10.7
Reserves to external debt stocks (%)	12.3	26.2	80.3	116.5	149.2	158.3	131.1	98.9

Notes:

Short-term debt before 2009 is based on data from the BIS.

ARMENIA

(US$ million, unless otherwise indicated)

	2000	2005	2009	2010	2011	2012	2013	2014
Summary external debt data								
External debt stocks	**1,010**	**1,968**	**4,933**	**6,304**	**7,407**	**7,637**	**8,678**	**8,551**
Long-term external debt	675	1,368	3,679	4,772	5,541	5,884	6,807	7,073
Short-term external debt	44	298	529	656	904	842	1,150	908
interest arrears on long-term	6	0	0	0	0	0	0	0
Use of IMF credit	290	302	725	876	963	911	720	570
Long-term external debt								
Debt outstanding and disbursed	**675**	**1,368**	**3,679**	**4,772**	**5,541**	**5,884**	**6,807**	**7,073**
Public and publicly guaranteed	675	923	2,376	2,557	2,736	2,956	3,312	3,376
Official creditors	658	921	2,375	2,556	2,733	2,942	2,594	2,658
Private creditors	17	1	1	1	4	14	718	718
of which: Bonds	0	0	0	0	0	0	700	700
Private nonguaranteed	..	446	1,302	2,216	2,805	2,928	3,495	3,698
of which: Bonds	..	..	..	..	..	..	..	..
Disbursements	**63**	**168**	**1,247**	**1,734**	**1,490**	**1,633**	**2,817**	**2,080**
Public and publicly guaranteed	63	50	941	198	206	280	937	283
Official creditors	62	50	941	198	203	270	234	281
Private creditors	1	0	0	0	2	10	703	2
of which: Bonds	0	0	0	0	0	0	700	0
Private nonguaranteed	..	117	306	1,536	1,285	1,353	1,880	1,797
of which: Bonds	..	..	..	..	..	..	..	..
Principal repayments	**15**	**69**	**300**	**857**	**742**	**854**	**1,599**	**1,077**
Public and publicly guaranteed	15	16	21	24	28	30	537	42
Official creditors	13	16	21	24	28	30	537	42
Private creditors	2	0	0	0	0	0	0	0
of which: Bonds	0	0	0	0	0	0	0	0
Private nonguaranteed	..	53	279	833	714	824	1,063	1,035
of which: Bonds	..	..	..	..	..	..	..	..
Interest payments	**9**	**23**	**79**	**60**	**128**	**128**	**126**	**176**
Public and publicly guaranteed	9	9	23	35	38	43	42	71
Official creditors	9	9	23	35	38	43	42	29
Private creditors	0	0	0	0	0	0	0	42
of which: Bonds	0	0	0	0	0	0	0	42
Private nonguaranteed	..	14	56	25	91	84	84	105
of which: Bonds	..	..	..	..	..	..	..	..
Net financial flows								
Net debt inflows	21	-38	1,398	1,167	1,087	665	1,335	648
Official creditors (incl. IMF)	34	10	1,362	337	266	188	-494	126
Private creditors	-13	-48	36	829	821	478	1,828	522
Long-term	-2	64	28	703	573	539	1,521	764
Public and publicly guaranteed	-2	..	0	0	2	10	703	2
Private nonguaranteed	..	64	28	703	571	529	817	762
Short-term	-11	-112	8	127	248	-62	308	-242
Net equity inflows								
Foreign direct investment	104	278	718	361	386	589	363	335
Portfolio equity	0	0	1	7	3	2	-2	1
Major economic aggregates								
Gross national income (GNI)	1,964	5,106	9,007	9,719	10,502	10,381	10,972	11,437
Exports of goods, services & prim. income	551	1,944	2,435	3,260	3,808	4,033	4,415	4,532
Imports of goods, services & prim. income	1,017	2,520	4,443	5,128	5,623	5,824	6,085	6,125
Primary income on FDI	22	170	352	362	379	335	324	169
Personal transfers & comp. of employees	87	915	1,440	1,669	1,799	1,915	2,192	2,079
International reserves	302	669	2,004	1,866	1,932	1,799	2,252	1,489
Ratios								
External debt stocks to exports (%)	183.4	101.3	202.6	193.4	194.5	189.4	196.5	188.7
External debt stocks to GNI (%)	51.4	38.5	54.8	64.9	70.5	73.6	79.1	74.8
Debt service to exports (%)	9.2	7.3	17.4	29.7	24.6	29.1	46.4	31.7
Reserves to external debt stocks (%)	29.9	34.0	40.6	29.6	26.1	23.6	25.9	17.4

Notes:

Long-term private nonguaranteed debt data from 2011 are World Bank staff estimates based on reports provided by the country.

AZERBAIJAN

(US$ million, unless otherwise indicated)

	2000	2005	2009	2010	2011	2012	2013	2014
Summary external debt data								
External debt stocks	**1,524**	**2,118**	**4,755**	**7,029**	**8,085**	**9,551**	**10,294**	**11,693**
Long-term external debt	832	1,549	3,642	5,869	6,929	8,448	8,218	9,543
Short-term external debt	156	186	810	878	891	852	1,834	1,926
interest arrears on long-term	0	0	0	0	0	0	0	0
Use of IMF credit	536	383	303	282	265	252	242	224
Long-term external debt								
Debt outstanding and disbursed	**832**	**1,549**	**3,642**	**5,869**	**6,929**	**8,448**	**8,218**	**9,543**
Public and publicly guaranteed	734	1,362	3,328	3,711	4,312	5,695	6,075	8,094
Official creditors	643	1,102	2,172	2,562	3,144	4,033	4,192	4,464
Private creditors	90	260	1,157	1,149	1,168	1,662	1,884	3,630
of which: Bonds	0	0	0	0	0	500	500	2,250
Private nonguaranteed	99	187	314	2,158	2,616	2,752	2,142	1,448
of which: Bonds	..	..	..	..	..	..	..	..
Disbursements	**269**	**431**	**870**	**2,547**	**1,941**	**2,477**	**1,327**	**3,190**
Public and publicly guaranteed	263	307	820	633	878	1,659	1,073	2,873
Official creditors	204	71	431	453	698	1,069	741	761
Private creditors	59	236	389	180	180	590	333	2,112
of which: Bonds	0	0	0	0	0	500	0	1,750
Private nonguaranteed	6	124	50	1,914	1,063	818	253	317
of which: Bonds	..	..	..	..	..	..	..	..
Principal repayments	**22**	**134**	**230**	**300**	**856**	**922**	**1,511**	**1,498**
Public and publicly guaranteed	14	37	178	228	249	239	646	504
Official creditors	12	34	101	97	116	127	494	259
Private creditors	2	3	76	131	133	111	152	245
of which: Bonds	0	0	0	0	0	0	0	0
Private nonguaranteed	7	97	53	72	608	684	866	995
of which: Bonds	..	..	..	..	..	..	..	..
Interest payments	**37**	**24**	**67**	**80**	**948**	**945**	**930**	**260**
Public and publicly guaranteed	32	17	55	67	77	97	104	106
Official creditors	31	15	35	33	42	43	52	45
Private creditors	1	2	21	35	35	53	52	61
of which: Bonds	0	0	0	0	0	14	27	27
Private nonguaranteed	5	7	12	13	871	848	826	154
of which: Bonds	..	..	..	..	..	..	..	..
Net financial flows								
Net debt inflows	323	316	262	2,300	1,080	1,502	788	1,780
Official creditors (incl. IMF)	141	8	312	341	565	928	237	499
Private creditors	182	308	-49	1,959	515	574	551	1,281
Long-term	55	260	310	1,891	502	613	-431	1,189
Public and publicly guaranteed	57	233	312	50	47	479	181	1,867
Private nonguaranteed	-2	27	-2	1,842	455	134	-612	-678
Short-term	127	48	-359	68	13	-39	982	92
Net equity inflows								
Foreign direct investment	130	4,476	2,525	3,353	4,485	5,293	2,619	4,430
Portfolio equity	..	..	..	1	0	0	30	10
Major economic aggregates								
Gross national income (GNI)	4,987	11,599	40,772	49,436	61,092	63,181	69,440	72,617
Exports of goods, services & prim. income	2,174	8,341	23,311	28,910	38,058	37,837	36,941	34,231
Imports of goods, services & prim. income	2,415	8,658	13,858	14,379	21,586	22,811	24,650	23,974
Primary income on FDI	317	1,582	3,664	3,815	5,488	4,906	4,507	3,359
Personal transfers & comp. of employees	57	623	1,255	1,410	1,893	1,990	1,733	1,846
International reserves	680	1,178	5,364	6,409	10,274	11,277	14,401	14,647
Ratios								
External debt stocks to exports (%)	70.1	25.4	20.4	24.3	21.2	25.2	27.9	34.2
External debt stocks to GNI (%)	30.6	18.3	11.7	14.2	13.2	15.1	14.8	16.1
Debt service to exports (%)	6.4	2.7	1.4	1.4	4.8	5.0	6.7	5.2
Reserves to external debt stocks (%)	44.6	55.6	112.8	91.2	127.1	118.1	139.9	125.3

Notes:

Long-term private nonguaranteed debt data are World Bank staff estimates based on the market data. Short-term debt is based on data from the BIS.

BANGLADESH

(US$ million, unless otherwise indicated)

	2000	2005	2009	2010	2011	2012	2013	2014
Summary external debt data								
External debt stocks	**15,596**	**18,449**	**24,596**	**25,752**	**27,180**	**28,300**	**33,535**	**34,925**
Long-term external debt	14,985	17,385	21,187	21,400	23,804	25,128	28,304	29,302
Short-term external debt	334	688	1,934	2,949	2,105	1,959	3,735	4,153
interest arrears on long-term	0	16	1	2	2	2	2	2
Use of IMF credit	277	376	1,475	1,403	1,271	1,213	1,496	1,470
Long-term external debt								
Debt outstanding and disbursed	**14,985**	**17,385**	**21,187**	**21,400**	**23,804**	**25,128**	**28,304**	**29,302**
Public and publicly guaranteed	14,985	17,385	21,187	21,400	22,350	23,339	26,113	26,433
Official creditors	14,809	17,209	21,144	21,367	22,328	23,325	26,102	26,423
Private creditors	176	176	43	33	22	13	12	10
of which: Bonds	0	0	0	0	0	0	0	0
Private nonguaranteed	..	..	..	..	1,454	1,789	2,191	2,869
of which: Bonds	..	..	..	..	..	..	..	..
Disbursements	**863**	**880**	**1,497**	**978**	**1,028**	**2,177**	**4,303**	**3,440**
Public and publicly guaranteed	863	880	1,497	978	1,028	2,177	4,303	3,440
Official creditors	796	880	1,497	978	1,028	2,177	4,303	3,440
Private creditors	67	0	0	0	0	0	0	0
of which: Bonds	0	0	0	0	0	0	0	0
Private nonguaranteed	..	..	..	..	..	..	..	..
of which: Bonds	..	..	..	..	..	..	..	..
Principal repayments	**488**	**575**	**699**	**737**	**1,050**	**988**	**1,242**	**1,355**
Public and publicly guaranteed	488	575	699	737	1,050	988	1,242	1,355
Official creditors	467	559	687	726	1,039	980	1,240	1,354
Private creditors	22	16	12	11	11	9	2	2
of which: Bonds	0	0	0	0	0	0	0	0
Private nonguaranteed	..	..	..	..	..	..	..	..
of which: Bonds	..	..	..	..	..	..	..	..
Interest payments	**165**	**199**	**196**	**200**	**258**	**243**	**249**	**260**
Public and publicly guaranteed	165	199	196	200	258	243	249	260
Official creditors	156	197	195	199	257	242	248	260
Private creditors	9	2	1	2	1	1	1	1
of which: Bonds	0	0	0	0	0	0	0	0
Private nonguaranteed	..	..	..	..	..	..	..	..
of which: Bonds	..	..	..	..	..	..	..	..
Net financial flows								
Net debt inflows	368	365	814	1,209	-997	983	5,115	2,569
Official creditors (incl. IMF)	242	421	787	206	-142	1,138	3,341	2,152
Private creditors	125	-56	28	1,003	-855	-155	1,774	417
Long-term	46	-16	-12	-11	-11	-9	-2	-2
Public and publicly guaranteed	46	-16	-12	-11	-11	-9	-2	-2
Private nonguaranteed	..	..	..	..	..	..	..	..
Short-term	80	-40	40	1,014	-844	-146	1,776	418
Net equity inflows								
Foreign direct investment	280	626	754	805	924	1,030	1,238	1,304
Portfolio equity	1	20	-104	-104	-16	81	270	413
Major economic aggregates								
Gross national income (GNI)	55,102	72,521	110,603	124,617	138,823	144,642	162,054	185,401
Exports of goods, services & prim. income	7,293	11,322	17,622	23,756	27,148	27,768	31,768	33,214
Imports of goods, services & prim. income	10,018	15,970	24,984	34,315	39,553	39,740	44,208	50,470
Primary income on FDI	149	669	1,083	1,258	1,298	1,622	2,104	2,328
Personal transfers & comp. of employees	1,968	4,642	10,739	11,282	12,071	14,120	13,867	14,983
International reserves	1,486	2,767	10,219	10,564	8,510	12,031	17,564	21,785
Ratios								
External debt stocks to exports (%)	213.9	162.9	139.6	108.4	100.1	101.9	105.6	105.2
External debt stocks to GNI (%)	28.3	25.4	22.2	20.7	19.6	19.6	20.7	18.8
Debt service to exports (%)	10.6	7.2	5.4	4.3	5.5	5.2	5.3	5.2
Reserves to external debt stocks (%)	9.5	15.0	41.5	41.0	31.3	42.5	52.4	62.4

Notes:

Short-term debt before 2012 is based on data from the BIS. Long-term private nonguaranteed debt data from 2011 are World Bank staff estimates based on reports provided by the country and are not available prior to 2011.

BELARUS

(US$ million, unless otherwise indicated)

	2000	2005	2009	2010	2011	2012	2013	2014
Summary external debt data								
External debt stocks	**2,604**	**5,284**	**22,054**	**28,397**	**33,926**	**33,756**	**39,573**	**40,014**
Long-term external debt	771	1,254	9,528	12,470	16,430	18,532	23,579	26,573
Short-term external debt	1,239	3,503	9,076	11,864	13,446	11,635	14,062	12,827
interest arrears on long-term	14	1	3	4	4	4	4	5
Use of IMF credit	594	527	3,449	4,063	4,050	3,588	1,932	613
Long-term external debt								
Debt outstanding and disbursed	**771**	**1,254**	**9,528**	**12,470**	**16,430**	**18,532**	**23,579**	**26,573**
Public and publicly guaranteed	673	769	6,217	7,999	10,609	12,559	14,622	15,628
Official creditors	384	552	4,689	5,725	8,380	7,303	8,540	10,114
Private creditors	289	217	1,529	2,274	2,228	5,256	6,082	5,514
of which: Bonds	0	0	19	1,019	1,800	1,800	1,800	1,800
Private nonguaranteed	98	485	3,311	4,471	5,821	5,973	8,957	10,945
of which: Bonds	..	..	..	..	..	..	..	..
Disbursements	**237**	**647**	**1,984**	**3,810**	**5,406**	**3,542**	**4,675**	**5,276**
Public and publicly guaranteed	131	252	1,264	2,679	3,926	2,223	3,108	3,696
Official creditors	13	188	1,254	1,580	2,826	1,050	1,603	3,046
Private creditors	118	64	10	1,099	1,100	1,173	1,505	650
of which: Bonds	0	0	0	1,000	800	0	0	0
Private nonguaranteed	106	395	720	1,132	1,479	1,320	1,567	1,580
of which: Bonds	..	..	..	..	..	..	..	..
Principal repayments	**193**	**508**	**1,275**	**1,257**	**2,339**	**3,412**	**1,938**	**2,976**
Public and publicly guaranteed	121	175	450	455	1,310	2,649	1,064	2,099
Official creditors	39	92	97	108	167	2,551	379	894
Private creditors	82	83	352	347	1,143	97	685	1,205
of which: Bonds	0	0	0	0	19	0	0	0
Private nonguaranteed	71	333	825	802	1,029	763	874	877
of which: Bonds	..	..	..	..	..	..	..	..
Interest payments	**37**	**53**	**185**	**208**	**572**	**851**	**783**	**885**
Public and publicly guaranteed	36	37	114	127	460	729	603	691
Official creditors	17	16	96	114	312	431	267	313
Private creditors	19	21	17	14	148	298	336	379
of which: Bonds	0	0	2	4	129	159	159	159
Private nonguaranteed	1	15	71	80	112	121	181	193
of which: Bonds	..	..	..	..	..	..	..	..
Net financial flows								
Net debt inflows	-87	696	5,051	6,008	4,648	-2,143	3,515	-198
Official creditors (incl. IMF)	-81	87	3,982	2,141	2,659	-1,965	-423	890
Private creditors	-6	608	1,069	3,867	1,990	-178	3,939	-1,087
Long-term	70	42	-448	1,081	408	1,632	1,512	148
Public and publicly guaranteed	36	-19	-343	752	-42	1,075	820	-555
Private nonguaranteed	35	61	-105	329	450	556	693	703
Short-term	-76	566	1,517	2,786	1,582	-1,810	2,426	-1,236
Net equity inflows								
Foreign direct investment	119	314	1,823	1,348	3,773	1,251	1,772	1,491
Portfolio equity	1	1	1	1	0	-4	2	5
Major economic aggregates								
Gross national income (GNI)	12,690	30,266	48,095	54,058	59,052	62,145	70,389	73,732
Exports of goods, services & prim. income	7,667	17,705	24,818	29,805	47,242	52,803	44,905	44,448
Imports of goods, services & prim. income	8,160	17,411	31,224	38,402	49,812	51,442	49,930	47,246
Primary income on FDI	5	135	872	1,039	1,186	1,258	2,373	2,020
Personal transfers & comp. of employees	139	199	504	575	891	1,053	1,214	1,248
International reserves	350	1,137	4,831	3,431	6,011	5,809	4,938	3,422
Ratios								
External debt stocks to exports (%)	34.0	29.8	88.9	95.3	71.8	63.9	88.1	90.0
External debt stocks to GNI (%)	20.5	17.5	45.9	52.5	57.5	54.3	56.2	54.3
Debt service to exports (%)	4.9	3.9	6.5	5.8	6.8	9.4	10.3	12.0
Reserves to external debt stocks (%)	13.5	21.5	21.9	12.1	17.7	17.2	12.5	8.6

Notes:

Long-term private nonguaranteed debt data for 2014 are World Bank staff estimates based on reports provided by the country.

BELIZE

(US$ million, unless otherwise indicated)

	2000	2005	2009	2010	2011	2012	2013	2014
Summary external debt data								
External debt stocks	**528**	**989**	**1,271**	**1,287**	**1,261**	**1,196**	**1,249**	**1,288**
Long-term external debt	455	956	1,226	1,245	1,219	1,158	1,214	1,255
Short-term external debt	50	7	10	7	8	6	7	7
interest arrears on long-term	0	7	10	7	8	6	7	7
Use of IMF credit	23	26	35	35	35	32	28	26
Long-term external debt								
Debt outstanding and disbursed	**455**	**956**	**1,226**	**1,245**	**1,219**	**1,158**	**1,214**	**1,255**
Public and publicly guaranteed	455	956	1,017	1,002	1,001	984	1,052	1,101
Official creditors	228	348	412	402	406	412	504	557
Private creditors	226	608	605	600	595	573	548	544
of which: Bonds	75	482	21	21	21	3	527	527
Private nonguaranteed	..	..	209	243	218	173	162	154
of which: Bonds	..	..	..	..	..	..	..	..
Disbursements	**195**	**213**	**79**	**39**	**53**	**41**	**166**	**87**
Public and publicly guaranteed	195	213	66	32	36	37	164	87
Official creditors	27	48	65	32	36	37	123	87
Private creditors	169	165	1	0	0	0	41	0
of which: Bonds	86	143	0	0	0	0	41	0
Private nonguaranteed	..	..	13	7	18	4	2	0
of which: Bonds	..	..	..	..	..	..	..	..
Principal repayments	**41**	**152**	**66**	**66**	**69**	**103**	**102**	**47**
Public and publicly guaranteed	41	152	47	46	37	54	89	37
Official creditors	20	21	39	41	32	31	31	33
Private creditors	21	131	9	5	5	22	58	4
of which: Bonds	11	36	1	0	0	18	54	0
Private nonguaranteed	..	..	18	20	32	49	13	10
of which: Bonds	..	..	..	..	..	..	..	..
Interest payments	**22**	**70**	**54**	**56**	**57**	**49**	**30**	**44**
Public and publicly guaranteed	22	70	43	45	46	40	22	37
Official creditors	12	15	15	13	10	9	10	10
Private creditors	11	54	28	32	36	31	12	27
of which: Bonds	1	41	2	2	2	1	11	26
Private nonguaranteed	..	..	11	11	11	9	8	7
of which: Bonds	..	..	..	..	..	..	..	..
Net financial flows								
Net debt inflows	153	61	21	-26	-16	-64	61	40
Official creditors (incl. IMF)	7	27	33	-9	3	3	89	53
Private creditors	146	34	-13	-17	-19	-67	-28	-13
Long-term	147	34	-13	-17	-19	-67	-28	-13
Public and publicly guaranteed	147	34	-7	-5	-5	-22	-17	-4
Private nonguaranteed	..	..	-6	-12	-14	-45	-11	-10
Short-term	-1	..	..	..	..	..	..	..
Net equity inflows								
Foreign direct investment	23	106	102	94	94	194	92	141
Portfolio equity	..	..	-10	..	..	..	..	..
Major economic aggregates								
Gross national income (GNI)	779	1,000	1,246	1,259	1,389	1,454	1,506	..
Exports of goods, services & prim. income	441	622	733	834	949	1,040	1,062	1,091
Imports of goods, services & prim. income	661	824	895	972	1,052	1,148	1,208	1,301
Primary income on FDI	31	35	56	102	40	68	85	98
Personal transfers & comp. of employees	26	45	79	78	75	76	74	80
International reserves	123	71	214	218	237	289	403	487
Ratios								
External debt stocks to exports (%)	119.6	159.0	173.4	154.3	133.0	115.0	117.6	118.1
External debt stocks to GNI (%)	67.8	98.9	102.0	102.2	90.8	82.3	82.9	..
Debt service to exports (%)	15.3	35.7	16.3	14.6	13.3	14.9	12.7	8.4
Reserves to external debt stocks (%)	23.3	7.2	16.8	16.9	18.8	24.2	32.2	37.8

Notes:

Long-term private nonguaranteed debt data from 2008 are based on Central Bank data.

BENIN

(US$ million, unless otherwise indicated)

	2000	2005	2009	2010	2011	2012	2013	2014
Summary external debt data								
External debt stocks	**1,370**	**1,536**	**1,317**	**1,599**	**1,869**	**2,054**	**2,367**	**1,984**
Long-term external debt	1,207	1,429	972	1,113	1,194	1,302	1,593	1,742
Short-term external debt	66	41	213	341	497	542	549	22
interest arrears on long-term	1	2	32	25	28	47	54	22
Use of IMF credit	96	66	132	146	177	210	225	220
Long-term external debt								
Debt outstanding and disbursed	**1,207**	**1,429**	**972**	**1,113**	**1,194**	**1,302**	**1,593**	**1,742**
Public and publicly guaranteed	1,207	1,429	972	1,113	1,194	1,302	1,593	1,742
Official creditors	1,205	1,429	972	1,113	1,194	1,302	1,593	1,742
Private creditors	3	0	0	0	0	0	0	0
of which: Bonds	0	0	0	0	0	0	0	0
Private nonguaranteed	..	..	..	..	..	..	..	..
of which: Bonds	..	..	..	..	..	..	..	..
Disbursements	**39**	**97**	**142**	**184**	**116**	**116**	**337**	**331**
Public and publicly guaranteed	39	97	142	184	116	116	337	331
Official creditors	39	97	142	184	116	116	337	331
Private creditors	0	0	0	0	0	0	0	0
of which: Bonds	0	0	0	0	0	0	0	0
Private nonguaranteed	..	..	..	..	..	..	..	..
of which: Bonds	..	..	..	..	..	..	..	..
Principal repayments	**43**	**24**	**25**	**25**	**29**	**39**	**68**	**73**
Public and publicly guaranteed	43	24	25	25	29	39	68	73
Official creditors	43	20	25	25	29	39	68	73
Private creditors	0	4	0	0	0	0	0	0
of which: Bonds	0	0	0	0	0	0	0	0
Private nonguaranteed	..	..	..	..	..	..	..	..
of which: Bonds	..	..	..	..	..	..	..	..
Interest payments	**16**	**14**	**12**	**13**	**13**	**16**	**18**	**25**
Public and publicly guaranteed	16	14	12	13	13	16	18	25
Official creditors	16	14	12	13	13	16	18	24
Private creditors	0	0	0	0	0	0	0	0
of which: Bonds	0	0	0	0	0	0	0	0
Private nonguaranteed	..	..	..	..	..	..	..	..
of which: Bonds	..	..	..	..	..	..	..	..
Net financial flows								
Net debt inflows	-54	82	229	309	274	135	284	-227
Official creditors (incl. IMF)	-6	71	133	175	120	109	284	267
Private creditors	-48	11	96	134	154	26	0	-494
Long-term	..	-4	..	..	..	..	..	..
Public and publicly guaranteed	..	-4	..	..	..	..	..	..
Private nonguaranteed	..	..	..	..	..	..	..	..
Short-term	-48	15	96	134	154	26	0	-494
Net equity inflows								
Foreign direct investment	60	-31	-32	-26	149	198	360	377
Portfolio equity	0	2	9	5	1	1	..	..
Major economic aggregates								
Gross national income (GNI)	2,347	4,340	6,551	6,508	7,274	7,495	8,247	8,684
Exports of goods, services & prim. income	552	797	1,489	1,707	1,765	1,969	2,203	..
Imports of goods, services & prim. income	744	1,188	2,310	2,393	2,423	2,746	3,150	..
Primary income on FDI	-1	9	32	55	66	91	..	..
Personal transfers & comp. of employees	87	147	126	139	172	208	..	..
International reserves	459	655	1,230	1,200	887	713	695	726
Ratios								
External debt stocks to exports (%)	248.2	192.7	88.5	93.7	105.8	104.3	107.4	..
External debt stocks to GNI (%)	58.4	35.4	20.1	24.6	25.7	27.4	28.7	22.8
Debt service to exports (%)	13.6	6.0	3.6	3.3	4.0	4.3	5.1	..
Reserves to external debt stocks (%)	33.5	42.6	93.4	75.0	47.5	34.7	29.4	36.6

Notes:

Data include the effects of Paris Club debt restructuring agreement and HIPC and MDRI debt relief.

BHUTAN

(US$ million, unless otherwise indicated)

	2000	2005	2009	2010	2011	2012	2013	2014
Summary external debt data								
External debt stocks	**212**	**657**	**787**	**935**	**1,072**	**1,475**	**1,528**	**1,840**
Long-term external debt	202	636	772	919	1,054	1,365	1,519	1,821
Short-term external debt	2	12	5	6	8	100	0	10
interest arrears on long-term	0	4	0	0	0	0	0	0
Use of IMF credit	8	9	9	9	9	9	9	9
Long-term external debt								
Debt outstanding and disbursed	**202**	**636**	**772**	**919**	**1,054**	**1,365**	**1,519**	**1,821**
Public and publicly guaranteed	202	636	772	919	1,045	1,358	1,514	1,820
Official creditors	202	636	767	899	1,016	1,320	1,464	1,769
Private creditors	0	0	5	21	29	38	49	50
of which: Bonds	0	0	0	0	0	0	0	0
Private nonguaranteed	..	..	..	..	10	8	5	2
of which: Bonds	..	..	..	..	..	..	..	..
Disbursements	**35**	**82**	**118**	**178**	**270**	**409**	**293**	**424**
Public and publicly guaranteed	35	82	118	178	260	409	293	424
Official creditors	35	82	113	162	251	400	283	417
Private creditors	0	0	5	16	9	9	9	7
of which: Bonds	0	0	0	0	0	0	0	0
Private nonguaranteed	..	..	..	..	10	..	..	..
of which: Bonds	..	..	..	..	..	..	..	..
Principal repayments	**5**	**5**	**41**	**47**	**45**	**69**	**39**	**42**
Public and publicly guaranteed	5	5	41	47	45	67	37	40
Official creditors	5	5	41	47	45	67	37	40
Private creditors	0	0	0	0	0	0	0	0
of which: Bonds	0	0	0	0	0	0	0	0
Private nonguaranteed	..	..	..	..	..	2	2	2
of which: Bonds	..	..	..	..	..	..	..	..
Interest payments	**2**	**2**	**34**	**41**	**40**	**60**	**38**	**41**
Public and publicly guaranteed	2	2	34	41	40	60	38	40
Official creditors	2	2	34	40	38	58	35	37
Private creditors	0	0	0	1	2	2	2	3
of which: Bonds	0	0	0	0	0	0	0	0
Private nonguaranteed	..	..	..	..	..	0	0	0
of which: Bonds	..	..	..	..	..	..	..	..
Net financial flows								
Net debt inflows	30	85	74	132	227	432	153	392
Official creditors (incl. IMF)	30	77	72	115	206	334	246	377
Private creditors	0	8	2	17	21	98	-93	15
Long-term	..	..	5	16	19	6	7	5
Public and publicly guaranteed	..	..	5	16	9	9	9	7
Private nonguaranteed	..	..	..	..	10	-2	-2	-2
Short-term	0	8	-3	1	2	92	-100	10
Net equity inflows								
Foreign direct investment	..	6	6	20	20	11	49	10
Portfolio equity	..	..	..	..	..	..	..	..
Major economic aggregates								
Gross national income (GNI)	439	807	1,214	1,497	1,706	1,682	1,665	1,751
Exports of goods, services & prim. income	..	..	595	607	762	746	685	686
Imports of goods, services & prim. income	..	..	735	1,024	1,425	1,343	1,316	1,257
Primary income on FDI	..	..	-1	4	5	2	20	..
Personal transfers & comp. of employees	..	..	5	8	10	18	12	14
International reserves	318	467	891	1,002	790	955	991	1,245
Ratios								
External debt stocks to exports (%)	..	..	132.1	154.0	140.6	197.6	223.0	268.2
External debt stocks to GNI (%)	48.2	81.3	64.8	62.4	62.8	87.7	91.8	105.1
Debt service to exports (%)	..	..	12.7	14.4	11.2	17.4	11.3	12.1
Reserves to external debt stocks (%)	150.1	71.2	113.3	107.2	73.7	64.7	64.9	67.7

Notes:

Short-term debt is based on data from the BIS.

BOLIVIA, PLURINATIONAL STATE OF

(US$ million, unless otherwise indicated)

	2000	2005	2009	2010	2011	2012	2013	2014
Summary external debt data								
External debt stocks	**5,875**	**6,908**	**5,731**	**5,726**	**6,136**	**6,566**	**8,009**	**8,781**
Long-term external debt	5,218	6,445	5,170	5,137	5,561	5,984	7,505	8,254
Short-term external debt	402	182	304	336	324	330	250	289
interest arrears on long-term	2	0	0	0	0	0	0	0
Use of IMF credit	255	282	257	253	252	252	253	238
Long-term external debt								
Debt outstanding and disbursed	**5,218**	**6,445**	**5,170**	**5,137**	**5,561**	**5,984**	**7,505**	**8,254**
Public and publicly guaranteed	4,192	4,531	2,523	2,779	3,388	4,138	5,148	5,642
Official creditors	4,159	4,504	2,431	2,755	3,299	3,618	4,130	4,626
Private creditors	33	27	92	24	89	520	1,019	1,015
of which: Bonds	0	0	0	0	0	500	1,000	1,000
Private nonguaranteed	1,026	1,914	2,647	2,358	2,173	1,846	2,357	2,612
of which: Bonds	..	..	..	..	..	..	..	..
Disbursements	**745**	**880**	**512**	**538**	**776**	**1,250**	**1,405**	**1,628**
Public and publicly guaranteed	277	434	415	509	776	1,250	1,180	787
Official creditors	264	429	408	506	709	683	680	786
Private creditors	13	4	7	3	67	567	500	0
of which: Bonds	0	0	0	0	0	500	500	0
Private nonguaranteed	468	447	97	30	..	..	225	842
of which: Bonds	..	..	..	..	..	..	..	..
Principal repayments	**438**	**309**	**448**	**562**	**351**	**551**	**419**	**830**
Public and publicly guaranteed	156	178	190	240	166	368	179	243
Official creditors	153	176	178	170	164	366	177	241
Private creditors	4	2	13	70	2	2	2	2
of which: Bonds	0	0	10	0	0	0	0	0
Private nonguaranteed	281	131	257	322	185	183	240	586
of which: Bonds	..	..	..	..	..	..	..	..
Interest payments	**160**	**155**	**117**	**75**	**77**	**79**	**113**	**157**
Public and publicly guaranteed	113	96	69	52	57	65	95	139
Official creditors	111	96	65	49	53	64	71	85
Private creditors	1	0	4	4	4	0	25	54
of which: Bonds	0	0	0	0	0	0	24	54
Private nonguaranteed	47	59	48	22	20	14	18	18
of which: Bonds	..	..	..	..	..	..	..	..
Net financial flows								
Net debt inflows	292	454	99	9	412	704	906	837
Official creditors (incl. IMF)	106	227	231	336	545	317	502	545
Private creditors	186	227	-132	-327	-133	387	404	292
Long-term	196	318	-166	-359	-120	381	483	254
Public and publicly guaranteed	9	2	-6	-67	65	564	498	-2
Private nonguaranteed	187	316	-161	-292	-185	-183	-15	256
Short-term	-10	-91	34	32	-13	6	-79	39
Net equity inflows								
Foreign direct investment	736	-91	505	774	902	1,224	1,699	648
Portfolio equity	..	..	..	..	..	..	..	..
Major economic aggregates								
Gross national income (GNI)	8,172	9,173	16,666	18,786	22,788	25,406	28,693	32,469
Exports of goods, services & prim. income	1,610	3,401	5,663	6,919	9,260	12,399	12,923	13,663
Imports of goods, services & prim. income	2,443	3,362	6,062	7,126	9,900	11,690	13,139	14,864
Primary income on FDI	148	271	769	863	977	1,649	1,916	1,690
Personal transfers & comp. of employees	127	337	1,058	960	1,043	1,111	1,201	1,184
International reserves	926	1,328	7,584	8,134	9,911	11,659	12,783	13,481
Ratios								
External debt stocks to exports (%)	365.0	203.2	101.2	82.8	66.3	53.0	62.0	64.3
External debt stocks to GNI (%)	71.9	75.3	34.4	30.5	26.9	25.8	27.9	27.0
Debt service to exports (%)	39.8	15.4	10.2	9.4	4.7	5.2	4.2	7.3
Reserves to external debt stocks (%)	15.8	19.2	132.3	142.1	161.5	177.6	159.6	153.5

BOSNIA AND HERZEGOVINA

(US$ million, unless otherwise indicated)

	2000	2005	2009	2010	2011	2012	2013	2014
Summary external debt data								
External debt stocks	**2,800**	**6,378**	**11,328**	**9,935**	**10,165**	**10,576**	**11,078**	**10,591**
Long-term external debt	2,619	5,326	9,111	8,128	8,091	8,426	8,920	8,833
Short-term external debt	49	960	1,678	1,038	1,308	1,262	1,309	865
interest arrears on long-term	1	0	0	0	0	0	0	0
Use of IMF credit	131	91	539	769	766	888	848	892
Long-term external debt								
Debt outstanding and disbursed	**2,619**	**5,326**	**9,111**	**8,128**	**8,091**	**8,426**	**8,920**	**8,833**
Public and publicly guaranteed	1,957	2,559	3,570	3,733	3,874	4,201	4,732	4,681
Official creditors	1,832	2,404	3,042	3,267	3,451	3,797	4,337	4,354
Private creditors	125	155	527	466	423	404	395	328
of which: Bonds	0	0	322	273	241	221	205	158
Private nonguaranteed	663	2,767	5,541	4,395	4,216	4,225	4,188	4,152
of which: Bonds	..	..	..	..	..	..	..	..
Disbursements	**103**	**540**	**394**	**510**	**491**	**525**	**729**	**639**
Public and publicly guaranteed	98	153	321	441	382	448	644	639
Official creditors	98	153	309	427	370	431	625	612
Private creditors	0	0	12	14	12	17	19	27
of which: Bonds	0	0	0	0	0	0	0	0
Private nonguaranteed	5	386	73	69	108	77	85	..
of which: Bonds	..	..	..	..	..	..	..	..
Principal repayments	**170**	**95**	**171**	**537**	**594**	**758**	**669**	**262**
Public and publicly guaranteed	170	54	110	145	171	167	200	226
Official creditors	170	51	97	108	129	124	155	176
Private creditors	0	3	13	37	43	43	46	49
of which: Bonds	0	0	0	25	26	24	25	25
Private nonguaranteed	1	41	61	392	423	591	468	37
of which: Bonds	..	..	..	..	..	..	..	..
Interest payments	**119**	**136**	**217**	**177**	**186**	**183**	**178**	**249**
Public and publicly guaranteed	89	53	63	55	66	65	58	81
Official creditors	86	48	56	47	55	56	53	77
Private creditors	2	6	8	9	11	9	5	5
of which: Bonds	0	0	0	5	6	5	2	2
Private nonguaranteed	30	83	153	121	120	118	120	168
of which: Bonds	..	..	..	..	..	..	..	..
Net financial flows								
Net debt inflows	-41	1,052	1,276	-429	166	-159	66	32
Official creditors (incl. IMF)	-56	63	494	556	241	427	429	535
Private creditors	15	989	782	-985	-75	-586	-363	-502
Long-term	4	342	11	-345	-345	-540	-410	-58
Public and publicly guaranteed	..	-3	-1	-23	-30	-26	-27	-22
Private nonguaranteed	4	346	12	-322	-315	-514	-384	-37
Short-term	11	647	771	-640	270	-46	47	-444
Net equity inflows								
Foreign direct investment	146	314	-202	149	343	162	292	281
Portfolio equity	..	..	..	..	..	..	..	..
Major economic aggregates								
Gross national income (GNI)	6,096	11,372	17,943	17,127	18,467	17,061	18,078	18,557
Exports of goods, services & prim. income	2,247	4,227	5,328	5,691	6,646	6,106	6,677	6,909
Imports of goods, services & prim. income	4,234	8,103	8,843	9,111	10,931	10,021	10,198	10,953
Primary income on FDI	..	97	-104	79	276	207	187	263
Personal transfers & comp. of employees	1,607	2,038	2,127	1,822	1,958	1,846	1,929	2,062
International reserves	497	2,548	4,529	4,366	4,150	4,283	4,868	4,744
Ratios								
External debt stocks to exports (%)	124.6	150.9	212.6	174.6	152.9	173.2	165.9	153.3
External debt stocks to GNI (%)	45.9	56.1	63.1	58.0	55.0	62.0	61.3	57.1
Debt service to exports (%)	14.2	7.3	8.8	14.1	13.1	17.4	16.8	11.8
Reserves to external debt stocks (%)	17.7	39.9	40.0	43.9	40.8	40.5	43.9	44.8

Notes:

Long-term private nonguaranteed debt data from 2005 are World Bank staff estimates. Short-term debt is based on data from the BIS.

BOTSWANA

(US$ million, unless otherwise indicated)

	2000	2005	2009	2010	2011	2012	2013	2014
Summary external debt data								
External debt stocks	**458**	**454**	**1,706**	**1,797**	**2,396**	**2,488**	**2,427**	**2,384**
Long-term external debt	438	412	1,387	1,352	1,897	2,015	1,892	1,884
Short-term external debt	15	35	229	357	411	385	446	417
interest arrears on long-term	0	0	0	0	0	0	0	0
Use of IMF credit	6	6	90	88	88	88	88	83
Long-term external debt								
Debt outstanding and disbursed	**438**	**412**	**1,387**	**1,352**	**1,897**	**2,015**	**1,892**	**1,884**
Public and publicly guaranteed	438	412	1,387	1,352	1,897	1,935	1,813	1,804
Official creditors	410	401	1,385	1,351	1,896	1,935	1,813	1,804
Private creditors	28	12	2	1	1	0	0	0
of which: Bonds	0	0	0	0	0	0	0	0
Private nonguaranteed	..	..	..	..	..	80	80	80
of which: Bonds	..	..	..	..	..	80	80	80
Disbursements	**28**	**11**	**1,006**	**17**	**595**	**149**	**29**	**79**
Public and publicly guaranteed	28	11	1,006	17	595	69	29	39
Official creditors	24	11	1,006	17	595	69	29	39
Private creditors	4	0	0	0	0	0	0	0
of which: Bonds	0	0	0	0	0	0	0	0
Private nonguaranteed	..	..	..	..	..	80	..	40
of which: Bonds	..	..	..	..	..	80	..	..
Principal repayments	**52**	**40**	**36**	**56**	**51**	**28**	**152**	**32**
Public and publicly guaranteed	52	40	36	56	51	28	152	32
Official creditors	45	38	35	55	51	27	152	32
Private creditors	7	2	1	1	0	1	0	0
of which: Bonds	0	0	0	0	0	0	0	0
Private nonguaranteed	..	..	..	..	..	..	..	..
of which: Bonds	..	..	..	..	..	..	..	..
Interest payments	**15**	**12**	**9**	**16**	**16**	**20**	**32**	**18**
Public and publicly guaranteed	15	12	9	16	16	20	28	16
Official creditors	14	11	9	16	16	20	28	16
Private creditors	1	0	0	0	0	0	0	0
of which: Bonds	0	0	0	0	0	0	0	0
Private nonguaranteed	..	..	..	..	..	..	5	2
of which: Bonds	..	..	..	..	..	..	5	2
Net financial flows								
Net debt inflows	-29	-17	1,156	89	598	94	-62	18
Official creditors (incl. IMF)	-21	-27	971	-38	544	42	-123	7
Private creditors	-8	11	186	128	54	53	61	11
Long-term	-3	-2	-1	-1	0	79	..	40
Public and publicly guaranteed	-3	-2	-1	-1	0	-1	..	..
Private nonguaranteed	..	..	..	..	..	80	..	40
Short-term	-5	13	186	128	54	-26	61	-29
Net equity inflows								
Foreign direct investment	57	211	133	141	1,134	134	200	393
Portfolio equity	-6	27	18	11	-17	-9	2	..
Major economic aggregates								
Gross national income (GNI)	5,436	9,096	10,029	12,237	15,570	14,815	14,873	15,746
Exports of goods, services & prim. income	3,378	5,739	3,870	5,169	7,214	6,491	8,357	..
Imports of goods, services & prim. income	3,050	4,737	5,862	7,162	8,394	8,758	8,225	..
Primary income on FDI	658	1,066	471	731	285	116	151	..
Personal transfers & comp. of employees	26	118	15	22	20	18	36	48
International reserves	6,318	6,309	8,704	7,885	8,082	7,628	7,726	8,323
Ratios								
External debt stocks to exports (%)	13.6	7.9	44.1	34.8	33.2	38.3	29.0	..
External debt stocks to GNI (%)	8.4	5.0	17.0	14.7	15.4	16.8	16.3	15.1
Debt service to exports (%)	2.0	0.9	1.2	1.5	1.0	0.8	2.3	..
Reserves to external debt stocks (%)	1,378.2	1,391.1	510.3	438.8	337.3	306.6	318.4	349.1

Notes:

Long-term public and publicly guaranteed debt data are World Bank staff estimates. Short-term debt is based on data from the BIS.

BRAZIL

(US$ million, unless otherwise indicated)

	2000	2005	2009	2010	2011	2012	2013	2014
Summary external debt data								
External debt stocks	**242,432**	**188,351**	**281,651**	**352,364**	**404,046**	**440,513**	**483,814**	**556,871**
Long-term external debt	209,223	163,846	237,339	282,426	357,473	403,493	445,861	494,511
Short-term external debt	30,973	23,993	39,786	65,492	42,140	32,583	33,507	58,177
interest arrears on long-term	176	0	0	0	0	0	27	17
Use of IMF credit	2,235	513	4,526	4,446	4,432	4,437	4,446	4,183
Long-term external debt								
Debt outstanding and disbursed	**209,223**	**163,846**	**237,339**	**282,426**	**357,473**	**403,493**	**445,861**	**494,511**
Public and publicly guaranteed	96,542	94,341	87,513	97,486	94,712	116,663	136,603	174,273
Official creditors	29,765	26,160	32,655	41,517	36,568	39,005	39,373	42,066
Private creditors	66,776	68,181	54,858	55,968	58,144	77,658	97,230	132,206
of which: Bonds	54,096	59,077	47,350	46,806	45,408	48,471	52,125	53,855
Private nonguaranteed	112,682	69,505	149,826	184,940	262,761	286,830	309,258	320,239
of which: Bonds	16,846	35,969	53,342	83,032	79,363	69,053	61,384	55,073
Disbursements	**44,079**	**27,414**	**57,675**	**85,379**	**111,458**	**79,638**	**107,238**	**115,770**
Public and publicly guaranteed	19,664	13,207	13,732	19,957	13,655	27,987	36,344	41,798
Official creditors	5,272	3,327	6,845	11,317	3,250	4,985	5,253	5,232
Private creditors	14,391	9,880	6,887	8,640	10,405	23,002	31,091	36,566
of which: Bonds	10,836	8,252	5,100	5,433	3,631	6,587	8,680	6,319
Private nonguaranteed	24,415	14,207	43,943	65,422	97,803	51,652	70,894	73,972
of which: Bonds	2,886	6,579	17,015	32,384	30,765	8,822	4,780	8,163
Principal repayments	**34,746**	**25,788**	**30,471**	**32,026**	**41,778**	**30,592**	**63,771**	**42,672**
Public and publicly guaranteed	10,932	9,481	7,786	9,628	15,852	6,691	14,918	6,786
Official creditors	7,093	3,334	3,447	2,665	8,355	2,322	4,476	1,969
Private creditors	3,839	6,147	4,339	6,963	7,498	4,369	10,442	4,817
of which: Bonds	2,056	4,187	2,760	5,770	4,281	3,269	4,325	2,936
Private nonguaranteed	23,813	16,306	22,685	22,398	25,925	23,901	48,853	35,886
of which: Bonds	2,775	7,063	1,585	2,656	3,666	7,154	11,459	9,588
Interest payments	**15,297**	**10,314**	**13,554**	**13,157**	**16,615**	**14,259**	**17,833**	**16,448**
Public and publicly guaranteed	6,943	6,700	5,656	5,172	5,446	5,019	6,010	5,717
Official creditors	1,932	1,058	1,085	968	1,013	963	921	800
Private creditors	5,010	5,642	4,571	4,204	4,433	4,057	5,089	4,917
of which: Bonds	4,212	5,033	4,148	3,864	3,902	3,392	3,805	3,662
Private nonguaranteed	8,355	3,614	7,898	7,985	11,169	9,240	11,823	10,731
of which: Bonds	1,562	2,161	2,936	4,207	5,859	3,107	3,722	3,354
Net financial flows								
Net debt inflows	4,471	-23,457	30,345	79,059	46,329	39,489	44,363	97,778
Official creditors (incl. IMF)	-8,514	-23,817	3,399	8,652	-5,104	2,663	777	3,262
Private creditors	12,985	360	26,947	70,407	51,433	36,827	43,586	94,516
Long-term	11,154	1,634	23,805	44,700	74,785	46,384	42,690	69,836
Public and publicly guaranteed	10,552	3,733	2,547	1,676	2,907	18,633	20,649	31,749
Private nonguaranteed	602	-2,099	21,257	43,024	71,878	27,750	22,041	38,087
Short-term	1,831	-1,274	3,142	25,706	-23,352	-9,557	897	24,680
Net equity inflows								
Foreign direct investment	32,779	15,045	19,906	40,117	54,782	52,838	41,644	57,874
Portfolio equity	3,076	6,451	37,071	37,671	7,174	5,600	11,636	11,773
Major economic aggregates								
Gross national income (GNI)	626,889	856,746	1,588,117	2,172,734	2,570,959	2,380,575	2,356,039	2,309,375
Exports of goods, services & prim. income	68,205	136,200	189,564	240,920	305,002	293,331	291,232	277,662
Imports of goods, services & prim. income	93,950	125,773	217,207	291,094	360,466	350,424	375,706	383,679
Primary income on FDI	4,238	11,035	21,029	26,584	31,716	24,564	27,536	35,803
Personal transfers & comp. of employees	1,649	2,805	2,889	2,754	2,798	2,583	2,537	2,645
International reserves	32,434	53,245	237,364	287,056	350,356	369,566	356,214	360,965
Ratios								
External debt stocks to exports (%)	355.4	138.3	148.6	146.3	132.5	150.2	166.1	200.6
External debt stocks to GNI (%)	38.7	22.0	17.7	16.2	15.7	18.5	20.5	24.1
Debt service to exports (%)	85.9	46.2	23.5	19.0	19.4	15.5	28.2	21.6
Reserves to external debt stocks (%)	13.4	28.3	84.3	81.5	86.7	83.9	73.6	64.8

BULGARIA

(US$ million, unless otherwise indicated)

	2000	2005	2009	2010	2011	2012	2013	2014
Summary external debt data								
External debt stocks	**12,009**	**18,507**	**55,670**	**50,635**	**47,642**	**50,703**	**51,978**	**48,742**
Long-term external debt	8,440	12,532	36,916	34,551	33,857	35,984	37,869	35,638
Short-term external debt	1,451	4,442	17,797	15,143	12,848	13,780	13,168	12,219
interest arrears on long-term	1	0	0	0	0	0	0	0
Use of IMF credit	2,118	1,533	958	941	938	939	941	885
Long-term external debt								
Debt outstanding and disbursed	**8,440**	**12,532**	**36,916**	**34,551**	**33,857**	**35,984**	**37,869**	**35,638**
Public and publicly guaranteed	7,671	5,075	5,068	4,782	4,579	5,132	5,282	6,069
Official creditors	2,603	3,045	3,322	3,151	3,140	3,094	3,232	2,745
Private creditors	5,068	2,030	1,746	1,631	1,440	2,037	2,050	3,323
of which: Bonds	4,982	1,920	1,725	1,618	1,434	2,032	2,044	3,318
Private nonguaranteed	769	7,457	31,848	29,768	29,277	30,852	32,587	29,569
of which: Bonds	..	526	146	134	24	274	1,519	1,339
Disbursements	**719**	**4,895**	**8,625**	**1,569**	**10,803**	**6,182**	**6,069**	**5,674**
Public and publicly guaranteed	405	402	520	199	292	1,439	770	2,130
Official creditors	381	383	520	199	292	228	380	179
Private creditors	24	19	0	0	0	1,211	389	1,951
of which: Bonds	0	0	0	0	0	1,211	389	1,951
Private nonguaranteed	313	4,493	8,105	1,370	10,511	4,743	5,300	3,544
of which: Bonds	..	249	..	..	..	340	539	..
Principal repayments	**573**	**3,349**	**3,989**	**3,550**	**3,567**	**3,777**	**3,821**	**4,771**
Public and publicly guaranteed	345	1,761	404	268	258	263	269	630
Official creditors	297	255	266	261	251	263	269	296
Private creditors	48	1,507	138	7	7	0	0	334
of which: Bonds	46	1,496	123	0	0	0	0	334
Private nonguaranteed	229	1,588	3,585	3,282	3,308	3,514	3,551	4,142
of which: Bonds	..	10	372	..	109	57	..	150
Interest payments	**456**	**479**	**800**	**607**	**785**	**749**	**838**	**827**
Public and publicly guaranteed	424	327	208	177	188	161	210	230
Official creditors	139	93	106	71	83	82	69	69
Private creditors	285	234	102	106	105	79	141	160
of which: Bonds	284	229	101	106	105	79	141	160
Private nonguaranteed	32	152	592	430	598	588	628	598
of which: Bonds	..	30	29	11	6	..	12	42
Net financial flows								
Net debt inflows	465	2,308	4,099	-4,635	4,941	3,337	1,637	-46
Official creditors (incl. IMF)	221	-315	254	-62	41	-35	111	-117
Private creditors	244	2,623	3,845	-4,573	4,901	3,372	1,232	71
Long-term	61	1,418	4,382	-1,919	7,196	2,439	1,844	1,020
Public and publicly guaranteed	-24	-1,488	-138	-7	-7	1,211	389	1,617
Private nonguaranteed	85	2,905	4,520	-1,912	7,203	1,229	1,748	-597
Short-term	183	1,206	-537	-2,654	-2,296	932	-611	-949
Net equity inflows								
Foreign direct investment	1,002	2,017	2,249	1,528	1,268	889	1,554	978
Portfolio equity	5	449	8	9	-42	5	-19	-77
Major economic aggregates								
Gross national income (GNI)	13,030	29,383	48,495	47,168	53,247	50,880	52,083	54,128
Exports of goods, services & prim. income	7,321	17,674	24,384	27,944	36,606	34,960	38,305	39,247
Imports of goods, services & prim. income	8,314	22,034	29,966	30,711	38,836	38,137	40,482	40,906
Primary income on FDI	107	912	1,823	1,573	2,521	1,876	2,273	1,690
Personal transfers & comp. of employees	58	1,613	1,592	1,333	1,483	1,449	1,667	1,684
International reserves	3,155	8,041	17,127	15,421	15,252	18,371	18,335	18,576
Ratios								
External debt stocks to exports (%)	164.0	104.7	228.3	181.2	130.1	145.0	135.7	124.2
External debt stocks to GNI (%)	92.2	63.0	114.8	107.4	89.5	99.7	99.8	90.1
Debt service to exports (%)	18.2	25.3	20.0	15.1	12.2	13.3	13.3	14.7
Reserves to external debt stocks (%)	26.3	43.4	30.8	30.5	32.0	36.2	35.3	38.1

Notes:

Long-term private nonguaranteed debt data from 2008 are World Bank staff estimates based on reports provided by the country. Short-term debt before 2009 is World Bank staff estimates based on Central Bank data. The data may include long-term public and publicly guaranteed debt owed by the state-owned railway.

BURKINA FASO

(US$ million, unless otherwise indicated)

	2000	2005	2009	2010	2011	2012	2013	2014
Summary external debt data								
External debt stocks	**1,435**	**2,000**	**1,917**	**2,148**	**2,290**	**2,519**	**2,565**	**2,544**
Long-term external debt	1,226	1,861	1,716	1,931	2,057	2,218	2,261	2,261
Short-term external debt	84	22	0	0	0	0	0	0
interest arrears on long-term	5	0	0	0	0	0	0	0
Use of IMF credit	124	117	201	217	233	301	304	283
Long-term external debt								
Debt outstanding and disbursed	**1,226**	**1,861**	**1,716**	**1,931**	**2,057**	**2,218**	**2,261**	**2,261**
Public and publicly guaranteed	1,226	1,861	1,716	1,931	2,057	2,218	2,261	2,261
Official creditors	1,223	1,861	1,694	1,913	2,043	2,205	2,250	2,254
Private creditors	3	0	22	18	15	13	11	7
of which: Bonds	0	0	0	0	0	0	0	0
Private nonguaranteed	..	..	..	..	..	..	..	..
of which: Bonds	..	..	..	..	..	..	..	..
Disbursements	**91**	**208**	**217**	**276**	**171**	**159**	**60**	**217**
Public and publicly guaranteed	91	208	217	276	171	159	60	217
Official creditors	91	208	217	276	171	159	60	217
Private creditors	0	0	0	0	0	0	0	0
of which: Bonds	0	0	0	0	0	0	0	0
Private nonguaranteed	..	..	..	..	..	..	..	..
of which: Bonds	..	..	..	..	..	..	..	..
Principal repayments	**26**	**24**	**28**	**30**	**43**	**43**	**48**	**57**
Public and publicly guaranteed	26	24	28	30	43	43	48	57
Official creditors	26	24	28	27	40	41	46	55
Private creditors	0	0	0	2	3	2	2	2
of which: Bonds	0	0	0	0	0	0	0	0
Private nonguaranteed	..	..	..	..	..	..	..	..
of which: Bonds	..	..	..	..	..	..	..	..
Interest payments	**12**	**16**	**15**	**18**	**21**	**21**	**22**	**23**
Public and publicly guaranteed	12	16	15	18	21	21	22	23
Official creditors	12	16	15	18	21	21	22	23
Private creditors	0	0	0	0	0	0	0	0
of which: Bonds	0	0	0	0	0	0	0	0
Private nonguaranteed	..	..	..	..	..	..	..	..
of which: Bonds	..	..	..	..	..	..	..	..
Net financial flows								
Net debt inflows	47	194	235	266	145	184	14	157
Official creditors (incl. IMF)	66	196	244	269	147	186	17	159
Private creditors	-19	-2	-9	-2	-3	-2	-2	-2
Long-term	0	0	0	-2	-3	-2	-2	-2
Public and publicly guaranteed	0	0	0	-2	-3	-2	-2	-2
Private nonguaranteed	..	..	..	..	..	..	..	..
Short-term	-19	-2	-8	..	..	..	..	..
Net equity inflows								
Foreign direct investment	23	1	9	-32	144	329	490	342
Portfolio equity	-3	-4	0	3	-132	209	..	..
Major economic aggregates								
Gross national income (GNI)	2,606	5,442	8,343	9,203	10,392	10,721	11,030	12,400
Exports of goods, services & prim. income	251	583	1,140	1,981	2,913	3,484	2,809	..
Imports of goods, services & prim. income	691	1,452	2,035	2,655	3,618	4,165	4,337	..
Primary income on FDI	3	7	35	26	..	..	..	..
Personal transfers & comp. of employees	67	57	96	120	..	..	..	..
International reserves	243	438	1,296	1,068	957	1,025	628	297
Ratios								
External debt stocks to exports (%)	572.8	343.0	168.1	108.5	78.6	72.3	91.3	..
External debt stocks to GNI (%)	55.1	36.8	23.0	23.3	22.0	23.5	23.3	20.5
Debt service to exports (%)	18.8	7.8	3.8	2.5	2.3	2.0	2.8	..
Reserves to external debt stocks (%)	16.9	21.9	67.6	49.7	41.8	40.7	24.5	11.7

Notes:
Short-term debt before 2009 is based on data from the BIS. Data include HIPC and MDRI debt relief.

BURUNDI

(US$ million, unless otherwise indicated)

	2000	2005	2009	2010	2011	2012	2013	2014
Summary external debt data								
External debt stocks	**1,125.9**	**1,287.9**	**607.2**	**620.9**	**604.4**	**667.3**	**683.6**	**690.2**
Long-term external debt	1,036.0	1,176.1	393.5	381.8	363.2	411.4	398.1	403.6
Short-term external debt	65.0	34.1	7.0	15.7	0.4	7.3	31.3	48.3
interest arrears on long-term	19.7	33.1	0.0	0.7	0.4	0.3	0.3	0.3
Use of IMF credit	24.9	77.7	206.7	223.4	240.7	248.7	254.2	238.3
Long-term external debt								
Debt outstanding and disbursed	**1,036.0**	**1,176.1**	**393.5**	**381.8**	**363.2**	**411.4**	**398.1**	**403.6**
Public and publicly guaranteed	1,036.0	1,176.1	393.5	381.8	363.2	411.4	398.1	403.6
Official creditors	1,032.0	1,174.0	388.5	376.8	358.2	407.0	393.8	399.2
Private creditors	4.0	2.1	5.0	5.0	5.0	4.4	4.4	4.4
of which: Bonds	0.0	0.0	0.0	0.0	0.0	0.0	0.0	0.0
Private nonguaranteed	..	..	..	..	..	..	..	..
of which: Bonds	..	..	..	..	..	..	..	..
Disbursements	**41.3**	**42.1**	**29.3**	**31.6**	**28.0**	**60.2**	**6.9**	**39.9**
Public and publicly guaranteed	41.3	42.1	29.3	31.6	28.0	60.2	6.9	39.9
Official creditors	38.2	42.1	24.3	31.6	28.0	60.2	6.9	39.9
Private creditors	3.0	0.0	5.0	0.0	0.0	0.0	0.0	0.0
of which: Bonds	0.0	0.0	0.0	0.0	0.0	0.0	0.0	0.0
Private nonguaranteed	..	..	..	..	..	..	..	..
of which: Bonds	..	..	..	..	..	..	..	..
Principal repayments	**9.4**	**27.2**	**8.5**	**2.4**	**5.8**	**10.2**	**18.3**	**8.7**
Public and publicly guaranteed	9.4	27.2	8.5	2.4	5.8	10.2	18.3	8.7
Official creditors	9.4	22.6	8.5	2.4	5.8	9.6	18.3	8.7
Private creditors	0.0	4.6	0.0	0.0	0.0	0.6	0.0	0.0
of which: Bonds	0.0	0.0	0.0	0.0	0.0	0.0	0.0	0.0
Private nonguaranteed	..	..	..	..	..	..	..	..
of which: Bonds	..	..	..	..	..	..	..	..
Interest payments	**4.5**	**11.9**	**3.6**	**1.4**	**2.0**	**3.0**	**3.2**	**3.7**
Public and publicly guaranteed	4.5	11.9	3.6	1.4	2.0	3.0	3.2	3.7
Official creditors	4.5	11.9	3.6	1.4	2.0	3.0	3.2	3.7
Private creditors	0.0	0.0	0.0	0.0	0.0	0.0	0.0	0.0
of which: Bonds	0.0	0.0	0.0	0.0	0.0	0.0	0.0	0.0
Private nonguaranteed	..	..	..	..	..	..	..	..
of which: Bonds	..	..	..	..	..	..	..	..
Net financial flows								
Net debt inflows	18.4	34.1	27.2	57.3	25.8	64.6	17.6	47.4
Official creditors (incl. IMF)	24.3	40.7	29.2	49.3	40.8	58.2	-6.4	30.4
Private creditors	-5.9	-6.6	-2.0	8.0	-15.0	6.4	24.0	17.0
Long-term	3.0	-4.6	5.0	..	..	-0.6	..	..
Public and publicly guaranteed	3.0	-4.6	5.0	..	..	-0.6	..	..
Private nonguaranteed	..	..	..	..	..	..	..	..
Short-term	-8.9	-2.0	-7.0	8.0	-15.0	7.0	24.0	17.0
Net equity inflows								
Foreign direct investment	11.7	0.6	0.3	0.8	3.4	0.6	6.9	..
Portfolio equity	..	..	..	..	..	..	..	..
Major economic aggregates								
Gross national income (GNI)	884.8	1,099.6	1,722.8	2,014.8	2,338.2	2,463.3	2,713.1	3,093.8
Exports of goods, services & prim. income	55.4	98.7	119.7	181.9	243.1	239.0	236.1	..
Imports of goods, services & prim. income	164.9	343.9	538.0	618.7	790.3	940.6	921.9	..
Primary income on FDI	0.4	2.1	..	..	..	..	..	..
Personal transfers & comp. of employees	..	0.1	28.2	34.5	45.5	46.4	48.6	50.8
International reserves	32.9	100.1	322.0	330.7	294.0	307.2	328.2	316.0
Ratios								
External debt stocks to exports (%)	2031.9	1304.3	507.2	341.4	248.6	279.3	289.5	..
External debt stocks to GNI (%)	127.2	117.1	35.2	30.8	25.8	27.1	25.2	22.3
Debt service to exports (%)	40.9	40.5	16.6	2.4	4.2	8.8	13.7	..
Reserves to external debt stocks (%)	2.9	7.8	53.0	53.3	48.6	46.0	48.0	45.8

Notes:
Short-term debt is based on data from the BIS. Data include the effects of Paris Club debt restructuring agreement and HIPC and MDRI debt relief.

CABO VERDE

(US$ million, unless otherwise indicated)

	2000	2005	2009	2010	2011	2012	2013	2014
Summary external debt data								
External debt stocks	**320**	**477**	**727**	**892**	**1,039**	**1,245**	**1,486**	**1,537**
Long-term external debt	315	463	700	868	1,017	1,226	1,469	1,522
Short-term external debt	4	0	2	2	2	2	2	2
interest arrears on long-term	4	0	2	2	2	2	2	2
Use of IMF credit	1	13	25	23	20	18	16	14
Long-term external debt								
Debt outstanding and disbursed	**315**	**463**	**700**	**868**	**1,017**	**1,226**	**1,469**	**1,522**
Public and publicly guaranteed	315	463	700	868	1,017	1,226	1,469	1,522
Official creditors	308	442	693	816	944	1,108	1,279	1,265
Private creditors	7	22	6	53	73	118	190	257
of which: Bonds	0	0	0	0	0	0	0	0
Private nonguaranteed	..	..	..	..	..	..	..	..
of which: Bonds	..	..	..	..	..	..	..	..
Disbursements	**29**	**74**	**102**	**208**	**191**	**222**	**243**	**227**
Public and publicly guaranteed	29	74	102	208	191	222	243	227
Official creditors	29	65	102	158	165	179	178	129
Private creditors	0	9	0	50	25	43	64	98
of which: Bonds	0	0	0	0	0	0	0	0
Private nonguaranteed	..	..	..	..	..	..	..	..
of which: Bonds	..	..	..	..	..	..	..	..
Principal repayments	**11**	**29**	**25**	**26**	**26**	**20**	**22**	**24**
Public and publicly guaranteed	11	29	25	26	26	20	22	24
Official creditors	10	23	21	22	24	20	22	24
Private creditors	2	5	4	3	2	0	0	0
of which: Bonds	0	0	0	0	0	0	0	0
Private nonguaranteed	..	..	..	..	..	..	..	..
of which: Bonds	..	..	..	..	..	..	..	..
Interest payments	**5**	**7**	**7**	**8**	**10**	**13**	**16**	**18**
Public and publicly guaranteed	5	7	7	8	10	13	16	18
Official creditors	4	6	7	8	9	12	13	14
Private creditors	1	1	0	0	1	2	2	4
of which: Bonds	0	0	0	0	0	0	0	0
Private nonguaranteed	..	..	..	..	..	..	..	..
of which: Bonds	..	..	..	..	..	..	..	..
Net financial flows								
Net debt inflows	2	49	76	180	162	199	219	201
Official creditors (incl. IMF)	19	45	79	134	138	156	154	104
Private creditors	-18	4	-4	46	23	43	64	98
Long-term	-2	4	-4	46	23	43	64	98
Public and publicly guaranteed	-2	4	-4	46	23	43	64	98
Private nonguaranteed	..	..	..	..	..	..	..	..
Short-term	-16	..	..	..	..	..	..	..
Net equity inflows								
Foreign direct investment	33	63	124	95	91	112	111	119
Portfolio equity	..	..	2	..	..	..	..	..
Major economic aggregates								
Gross national income (GNI)	525	938	1,668	1,591	1,792	1,677	1,773	1,778
Exports of goods, services & prim. income	151	373	590	644	796	796	879	915
Imports of goods, services & prim. income	344	695	1,149	1,207	1,459	1,275	1,236	1,345
Primary income on FDI	5	11	26	56	42	32	16	36
Personal transfers & comp. of employees	87	137	137	131	177	178	176	189
International reserves	28	174	398	382	339	376	475	511
Ratios								
External debt stocks to exports (%)	211.8	127.8	123.1	138.6	130.5	156.4	169.2	168.0
External debt stocks to GNI (%)	60.9	50.8	43.6	56.1	58.0	74.2	83.8	86.4
Debt service to exports (%)	10.7	9.6	5.7	5.6	4.9	4.5	4.5	4.8
Reserves to external debt stocks (%)	8.8	36.5	54.8	42.8	32.6	30.2	32.0	33.2

CAMBODIA

(US$ million, unless otherwise indicated)

	2000	2005	2009	2010	2011	2012	2013	2014
Summary external debt data								
External debt stocks	**2,648**	**3,525**	**3,430**	**3,745**	**4,346**	**5,717**	**6,472**	**6,811**
Long-term external debt	2,328	3,141	3,027	3,335	3,732	4,549	5,139	5,566
Short-term external debt	227	280	272	281	486	1,038	1,204	1,124
interest arrears on long-term	131	243	208	215	221	209	152	138
Use of IMF credit	93	103	132	129	129	129	129	122
Long-term external debt								
Debt outstanding and disbursed	**2,328**	**3,141**	**3,027**	**3,335**	**3,732**	**4,549**	**5,139**	**5,566**
Public and publicly guaranteed	2,328	3,141	3,027	3,335	3,732	4,549	5,139	5,566
Official creditors	2,328	3,141	3,027	3,335	3,732	4,549	5,139	5,566
Private creditors	0	0	0	0	0	0	0	0
of which: Bonds	0	0	0	0	0	0	0	0
Private nonguaranteed	..	..	..	..	..	..	..	..
of which: Bonds	..	..	..	..	..	..	..	..
Disbursements	**79**	**155**	**207**	**344**	**431**	**863**	**603**	**648**
Public and publicly guaranteed	79	155	207	344	431	863	603	648
Official creditors	79	155	207	344	431	863	603	648
Private creditors	0	0	0	0	0	0	0	0
of which: Bonds	0	0	0	0	0	0	0	0
Private nonguaranteed	..	..	..	..	..	..	..	..
of which: Bonds	..	..	..	..	..	..	..	..
Principal repayments	**7**	**8**	**26**	**33**	**41**	**47**	**60**	**77**
Public and publicly guaranteed	7	8	26	33	41	47	60	77
Official creditors	7	8	26	33	41	47	60	77
Private creditors	0	0	0	0	0	0	0	0
of which: Bonds	0	0	0	0	0	0	0	0
Private nonguaranteed	..	..	..	..	..	..	..	..
of which: Bonds	..	..	..	..	..	..	..	..
Interest payments	**12**	**12**	**21**	**26**	**31**	**42**	**52**	**57**
Public and publicly guaranteed	12	12	21	26	31	42	52	57
Official creditors	12	12	21	26	31	42	52	57
Private creditors	0	0	0	0	0	0	0	0
of which: Bonds	0	0	0	0	0	0	0	0
Private nonguaranteed	..	..	..	..	..	..	..	..
of which: Bonds	..	..	..	..	..	..	..	..
Net financial flows								
Net debt inflows	128	141	117	313	589	1,380	766	505
Official creditors (incl. IMF)	76	138	181	311	390	816	543	571
Private creditors	52	3	-64	2	199	564	223	-66
Long-term	..	..	..	..	..	..	..	..
Public and publicly guaranteed	..	..	..	..	..	..	..	..
Private nonguaranteed	..	..	..	..	..	..	..	..
Short term	52	3	-64	2	199	564	223	-66
Net equity inflows								
Foreign direct investment	149	379	511	735	795	1,441	1,345	1,730
Portfolio equity	..	..	..	..	..	..	..	..
Major economic aggregates								
Gross national income (GNI)	3,534	6,006	9,931	10,698	12,261	13,403	14,470	15,883
Exports of goods, services & prim. income	1,893	4,094	5,015	6,026	7,826	8,893	10,087	11,262
Imports of goods, services & prim. income	2,453	4,935	5,981	7,075	8,882	10,343	12,075	..
Primary income on FDI	123	227	351	414	460	617	700	..
Personal transfers & comp. of employees	121	164	142	153	160	172	176	304
International reserves	502	953	2,851	3,255	3,450	4,267	4,516	5,626
Ratios								
External debt stocks to exports (%)	139.9	86.1	68.4	62.2	55.5	64.3	64.2	60.5
External debt stocks to GNI (%)	74.9	58.7	34.5	35.0	35.4	42.7	44.7	42.9
Debt service to exports (%)	1.7	0.8	1.0	1.0	1.1	1.4	1.5	1.5
Reserves to external debt stocks (%)	18.9	27.0	83.1	86.9	79.4	74.6	69.8	82.6

Notes:

Short term debt is based on data from the BIS. Data include MDRI debt relief.

CAMEROON

(US$ million, unless otherwise indicated)

	2000	2005	2009	2010	2011	2012	2013	2014
Summary external debt data								
External debt stocks	**10,561**	**7,700**	**3,238**	**3,189**	**3,095**	**3,737**	**4,903**	**5,289**
Long-term external debt	9,070	7,059	2,783	2,735	2,582	3,140	4,023	4,706
Short-term external debt	1,224	334	3	9	70	157	442	177
interest arrears on long-term	205	280	3	9	2	24	60	1
Use of IMF credit	267	307	453	445	442	440	437	406
Long-term external debt								
Debt outstanding and disbursed	**9,070**	**7,059**	**2,783**	**2,735**	**2,582**	**3,140**	**4,023**	**4,706**
Public and publicly guaranteed	8,753	6,467	2,167	2,158	2,121	2,772	3,798	4,463
Official creditors	8,436	6,384	2,153	2,138	2,098	2,727	3,560	4,080
Private creditors	317	83	14	20	23	45	239	383
of which: Bonds	0	0	0	0	0	0	0	0
Private nonguaranteed	317	592	615	577	461	368	225	243
of which: Bonds	..	..	..	..	..	..	..	..
Disbursements	**286**	**227**	**356**	**278**	**178**	**608**	**1,005**	**1,240**
Public and publicly guaranteed	247	130	147	278	178	608	1,005	1,194
Official creditors	247	130	139	272	174	586	814	963
Private creditors	0	0	8	6	5	22	191	231
of which: Bonds	0	0	0	0	0	0	0	17
Private nonguaranteed	39	98	209	..	..	..	..	46
of which: Bonds	..	..	..	..	..	..	..	..
Principal repayments	**253**	**537**	**344**	**159**	**244**	**173**	**156**	**290**
Public and publicly guaranteed	166	396	115	121	133	80	63	262
Official creditors	162	396	115	121	133	79	59	227
Private creditors	4	0	0	0	1	1	4	36
of which: Bonds	0	0	0	0	0	0	0	17
Private nonguaranteed	86	141	229	38	111	93	93	28
of which: Bonds	..	..	..	..	..	..	..	..
Interest payments	**215**	**228**	**57**	**42**	**86**	**60**	**55**	**147**
Public and publicly guaranteed	198	178	26	27	57	35	29	135
Official creditors	198	177	26	27	56	34	28	127
Private creditors	1	1	0	0	1	1	2	8
of which: Bonds	0	0	0	0	0	0	0	1
Private nonguaranteed	17	51	31	15	28	25	25	12
of which: Bonds	..	..	..	..	..	..	..	..
Net financial flows								
Net debt inflows	-21	-683	159	119	1	497	1,094	739
Official creditors (incl. IMF)	136	-301	172	151	40	505	751	732
Private creditors	-157	-382	-12	-32	-39	-8	343	7
Long-term	-52	-44	-12	-32	-107	-73	94	213
Public and publicly guaranteed	-4	..	8	6	4	20	187	195
Private nonguaranteed	-48	-44	-20	-38	-111	-93	-93	18
Short-term	-105	-339	..	..	68	65	249	-206
Net equity inflows								
Foreign direct investment	159	120	814	525	138	277	143	501
Portfolio equity	0	-4	0	0	0	0	0	..
Major economic aggregates								
Gross national income (GNI)	8,694	16,099	23,267	23,358	26,284	26,027	28,948	32,259
Exports of goods, services & prim. income	2,694	4,280	5,445	5,701	7,674	7,591	8,226	..
Imports of goods, services & prim. income	3,021	5,012	6,842	6,703	8,680	8,810	9,658	..
Primary income on FDI	41	289	436	166	282	503	648	..
Personal transfers & comp. of employees	30	77	184	115	219	210	244	251
International reserves	212	949	3,676	3,643	3,199	3,381	3,472	3,168
Ratios								
External debt stocks to exports (%)	392.0	179.9	59.5	55.9	40.3	49.2	59.6	..
External debt stocks to GNI (%)	121.5	47.8	13.9	13.7	11.8	14.4	16.9	16.4
Debt service to exports (%)	20.8	19.1	7.4	3.6	4.3	3.1	2.7	..
Reserves to external debt stocks (%)	2.0	12.3	113.5	114.2	103.4	90.5	70.8	59.9

Notes:

Short-term debt is based on data from the BIS. Data include the effects of HIPC and MDRI debt relief.

CENTRAL AFRICAN REPUBLIC

(US$ million, unless otherwise indicated)

	2000	2005	2009	2010	2011	2012	2013	2014
Summary external debt data								
External debt stocks	**872.1**	**1,033.0**	**537.6**	**614.2**	**547.3**	**551.5**	**574.7**	**657.4**
Long-term external debt	797.3	877.2	293.8	361.9	271.2	288.3	307.3	393.9
Short-term external debt	41.2	106.6	81.7	79.7	104.1	80.3	86.4	86.2
interest arrears on long-term	26.1	97.6	77.7	77.7	71.1	73.3	80.4	83.2
Use of IMF credit	33.6	49.2	162.1	172.6	172.0	182.9	181.0	177.3
Long-term external debt								
Debt outstanding and disbursed	**797.3**	**877.2**	**293.8**	**361.9**	**271.2**	**288.3**	**307.3**	**393.9**
Public and publicly guaranteed	797.3	877.2	293.8	361.9	271.2	288.3	307.3	393.9
Official creditors	764.8	843.1	259.4	325.3	244.1	261.2	281.1	370.2
Private creditors	32.6	34.1	34.4	36.6	27.1	27.1	26.2	23.7
of which: Bonds	0.0	0.0	0.0	0.0	0.0	0.0	0.0	0.0
Private nonguaranteed	..	..	..	..	..	..	..	..
of which: Bonds	..	..	..	..	..	..	..	..
Disbursements	**16.1**	**0.0**	**18.7**	**19.2**	**17.1**	**18.4**	**20.2**	**93.9**
Public and publicly guaranteed	16.1	0.0	18.7	19.2	17.1	18.4	20.2	93.9
Official creditors	16.1	0.0	18.7	19.2	17.1	18.4	20.2	93.9
Private creditors	0.0	0.0	0.0	0.0	0.0	0.0	0.0	0.0
of which: Bonds	0.0	0.0	0.0	0.0	0.0	0.0	0.0	0.0
Private nonguaranteed	..	..	..	..	..	..	..	..
of which: Bonds	..	..	..	..	..	..	..	..
Principal repayments	**7.5**	**0.7**	**8.4**	**1.0**	**0.8**	**2.1**	**3.5**	**7.3**
Public and publicly guaranteed	7.5	0.7	8.4	1.0	0.8	2.1	3.5	7.3
Official creditors	7.4	0.7	8.4	1.0	0.7	2.1	2.3	5.1
Private creditors	0.0	0.0	0.0	0.0	0.1	0.1	1.2	2.2
of which: Bonds	0.0	0.0	0.0	0.0	0.0	0.0	0.0	0.0
Private nonguaranteed	..	..	..	..	..	..	..	..
of which: Bonds	..	..	..	..	..	..	..	..
Interest payments	**4.3**	**0.2**	**3.0**	**1.2**	**0.2**	**1.9**	**0.5**	**2.6**
Public and publicly guaranteed	4.3	0.2	3.0	1.2	0.2	1.9	0.5	2.6
Official creditors	4.3	0.2	3.0	1.2	0.2	1.9	0.5	2.6
Private creditors	0.0	0.0	0.0	0.0	0.0	0.0	0.0	0.0
of which: Bonds	0.0	0.0	0.0	0.0	0.0	0.0	0.0	0.0
Private nonguaranteed	..	..	..	..	..	..	..	..
of which: Bonds	..	..	..	..	..	..	..	..
Net financial flows								
Net debt inflows	-13.8	-5.6	22.6	29.4	47.3	0.9	13.4	91.0
Official creditors (incl. IMF)	7.8	-5.6	30.6	31.4	16.4	26.9	15.7	96.2
Private creditors	-21.6	..	-8.0	-2.0	30.9	-26.1	-2.2	-5.2
Long-term	0.0	..	..	..	-0.1	-0.1	-1.2	-2.2
Public and publicly guaranteed	0.0	..	..	..	-0.1	-0.1	-1.2	-2.2
Private nonguaranteed	..	..	..	..	..	..	..	..
Short-term	-21.6	..	-8.0	-2.0	31.0	-26.0	-1.0	-3.0
Net equity inflows								
Foreign direct investment	0.9	10.1	42.3	61.5	36.9	70.0	1.9	3.5
Portfolio equity	..	..	..	..	..	..	..	..
Major economic aggregates								
Gross national income (GNI)	901.4	1,340.1	1,975.9	1,995.6	2,205.3	2,181.2	1,550.3	1,790.2
Exports of goods, services & prim. income	..	..	..	..	..	..	..	..
Imports of goods, services & prim. income	..	..	..	..	..	..	..	..
Primary income on FDI	..	..	..	..	..	..	..	..
Personal transfers & comp. of employees	..	..	..	..	..	..	..	..
International reserves	133.3	139.2	210.6	181.2	154.5	157.9	193.7	259.6
Ratios								
External debt stocks to exports (%)	..	..	..	..	..	..	..	..
External debt stocks to GNI (%)	96.7	77.1	27.2	30.8	24.8	25.3	37.1	36.7
Debt service to exports (%)	..	..	..	..	..	..	..	..
Reserves to external debt stocks (%)	15.3	13.5	39.2	29.5	28.2	28.6	33.7	39.5

Notes:

Short-term debt is based on data from the BIS. Data include the effects of HIPC and MDRI debt relief.

CHAD

(US$ million, unless otherwise indicated)

	2000	2005	2009	2010	2011	2012	2013	2014
Summary external debt data								
External debt stocks	**1,101**	**1,630**	**1,866**	**2,157**	**2,346**	**2,379**	**2,922**	**2,857**
Long-term external debt	986	1,526	1,750	2,049	2,235	2,265	2,829	2,752
Short-term external debt	25	11	4	8	20	27	8	8
interest arrears on long-term	10	6	4	7	8	8	8	8
Use of IMF credit	90	93	113	99	91	87	85	98
Long-term external debt								
Debt outstanding and disbursed	**986**	**1,526**	**1,750**	**2,049**	**2,235**	**2,265**	**2,829**	**2,752**
Public and publicly guaranteed	986	1,526	1,750	2,049	2,235	2,265	2,829	2,752
Official creditors	971	1,494	1,718	2,019	2,211	2,242	2,210	2,135
Private creditors	15	32	32	30	24	22	620	617
of which: Bonds	0	0	0	0	0	0	0	0
Private nonguaranteed	..	..	..	..	..	..	..	..
of which: Bonds	..	..	..	..	..	..	..	..
Disbursements	**46**	**143**	**34**	**366**	**254**	**95**	**660**	**147**
Public and publicly guaranteed	46	143	34	366	254	95	660	147
Official creditors	46	143	34	366	254	95	60	147
Private creditors	0	0	0	0	0	0	600	0
of which: Bonds	0	0	0	0	0	0	0	0
Private nonguaranteed	..	..	..	..	..	..	..	..
of which: Bonds	..	..	..	..	..	..	..	..
Principal repayments	**13**	**24**	**42**	**46**	**57**	**59**	**95**	**96**
Public and publicly guaranteed	13	24	42	46	57	59	95	96
Official creditors	13	23	41	44	51	57	93	94
Private creditors	1	1	1	2	6	2	3	2
of which: Bonds	0	0	0	0	0	0	0	0
Private nonguaranteed	..	..	..	..	..	..	..	..
of which: Bonds	..	..	..	..	..	..	..	..
Interest payments	**9**	**16**	**23**	**17**	**18**	**21**	**23**	**28**
Public and publicly guaranteed	9	16	23	17	18	21	23	28
Official creditors	9	16	23	17	18	21	23	28
Private creditors	0	0	0	0	0	0	0	0
of which: Bonds	0	0	0	0	0	0	0	0
Private nonguaranteed	..	..	..	..	..	..	..	..
of which: Bonds	..	..	..	..	..	..	..	..
Net financial flows								
Net debt inflows	44	109	-20	311	200	39	543	69
Official creditors (incl. IMF)	46	114	-19	312	194	34	-36	71
Private creditors	-2	-4	-1	-1	5	5	578	-2
Long-term	-1	-1	-1	-2	-6	-2	597	-2
Public and publicly guaranteed	-1	-1	-1	-2	-6	-2	597	-2
Private nonguaranteed	..	..	..	..	..	..	..	..
Short-term	-2	-3	..	1	11	7	-19	..
Net equity inflows								
Foreign direct investment	115	-99	375	313	282	343	538	761
Portfolio equity	..	..	..	..	..	..	..	..
Major economic aggregates								
Gross national income (GNI)	1,368	5,622	8,868	10,302	11,841	12,068	12,359	13,233
Exports of goods, services & prim. income	..	..	..	..	..	..	..	..
Imports of goods, services & prim. income	..	..	..	..	..	..	..	..
Primary income on FDI	..	..	..	..	..	..	..	..
Personal transfers & comp. of employees	..	..	..	..	..	..	..	..
International reserves	111	226	617	632	951	1,156	1,183	1,076
Ratios								
External debt stocks to exports (%)	..	..	..	..	..	..	..	..
External debt stocks to GNI (%)	80.5	29.0	21.0	20.9	19.8	19.7	23.6	21.6
Debt service to exports (%)	..	..	..	..	..	..	..	..
Reserves to external debt stocks (%)	10.1	13.8	33.0	29.3	40.5	48.6	40.5	37.7

Notes:

Long-term public and publicly guaranteed debt data for 2014 are World Bank staff estimates. Short-term debt is based on data from the BIS. Data include the effects of HIPC debt relief.

CHINA

(US$ million, unless otherwise indicated)

	2000	2005	2009	2010	2011	2012	2013	2014
Summary external debt data								
External debt stocks	**145,648**	**281,113**	**445,942**	**559,772**	**710,234**	**750,746**	**870,848**	**959,510**
Long-term external debt	132,259	132,507	194,475	201,484	222,592	230,411	238,981	266,020
Short-term external debt	13,080	148,267	240,509	347,524	476,911	509,592	621,103	683,363
interest arrears on long-term	0	0	0	0	0	0	0	0
Use of IMF credit	309	338	10,958	10,764	10,731	10,743	10,764	10,127
Long-term external debt								
Debt outstanding and disbursed	**132,259**	**132,507**	**194,475**	**201,484**	**222,592**	**230,411**	**238,981**	**266,020**
Public and publicly guaranteed	94,470	82,015	92,318	90,637	75,176	70,741	78,211	83,306
Official creditors	50,374	52,421	68,358	67,204	67,684	66,201	60,532	59,268
Private creditors	44,096	29,595	23,960	23,433	7,492	4,540	17,679	24,039
of which: Bonds	11,371	13,859	9,905	10,730	2,486	2,630	8,130	11,161
Private nonguaranteed	37,789	50,492	102,157	110,847	147,416	159,671	160,771	182,714
of which: Bonds	1,068	3,574	7,020	17,153	28,203	38,819	49,133	73,351
Disbursements	**19,006**	**28,228**	**23,648**	**42,423**	**46,950**	**37,375**	**56,798**	**66,903**
Public and publicly guaranteed	11,924	8,776	6,481	10,125	7,785	3,629	16,868	18,921
Official creditors	5,790	2,170	3,310	4,348	3,848	3,408	2,713	4,902
Private creditors	6,133	6,606	3,171	5,777	3,937	222	14,155	14,018
of which: Bonds	848	3,208	0	0	3,098	0	5,500	7,832
Private nonguaranteed	7,082	19,452	17,167	32,298	39,165	33,746	39,930	47,982
of which: Bonds	390	1,622	925	11,592	12,133	10,903	25,897	24,871
Principal repayments	**19,362**	**20,936**	**33,448**	**27,237**	**36,277**	**35,519**	**33,395**	**43,975**
Public and publicly guaranteed	10,235	6,659	6,473	8,400	12,199	8,132	6,680	12,763
Official creditors	4,270	1,413	2,594	3,643	5,301	4,491	5,650	5,134
Private creditors	5,965	5,246	3,878	4,757	6,898	3,641	1,029	7,628
of which: Bonds	443	550	500	0	2,092	318	0	4,801
Private nonguaranteed	9,127	14,277	26,976	18,837	24,078	27,387	26,715	31,212
of which: Bonds	534	370	464	..	1,083	..	1,821	405
Interest payments	**6,064**	**3,157**	**3,045**	**5,316**	**6,890**	**4,312**	**4,822**	**7,757**
Public and publicly guaranteed	4,140	2,140	2,030	1,651	1,792	2,139	1,775	1,524
Official creditors	2,386	1,375	1,090	944	1,070	1,832	1,552	1,088
Private creditors	1,754	765	940	707	722	307	223	436
of which: Bonds	521	369	480	317	310	59	151	349
Private nonguaranteed	1,924	1,017	1,015	3,665	5,097	2,173	3,047	6,233
of which: Bonds	93	248	445	672	1,942	1,117	2,292	3,830
Net financial flows								
Net debt inflows	-2,457	39,789	43,521	122,201	140,060	34,538	134,915	85,188
Official creditors (incl. IMF)	1,520	757	716	705	-1,453	-1,083	-2,937	-232
Private creditors	-3,977	39,032	42,805	121,496	141,513	35,621	137,852	85,420
Long-term	-1,877	6,535	-10,516	14,481	12,126	2,940	26,341	23,160
Public and publicly guaranteed	168	1,360	-707	1,020	-2,961	-3,419	13,126	6,390
Private nonguaranteed	-2,045	5,175	-9,809	13,461	15,087	6,359	13,215	16,770
Short-term	-2,100	32,497	53,321	107,015	129,387	32,681	111,511	62,260
Net equity inflows								
Foreign direct investment	38,399	94,959	147,356	240,537	279,762	241,544	273,189	289,100
Portfolio equity	6,912	20,569	29,117	31,357	5,308	29,903	32,595	51,900
Major economic aggregates								
Gross national income (GNI)	1,190,595	2,252,486	5,050,889	6,013,586	7,422,055	8,441,806	9,447,316	10,295,771
Exports of goods, services & prim. income	292,111	809,731	1,368,583	1,790,140	2,134,931	2,355,310	2,548,141	2,758,100
Imports of goods, services & prim. income	277,904	701,218	1,156,985	1,593,015	2,023,344	2,143,352	2,356,600	2,508,200
Primary income on FDI	20,198	47,566	105,948	159,637	204,476	171,845	206,381	..
Personal transfers & comp. of employees	5,237	8,832	22,903	33,440	40,483	39,221	38,819	64,140
International reserves	168,278	821,514	2,416,044	2,866,079	3,202,789	3,331,120	3,839,548	3,859,168
Ratios								
External debt stocks to exports (%)	49.9	34.7	32.6	31.3	33.3	31.9	34.2	34.8
External debt stocks to GNI (%)	12.2	12.5	8.8	9.3	9.6	8.9	9.2	9.3
Debt service to exports (%)	9.1	3.4	2.9	3.4	3.5	3.2	1.5	1.9
Reserves to external debt stocks (%)	115.5	292.2	541.8	512.0	450.9	443.7	440.9	402.2

Notes:

Long-term private nonguaranteed and short-term debt data are World Bank staff estimates based on reports provided by the country and market data.

COLOMBIA

(US$ million, unless otherwise indicated)

	2000	2005	2009	2010	2011	2012	2013	2014
Summary external debt data								
External debt stocks	**33,231**	**36,656**	**53,054**	**63,819**	**73,582**	**76,558**	**89,265**	**102,345**
Long-term external debt	30,211	30,855	47,884	54,770	61,853	65,089	77,237	89,054
Short-term external debt	2,871	5,637	4,013	7,912	10,596	10,334	10,891	12,221
interest arrears on long-term	0	0	0	0	0	0	0	0
Use of IMF credit	149	163	1,157	1,137	1,134	1,135	1,137	1,070
Long-term external debt								
Debt outstanding and disbursed	**30,211**	**30,855**	**47,884**	**54,770**	**61,853**	**65,089**	**77,237**	**89,054**
Public and publicly guaranteed	19,952	21,866	35,135	36,692	39,254	43,722	50,491	58,108
Official creditors	6,868	9,862	14,991	16,154	16,685	19,697	20,738	21,350
Private creditors	13,084	12,005	20,145	20,539	22,569	24,025	29,753	36,758
of which: Bonds	8,201	10,927	17,159	17,686	20,099	21,729	25,555	31,450
Private nonguaranteed	10,259	8,989	12,749	18,078	22,599	21,368	26,746	30,946
of which: Bonds	762	370	2,709	3,329	2,720	5,320	8,420	10,170
Disbursements	**3,753**	**6,522**	**13,148**	**12,831**	**16,529**	**17,598**	**20,745**	**19,097**
Public and publicly guaranteed	2,889	4,401	8,107	3,491	4,690	7,150	9,061	10,857
Official creditors	610	1,469	2,415	2,125	1,559	4,040	2,228	2,319
Private creditors	2,279	2,932	5,691	1,365	3,131	3,110	6,833	8,538
of which: Bonds	1,804	2,304	5,491	1,335	2,829	2,489	4,778	7,220
Private nonguaranteed	865	2,121	5,041	9,340	11,839	10,448	11,683	8,240
of which: Bonds	..	..	1,900	620	2,720	2,600	3,100	1,750
Principal repayments	**2,890**	**7,275**	**5,785**	**6,435**	**6,398**	**11,355**	**6,129**	**8,694**
Public and publicly guaranteed	2,058	4,583	1,660	2,188	2,205	2,782	2,011	2,493
Official creditors	547	2,096	809	985	1,022	1,067	1,114	1,420
Private creditors	1,511	2,487	851	1,203	1,183	1,716	897	1,073
of which: Bonds	469	1,723	623	983	481	847	809	1,015
Private nonguaranteed	832	2,692	4,126	4,248	4,193	8,573	4,118	6,201
of which: Bonds	110	..	..	..	..	..	..	..
Interest payments	**1,952**	**2,513**	**2,695**	**2,824**	**3,187**	**3,381**	**3,276**	**3,964**
Public and publicly guaranteed	1,334	1,876	1,977	2,118	2,087	2,145	2,155	2,588
Official creditors	461	502	574	540	516	531	558	526
Private creditors	873	1,374	1,403	1,577	1,571	1,614	1,597	2,062
of which: Bonds	515	1,284	1,073	1,282	1,315	1,395	1,392	1,763
Private nonguaranteed	618	637	718	707	1,100	1,236	1,121	1,376
of which: Bonds	84	36	129	221	308	202	333	486
Net financial flows								
Net debt inflows	-231	-236	5,743	10,295	12,815	5,981	15,173	11,733
Official creditors (incl. IMF)	63	-628	1,607	1,140	537	2,973	1,114	899
Private creditors	-294	392	4,136	9,155	12,279	3,008	14,059	10,835
Long-term	800	-126	5,756	5,256	9,595	3,270	13,502	9,504
Public and publicly guaranteed	768	446	4,840	163	1,949	1,394	5,937	7,466
Private nonguaranteed	32	-571	916	5,093	7,646	1,875	7,565	2,039
Short-term	-1,094	517	-1,620	3,900	2,684	-262	557	1,331
Net equity inflows								
Foreign direct investment	2,436	10,267	7,303	7,065	12,776	13,800	13,831	13,561
Portfolio equity	17	86	67	1,318	2,288	3,180	1,926	3,833
Major economic aggregates								
Gross national income (GNI)	97,730	141,300	225,455	275,791	319,928	354,614	365,886	364,892
Exports of goods, services & prim. income	16,850	25,787	40,137	47,542	66,664	71,874	70,753	67,962
Imports of goods, services & prim. income	17,728	31,761	49,343	60,652	81,208	87,759	87,677	92,100
Primary income on FDI	655	3,566	7,294	9,875	14,866	14,954	13,695	12,315
Personal transfers & comp. of employees	1,610	3,346	4,125	4,031	4,101	4,019	4,450	4,166
International reserves	8,916	14,787	24,748	27,766	31,386	36,444	42,758	46,408
Ratios								
External debt stocks to exports (%)	197.2	142.1	132.2	134.2	110.4	106.5	126.2	150.6
External debt stocks to GNI (%)	34.0	25.9	23.5	23.1	23.0	21.6	24.4	28.0
Debt service to exports (%)	29.8	38.9	21.6	20.3	15.1	21.2	14.0	19.5
Reserves to external debt stocks (%)	26.8	40.3	46.6	43.5	42.7	47.6	47.9	45.3

COMOROS

(US$ million, unless otherwise indicated)

	2000	2005	2009	2010	2011	2012	2013	2014
Summary external debt data								
External debt stocks	**226.7**	**280.8**	**288.4**	**280.6**	**277.9**	**255.7**	**151.1**	**145.0**
Long-term external debt	204.0	255.3	260.2	250.7	245.5	223.5	116.6	112.5
Short-term external debt	20.3	24.5	4.7	4.4	4.7	4.1	1.6	1.6
interest arrears on long-term	11.3	21.5	4.7	4.4	4.7	4.1	1.6	1.6
Use of IMF credit	2.4	1.0	23.4	25.4	27.7	28.0	32.9	30.9
Long-term external debt								
Debt outstanding and disbursed	**204.0**	**255.3**	**260.2**	**250.7**	**245.5**	**223.5**	**116.6**	**112.5**
Public and publicly guaranteed	204.0	255.3	260.2	250.7	245.5	223.5	116.6	112.5
Official creditors	204.0	255.3	260.2	250.7	245.5	223.5	116.6	112.5
Private creditors	0.0	0.0	0.0	0.0	0.0	0.0	0.0	0.0
of which: Bonds	0.0	0.0	0.0	0.0	0.0	0.0	0.0	0.0
Private nonguaranteed	..	..	..	..	..	..	..	..
of which: Bonds	..	..	..	..	..	..	..	..
Disbursements	**2.1**	**3.3**	**0.3**	**0.0**	**0.0**	**0.0**	**0.0**	**0.0**
Public and publicly guaranteed	2.1	3.3	0.3	0.0	0.0	0.0	0.0	0.0
Official creditors	2.1	3.3	0.3	0.0	0.0	0.0	0.0	0.0
Private creditors	0.0	0.0	0.0	0.0	0.0	0.0	0.0	0.0
of which: Bonds	0.0	0.0	0.0	0.0	0.0	0.0	0.0	0.0
Private nonguaranteed	..	..	..	..	..	..	..	..
of which: Bonds	..	..	..	..	..	..	..	..
Principal repayments	**1.2**	**2.6**	**7.2**	**3.1**	**2.2**	**5.1**	**0.3**	**0.5**
Public and publicly guaranteed	1.2	2.6	7.2	3.1	2.2	5.1	0.3	0.5
Official creditors	1.2	2.6	7.2	3.1	2.2	5.1	0.3	0.5
Private creditors	0.0	0.0	0.0	0.0	0.0	0.0	0.0	0.0
of which: Bonds	0.0	0.0	0.0	0.0	0.0	0.0	0.0	0.0
Private nonguaranteed	..	..	..	..	..	..	..	..
of which: Bonds	..	..	..	..	..	..	..	..
Interest payments	**0.8**	**1.3**	**2.9**	**1.1**	**1.7**	**2.3**	**0.1**	**0.1**
Public and publicly guaranteed	0.8	1.3	2.9	1.1	1.7	2.3	0.1	0.1
Official creditors	0.8	1.3	2.9	1.1	1.7	2.3	0.1	0.1
Private creditors	0.0	0.0	0.0	0.0	0.0	0.0	0.0	0.0
of which: Bonds	0.0	0.0	0.0	0.0	0.0	0.0	0.0	0.0
Private nonguaranteed	..	..	..	..	..	..	..	..
of which: Bonds	..	..	..	..	..	..	..	..
Net financial flows								
Net debt inflows	2.3	0.7	-2.1	-0.7	0.2	-4.9	4.4	-0.5
Official creditors (incl. IMF)	0.3	0.7	-2.1	-0.7	0.2	-4.9	4.4	-0.5
Private creditors	2.0	..	..	..	..	..	..	..
Long-term	..	..	..	..	..	..	..	..
Public and publicly guaranteed	..	..	..	..	..	..	..	..
Private nonguaranteed	..	..	..	..	..	..	..	..
Short-term	2.0	..	..	..	..	..	..	..
Net equity inflows								
Foreign direct investment	0.1	0.6	13.8	8.3	23.1	4.9	9.5	14.0
Portfolio equity	..	..	..	..	..	..	..	..
Major economic aggregates								
Gross national income (GNI)	202.2	378.7	523.0	529.4	585.1	569.7	617.4	646.5
Exports of goods, services & prim. income	..	59.5	80.9	90.7	103.4	93.3	109.1	90.5
Imports of goods, services & prim. income	..	144.3	258.0	275.4	311.6	327.1	350.8	310.0
Primary income on FDI	..	1.7	1.7	1.8	2.4	2.2	..	..
Personal transfers & comp. of employees	..	54.0	100.0	87.2	108.0	110.2	..	..
International reserves	43.2	85.8	150.3	145.3	155.2	194.1	173.4	170.5
Ratios								
External debt stocks to exports (%)	..	471.6	356.5	309.5	268.7	274.0	138.4	160.3
External debt stocks to GNI (%)	112.1	74.1	55.1	53.0	47.5	44.9	24.5	22.4
Debt service to exports (%)	..	6.8	14.7	4.7	3.8	12.8	0.4	0.7
Reserves to external debt stocks (%)	19.1	30.6	52.1	51.8	55.8	75.9	114.8	117.5

Notes:

Data include the effects of Paris Club debt restructuring agreements signed in 2010 and 2013, and the HIPC debt relief.

CONGO, DEMOCRATIC REPUBLIC OF

(US$ million, unless otherwise indicated)

	2000	2005	2009	2010	2011	2012	2013	2014
Summary external debt data								
External debt stocks	**11,805**	**10,714**	**13,083**	**6,188**	**5,531**	**5,591**	**6,180**	**5,508**
Long-term external debt	7,880	9,402	10,880	4,597	4,022	4,103	4,470	4,149
Short-term external debt	3,421	397	603	481	250	229	448	171
interest arrears on long-term	3,042	359	489	267	73	71	71	71
Use of IMF credit	503	914	1,601	1,110	1,258	1,260	1,262	1,188
Long-term external debt								
Debt outstanding and disbursed	**7,880**	**9,402**	**10,880**	**4,597**	**4,022**	**4,103**	**4,470**	**4,149**
Public and publicly guaranteed	7,880	9,402	10,880	4,597	4,022	4,103	4,470	4,149
Official creditors	7,384	9,033	10,548	4,472	4,008	4,075	4,452	4,140
Private creditors	496	369	332	126	14	27	18	9
of which: Bonds	3	0	0	0	0	0	0	0
Private nonguaranteed	..	..	..	..	..	..	..	..
of which: Bonds	..	..	..	..	..	..	..	..
Disbursements	**0**	**249**	**131**	**78**	**152**	**242**	**495**	**116**
Public and publicly guaranteed	0	249	131	78	152	242	495	116
Official creditors	0	249	131	58	152	226	494	116
Private creditors	0	0	0	20	0	17	1	0
of which: Bonds	0	0	0	0	0	0	0	0
Private nonguaranteed	..	..	..	..	..	..	..	..
of which: Bonds	..	..	..	..	..	..	..	..
Principal repayments	**0**	**112**	**226**	**89**	**133**	**108**	**242**	**262**
Public and publicly guaranteed	0	112	226	89	133	108	242	262
Official creditors	0	110	205	85	128	105	232	255
Private creditors	0	2	21	4	5	4	10	8
of which: Bonds	0	1	0	0	0	0	0	0
Private nonguaranteed	..	..	..	..	..	..	..	..
of which: Bonds	..	..	..	..	..	..	..	..
Interest payments	**0**	**97**	**242**	**125**	**120**	**168**	**153**	**146**
Public and publicly guaranteed	0	97	242	125	120	168	153	146
Official creditors	0	95	240	124	120	168	153	146
Private creditors	0	1	2	0	0	0	0	0
of which: Bonds	0	0	0	0	0	0	0	0
Private nonguaranteed	..	..	..	..	..	..	..	..
of which: Bonds	..	..	..	..	..	..	..	..
Net financial flows								
Net debt inflows	20	95	-55	107	138	115	471	-423
Official creditors (incl. IMF)	0	178	58	-8	180	121	262	-139
Private creditors	20	-83	-113	116	-42	-6	209	-285
Long-term	..	-2	-21	16	-5	13	-10	-8
Public and publicly guaranteed	..	-2	-21	16	-5	13	-10	-8
Private nonguaranteed	..	..	..	..	..	..	..	..
Short-term	20	-81	-92	100	-37	-19	219	-277
Net equity inflows								
Foreign direct investment	72	180	-243	2,736	1,687	3,312	2,098	2,063
Portfolio equity	..	..	..	..	..	..	-3	-17
Major economic aggregates								
Gross national income (GNI)	18,700	11,457	17,477	19,613	22,553	25,867	27,204	28,812
Exports of goods, services & prim. income	..	2,756	5,047	8,915	10,379	9,049	12,054	13,257
Imports of goods, services & prim. income	..	3,892	7,571	11,931	13,071	12,075	16,428	18,118
Primary income on FDI	..	..	..	131	..	..	..	..
Personal transfers & comp. of employees	..	9	20	16	115	12	33	22
International reserves	..	131	1,035	1,300	1,268	1,633	1,678	1,557
Ratios								
External debt stocks to exports (%)	..	388.8	259.2	69.4	53.3	61.8	51.3	41.5
External debt stocks to GNI (%)	63.1	93.5	74.9	31.6	24.5	21.6	22.7	19.1
Debt service to exports (%)	..	7.9	12.4	3.1	2.5	3.1	3.3	3.1
Reserves to external debt stocks (%)	..	1.2	7.9	21.0	22.9	29.2	27.2	28.3

Notes:

Short-term debt is based on data from the BIS. Data include the effects of Paris Club debt restructuring agreement and HIPC and MDRI debt relief.

CONGO, REPUBLIC OF

(US$ million, unless otherwise indicated)

	2000	2005	2009	2010	2011	2012	2013	2014
Summary external debt data								
External debt stocks	**4,864**	**6,252**	**4,938**	**2,406**	**2,638**	**2,829**	**3,448**	**3,901**
Long-term external debt	3,733	5,465	4,610	2,063	2,329	2,492	3,072	3,559
Short-term external debt	1,076	746	161	193	155	185	228	208
interest arrears on long-term	655	735	94	76	61	60	69	68
Use of IMF credit	54	40	168	150	155	152	148	134
Long-term external debt								
Debt outstanding and disbursed	**3,733**	**5,465**	**4,610**	**2,063**	**2,329**	**2,492**	**3,072**	**3,559**
Public and publicly guaranteed	3,733	5,465	4,610	2,063	2,329	2,492	3,072	3,559
Official creditors	2,919	3,287	3,656	1,224	1,402	1,479	1,977	2,435
Private creditors	815	2,179	954	840	927	1,013	1,095	1,124
of which: Bonds	0	0	454	454	454	449	436	418
Private nonguaranteed	..	..	..	..	..	..	..	..
of which: Bonds	..	..	..	..	..	..	..	..
Disbursements	**1**	**183**	**7**	**504**	**356**	**472**	**836**	**844**
Public and publicly guaranteed	1	183	7	504	356	472	836	844
Official creditors	1	183	7	502	244	251	632	623
Private creditors	0	0	0	2	112	221	204	221
of which: Bonds	0	0	0	0	0	0	0	0
Private nonguaranteed	..	..	..	..	..	..	..	..
of which: Bonds	..	..	..	..	..	..	..	..
Principal repayments	**6**	**65**	**114**	**116**	**114**	**141**	**265**	**262**
Public and publicly guaranteed	6	65	114	116	114	141	265	262
Official creditors	6	65	80	104	92	106	138	135
Private creditors	0	0	34	12	22	35	126	128
of which: Bonds	0	0	0	0	0	5	14	18
Private nonguaranteed	..	..	..	..	..	..	..	..
of which: Bonds	..	..	..	..	..	..	..	..
Interest payments	**7**	**34**	**63**	**23**	**20**	**23**	**31**	**34**
Public and publicly guaranteed	7	34	63	23	20	23	31	34
Official creditors	7	34	48	9	6	7	13	12
Private creditors	0	0	14	14	14	16	18	22
of which: Bonds	0	0	14	14	14	14	16	15
Private nonguaranteed	..	..	..	..	..	..	..	..
of which: Bonds	..	..	..	..	..	..	..	..
Net financial flows								
Net debt inflows	-52	128	-174	439	224	359	601	557
Official creditors (incl. IMF)	9	117	-70	400	158	142	489	483
Private creditors	-61	11	-104	39	66	217	112	75
Long-term	..	..	-34	-11	89	186	78	94
Public and publicly guaranteed	..	..	-34	-11	89	186	78	94
Private nonguaranteed	..	..	..	..	..	..	..	..
Short-term	-61	11	-70	50	-23	31	34	-19
Net equity inflows								
Foreign direct investment	166	801	1,274	928	2,180	2,152	2,914	5,502
Portfolio equity	0	..	..	..	..	..	..	..
Major economic aggregates								
Gross national income (GNI)	2,275	4,032	6,979	9,024	10,713	10,542	11,050	11,697
Exports of goods, services & prim. income	2,642	4,983	..	..	..	..	..	..
Imports of goods, services & prim. income	2,013	4,318	..	..	..	..	..	..
Primary income on FDI	466	1,296	..	..	..	..	..	..
Personal transfers & comp. of employees	10	11	..	..	..	..	..	..
International reserves	222	732	3,806	4,447	5,641	5,550	5,245	4,926
Ratios								
External debt stocks to exports (%)	184.1	125.5	..	..	..	..	..	..
External debt stocks to GNI (%)	213.8	155.0	70.8	26.7	24.6	26.8	31.2	33.3
Debt service to exports (%)	1.7	2.3	..	..	..	..	..	..
Reserves to external debt stocks (%)	4.6	11.7	77.1	184.8	213.8	196.1	152.1	126.3

Notes:

Short-term debt is based on data from the BIS. Data include the effects of Paris Club debt restructuring agreement and HIPC and MDRI debt relief.

COSTA RICA

(US$ million, unless otherwise indicated)

	2000	2005	2009	2010	2011	2012	2013	2014
Summary external debt data								
External debt stocks	**4,688**	**6,483**	**7,760**	**8,154**	**10,271**	**14,310**	**18,735**	**20,974**
Long-term external debt	3,695	4,352	5,271	5,482	7,221	11,166	16,083	18,647
Short-term external debt	962	2,097	2,243	2,431	2,810	2,904	2,411	2,100
interest arrears on long-term	27	2	0	0	0	0	0	0
Use of IMF credit	31	34	245	241	240	241	241	227
Long-term external debt								
Debt outstanding and disbursed	**3,695**	**4,352**	**5,271**	**5,482**	**7,221**	**11,166**	**16,083**	**18,647**
Public and publicly guaranteed	3,509	3,157	3,208	3,822	3,968	4,977	7,467	8,737
Official creditors	1,918	1,366	1,578	2,196	2,196	2,192	1,933	2,310
Private creditors	1,591	1,791	1,630	1,626	1,773	2,786	5,534	6,427
of which: Bonds	1,542	1,669	1,435	1,435	1,435	2,435	4,185	4,875
Private nonguaranteed	187	1,195	2,063	1,660	3,253	6,189	8,616	9,910
of which: Bonds	..	..	..	..	..	..	1,000	1,350
Disbursements	**749**	**982**	**1,329**	**1,455**	**1,797**	**3,811**	**7,440**	**4,972**
Public and publicly guaranteed	749	75	559	928	773	1,784	3,648	2,025
Official creditors	249	75	419	845	269	351	418	669
Private creditors	500	0	141	82	504	1,433	3,230	1,356
of which: Bonds	500	0	75	0	250	1,250	2,000	1,000
Private nonguaranteed	..	906	770	528	1,023	2,026	3,791	2,947
of which: Bonds	..	..	..	..	..	..	1,000	350
Principal repayments	**391**	**565**	**849**	**617**	**1,149**	**1,647**	**2,490**	**2,409**
Public and publicly guaranteed	374	365	573	342	641	742	1,126	756
Official creditors	338	306	250	256	283	323	646	294
Private creditors	37	59	323	86	357	420	480	462
of which: Bonds	30	41	300	0	250	250	250	310
Private nonguaranteed	17	200	276	275	508	904	1,364	1,653
of which: Bonds	..	..	..	..	..	..	..	..
Interest payments	**202**	**177**	**342**	**313**	**397**	**561**	**728**	**997**
Public and publicly guaranteed	191	105	218	213	200	202	253	387
Official creditors	105	62	77	86	85	77	70	57
Private creditors	86	43	142	127	115	125	183	330
of which: Bonds	80	39	131	116	105	111	169	260
Private nonguaranteed	12	72	124	100	197	359	475	610
of which: Bonds	..	..	..	..	..	..	..	65
Net financial flows								
Net debt inflows	537	842	-1,265	1,026	1,027	2,257	4,457	2,252
Official creditors (incl. IMF)	-88	-231	169	590	-14	29	-228	375
Private creditors	625	1,072	-1,434	437	1,041	2,228	4,685	1,877
Long-term	446	647	312	249	662	2,135	5,178	2,188
Public and publicly guaranteed	463	-59	-182	-4	147	1,013	2,751	894
Private nonguaranteed	-17	706	494	253	515	1,122	2,427	1,294
Short-term	179	425	-1,745	188	379	93	-493	-311
Net equity inflows								
Foreign direct investment	409	575	1,405	1,254	1,563	1,585	2,577	1,589
Portfolio equity	..	..	..	..	..	..	..	..
Major economic aggregates								
Gross national income (GNI)	14,694	19,756	28,299	35,553	40,648	43,997	47,794	47,914
Exports of goods, services & prim. income	7,992	7,535	10,806	12,457	14,066	15,204	15,796	16,407
Imports of goods, services & prim. income	8,793	8,787	11,720	13,938	16,445	17,941	18,398	18,945
Primary income on FDI	1,141	743	802	847	998	1,185	1,269	1,455
Personal transfers & comp. of employees	136	420	513	531	520	562	596	594
International reserves	1,318	2,313	4,066	4,627	4,756	6,857	7,331	7,211
Ratios								
External debt stocks to exports (%)	58.7	86.0	71.8	65.5	73.0	94.1	118.6	127.8
External debt stocks to GNI (%)	31.9	32.8	27.4	22.9	25.3	32.5	39.2	43.8
Debt service to exports (%)	8.1	11.1	11.6	8.0	11.5	15.0	20.8	21.1
Reserves to external debt stocks (%)	28.1	35.7	52.4	56.7	46.3	47.9	39.1	34.4

Notes:

Long-term private nonguaranteed debt data are World Bank staff estimates based on reports provided by the country. Short-term debt before 2005 is based on data from the BIS, and 2014 is based on Central Bank data.

CÔTE D'IVOIRE

(US$ million, unless otherwise indicated)

	2000	2005	2009	2010	2011	2012	2013	2014
Summary external debt data								
External debt stocks	**12,187**	**11,178**	**13,431**	**10,665**	**12,334**	**9,166**	**11,082**	**10,857**
Long-term external debt	10,546	10,129	12,530	9,489	10,424	7,728	9,664	9,365
Short-term external debt	1,043	797	62	314	821	173	0	0
interest arrears on long-term	79	797	62	7	5	0	0	0
Use of IMF credit	599	252	839	861	1,090	1,265	1,418	1,492
Long-term external debt								
Debt outstanding and disbursed	**10,546**	**10,129**	**12,530**	**9,489**	**10,424**	**7,728**	**9,664**	**9,365**
Public and publicly guaranteed	9,063	9,228	11,682	8,472	9,092	5,237	7,597	7,671
Official creditors	6,669	6,977	9,690	8,426	9,023	4,017	4,969	4,295
Private creditors	2,394	2,252	1,992	46	68	1,221	2,628	3,377
of which: Bonds	2,343	2,159	1,931	0	0	0	0	750
Private nonguaranteed	1,482	900	848	1,018	1,332	2,490	2,067	1,693
of which: Bonds	..	..	..	..	..	..	..	..
Disbursements	**148**	**55**	**423**	**715**	**1,243**	**2,104**	**3,273**	**1,661**
Public and publicly guaranteed	148	21	103	360	840	1,284	3,273	1,661
Official creditors	148	21	103	334	806	106	1,830	899
Private creditors	0	0	0	26	34	1,178	1,443	762
of which: Bonds	0	0	0	0	0	0	0	750
Private nonguaranteed	..	34	320	355	402	820	..	..
of which: Bonds	..	..	..	..	..	..	..	..
Principal repayments	**442**	**164**	**696**	**615**	**561**	**565**	**966**	**1,480**
Public and publicly guaranteed	329	21	531	430	341	299	542	1,107
Official creditors	283	21	531	430	332	290	507	1,093
Private creditors	46	0	0	0	9	10	35	14
of which: Bonds	46	0	0	0	0	0	0	0
Private nonguaranteed	113	143	165	185	220	266	423	374
of which: Bonds	..	..	..	..	..	..	..	..
Interest payments	**462**	**46**	**287**	**113**	**130**	**169**	**291**	**179**
Public and publicly guaranteed	342	3	240	57	60	50	200	155
Official creditors	189	3	240	57	59	50	55	117
Private creditors	153	0	0	0	0	0	145	38
of which: Bonds	153	0	0	0	0	0	0	0
Private nonguaranteed	120	43	48	56	70	119	91	24
of which: Bonds	..	..	..	..	..	..	..	..
Net financial flows								
Net debt inflows	-617	-307	-116	452	1,429	1,068	2,283	347
Official creditors (incl. IMF)	-174	-90	-271	-51	713	-12	1,471	-28
Private creditors	-442	-217	155	503	716	1,079	811	375
Long-term	-159	-109	155	196	207	1,722	984	375
Public and publicly guaranteed	-46	0	..	26	25	1,168	1,408	749
Private nonguaranteed	-113	-109	155	170	182	554	-423	-374
Short-term	-283	-108	..	307	509	-643	-173	..
Net equity inflows								
Foreign direct investment	235	302	400	371	322	155	134	462
Portfolio equity	1	14	2	2	..	30	1	..
Major economic aggregates								
Gross national income (GNI)	9,715	16,433	23,343	23,972	24,393	26,178	29,882	32,930
Exports of goods, services & prim. income	4,512	8,717	12,562	12,811	13,859	13,316	13,192	14,432
Imports of goods, services & prim. income	4,423	8,215	10,845	11,907	10,664	13,116	13,175	15,185
Primary income on FDI	284	370	572	562	612	578	651	..
Personal transfers & comp. of employees	119	163	315	373	397	367	385	378
International reserves	674	1,367	3,267	3,624	4,316	3,928	4,243	4,478
Ratios								
External debt stocks to exports (%)	270.1	128.2	106.9	83.2	89.0	68.8	84.0	75.2
External debt stocks to GNI (%)	125.4	68.0	57.5	44.5	50.6	35.0	37.1	33.0
Debt service to exports (%)	22.7	3.5	9.0	5.8	5.2	5.8	9.5	11.6
Reserves to external debt stocks (%)	5.5	12.2	24.3	34.0	35.0	42.9	38.3	41.2

Notes:

Long-term public and publicly guaranteed debt data for 2012 and 2014 are World Bank staff estimates based on the original terms of the loans. Long-term private nonguaranteed debt data are World Bank staff estimates. Short-term debt is based on data from the BIS. Data include the effects of Paris Club agreement signed in 2011, 2012 and HIPC and MDRI debt relief.

DJIBOUTI

(US$ million, unless otherwise indicated)

	2000	2005	2009	2010	2011	2012	2013	2014
Summary external debt data								
External debt stocks	**298.6**	**485.1**	**894.1**	**769.7**	**775.8**	**807.7**	**831.8**	**957.5**
Long-term external debt	238.3	376.9	735.3	619.7	650.6	641.9	672.7	817.5
Short-term external debt	45.4	87.9	119.3	114.5	85.6	108.3	101.4	87.1
interest arrears on long-term	6.4	8.9	2.3	0.5	0.6	1.3	1.4	3.1
Use of IMF credit	14.9	20.4	39.5	35.5	39.7	57.5	57.6	52.9
Long-term external debt								
Debt outstanding and disbursed	**238.3**	**376.9**	**735.3**	**619.7**	**650.6**	**641.9**	**672.7**	**817.5**
Public and publicly guaranteed	238.3	376.9	735.3	619.7	650.6	641.9	672.7	817.5
Official creditors	238.3	371.3	711.1	599.3	633.4	628.1	662.3	809.6
Private creditors	0.0	5.6	24.2	20.4	17.2	13.8	10.4	7.9
of which: Bonds	0.0	0.0	0.0	0.0	0.0	0.0	0.0	0.0
Private nonguaranteed	..	..	..	..	..	..	..	..
of which: Bonds	..	..	..	..	..	..	..	..
Disbursements	**7.7**	**26.5**	**67.4**	**35.2**	**55.7**	**25.2**	**63.9**	**211.6**
Public and publicly guaranteed	7.7	26.5	67.4	35.2	55.7	25.2	63.9	211.6
Official creditors	7.7	26.5	67.4	35.2	55.7	25.2	63.9	211.6
Private creditors	0.0	0.0	0.0	0.0	0.0	0.0	0.0	0.0
of which: Bonds	0.0	0.0	0.0	0.0	0.0	0.0	0.0	0.0
Private nonguaranteed	..	..	..	..	..	..	..	..
of which: Bonds	..	..	..	..	..	..	..	..
Principal repayments	**8.4**	**11.0**	**22.3**	**22.2**	**24.8**	**30.8**	**31.7**	**29.7**
Public and publicly guaranteed	8.4	11.0	22.3	22.2	24.8	30.8	31.7	29.7
Official creditors	8.4	11.0	17.3	19.8	21.9	27.3	28.1	27.7
Private creditors	0.0	0.0	5.1	2.4	2.9	3.5	3.7	2.0
of which: Bonds	0.0	0.0	0.0	0.0	0.0	0.0	0.0	0.0
Private nonguaranteed	..	..	..	..	..	..	..	..
of which: Bonds	..	..	..	..	..	..	..	..
Interest payments	**2.2**	**3.7**	**8.1**	**8.2**	**9.2**	**9.3**	**9.5**	**9.3**
Public and publicly guaranteed	2.2	3.7	8.1	8.2	9.2	9.3	9.5	9.3
Official creditors	2.2	3.7	7.6	7.5	8.5	8.8	9.1	9.1
Private creditors	0.0	0.0	0.6	0.6	0.7	0.5	0.4	0.2
of which: Bonds	0.0	0.0	0.0	0.0	0.0	0.0	0.0	0.0
Private nonguaranteed	..	..	..	..	..	..	..	..
of which: Bonds	..	..	..	..	..	..	..	..
Net financial flows								
Net debt inflows	39.7	56.7	15.1	6.6	6.2	34.1	25.2	164.5
Official creditors (incl. IMF)	0.7	14.7	48.2	12.0	38.2	15.7	35.9	182.5
Private creditors	39.0	42.0	-33.1	-5.4	-31.9	18.5	-10.7	-18.0
Long-term	..	..	-5.1	-2.4	-2.9	-3.5	-3.7	-2.0
Public and publicly guaranteed	..	..	-5.1	-2.4	-2.9	-3.5	-3.7	-2.0
Private nonguaranteed	..	..	..	..	..	..	..	..
Short-term	39.0	42.0	-28.0	-3.0	-29.0	22.0	-7.0	-16.0
Net equity inflows								
Foreign direct investment	3.3	22.2	96.9	36.5	79.0	110.0	286.0	153.0
Portfolio equity	..	..	..	..	..	..	..	..
Major economic aggregates								
Gross national income (GNI)	567.0	775.8	..	..	..	..	..	..
Exports of goods, services & prim. income	218.4	319.8	422.7	439.0	440.3	487.7	517.0	683.4
Imports of goods, services & prim. income	287.1	372.3	580.0	493.8	686.3	727.0	918.5	1,044.6
Primary income on FDI	4.2	5.9	6.5	6.8	18.0	7.2	10.8	..
Personal transfers & comp. of employees	12.3	25.8	32.5	32.6	32.4	33.3	35.6	35.9
International reserves	67.8	89.3	241.8	249.0	244.1	248.6	425.0	393.1
Ratios								
External debt stocks to exports (%)	136.7	151.7	211.5	175.3	176.2	165.6	160.9	140.1
External debt stocks to GNI (%)	52.7	62.5	..	..	..	..	..	..
Debt service to exports (%)	6.9	5.6	8.5	8.1	8.6	8.8	8.2	6.1
Reserves to external debt stocks (%)	22.7	18.4	27.0	32.4	31.5	30.8	51.1	41.1

Notes:

Short-term debt is based on data from the BIS. Data include the effects of Paris Club debt restructuring agreement signed in 2008.

DOMINICA

(US$ million, unless otherwise indicated)

	2000	2005	2009	2010	2011	2012	2013	2014
Summary external debt data								
External debt stocks	**183.3**	**277.4**	**255.0**	**254.5**	**263.6**	**287.9**	**293.0**	**291.4**
Long-term external debt	163.6	224.4	201.1	218.8	230.7	255.8	263.6	264.9
Short-term external debt	19.0	40.6	22.0	5.5	5.6	5.6	5.6	5.5
interest arrears on long-term	0.0	8.6	17.9	1.5	1.5	1.5	1.5	1.5
Use of IMF credit	0.8	12.4	31.9	30.2	27.3	26.6	23.8	20.9
Long-term external debt								
Debt outstanding and disbursed	**163.6**	**224.4**	**201.1**	**218.8**	**230.7**	**255.8**	**263.6**	**264.9**
Public and publicly guaranteed	163.6	224.4	201.1	218.8	230.7	255.8	263.6	264.9
Official creditors	114.3	173.0	155.3	173.0	182.3	216.6	227.1	233.0
Private creditors	49.2	51.4	45.8	45.8	48.4	39.2	36.5	31.9
of which: Bonds	49.2	48.9	40.3	40.3	42.1	11.5	11.5	8.9
Private nonguaranteed	..	..	..	..	..	..	..	..
of which: Bonds	..	..	..	..	..	..	..	..
Disbursements	**56.2**	**4.5**	**8.9**	**29.7**	**21.1**	**36.3**	**21.5**	**20.3**
Public and publicly guaranteed	56.2	4.5	8.9	29.7	21.1	36.3	21.5	20.3
Official creditors	25.7	4.5	8.6	29.7	18.3	36.3	21.5	20.3
Private creditors	30.5	0.0	0.3	0.0	2.8	0.0	0.0	0.0
of which: Bonds	30.5	0.0	0.0	0.0	1.8	0.0	0.0	0.0
Private nonguaranteed	..	..	..	..	..	..	..	..
of which: Bonds	..	..	..	..	..	..	..	..
Principal repayments	**6.8**	**9.6**	**14.8**	**9.8**	**9.4**	**7.8**	**9.9**	**11.5**
Public and publicly guaranteed	6.8	9.6	14.8	9.8	9.4	7.8	9.9	11.5
Official creditors	6.8	9.6	12.9	9.8	9.2	7.6	8.0	9.2
Private creditors	0.0	0.0	1.9	0.1	0.2	0.2	1.9	2.3
of which: Bonds	0.0	0.0	1.9	0.0	0.0	0.0	0.0	0.4
Private nonguaranteed	..	..	..	..	..	..	..	..
of which: Bonds	..	..	..	..	..	..	..	..
Interest payments	**3.1**	**4.7**	**4.5**	**4.3**	**4.2**	**7.8**	**5.9**	**6.1**
Public and publicly guaranteed	3.1	4.7	4.5	4.3	4.2	7.8	5.9	6.1
Official creditors	2.9	4.3	3.9	3.8	3.9	4.2	4.7	5.1
Private creditors	0.2	0.4	0.6	0.5	0.3	3.7	1.1	1.0
of which: Bonds	0.2	0.4	0.3	0.4	0.3	2.7	0.3	0.2
Private nonguaranteed	..	..	..	..	..	..	..	..
of which: Bonds	..	..	..	..	..	..	..	..
Net financial flows								
Net debt inflows	49.5	-37.0	-3.1	18.7	8.7	27.7	8.8	7.2
Official creditors (incl. IMF)	18.8	-2.0	0.0	18.8	6.1	27.9	10.8	9.6
Private creditors	30.7	-35.0	-3.1	-0.1	2.6	-0.2	-1.9	-2.4
Long-term	30.5	0.0	-1.6	0.0	2.6	-0.2	-1.9	-2.3
Public and publicly guaranteed	30.5	0.0	-1.6	0.0	2.6	-0.2	-1.9	-2.3
Private nonguaranteed	..	..	..	..	..	..	..	..
Short-term	0.2	-35.0	-1.5	0.0	0.0	..	0.0	-0.1
Net equity inflows								
Foreign direct investment	17.6	21.7	26.3	10.0	6.8	15.7	10.0	22.2
Portfolio equity	..	..	..	..	..	..	..	..
Major economic aggregates								
Gross national income (GNI)	296.5	341.5	485.2	483.7	497.9	496.4	497.2	517.5
Exports of goods, services & prim. income	149.2	135.3	154.5	180.2	195.9	165.0	174.3	183.4
Imports of goods, services & prim. income	227.1	231.0	284.7	280.1	280.3	274.0	267.7	272.6
Primary income on FDI	33.0	22.7	13.4	7.8	5.0	5.1	5.4	..
Personal transfers & comp. of employees	16.3	21.8	22.1	22.9	22.9	23.2	23.6	23.6
International reserves	29.4	49.2	75.5	76.1	81.1	94.6	87.1	101.4
Ratios								
External debt stocks to exports (%)	122.9	205.0	165.1	141.3	134.6	174.5	168.1	158.8
External debt stocks to GNI (%)	61.8	81.2	52.6	52.6	52.9	58.0	58.9	56.3
Debt service to exports (%)	7.4	12.1	13.5	8.6	8.5	11.9	10.7	10.5
Reserves to external debt stocks (%)	16.0	17.7	29.6	29.9	30.8	32.8	29.7	34.8

DOMINICAN REPUBLIC

(US$ million, unless otherwise indicated)

	2000	2005	2009	2010	2011	2012	2013	2014
Summary external debt data								
External debt stocks	**4,652**	**7,752**	**11,854**	**13,499**	**15,097**	**22,102**	**24,527**	**26,708**
Long-term external debt	3,381	6,419	9,005	10,283	11,675	18,835	21,457	23,419
Short-term external debt	1,178	887	1,755	1,754	1,800	1,753	1,753	2,486
interest arrears on long-term	28	20	0	0	0	0	0	0
Use of IMF credit	93	446	1,094	1,461	1,623	1,513	1,317	803
Long-term external debt								
Debt outstanding and disbursed	**3,381**	**6,419**	**9,005**	**10,283**	**11,675**	**18,835**	**21,457**	**23,419**
Public and publicly guaranteed	3,381	6,418	8,162	9,441	10,762	11,983	14,175	15,689
Official creditors	2,625	3,257	5,505	6,376	7,119	8,159	9,088	9,020
Private creditors	756	3,160	2,657	3,065	3,643	3,824	5,086	6,669
of which: Bonds	506	561	490	1,134	1,826	1,826	3,312	4,812
Private nonguaranteed	..	2	843	843	913	6,852	7,282	7,730
of which: Bonds	..	..	843	843	843	1,137	965	1,454
Disbursements	**314**	**665**	**1,483**	**2,111**	**2,165**	**2,840**	**3,571**	**3,965**
Public and publicly guaranteed	314	664	1,483	2,111	2,120	1,843	3,112	2,824
Official creditors	150	372	1,392	1,176	1,117	1,458	1,554	795
Private creditors	164	292	92	935	1,003	385	1,558	2,029
of which: Bonds	0	0	0	750	750	0	1,500	1,500
Private nonguaranteed	..	2	..	..	45	998	459	1,141
of which: Bonds	..	..	..	..	..	550	13	499
Principal repayments	**264**	**462**	**896**	**799**	**796**	**1,521**	**1,657**	**1,917**
Public and publicly guaranteed	264	462	896	798	788	625	932	1,225
Official creditors	223	184	354	311	376	407	608	847
Private creditors	40	278	541	487	412	218	324	378
of which: Bonds	4	20	125	105	58	0	14	0
Private nonguaranteed	..	..	0	0	8	897	725	692
of which: Bonds	..	..	..	..	..	431	260	11
Interest payments	**211**	**212**	**433**	**444**	**584**	**919**	**963**	**827**
Public and publicly guaranteed	211	212	325	336	473	448	484	573
Official creditors	159	109	150	156	176	198	204	197
Private creditors	53	103	174	181	297	250	280	377
of which: Bonds	38	16	55	76	191	140	172	281
Private nonguaranteed	..	0	108	108	111	471	480	253
of which: Bonds	..	..	108	108	108	90	100	88
Net financial flows								
Net debt inflows	316	400	666	1,695	1,585	1,162	1,716	2,323
Official creditors (incl. IMF)	-73	407	1,299	1,247	912	941	748	-509
Private creditors	389	-7	-632	447	674	221	969	2,832
Long-term	124	16	-450	448	628	268	969	2,099
Public and publicly guaranteed	124	14	-450	448	590	167	1,234	1,651
Private nonguaranteed	..	2	0	0	37	101	-266	449
Short-term	265	-23	-182	-1	46	-47	0	733
Net equity inflows								
Foreign direct investment	953	1,172	1,070	1,419	2,198	3,416	1,600	2,208
Portfolio equity	..	..	..	..	..	..	..	..
Major economic aggregates								
Gross national income (GNI)	22,955	31,559	46,168	51,356	55,923	58,212	58,391	60,760
Exports of goods, services & prim. income	9,264	8,013	8,444	13,525	14,889	15,754	16,851	17,519
Imports of goods, services & prim. income	12,193	11,183	13,986	20,983	23,081	23,634	23,463	23,871
Primary income on FDI	1,068	1,765	1,518	1,698	1,949	1,972	2,670	..
Personal transfers & comp. of employees	1,839	2,719	3,415	3,887	4,241	4,262	4,486	4,650
International reserves	627	1,920	3,560	3,849	4,086	3,528	4,679	4,840
Ratios								
External debt stocks to exports (%)	50.2	96.7	140.4	99.8	101.4	140.3	145.6	152.5
External debt stocks to GNI (%)	20.3	24.6	25.7	26.3	27.0	38.0	42.0	44.0
Debt service to exports (%)	5.7	9.1	16.7	10.5	10.8	16.5	17.0	18.5
Reserves to external debt stocks (%)	13.5	24.8	30.0	28.5	27.1	16.0	19.1	18.1

Notes:

Long-term private nonguaranteed debt data are based on country reports. Short-term debt for 2014 and before 2009 is based on data from the BIS. Data include the effects of Paris Club debt restructuring agreement signed in 2005.

ECUADOR

(US$ million, unless otherwise indicated)

	2000	2005	2009	2010	2011	2012	2013	2014
Summary external debt data								
External debt stocks	**13,329**	**17,402**	**13,259**	**14,959**	**16,490**	**16,938**	**20,287**	**26,333**
Long-term external debt	12,341	15,558	11,421	13,711	15,303	15,822	19,190	25,216
Short-term external debt	797	1,719	1,386	804	745	673	653	699
interest arrears on long-term	3	1	37	37	46	44	43	37
Use of IMF credit	191	125	452	444	443	443	444	418
Long-term external debt								
Debt outstanding and disbursed	**12,341**	**15,558**	**11,421**	**13,711**	**15,303**	**15,822**	**19,190**	**25,216**
Public and publicly guaranteed	10,906	10,890	6,955	8,630	9,922	10,072	12,035	16,882
Official creditors	5,913	5,987	5,890	7,607	8,932	9,113	11,004	11,571
Private creditors	4,993	4,902	1,065	1,023	990	959	1,031	5,311
of which: Bonds	3,950	4,600	873	868	868	868	868	2,868
Private nonguaranteed	1,435	4,668	4,466	5,082	5,380	5,750	7,154	8,334
of which: Bonds	..	..	..	..	..	..	..	..
Disbursements	**983**	**3,154**	**1,180**	**2,977**	**3,370**	**2,322**	**5,608**	**8,998**
Public and publicly guaranteed	602	991	384	2,307	2,342	1,336	3,145	6,160
Official creditors	531	318	382	2,305	2,342	1,336	3,044	1,851
Private creditors	71	674	2	2	1	0	101	4,309
of which: Bonds	0	650	0	0	0	0	0	2,000
Private nonguaranteed	381	2,162	796	670	1,028	986	2,463	2,837
of which: Bonds	..	..	..	..	..	..	..	..
Principal repayments	**1,067**	**3,048**	**4,187**	**1,259**	**1,836**	**1,895**	**2,264**	**3,034**
Public and publicly guaranteed	549	922	3,528	636	1,048	1,174	1,173	1,262
Official creditors	399	802	503	592	1,015	1,143	1,143	1,233
Private creditors	151	120	3,025	44	33	31	30	29
of which: Bonds	0	0	2,987	6	0	0	0	0
Private nonguaranteed	517	2,125	659	623	789	720	1,091	1,772
of which: Bonds	..	..	..	..	..	..	..	..
Interest payments	**708**	**843**	**521**	**464**	**534**	**674**	**839**	**941**
Public and publicly guaranteed	536	658	330	326	360	481	647	735
Official creditors	296	275	227	255	292	414	575	534
Private creditors	240	383	103	71	69	67	72	200
of which: Bonds	140	367	91	61	61	61	61	140
Private nonguaranteed	172	185	191	139	174	193	192	206
of which: Bonds	..	..	..	..	..	..	..	..
Net financial flows								
Net debt inflows	-188	-234	-3,310	1,136	1,466	357	3,326	6,015
Official creditors (incl. IMF)	282	-679	-121	1,713	1,327	193	1,901	618
Private creditors	-471	445	-3,189	-577	139	164	1,426	5,397
Long-term	-216	590	-2,886	5	207	235	1,444	5,345
Public and publicly guaranteed	-80	553	-3,023	-42	-33	-31	72	4,280
Private nonguaranteed	-136	37	138	47	239	266	1,372	1,065
Short-term	-254	-145	-303	-582	-68	-71	-18	52
Net equity inflows								
Foreign direct investment	-23	519	534	178	580	528	734	774
Portfolio equity	0	2	2	0	2	5	2	1
Major economic aggregates								
Gross national income (GNI)	16,916	39,692	61,246	68,515	78,017	86,321	93,078	98,964
Exports of goods, services & prim. income	6,163	11,693	15,948	19,687	24,754	26,481	27,835	29,059
Imports of goods, services & prim. income	6,403	13,880	18,366	23,752	27,697	29,145	31,403	31,921
Primary income on FDI	329	1,004	838	546	701	676	684	..
Personal transfers & comp. of employees	1,322	2,460	2,742	2,599	2,681	2,476	2,459	2,462
International reserves	947	1,714	2,873	1,435	1,664	1,080	3,328	3,484
Ratios								
External debt stocks to exports (%)	216.3	148.8	83.1	76.0	66.6	64.0	72.9	90.6
External debt stocks to GNI (%)	78.8	43.8	21.6	21.8	21.1	19.6	21.8	26.6
Debt service to exports (%)	30.5	35.9	30.0	9.1	9.7	9.8	11.2	13.8
Reserves to external debt stocks (%)	7.1	9.9	21.7	9.6	10.1	6.4	16.4	13.2

Notes:

Short-term debt is World Bank staff estimates based on Central Bank data.

EGYPT, ARAB REPUBLIC OF

(US$ million, unless otherwise indicated)

	2000	2005	2009	2010	2011	2012	2013	2014
Summary external debt data								
External debt stocks	**29,178**	**29,948**	**35,068**	**36,542**	**35,145**	**39,997**	**44,444**	**39,624**
Long-term external debt	24,897	28,098	31,098	32,009	30,740	31,959	40,244	35,001
Short-term external debt	4,104	1,656	2,561	3,149	3,026	6,657	2,816	3,321
interest arrears on long-term	0	2	0	0	0	0	0	0
Use of IMF credit	177	194	1,408	1,384	1,379	1,381	1,384	1,302
Long-term external debt								
Debt outstanding and disbursed	**24,897**	**28,098**	**31,098**	**32,009**	**30,740**	**31,959**	**40,244**	**35,001**
Public and publicly guaranteed	24,325	28,005	31,024	31,955	30,724	31,939	40,232	34,980
Official creditors	23,785	25,777	28,675	28,236	27,452	28,685	34,022	31,358
Private creditors	540	2,228	2,350	3,719	3,272	3,254	6,210	3,623
of which: Bonds	0	1,250	1,883	3,133	2,750	2,750	5,850	3,350
Private nonguaranteed	573	93	74	54	16	20	12	21
of which: Bonds	100	..	..	..	..	..	..	..
Disbursements	**569**	**3,090**	**2,131**	**3,617**	**1,510**	**3,681**	**11,100**	**1,648**
Public and publicly guaranteed	362	3,090	2,122	3,612	1,480	3,656	11,082	1,623
Official creditors	218	1,114	2,016	1,903	1,459	3,601	7,957	1,603
Private creditors	144	1,976	107	1,709	21	55	3,125	20
of which: Bonds	0	1,250	0	1,500	0	0	3,100	0
Private nonguaranteed	207	..	9	5	30	25	17	25
of which: Bonds	..	..	..	..	..	..	..	..
Principal repayments	**1,097**	**1,573**	**2,050**	**2,162**	**2,652**	**2,246**	**2,601**	**5,163**
Public and publicly guaranteed	982	1,573	2,030	2,137	2,585	2,224	2,576	5,147
Official creditors	860	1,344	1,911	2,063	2,125	2,150	2,398	2,574
Private creditors	121	229	119	74	460	74	178	2,573
of which: Bonds	0	0	0	0	383	0	0	2,500
Private nonguaranteed	116	..	20	25	68	22	25	16
of which: Bonds	..	..	..	..	..	..	..	..
Interest payments	**618**	**569**	**779**	**719**	**718**	**680**	**665**	**692**
Public and publicly guaranteed	602	565	776	717	717	679	665	692
Official creditors	572	547	654	581	563	557	531	494
Private creditors	31	18	123	136	154	122	134	198
of which: Bonds	0	0	112	123	142	108	121	188
Private nonguaranteed	16	4	2	1	0	0	0	0
of which: Bonds	12	..	..	..	..	..	..	..
Net financial flows								
Net debt inflows	-717	1,453	-200	2,043	-1,266	5,067	4,658	-3,014
Official creditors (incl. IMF)	-643	-230	105	-160	-665	1,451	5,559	-975
Private creditors	-75	1,683	-305	2,203	-600	3,616	-902	-2,039
Long-term	115	1,747	-24	1,615	-477	-15	2,939	-2,544
Public and publicly guaranteed	23	1,747	-13	1,635	-439	-19	2,947	-2,553
Private nonguaranteed	91	..	-11	-20	-38	4	-8	9
Short-term	-189	-64	-281	588	-123	3,632	-3,841	505
Net equity inflows								
Foreign direct investment	1,235	..	1,008	1,360	540	209	339	202
Portfolio equity	269	729	393	1,724	-711	-983	-431	485
Major economic aggregates								
Gross national income (GNI)	100,770	89,432	189,136	214,526	229,952	256,357	264,563	279,242
Exports of goods, services & prim. income	18,735	32,141	45,601	49,365	47,371	48,834	44,992	47,300
Imports of goods, services & prim. income	23,878	35,787	56,910	66,308	68,076	75,597	72,686	80,780
Primary income on FDI	92	647	2,101	5,268	5,079	5,704	6,376	6,089
Personal transfers & comp. of employees	2,852	5,017	7,150	12,453	14,324	19,236	17,833	19,570
International reserves	13,118	20,609	32,253	33,612	14,916	11,628	13,608	11,995
Ratios								
External debt stocks to exports (%)	155.7	93.2	76.9	74.0	74.2	81.9	98.8	83.8
External debt stocks to GNI (%)	29.0	33.5	18.5	17.0	15.3	15.6	16.8	14.2
Debt service to exports (%)	9.8	6.9	6.4	6.1	7.4	6.5	7.5	12.7
Reserves to external debt stocks (%)	45.0	68.8	92.0	92.0	42.4	29.1	30.6	30.3

EL SALVADOR

(US$ million, unless otherwise indicated)

	2000	2005	2009	2010	2011	2012	2013	2014
Summary external debt data								
External debt stocks	**4,535**	**9,317**	**10,368**	**11,060**	**11,996**	**13,035**	**13,539**	**14,536**
Long-term external debt	2,858	7,425	9,248	9,972	10,521	11,257	11,434	12,280
Short-term external debt	1,645	1,856	863	836	1,223	1,526	1,853	2,018
interest arrears on long-term	0	0	0	0	0	0	0	0
Use of IMF credit	33	36	257	252	251	252	252	237
Long-term external debt								
Debt outstanding and disbursed	**2,858**	**7,425**	**9,248**	**9,972**	**10,521**	**11,257**	**11,434**	**12,280**
Public and publicly guaranteed	2,746	4,802	6,109	6,403	6,538	7,372	7,275	8,058
Official creditors	2,541	3,083	3,845	4,183	4,301	4,339	4,242	4,044
Private creditors	205	1,719	2,264	2,220	2,237	3,033	3,033	4,014
of which: Bonds	82	1,636	2,174	2,199	2,217	2,362	2,336	3,269
Private nonguaranteed	111	2,622	3,139	3,569	3,983	3,885	4,159	4,223
of which: Bonds	..	..	..	..	..	38	38	38
Disbursements	**372**	**1,222**	**1,216**	**1,055**	**874**	**1,448**	**1,006**	**1,768**
Public and publicly guaranteed	321	682	910	707	476	1,173	364	1,135
Official creditors	201	337	910	707	476	522	337	284
Private creditors	120	345	0	0	0	652	27	851
of which: Bonds	32	343	0	0	0	0	0	800
Private nonguaranteed	51	540	306	348	398	274	642	633
of which: Bonds	..	..	..	..	..	38	..	..
Principal repayments	**163**	**406**	**687**	**604**	**757**	**628**	**559**	**680**
Public and publicly guaranteed	130	245	559	455	587	453	392	410
Official creditors	126	230	555	388	367	452	391	409
Private creditors	4	16	4	68	220	1	1	1
of which: Bonds	0	0	0	0	219	0	0	0
Private nonguaranteed	33	160	127	149	170	175	167	269
of which: Bonds	..	..	..	..	..	..	..	..
Interest payments	**140**	**344**	**475**	**465**	**515**	**503**	**532**	**543**
Public and publicly guaranteed	133	257	374	350	386	373	403	414
Official creditors	124	119	139	117	119	121	121	116
Private creditors	9	139	235	233	267	252	282	299
of which: Bonds	8	133	232	232	266	251	251	251
Private nonguaranteed	7	87	102	115	129	130	129	129
of which: Bonds	..	..	..	..	..	..	2	..
Net financial flows								
Net debt inflows	802	892	-150	423	504	1,123	774	1,253
Official creditors (incl. IMF)	75	107	355	320	109	70	-54	-125
Private creditors	726	785	-504	104	395	1,053	827	1,378
Long-term	134	709	175	131	8	749	501	1,213
Public and publicly guaranteed	116	329	-4	-68	-220	650	26	850
Private nonguaranteed	18	380	178	199	229	99	475	364
Short-term	592	77	-679	-27	387	304	327	165
Net equity inflows								
Foreign direct investment	173	512	241	282	169	533	148	328
Portfolio equity	..	..	..	..	..	..	..	..
Major economic aggregates								
Gross national income (GNI)	12,881	16,604	20,105	20,868	22,507	22,932	23,418	24,388
Exports of goods, services & prim. income	3,803	3,517	4,293	5,028	5,940	6,170	6,492	6,550
Imports of goods, services & prim. income	6,031	7,173	8,047	9,190	10,882	11,425	12,166	12,068
Primary income on FDI	60	181	175	190	203	547	646	699
Personal transfers & comp. of employees	1,765	3,029	3,402	3,472	3,644	3,910	3,971	4,235
International reserves	1,773	1,721	2,867	2,568	2,151	2,805	2,476	2,430
Ratios								
External debt stocks to exports (%)	119.3	264.9	241.5	220.0	201.9	211.3	208.6	221.9
External debt stocks to GNI (%)	35.2	56.1	51.6	53.0	53.3	56.8	57.8	59.6
Debt service to exports (%)	9.9	24.2	27.4	21.5	21.6	18.6	17.1	19.0
Reserves to external debt stocks (%)	39.1	18.5	27.7	23.2	17.9	21.5	18.3	16.7

Notes:

Long-term private nonguaranteed debt data from 2005 are World Bank staff estimates based on reports provided by the country.

ERITREA

(US$ million, unless otherwise indicated)

	2000	2005	2009	2010	2011	2012	2013	2014
Summary external debt data								
External debt stocks	**329.7**	**757.2**	**1,050.7**	**1,041.5**	**1,055.2**	**994.1**	**945.5**	**908.1**
Long-term external debt	298.0	723.0	1,013.0	1,002.0	1,013.6	952.1	895.9	829.5
Short-term external debt	12.0	12.6	13.9	16.2	18.4	18.6	26.3	56.6
interest arrears on long-term	2.0	1.6	5.9	6.2	7.4	12.6	16.3	18.6
Use of IMF credit	19.8	21.7	23.8	23.3	23.3	23.3	23.3	22.0
Long-term external debt								
Debt outstanding and disbursed	**298.0**	**723.0**	**1,013.0**	**1,002.0**	**1,013.6**	**952.1**	**895.9**	**829.5**
Public and publicly guaranteed	298.0	723.0	1,013.0	1,002.0	1,013.6	952.1	895.9	829.5
Official creditors	298.0	690.1	972.1	964.1	976.9	914.7	856.7	795.0
Private creditors	0.0	32.9	40.9	38.0	36.8	37.5	39.2	34.5
of which: Bonds	0.0	0.0	0.0	0.0	0.0	0.0	0.0	0.0
Private nonguaranteed	..	..	..	..	..	..	..	..
of which: Bonds	..	..	..	..	..	..	..	..
Disbursements	**50.7**	**70.6**	**57.6**	**8.6**	**24.2**	**26.8**	**26.7**	**20.2**
Public and publicly guaranteed	50.7	70.6	57.6	8.6	24.2	26.8	26.7	20.2
Official creditors	50.7	70.6	57.6	8.6	24.2	26.8	26.7	20.2
Private creditors	0.0	0.0	0.0	0.0	0.0	0.0	0.0	0.0
of which: Bonds	0.0	0.0	0.0	0.0	0.0	0.0	0.0	0.0
Private nonguaranteed	..	..	..	..	..	..	..	..
of which: Bonds	..	..	..	..	..	..	..	..
Principal repayments	**0.5**	**11.8**	**11.3**	**13.3**	**14.0**	**86.0**	**81.1**	**40.9**
Public and publicly guaranteed	0.5	11.8	11.3	13.3	14.0	86.0	81.1	40.9
Official creditors	0.5	11.8	11.3	13.3	14.0	86.0	81.1	40.9
Private creditors	0.0	0.0	0.0	0.0	0.0	0.0	0.0	0.0
of which: Bonds	0.0	0.0	0.0	0.0	0.0	0.0	0.0	0.0
Private nonguaranteed	..	..	..	..	..	..	..	..
of which: Bonds	..	..	..	..	..	..	..	..
Interest payments	**2.5**	**8.4**	**10.3**	**9.3**	**7.9**	**8.5**	**6.4**	**4.9**
Public and publicly guaranteed	2.5	8.4	10.3	9.3	7.9	8.5	6.4	4.9
Official creditors	2.5	8.4	10.3	9.3	7.9	8.3	6.2	4.7
Private creditors	0.0	0.0	0.0	0.0	0.0	0.2	0.2	0.2
of which: Bonds	0.0	0.0	0.0	0.0	0.0	0.0	0.0	0.0
Private nonguaranteed	..	..	..	..	..	..	..	..
of which: Bonds	..	..	..	..	..	..	..	..
Net financial flows								
Net debt inflows	60.2	38.9	41.3	-2.7	11.2	-64.3	-50.4	7.3
Official creditors (incl. IMF)	50.2	58.9	46.3	-4.7	10.2	-59.3	-54.4	-20.7
Private creditors	10.0	-20.0	-5.0	2.0	1.0	-5.0	4.0	28.0
Long-term	..	..	..	..	..	..	..	..
Public and publicly guaranteed	..	..	..	..	..	..	..	..
Private nonguaranteed	..	..	..	..	..	..	..	..
Short-term	10.0	-20.0	-5.0	2.0	1.0	-5.0	4.0	28.0
Net equity inflows								
Foreign direct investment	27.9	1.4	91.0	91.0	39.0	41.4	43.9	46.5
Portfolio equity	..	..	..	..	..	..	..	..
Major economic aggregates								
Gross national income (GNI)	706.8	1,089.0	1,840.5	2,097.4	2,584.2	3,063.9	3,412.9	3,822.9
Exports of goods, services & prim. income	106.9	..	..	..	..	..	..	..
Imports of goods, services & prim. income	510.3	..	..	..	..	..	..	..
Primary income on FDI	4.4	..	..	..	..	..	..	..
Personal transfers & comp. of employees	3.3	..	..	..	..	..	..	..
International reserves	25.5	27.9	90.0	114.1	114.8	..	..	..
Ratios								
External debt stocks to exports (%)	308.5	..	..	..	..	..	..	..
External debt stocks to GNI (%)	46.6	69.5	57.1	49.7	40.8	32.4	27.7	23.8
Debt service to exports (%)	4.3	..	..	..	..	..	..	..
Reserves to external debt stocks (%)	7.7	3.7	8.6	11.0	10.9	..	..	..

Notes:

Long-term public and publicly guaranteed debt from 2010 are World Bank staff estimates. Short-term debt is based on data from the BIS.

ETHIOPIA

(US$ million, unless otherwise indicated)

	2000	2005	2009	2010	2011	2012	2013	2014
Summary external debt data								
External debt stocks	**5,509**	**6,221**	**5,232**	**7,347**	**8,604**	**10,462**	**12,557**	**16,585**
Long-term external debt	5,339	5,925	4,819	6,547	7,945	9,941	11,886	15,846
Short-term external debt	79	120	45	314	175	37	186	288
interest arrears on long-term	65	36	32	30	30	26	28	28
Use of IMF credit	92	176	368	485	484	484	485	452
Long-term external debt								
Debt outstanding and disbursed	**5,339**	**5,925**	**4,819**	**6,547**	**7,945**	**9,941**	**11,886**	**15,846**
Public and publicly guaranteed	5,339	5,925	4,819	6,547	7,945	9,941	11,886	15,846
Official creditors	5,226	5,561	3,556	4,638	5,685	7,218	8,980	11,374
Private creditors	113	364	1,263	1,909	2,259	2,723	2,905	4,472
of which: Bonds	0	0	0	0	0	0	0	1,000
Private nonguaranteed	..	..	..	..	..	..	..	..
of which: Bonds	..	..	..	..	..	..	..	..
Disbursements	**185**	**527**	**2,148**	**1,760**	**1,693**	**2,309**	**2,399**	**4,915**
Public and publicly guaranteed	185	527	2,148	1,760	1,693	2,309	2,399	4,915
Official creditors	184	400	1,098	1,021	1,157	1,645	1,889	2,950
Private creditors	2	127	1,050	739	537	664	510	1,966
of which: Bonds	0	0	0	0	0	0	0	1,000
Private nonguaranteed	..	..	..	..	..	..	..	..
of which: Bonds	..	..	..	..	..	..	..	..
Principal repayments	**72**	**36**	**62**	**130**	**259**	**328**	**503**	**569**
Public and publicly guaranteed	72	36	62	130	259	328	503	569
Official creditors	62	25	34	39	80	122	162	205
Private creditors	10	11	27	91	179	206	341	365
of which: Bonds	0	0	0	0	0	0	0	0
Private nonguaranteed	..	..	..	..	..	..	..	..
of which: Bonds	..	..	..	..	..	..	..	..
Interest payments	**52**	**49**	**40**	**50**	**91**	**103**	**159**	**190**
Public and publicly guaranteed	52	49	40	50	91	103	159	190
Official creditors	48	40	33	35	52	58	96	130
Private creditors	4	10	8	15	38	46	63	60
of which: Bonds	0	0	0	0	0	0	0	0
Private nonguaranteed	..	..	..	..	..	..	..	..
of which: Bonds	..	..	..	..	..	..	..	..
Net financial flows								
Net debt inflows	90	478	2,246	2,023	1,295	1,847	2,043	4,443
Official creditors (incl. IMF)	109	371	1,228	1,105	1,077	1,524	1,727	2,740
Private creditors	-19	107	1,018	918	219	324	316	1,703
Long-term	-8	116	1,023	647	358	458	169	1,601
Public and publicly guaranteed	-8	116	1,023	647	358	458	169	1,601
Private nonguaranteed	..	..	..	..	..	..	..	..
Short-term	-11	-9	-5	271	-139	-134	147	102
Net equity inflows								
Foreign direct investment	135	265	221	288	627	279	953	1,200
Portfolio equity	..	..	..	..	..	..	..	..
Major economic aggregates								
Gross national income (GNI)	8,182	12,365	32,396	29,826	31,883	43,215	47,418	54,645
Exports of goods, services & prim. income	1,008	1,973	3,436	4,652	5,824	6,003	..	..
Imports of goods, services & prim. income	1,673	4,943	9,086	9,982	11,736	14,235	..	..
Primary income on FDI	9	21	18	35	23	6	..	..
Personal transfers & comp. of employees	53	174	262	345	513	624	..	..
International reserves	306	1,043	1,781	..	..	..	..	..
Ratios								
External debt stocks to exports (%)	546.3	315.3	152.3	157.9	147.7	174.3	..	..
External debt stocks to GNI (%)	67.3	50.3	16.2	24.6	27.0	24.2	26.5	30.4
Debt service to exports (%)	13.7	4.8	3.0	3.9	6.1	7.2	..	..
Reserves to external debt stocks (%)	5.6	16.8	34.0	..	..	..	..	..

Notes:

Short-term debt is based on data from the BIS. Data include the effects of HIPC and MDRI debt relief.

FIJI

(US$ million, unless otherwise indicated)

	2000	2005	2009	2010	2011	2012	2013	2014
Summary external debt data								
External debt stocks	**181.7**	**195.7**	**535.9**	**553.2**	**859.4**	**730.6**	**796.8**	**863.6**
Long-term external debt	172.4	185.4	360.7	388.8	544.3	609.4	653.9	701.3
Short-term external debt	0.2	0.4	70.1	61.1	212.1	18.1	39.6	65.0
interest arrears on long-term	0.2	0.4	0.1	0.1	0.1	0.1	0.6	0.0
Use of IMF credit	9.1	9.9	105.2	103.3	103.0	103.1	103.3	97.2
Long-term external debt								
Debt outstanding and disbursed	**172.4**	**185.4**	**360.7**	**388.8**	**544.3**	**609.4**	**653.9**	**701.3**
Public and publicly guaranteed	172.4	185.4	360.1	388.3	543.8	608.9	653.5	700.9
Official creditors	172.4	185.4	210.1	238.3	293.8	358.9	403.5	450.9
Private creditors	0.0	0.0	150.0	150.0	250.0	250.0	250.0	250.0
of which: Bonds	0.0	0.0	150.0	150.0	250.0	250.0	250.0	250.0
Private nonguaranteed	..	..	0.5	0.5	0.5	0.5	0.5	0.4
of which: Bonds	..	..	..	..	..	..	..	..
Disbursements	**7.1**	**14.1**	**15.2**	**32.6**	**315.4**	**78.3**	**59.8**	**70.5**
Public and publicly guaranteed	7.1	14.1	15.0	32.6	315.4	78.2	59.8	70.5
Official creditors	7.1	14.1	15.0	32.6	65.4	78.2	59.8	70.5
Private creditors	0.0	0.0	0.0	0.0	250.0	0.0	0.0	0.0
of which: Bonds	0.0	0.0	0.0	0.0	250.0	0.0	0.0	0.0
Private nonguaranteed	..	..	0.3	0.0	0.0	0.1	0.0	0.0
of which: Bonds	..	..	..	..	..	..	..	..
Principal repayments	**16.9**	**8.5**	**10.4**	**9.1**	**163.6**	**11.2**	**15.1**	**21.1**
Public and publicly guaranteed	16.9	8.5	10.3	9.1	163.6	11.2	15.0	21.0
Official creditors	16.9	8.5	10.3	9.1	13.6	11.2	15.0	21.0
Private creditors	0.0	0.0	0.0	0.0	150.0	0.0	0.0	0.0
of which: Bonds	0.0	0.0	0.0	0.0	150.0	0.0	0.0	0.0
Private nonguaranteed	..	..	0.0	0.0	0.1	0.1	0.1	0.1
of which: Bonds	..	..	..	..	..	..	..	..
Interest payments	**7.7**	**5.5**	**14.4**	**13.3**	**24.9**	**26.7**	**27.9**	**29.5**
Public and publicly guaranteed	7.7	5.5	14.4	13.3	24.9	26.7	27.9	29.5
Official creditors	7.7	5.5	4.1	3.0	3.3	4.2	5.4	7.0
Private creditors	0.0	0.0	10.3	10.3	21.6	22.5	22.5	22.5
of which: Bonds	0.0	0.0	10.3	10.3	21.6	22.5	22.5	22.5
Private nonguaranteed	..	..	0.0	0.0	0.0	0.0	0.0	0.0
of which: Bonds	..	..	..	..	..	..	..	..
Net financial flows								
Net debt inflows	-9.8	-47.5	55.9	14.5	302.8	-126.9	65.7	75.4
Official creditors (incl. IMF)	-9.8	5.5	4.6	23.5	51.8	67.1	44.8	49.5
Private creditors	0.0	-53.0	51.2	-9.0	251.0	-194.0	21.0	25.9
Long-term	0.0	..	0.2	0.0	100.0	0.0	0.0	-0.1
Public and publicly guaranteed	0.0	..	..	..	100.0	..	..	..
Private nonguaranteed	..	..	0.2	0.0	0.0	0.0	0.0	-0.1
Short-term	..	-53.0	51.0	-9.0	151.0	-194.0	21.0	26.0
Net equity inflows								
Foreign direct investment	0.6	155.5	136.9	350.3	404.6	261.0	127.7	278.9
Portfolio equity	..	1.7	-1.1	0.1	-0.1	..	..	..
Major economic aggregates								
Gross national income (GNI)	1,717.4	3,050.1	2,859.1	3,043.1	3,532.3	3,707.3	3,774.7	3,989.2
Exports of goods, services & prim. income	1,023.2	1,693.0	1,482.8	1,898.2	2,330.2	2,510.4	2,333.2	..
Imports of goods, services & prim. income	1,136.4	2,046.1	1,785.3	2,189.2	2,668.4	2,777.9	3,109.3	..
Primary income on FDI	7.5	132.8	48.0	143.4	171.2	172.7	108.2	..
Personal transfers & comp. of employees	44.0	203.7	171.2	173.8	160.4	190.6	203.6	209.4
International reserves	411.8	320.9	569.1	719.4	832.2	920.0	940.9	915.2
Ratios								
External debt stocks to exports (%)	17.8	11.6	36.1	29.1	36.9	29.1	34.2	..
External debt stocks to GNI (%)	10.6	6.4	18.7	18.2	24.3	19.7	21.1	21.6
Debt service to exports (%)	2.4	0.8	1.7	1.2	8.2	1.5	1.9	..
Reserves to external debt stocks (%)	226.7	164.0	106.2	130.0	96.8	125.9	118.1	106.0

Notes:

Long-term private nonguaranteed debt data for 2012 are World Bank staff estimates. Short-term debt is based on data from the BIS.

GABON

(US$ million, unless otherwise indicated)

	2000	2005	2009	2010	2011	2012	2013	2014
Summary external debt data								
External debt stocks	**3,920**	**3,895**	**2,324**	**2,524**	**2,798**	**2,870**	**4,316**	**4,326**
Long-term external debt	3,457	3,561	1,991	2,128	2,388	2,533	3,817	4,040
Short-term external debt	355	246	104	170	185	111	273	73
interest arrears on long-term	63	186	1	0	0	0	0	0
Use of IMF credit	107	88	230	226	225	225	226	213
Long-term external debt								
Debt outstanding and disbursed	**3,457**	**3,561**	**1,991**	**2,128**	**2,388**	**2,533**	**3,817**	**4,040**
Public and publicly guaranteed	3,457	3,561	1,991	2,128	2,388	2,533	3,817	4,040
Official creditors	3,338	3,441	893	884	929	981	1,250	1,395
Private creditors	119	119	1,098	1,244	1,459	1,552	2,567	2,646
of which: Bonds	0	0	901	879	879	875	1,718	1,718
Private nonguaranteed	..	..	..	..	..	..	..	..
of which: Bonds	..	..	..	..	..	..	..	..
Disbursements	**34**	**18**	**261**	**466**	**549**	**385**	**2,103**	**659**
Public and publicly guaranteed	34	18	261	466	549	385	2,103	659
Official creditors	13	18	147	189	216	165	308	295
Private creditors	21	0	114	276	333	221	1,795	364
of which: Bonds	0	0	0	0	0	0	1,500	0
Private nonguaranteed	..	..	..	..	..	..	..	..
of which: Bonds	..	..	..	..	..	..	..	..
Principal repayments	**188**	**112**	**261**	**291**	**256**	**259**	**877**	**259**
Public and publicly guaranteed	188	112	261	291	256	259	877	259
Official creditors	160	63	222	171	165	118	64	90
Private creditors	27	48	39	120	91	142	813	169
of which: Bonds	0	0	0	23	0	4	657	0
Private nonguaranteed	..	..	..	..	..	..	..	..
of which: Bonds	..	..	..	..	..	..	..	..
Interest payments	**124**	**52**	**141**	**131**	**127**	**130**	**246**	**160**
Public and publicly guaranteed	124	52	141	131	127	130	246	160
Official creditors	118	46	49	32	30	28	31	30
Private creditors	7	7	91	99	97	102	215	130
of which: Bonds	0	0	75	74	72	73	191	114
Private nonguaranteed	..	..	..	..	..	..	..	..
of which: Bonds	..	..	..	..	..	..	..	..
Net financial flows								
Net debt inflows	-363	-58	-7	242	307	52	1,388	200
Official creditors (incl. IMF)	-140	-70	-75	19	51	47	244	205
Private creditors	-223	12	69	223	257	5	1,144	-6
Long-term	-7	-48	76	156	242	79	982	194
Public and publicly guaranteed	-7	-48	76	156	242	79	982	194
Private nonguaranteed	..	..	..	..	..	..	..	..
Short-term	-216	60	-7	67	15	-74	162	-200
Net equity inflows								
Foreign direct investment	-43	321	573	499	696	832	968	973
Portfolio equity	..	..	..	..	..	..	..	..
Major economic aggregates								
Gross national income (GNI)	4,289	8,501	11,142	12,776	15,601	15,364	14,936	15,143
Exports of goods, services & prim. income	3,547	5,639	..	..	..	..	..	..
Imports of goods, services & prim. income	2,483	3,387	..	..	..	..	..	..
Primary income on FDI	473	765	..	..	..	..	..	..
Personal transfers & comp. of employees	6	11	..	..	..	..	..	..
International reserves	190	669	1,993	1,736	2,157	2,352	3,004	2,478
Ratios								
External debt stocks to exports (%)	110.5	69.1	..	..	..	..	..	..
External debt stocks to GNI (%)	91.4	45.8	20.9	19.8	17.9	18.7	28.9	28.6
Debt service to exports (%)	9.9	3.4	..	..	..	..	..	..
Reserves to external debt stocks (%)	4.8	17.2	85.8	68.8	77.1	81.9	69.6	57.3

Notes:

Long-term public and publicly guaranteed debt data before 2008 are World Bank staff estimates based on reports provided by the country. Long-term public and publicly guaranteed debt data for 2014 are based on World Bank staff estimates. Short-term debt is based on data from the BIS. Data include the effects of Paris Club debt buyback agreement signed in 2007.

GAMBIA, THE

(US$ million, unless otherwise indicated)

	2000	2005	2009	2010	2011	2012	2013	2014
Summary external debt data								
External debt stocks	**490.1**	**667.1**	**500.5**	**512.3**	**475.8**	**512.8**	**519.3**	**500.1**
Long-term external debt	438.0	616.5	382.0	391.0	394.4	395.8	412.0	400.8
Short-term external debt	27.3	22.4	43.3	44.3	1.1	22.6	11.8	12.5
interest arrears on long-term	0.0	1.4	2.3	2.3	1.1	1.6	1.8	3.5
Use of IMF credit	24.8	28.1	75.2	77.0	80.3	94.4	95.5	86.8
Long-term external debt								
Debt outstanding and disbursed	**438.0**	**616.5**	**382.0**	**391.0**	**394.4**	**395.8**	**412.0**	**400.8**
Public and publicly guaranteed	438.0	616.5	382.0	391.0	394.4	395.8	412.0	400.8
Official creditors	437.0	616.5	378.6	384.6	390.3	386.2	401.0	391.9
Private creditors	1.0	0.0	3.4	6.4	4.1	9.6	11.0	8.9
of which: Bonds	0.0	0.0	0.0	0.0	0.0	0.0	0.0	0.0
Private nonguaranteed	..	..	..	..	..	..	..	..
of which: Bonds	..	..	..	..	..	..	..	..
Disbursements	**20.7**	**54.3**	**33.5**	**43.2**	**24.3**	**25.2**	**37.1**	**39.6**
Public and publicly guaranteed	20.7	54.3	33.5	43.2	24.3	25.2	37.1	39.6
Official creditors	20.7	54.3	32.7	36.8	24.3	17.9	34.0	38.3
Private creditors	0.0	0.0	0.8	6.4	0.0	7.3	3.1	1.3
of which: Bonds	0.0	0.0	0.0	0.0	0.0	0.0	0.0	0.0
Private nonguaranteed	..	..	..	..	..	..	..	..
of which: Bonds	..	..	..	..	..	..	..	..
Principal repayments	**12.7**	**16.1**	**11.2**	**15.8**	**18.5**	**17.8**	**20.5**	**35.2**
Public and publicly guaranteed	12.7	16.1	11.2	15.8	18.5	17.8	20.5	35.2
Official creditors	12.3	15.8	11.2	12.6	16.2	15.8	18.4	33.0
Private creditors	0.4	0.3	0.0	3.2	2.2	2.1	2.2	2.1
of which: Bonds	0.0	0.0	0.0	0.0	0.0	0.0	0.0	0.0
Private nonguaranteed	..	..	..	..	..	..	..	..
of which: Bonds	..	..	..	..	..	..	..	..
Interest payments	**6.0**	**9.4**	**7.0**	**6.6**	**6.3**	**6.1**	**5.1**	**4.8**
Public and publicly guaranteed	6.0	9.4	7.0	6.6	6.3	6.1	5.1	4.8
Official creditors	5.9	9.4	7.0	6.6	6.2	5.9	4.9	4.8
Private creditors	0.1	0.0	0.0	0.0	0.1	0.2	0.1	0.1
of which: Bonds	0.0	0.0	0.0	0.0	0.0	0.0	0.0	0.0
Private nonguaranteed	..	..	..	..	..	..	..	..
of which: Bonds	..	..	..	..	..	..	..	..
Net financial flows								
Net debt inflows	20.6	33.2	65.1	31.5	-32.5	42.4	6.4	0.2
Official creditors (incl. IMF)	15.8	36.5	37.3	27.3	11.7	16.1	16.5	2.0
Private creditors	4.8	-3.3	27.8	4.2	-44.2	26.3	-10.1	-1.8
Long-term	-0.4	-0.3	0.8	3.2	-2.2	5.3	0.9	-0.8
Public and publicly guaranteed	-0.4	-0.3	0.8	3.2	-2.2	5.3	0.9	-0.8
Private nonguaranteed	..	..	..	..	..	..	..	..
Short-term	5.2	-3.0	27.0	1.0	-42.0	21.0	-11.0	-1.0
Net equity inflows								
Foreign direct investment	..	53.7	39.4	37.4	36.2	33.5	37.6	28.4
Portfolio equity	..	..	..	..	..	..	..	..
Major economic aggregates								
Gross national income (GNI)	752.7	601.7	872.6	921.9	871.2	884.7	863.9	782.3
Exports of goods, services & prim. income	..	189.8	290.1	284.9	318.9	343.8	..	..
Imports of goods, services & prim. income	..	305.0	362.3	341.3	392.8	467.6	..	..
Primary income on FDI	..	26.9	11.7	11.5	11.3	10.2	..	..
Personal transfers & comp. of employees	..	59.3	79.8	115.7	107.9	141.0	..	..
International reserves	109.4	98.3	224.2	201.6	223.2	236.2	210.6	159.3
Ratios								
External debt stocks to exports (%)	..	351.5	172.6	179.8	149.2	149.2	..	..
External debt stocks to GNI (%)	65.1	110.9	57.4	55.6	54.6	58.0	60.1	63.9
Debt service to exports (%)	..	15.1	6.5	8.1	7.9	7.1	..	..
Reserves to external debt stocks (%)	22.3	14.7	44.8	39.4	46.9	46.1	40.5	31.9

Notes:

Short-term debt is based on data from the BIS. Data include the effects of HIPC and MDRI debt relief.

GEORGIA

(US$ million, unless otherwise indicated)

	2000	2005	2009	2010	2011	2012	2013	2014
Summary external debt data								
External debt stocks	**1,825**	**2,151**	**8,673**	**9,656**	**11,360**	**12,383**	**13,724**	**13,912**
Long-term external debt	1,316	1,663	6,736	7,284	8,605	9,274	11,078	11,278
Short-term external debt	44	50	925	1,101	1,546	2,144	2,066	2,214
interest arrears on long-term	1	11	7	7	84	351	348	375
Use of IMF credit	466	438	1,012	1,272	1,210	965	580	420
Long-term external debt								
Debt outstanding and disbursed	**1,316**	**1,663**	**6,736**	**7,284**	**8,605**	**9,274**	**11,078**	**11,278**
Public and publicly guaranteed	1,274	1,531	3,529	4,141	4,343	4,876	4,986	5,338
Official creditors	1,272	1,529	2,155	2,450	2,706	3,097	3,384	3,532
Private creditors	2	2	1,375	1,691	1,637	1,778	1,603	1,806
of which: Bonds	0	0	500	750	815	1,065	1,000	1,000
Private nonguaranteed	42	132	3,207	3,143	4,262	4,399	6,091	5,940
of which: Bonds	..	..	..	..	..	750	900	900
Disbursements	**65**	**146**	**1,147**	**1,190**	**1,785**	**1,625**	**1,386**	**1,513**
Public and publicly guaranteed	37	76	678	815	843	690	332	672
Official creditors	37	76	427	401	343	431	326	467
Private creditors	0	0	250	414	500	258	6	205
of which: Bonds	0	0	0	250	500	250	0	0
Private nonguaranteed	28	69	469	375	942	935	1,054	841
of which: Bonds	..	..	..	..	..	750	150	..
Principal repayments	**42**	**103**	**474**	**510**	**1,199**	**933**	**811**	**1,090**
Public and publicly guaranteed	41	80	140	169	620	165	238	98
Official creditors	41	80	70	71	67	48	56	98
Private creditors	0	0	70	97	553	118	182	0
of which: Bonds	0	0	0	0	435	0	65	0
Private nonguaranteed	2	23	334	342	579	768	573	992
of which: Bonds	..	..	..	..	..	..	..	..
Interest payments	**43**	**28**	**251**	**247**	**307**	**404**	**427**	**480**
Public and publicly guaranteed	42	24	77	87	139	112	130	122
Official creditors	42	24	31	39	35	38	43	45
Private creditors	0	0	45	47	104	73	87	76
of which: Bonds	0	0	38	38	94	64	79	76
Private nonguaranteed	1	4	174	160	167	292	297	358
of which: Bonds	..	..	..	..	..	29	70	70
Net financial flows								
Net debt inflows	33	-30	874	1,131	895	778	116	412
Official creditors (incl. IMF)	-29	-17	670	605	216	139	-113	237
Private creditors	62	-14	204	526	679	639	229	175
Long-term	26	46	316	350	310	308	304	53
Public and publicly guaranteed	..	0	181	316	-53	141	-176	205
Private nonguaranteed	26	47	136	34	363	167	481	-152
Short-term	36	-60	-112	176	369	331	-76	121
Net equity inflows								
Foreign direct investment	131	383	564	696	798	508	745	1,109
Portfolio equity	..	3	12	-22	-7	74	1	210
Major economic aggregates								
Gross national income (GNI)	3,175	6,473	10,725	11,424	14,012	15,700	15,835	16,371
Exports of goods, services & prim. income	1,007	2,415	3,672	4,591	6,000	7,099	8,097	8,019
Imports of goods, services & prim. income	1,433	3,469	5,779	6,885	9,169	10,357	10,489	11,057
Primary income on FDI	36	116	262	470	800	747	770	688
Personal transfers & comp. of employees	274	446	1,112	1,184	1,547	1,770	1,945	1,986
International reserves	116	479	2,110	2,264	2,818	2,873	2,823	2,699
Ratios								
External debt stocks to exports (%)	181.3	89.1	236.2	210.3	189.3	174.5	169.5	173.5
External debt stocks to GNI (%)	57.5	33.2	80.9	84.5	81.1	78.9	86.7	85.0
Debt service to exports (%)	12.5	8.1	21.0	17.5	26.8	22.9	21.2	23.3
Reserves to external debt stocks (%)	6.4	22.2	24.3	23.4	24.8	23.2	20.6	19.4

GHANA

(US$ million, unless otherwise indicated)

	2000	2005	2009	2010	2011	2012	2013	2014
Summary external debt data								
External debt stocks	**6,254**	**7,165**	**7,177**	**9,296**	**11,279**	**12,565**	**15,801**	**17,612**
Long-term external debt	5,307	6,043	5,019	6,096	7,383	8,699	11,019	13,336
Short-term external debt	572	616	1,332	2,263	2,795	2,614	3,559	3,156
interest arrears on long-term	10	38	50	27	105	143	230	165
Use of IMF credit	375	507	826	937	1,101	1,253	1,223	1,120
Long-term external debt								
Debt outstanding and disbursed	**5,307**	**6,043**	**5,019**	**6,096**	**7,383**	**8,699**	**11,019**	**13,336**
Public and publicly guaranteed	5,050	6,043	5,019	6,096	7,383	8,699	11,019	13,083
Official creditors	4,705	5,492	3,320	4,213	5,130	6,113	6,886	7,478
Private creditors	345	551	1,699	1,882	2,253	2,585	4,133	5,605
of which: Bonds	0	0	750	750	750	750	1,531	2,531
Private nonguaranteed	257	..	..	..	..	..	..	253
of which: Bonds	250	..	..	..	..	..	..	253
Disbursements	**417**	**558**	**1,005**	**1,297**	**1,534**	**1,546**	**2,807**	**3,174**
Public and publicly guaranteed	417	558	1,005	1,297	1,534	1,546	2,807	2,921
Official creditors	342	483	726	998	1,025	1,073	900	1,104
Private creditors	75	74	279	299	509	473	1,907	1,817
of which: Bonds	0	0	0	0	0	0	1,000	1,000
Private nonguaranteed	..	..	..	..	..	..	..	253
of which: Bonds	..	..	..	..	..	..	..	253
Principal repayments	**217**	**188**	**135**	**145**	**197**	**270**	**568**	**406**
Public and publicly guaranteed	214	188	135	145	197	270	568	406
Official creditors	141	127	55	74	88	117	163	207
Private creditors	73	61	80	71	109	153	405	199
of which: Bonds	0	0	0	0	0	0	219	0
Private nonguaranteed	3	..	..	..	..	..	..	..
of which: Bonds	..	..	..	..	..	..	..	..
Interest payments	**95**	**87**	**107**	**159**	**97**	**170**	**265**	**280**
Public and publicly guaranteed	80	87	107	159	97	170	265	280
Official creditors	64	57	46	72	61	79	113	87
Private creditors	16	29	60	87	36	91	151	193
of which: Bonds	0	0	32	64	0	32	54	124
Private nonguaranteed	14	..	..	..	..	..	..	..
of which: Bonds	14	..	..	..	..	..	..	..
Net financial flows								
Net debt inflows	62	268	918	2,230	1,963	1,207	3,064	2,398
Official creditors (incl. IMF)	199	364	775	1,049	1,109	1,106	704	865
Private creditors	-137	-96	143	1,182	854	101	2,360	1,533
Long-term	-1	13	199	228	400	320	1,502	1,871
Public and publicly guaranteed	2	13	199	228	400	320	1,502	1,618
Private nonguaranteed	-3	..	..	..	..	..	..	253
Short-term	-136	-109	-56	954	454	-219	858	-338
Net equity inflows								
Foreign direct investment	166	145	1,940	2,527	3,222	3,295	3,227	3,357
Portfolio equity	..	..	535	18	1	..	..	..
Major economic aggregates								
Gross national income (GNI)	4,836	10,601	25,884	31,641	38,336	39,808	47,233	36,934
Exports of goods, services & prim. income	2,456	3,952	7,735	9,490	14,712	16,867	16,490	15,372
Imports of goods, services & prim. income	3,473	6,851	11,710	14,560	20,813	24,188	24,135	20,888
Primary income on FDI	17	94	495	396	1,062	1,915	1,219	..
Personal transfers & comp. of employees	32	99	114	136	152	138	119	126
International reserves	232	1,753	3,386	4,763	5,483	5,368	5,249	..
Ratios								
External debt stocks to exports (%)	254.6	181.3	92.8	98.0	76.7	74.5	95.8	114.6
External debt stocks to GNI (%)	129.3	67.6	27.7	29.4	29.4	31.6	33.5	47.7
Debt service to exports (%)	16.0	8.4	3.6	3.8	2.3	3.1	5.7	5.1
Reserves to external debt stocks (%)	3.7	24.5	47.2	51.2	48.6	42.7	33.2	..

Notes:

Long-term private nonguaranteed debt data only cover bonds. Short-term debt is based on data from the BIS. Data include the effects of MDRI debt relief.

GRENADA

(US$ million, unless otherwise indicated)

	2000	2005	2009	2010	2011	2012	2013	2014
Summary external debt data								
External debt stocks	**203.5**	**407.2**	**600.5**	**607.2**	**596.0**	**620.3**	**616.5**	**650.8**
Long-term external debt	180.7	391.3	523.7	522.4	516.3	519.0	518.9	539.0
Short-term external debt	21.6	6.3	36.3	38.6	33.8	55.9	52.5	66.1
interest arrears on long-term	4.5	4.3	13.3	14.6	15.8	39.9	48.5	58.1
Use of IMF credit	1.2	9.7	40.5	46.3	45.9	45.5	45.1	45.7
Long-term external debt								
Debt outstanding and disbursed	**180.7**	**391.3**	**523.7**	**522.4**	**516.3**	**519.0**	**518.9**	**539.0**
Public and publicly guaranteed	180.7	391.3	523.7	522.4	516.3	519.0	518.9	539.0
Official creditors	116.8	172.4	274.6	277.7	273.2	275.8	275.8	295.9
Private creditors	63.9	218.9	249.0	244.7	243.1	243.1	243.1	243.1
of which: Bonds	27.4	214.3	239.4	239.4	239.4	239.4	239.4	239.4
Private nonguaranteed	..	..	..	..	..	..	..	..
of which: Bonds	..	..	..	..	..	..	..	..
Disbursements	**77.6**	**38.5**	**25.7**	**21.1**	**6.3**	**8.7**	**28.3**	**33.7**
Public and publicly guaranteed	77.6	38.5	25.7	21.1	6.3	8.7	28.3	33.7
Official creditors	19.8	38.5	25.7	21.1	6.3	8.7	28.3	33.7
Private creditors	57.8	0.0	0.0	0.0	0.0	0.0	0.0	0.0
of which: Bonds	26.6	0.0	0.0	0.0	0.0	0.0	0.0	0.0
Private nonguaranteed	..	..	..	..	..	..	..	..
of which: Bonds	..	..	..	..	..	..	..	..
Principal repayments	**10.1**	**5.6**	**9.4**	**15.4**	**13.5**	**6.3**	**28.6**	**11.2**
Public and publicly guaranteed	10.1	5.6	9.4	15.4	13.5	6.3	28.6	11.2
Official creditors	6.3	5.3	9.4	11.0	10.6	6.3	28.6	11.2
Private creditors	3.7	0.4	0.0	4.4	2.9	0.0	0.0	0.0
of which: Bonds	0.0	0.0	0.0	0.0	0.0	0.0	0.0	0.0
Private nonguaranteed	..	..	..	..	..	..	..	..
of which: Bonds	..	..	..	..	..	..	..	..
Interest payments	**3.4**	**3.3**	**11.9**	**11.7**	**12.2**	**8.9**	**6.9**	**11.2**
Public and publicly guaranteed	3.4	3.3	11.9	11.7	12.2	8.9	6.9	11.2
Official creditors	2.3	3.3	5.8	5.7	6.4	3.6	5.8	5.7
Private creditors	1.1	0.0	6.1	5.9	5.9	5.3	1.0	5.5
of which: Bonds	0.0	0.0	5.8	5.9	5.8	5.3	1.0	5.5
Private nonguaranteed	..	..	..	..	..	..	..	..
of which: Bonds	..	..	..	..	..	..	..	..
Net financial flows								
Net debt inflows	63.4	-28.1	0.0	13.1	-13.4	-0.1	-12.8	29.9
Official creditors (incl. IMF)	13.4	33.2	26.0	16.5	-4.5	1.9	-0.8	25.9
Private creditors	50.0	-61.4	-26.0	-3.4	-8.9	-2.0	-12.0	4.0
Long-term	54.1	-0.4	..	-4.4	-2.9	..	..	..
Public and publicly guaranteed	54.1	-0.4	..	-4.4	-2.9	..	..	..
Private nonguaranteed	..	..	..	..	..	..	..	..
Short-term	-4.1	-61.0	-26.0	1.0	-6.0	-2.0	-12.0	4.0
Net equity inflows								
Foreign direct investment	37.4	49.6	82.8	42.3	29.4	16.5	58.0	40.4
Portfolio equity	..	..	..	..	..	..	..	..
Major economic aggregates								
Gross national income (GNI)	486.3	667.1	708.1	731.1	747.0	765.6	805.9	860.4
Exports of goods, services & prim. income	240.8	160.3	195.4	190.9	202.0	213.5	216.7	244.8
Imports of goods, services & prim. income	349.0	435.9	432.1	426.6	433.0	437.0	455.9	438.9
Primary income on FDI	27.8	22.7	55.4	30.8	20.6	18.8	19.6	..
Personal transfers & comp. of employees	46.4	26.8	27.7	28.5	28.9	29.3	29.6	..
International reserves	57.7	94.3	129.1	119.2	120.7	119.5	150.6	169.9
Ratios								
External debt stocks to exports (%)	84.5	254.0	307.4	318.1	295.1	290.6	284.5	265.8
External debt stocks to GNI (%)	41.8	61.0	84.8	83.1	79.8	81.0	76.5	75.6
Debt service to exports (%)	6.0	6.6	12.3	14.4	13.0	7.5	16.8	10.4
Reserves to external debt stocks (%)	28.3	23.1	21.5	19.6	20.3	19.3	24.4	26.1

Notes:

Short-term debt is based on data from the BIS.

GUATEMALA

(US$ million, unless otherwise indicated)

	2000	2005	2009	2010	2011	2012	2013	2014
Summary external debt data								
External debt stocks	**3,948**	**9,506**	**14,822**	**15,039**	**16,277**	**15,128**	**17,252**	**18,761**
Long-term external debt	2,740	8,014	13,281	13,144	13,703	14,124	16,229	17,694
Short-term external debt	1,172	1,453	1,226	1,585	2,265	695	714	776
interest arrears on long-term	317	414	0	0	0	0	0	0
Use of IMF credit	36	40	315	309	308	309	309	291
Long-term external debt								
Debt outstanding and disbursed	**2,740**	**8,014**	**13,281**	**13,144**	**13,703**	**14,124**	**16,229**	**17,694**
Public and publicly guaranteed	2,598	3,720	4,923	5,555	5,349	6,298	7,058	6,945
Official creditors	2,156	2,484	3,968	4,600	4,719	4,968	5,311	5,196
Private creditors	442	1,237	955	955	630	1,330	1,748	1,749
of which: Bonds	245	1,105	955	955	630	1,330	1,730	1,730
Private nonguaranteed	142	4,294	8,358	7,589	8,354	7,826	9,170	10,749
of which: Bonds	..	50	5	5	155	855	1,455	2,555
Disbursements	**220**	**1,639**	**941**	**1,471**	**1,025**	**1,947**	**2,300**	**1,872**
Public and publicly guaranteed	220	144	807	879	393	1,247	1,392	250
Official creditors	220	144	807	879	393	547	674	249
Private creditors	0	0	0	0	0	700	718	2
of which: Bonds	0	0	0	0	0	700	700	0
Private nonguaranteed	..	1,495	135	592	633	700	908	1,622
of which: Bonds	..	..	..	..	150	700	600	1,100
Principal repayments	**192**	**570**	**1,086**	**949**	**1,347**	**1,481**	**2,328**	**1,254**
Public and publicly guaranteed	172	200	269	264	604	273	596	325
Official creditors	139	199	269	264	279	273	296	325
Private creditors	32	1	0	0	325	0	300	0
of which: Bonds	31	0	0	0	325	0	300	0
Private nonguaranteed	20	371	817	685	743	1,208	1,732	928
of which: Bonds	..	..	50	..	..	..	..	..
Interest payments	**153**	**420**	**657**	**636**	**684**	**598**	**601**	**762**
Public and publicly guaranteed	134	203	258	284	284	274	291	314
Official creditors	112	102	170	196	196	199	207	211
Private creditors	23	101	88	88	88	75	84	102
of which: Bonds	22	101	88	88	88	75	84	101
Private nonguaranteed	19	217	399	352	401	324	310	448
of which: Bonds	..	5	0	0	7	20	26	63
Net financial flows								
Net debt inflows	62	906	-1,070	881	359	-1,105	-8	680
Official creditors (incl. IMF)	80	-56	537	615	114	273	378	-77
Private creditors	-18	961	-1,607	266	245	-1,379	-386	757
Long-term	-52	1,124	-682	-93	-435	192	-406	695
Public and publicly guaranteed	-32	-1	0	0	-325	700	418	2
Private nonguaranteed	-20	1,125	-682	-93	-110	-508	-824	693
Short-term	34	-163	-925	359	680	-1,570	19	62
Net equity inflows								
Foreign direct investment	230	392	581	907	968	1,026	880	1,080
Portfolio equity	..	..	..	..	..	..	..	..
Major economic aggregates								
Gross national income (GNI)	19,065	26,726	36,632	40,127	46,004	49,091	52,557	56,671
Exports of goods, services & prim. income	4,077	7,069	9,792	11,165	13,171	12,985	13,175	14,235
Imports of goods, services & prim. income	5,991	11,886	14,145	16,674	19,904	19,939	20,642	22,068
Primary income on FDI	248	370	951	1,001	1,453	1,112	986	1,363
Personal transfers & comp. of employees	596	3,067	4,019	4,232	4,524	5,031	5,379	5,837
International reserves	1,746	3,664	4,964	5,637	5,835	6,325	7,002	7,064
Ratios								
External debt stocks to exports (%)	96.8	134.5	151.4	134.7	123.6	116.5	130.9	131.8
External debt stocks to GNI (%)	20.7	35.6	40.5	37.5	35.4	30.8	32.8	33.1
Debt service to exports (%)	9.7	14.8	18.0	14.4	15.7	16.5	22.5	14.5
Reserves to external debt stocks (%)	44.2	38.5	33.5	37.5	35.8	41.8	40.6	37.7

Notes:

Long-term private nonguaranteed debt data are World Bank staff estimates based on reports provided by the country. Short-term debt before 2012 is based on data from the BIS.

GUINEA

(US$ million, unless otherwise indicated)

	2000	2005	2009	2010	2011	2012	2013	2014
Summary external debt data								
External debt stocks	**3,083**	**3,152**	**3,417**	**3,374**	**3,359**	**1,300**	**1,390**	**1,407**
Long-term external debt	2,650	2,982	3,157	3,045	3,069	1,048	1,041	1,009
Short-term external debt	298	57	40	124	91	37	106	77
interest arrears on long-term	81	57	38	56	80	37	37	37
Use of IMF credit	136	113	220	205	199	215	243	321
Long-term external debt								
Debt outstanding and disbursed	**2,650**	**2,982**	**3,157**	**3,045**	**3,069**	**1,048**	**1,041**	**1,009**
Public and publicly guaranteed	2,650	2,982	3,157	3,045	3,069	1,048	1,041	1,009
Official creditors	2,621	2,791	3,001	2,913	2,954	950	953	942
Private creditors	29	190	156	132	115	98	88	67
of which: Bonds	0	159	137	114	97	86	76	55
Private nonguaranteed	..	..	..	..	..	..	..	..
of which: Bonds	..	..	..	..	..	..	..	..
Disbursements	**71**	**249**	**42**	**32**	**33**	**42**	**54**	**93**
Public and publicly guaranteed	71	249	42	32	33	42	54	93
Official creditors	71	247	42	32	33	42	54	93
Private creditors	0	1	0	0	0	0	0	0
of which: Bonds	0	0	0	0	0	0	0	0
Private nonguaranteed	..	..	..	..	..	..	..	..
of which: Bonds	..	..	..	..	..	..	..	..
Principal repayments	**91**	**97**	**98**	**65**	**154**	**108**	**69**	**64**
Public and publicly guaranteed	91	97	98	65	154	108	69	64
Official creditors	91	84	84	52	140	95	56	50
Private creditors	0	12	14	13	14	13	13	13
of which: Bonds	0	12	14	13	14	13	13	13
Private nonguaranteed	..	..	..	..	..	..	..	..
of which: Bonds	..	..	..	..	..	..	..	..
Interest payments	**41**	**50**	**29**	**21**	**36**	**21**	**13**	**12**
Public and publicly guaranteed	41	50	29	21	36	21	13	12
Official creditors	41	50	29	21	36	21	13	12
Private creditors	0	0	0	0	0	0	0	0
of which: Bonds	0	0	0	0	0	0	0	0
Private nonguaranteed	..	..	..	..	..	..	..	..
of which: Bonds	..	..	..	..	..	..	..	..
Net financial flows								
Net debt inflows	-41	126	-223	22	-184	-62	81	97
Official creditors (incl. IMF)	-28	137	-55	-30	-113	-38	26	139
Private creditors	-13	-11	-168	53	-71	-24	56	-42
Long-term	0	-11	-14	-13	-14	-13	-13	-13
Public and publicly guaranteed	0	-11	-14	-13	-14	-13	-13	-13
Private nonguaranteed	..	..	..	..	..	..	..	..
Short-term	-12	..	-154	66	-57	-11	69	-29
Net equity inflows								
Foreign direct investment	10	105	50	101	955	0	3	..
Portfolio equity	..	..	..	..	..	..	..	..
Major economic aggregates								
Gross national income (GNI)	2,922	2,658	4,108	4,302	4,625	5,235	5,778	6,134
Exports of goods, services & prim. income	758	929	1,144	1,549	1,528	2,118	1,993	..
Imports of goods, services & prim. income	973	1,079	1,581	1,892	2,829	3,289	3,242	..
Primary income on FDI	8	..	88	0	26	39	47	..
Personal transfers & comp. of employees	1	42	52	46	65	66	93	95
International reserves	148	95	..	..	103	155	174	293
Ratios								
External debt stocks to exports (%)	406.9	339.3	298.6	217.9	219.8	61.4	69.8	..
External debt stocks to GNI (%)	105.5	118.6	83.2	78.4	72.6	24.8	24.1	22.9
Debt service to exports (%)	20.7	18.8	12.4	6.3	12.8	8.0	4.2	..
Reserves to external debt stocks (%)	4.8	3.0	..	..	3.1	11.9	12.5	20.8

Notes:

Long-term public and publicly guaranteed debt data are World Bank staff estimates based on the original terms of the loans. Short-term debt is based on data from the BIS. Data include the effects of Paris Club debt restructuring agreement signed in 2010, 2012 and HIPC debt relief.

GUINEA-BISSAU

(US$ million, unless otherwise indicated)

	2000	2005	2009	2010	2011	2012	2013	2014
Summary external debt data								
External debt stocks	**947.8**	**1,021.7**	**1,025.5**	**1,103.5**	**283.7**	**279.5**	**277.4**	**271.4**
Long-term external debt	821.1	887.8	874.0	977.3	218.5	213.4	212.2	203.2
Short-term external debt	100.4	120.7	120.3	101.6	33.1	34.1	33.1	32.9
interest arrears on long-term	87.4	118.7	113.3	100.6	33.1	33.1	33.1	32.9
Use of IMF credit	26.3	13.2	31.3	24.7	32.0	32.0	32.1	35.3
Long-term external debt								
Debt outstanding and disbursed	**821.1**	**887.8**	**874.0**	**977.3**	**218.5**	**213.4**	**212.2**	**203.2**
Public and publicly guaranteed	821.1	887.8	874.0	977.3	218.5	213.4	212.2	203.2
Official creditors	821.1	887.8	874.0	977.3	218.5	213.4	212.2	203.2
Private creditors	0.0	0.0	0.0	0.0	0.0	0.0	0.0	0.0
of which: Bonds	0.0	0.0	0.0	0.0	0.0	0.0	0.0	0.0
Private nonguaranteed	..	..	..	..	..	..	..	..
of which: Bonds	..	..	..	..	..	..	..	..
Disbursements	**13.6**	**15.6**	**6.0**	**4.0**	**9.1**	**2.7**	**1.0**	**2.5**
Public and publicly guaranteed	13.6	15.6	6.0	4.0	9.1	2.7	1.0	2.5
Official creditors	13.6	15.6	6.0	4.0	9.1	2.7	1.0	2.5
Private creditors	0.0	0.0	0.0	0.0	0.0	0.0	0.0	0.0
of which: Bonds	0.0	0.0	0.0	0.0	0.0	0.0	0.0	0.0
Private nonguaranteed	..	..	..	..	..	..	..	..
of which: Bonds	..	..	..	..	..	..	..	..
Principal repayments	**2.6**	**1.0**	**4.7**	**5.8**	**4.5**	**6.3**	**1.1**	**1.4**
Public and publicly guaranteed	2.6	1.0	4.7	5.8	4.5	6.3	1.1	1.4
Official creditors	2.4	1.0	4.7	5.8	4.5	6.3	1.1	1.4
Private creditors	0.2	0.0	0.0	0.0	0.0	0.0	0.0	0.0
of which: Bonds	0.0	0.0	0.0	0.0	0.0	0.0	0.0	0.0
Private nonguaranteed	..	..	..	..	..	..	..	..
of which: Bonds	..	..	..	..	..	..	..	..
Interest payments	**1.6**	**2.0**	**3.7**	**3.3**	**0.5**	**0.6**	**0.4**	**0.5**
Public and publicly guaranteed	1.6	2.0	3.7	3.3	0.5	0.6	0.4	0.5
Official creditors	1.6	2.0	3.7	3.3	0.5	0.6	0.4	0.5
Private creditors	0.0	0.0	0.0	0.0	0.0	0.0	0.0	0.0
of which: Bonds	0.0	0.0	0.0	0.0	0.0	0.0	0.0	0.0
Private nonguaranteed	..	..	..	..	..	..	..	..
of which: Bonds	..	..	..	..	..	..	..	..
Net financial flows								
Net debt inflows	29.4	10.4	7.4	-0.2	11.2	-2.7	-1.1	6.4
Official creditors (incl. IMF)	19.6	11.4	2.4	5.8	12.2	-3.7	-0.1	6.4
Private creditors	9.8	-1.0	5.0	-6.0	-1.0	1.0	-1.0	..
Long-term	-0.2	..	..	..	..	..	..	..
Public and publicly guaranteed	-0.2	..	..	..	..	..	..	..
Private nonguaranteed	..	..	..	..	..	..	..	..
Short-term	10.0	-1.0	5.0	-6.0	-1.0	1.0	-1.0	..
Net equity inflows								
Foreign direct investment	0.7	5.9	18.9	26.2	36.8	12.8	19.6	21.5
Portfolio equity	..	..	-0.2	2.7	0.0	..	..	..
Major economic aggregates								
Gross national income (GNI)	357.8	575.4	815.6	846.6	1,102.9	957.9	945.6	1,021.5
Exports of goods, services & prim. income	..	95.2	163.4	183.8	297.9	156.3	458.7	..
Imports of goods, services & prim. income	..	156.9	309.0	314.7	373.7	290.5	591.5	..
Primary income on FDI	..	..	5.6	5.7	31.8	31.2	..	..
Personal transfers & comp. of employees	8.0	19.9	48.9	45.9	52.1	45.6	..	..
International reserves	66.8	79.8	168.6	156.4	220.0	164.6	186.3	287.0
Ratios								
External debt stocks to exports (%)	..	1072.9	627.6	600.4	95.2	178.8	60.5	..
External debt stocks to GNI (%)	264.9	177.6	125.7	130.4	25.7	29.2	29.3	26.6
Debt service to exports (%)	..	6.7	6.2	9.5	1.7	4.4	0.3	..
Reserves to external debt stocks (%)	7.0	7.8	16.4	14.2	77.6	58.9	67.1	105.7

Notes:

Long-term public and publicly guaranteed debt data are World Bank staff estimates. Short-term debt is based on data from the BIS. Data include the effects of Paris Club debt restructuring agreement and HIPC and MDRI debt relief.

GUYANA

(US$ million, unless otherwise indicated)

	2000	2005	2009	2010	2011	2012	2013	2014
Summary external debt data								
External debt stocks	**1,384**	**1,237**	**1,172**	**1,485**	**1,846**	**1,974**	**2,303**	**2,379**
Long-term external debt	1,129	1,043	781	885	1,054	1,215	1,116	1,315
Short-term external debt	119	82	196	410	609	588	1,027	924
interest arrears on long-term	67	82	97	103	107	111	111	112
Use of IMF credit	136	112	195	190	182	171	160	140
Long-term external debt								
Debt outstanding and disbursed	**1,129**	**1,043**	**781**	**885**	**1,054**	**1,215**	**1,116**	**1,315**
Public and publicly guaranteed	1,125	1,041	779	885	1,054	1,215	1,116	1,130
Official creditors	1,080	1,033	758	864	1,034	1,194	1,095	1,109
Private creditors	45	9	21	21	21	21	21	21
of which: Bonds	27	0	0	0	0	0	0	0
Private nonguaranteed	4	2	2	0	0	..	0	185
of which: Bonds	..	..	..	..	..	..	..	..
Disbursements	**64**	**104**	**105**	**123**	**188**	**279**	**200**	**355**
Public and publicly guaranteed	64	104	105	123	188	279	200	170
Official creditors	64	104	105	123	188	279	200	170
Private creditors	0	0	0	0	0	0	0	0
of which: Bonds	0	0	0	0	0	0	0	0
Private nonguaranteed	..	..	..	0	0	..	..	185
of which: Bonds	..	..	..	..	..	..	..	..
Principal repayments	**23**	**16**	**8**	**16**	**20**	**119**	**21**	**24**
Public and publicly guaranteed	22	15	8	16	20	119	21	24
Official creditors	22	15	8	16	20	119	21	24
Private creditors	0	0	0	0	0	0	0	0
of which: Bonds	0	0	0	0	0	0	0	0
Private nonguaranteed	0	0	0	..	..	..	..	..
of which: Bonds	..	..	..	..	..	..	..	..
Interest payments	**26**	**10**	**11**	**11**	**13**	**13**	**14**	**16**
Public and publicly guaranteed	26	10	10	11	13	13	14	16
Official creditors	26	10	10	11	13	13	14	16
Private creditors	0	0	0	0	0	0	0	0
of which: Bonds	0	0	0	0	0	0	0	0
Private nonguaranteed	0	0	0	..	..	..	..	..
of which: Bonds	..	..	..	..	..	..	..	..
Net financial flows								
Net debt inflows	21	76	195	314	355	124	607	216
Official creditors (incl. IMF)	34	108	96	106	160	149	168	135
Private creditors	-14	-32	99	208	195	-25	439	81
Long-term	0	-1	0	0	0	..	0	185
Public and publicly guaranteed	0	0	..	..	..	..	0	..
Private nonguaranteed	0	0	0	0	0	..	..	185
Short-term	-13	-31	99	208	195	-25	439	-104
Net equity inflows								
Foreign direct investment	67	18	31	39	46	42	29	..
Portfolio equity	..	..	..	..	..	..	..	..
Major economic aggregates								
Gross national income (GNI)	661	777	2,009	2,272	2,567	2,875	3,019	3,259
Exports of goods, services & prim. income	684	697	978	1,183	1,479	1,764	1,594	..
Imports of goods, services & prim. income	813	960	1,509	1,709	2,265	2,550	2,364	..
Primary income on FDI	6	7	13	13	18	10	5	..
Personal transfers & comp. of employees	27	201	262	368	412	469	328	341
International reserves	305	252	631	782	802	864	784	668
Ratios								
External debt stocks to exports (%)	202.4	177.5	119.8	125.5	124.8	111.9	144.5	..
External debt stocks to GNI (%)	209.5	159.2	58.3	65.4	71.9	68.7	76.3	73.0
Debt service to exports (%)	10.2	5.0	2.1	2.7	3.1	8.6	4.9	..
Reserves to external debt stocks (%)	22.0	20.4	53.9	52.7	43.4	43.8	34.0	28.1

Notes:

Long-term private nonguaranteed debt data for 2014 are World Bank staff estimates based on market data. Principal payment shown from 2012 include rice for oil deal. Data include the effects of HIPC and MDRI debt relief.

HAITI

(US$ million, unless otherwise indicated)

	2000	2005	2009	2010	2011	2012	2013	2014
Summary external debt data								
External debt stocks	**1,203**	**1,347**	**1,448**	**957**	**771**	**1,156**	**1,556**	**1,937**
Long-term external debt	1,056	1,278	1,158	822	623	986	1,378	1,760
Short-term external debt	90	28	0	0	0	0	0	1
interest arrears on long-term	1	15	0	0	0	0	0	1
Use of IMF credit	57	41	291	135	148	169	178	177
Long-term external debt								
Debt outstanding and disbursed	**1,056**	**1,278**	**1,158**	**822**	**623**	**986**	**1,378**	**1,760**
Public and publicly guaranteed	1,056	1,278	1,158	822	623	986	1,378	1,758
Official creditors	1,056	1,278	1,158	822	623	986	1,378	1,758
Private creditors	0	0	0	0	0	0	0	0
of which: Bonds	0	0	0	0	0	0	0	0
Private nonguaranteed	..	..	..	..	..	..	..	2
of which: Bonds	..	..	..	..	..	..	..	..
Disbursements	**51**	**77**	**212**	**288**	**357**	**360**	**398**	**410**
Public and publicly guaranteed	51	77	212	288	357	360	398	408
Official creditors	51	77	212	288	357	360	398	408
Private creditors	0	0	0	0	0	0	0	0
of which: Bonds	0	0	0	0	0	0	0	0
Private nonguaranteed	..	..	..	..	..	..	..	2
of which: Bonds	..	..	..	..	..	..	..	..
Principal repayments	**19**	**34**	**26**	**122**	**2**	**0**	**6**	**20**
Public and publicly guaranteed	19	34	26	122	2	0	6	20
Official creditors	19	34	26	122	2	0	6	20
Private creditors	0	0	0	0	0	0	0	0
of which: Bonds	0	0	0	0	0	0	0	0
Private nonguaranteed	..	..	..	..	..	..	..	..
of which: Bonds	..	..	..	..	..	..	..	..
Interest payments	**15**	**17**	**15**	**8**	**3**	**3**	**4**	**5**
Public and publicly guaranteed	15	17	15	8	3	3	4	5
Official creditors	15	17	15	8	3	3	4	5
Private creditors	0	0	0	0	0	0	0	0
of which: Bonds	0	0	0	0	0	0	0	0
Private nonguaranteed	..	..	..	..	..	..	..	0
of which: Bonds	..	..	..	..	..	..	..	..
Net financial flows								
Net debt inflows	20	21	243	290	368	382	402	396
Official creditors (incl. IMF)	26	55	243	290	368	382	402	394
Private creditors	-6	-34	..	..	..	..	..	2
Long-term	..	..	..	..	..	..	..	2
Public and publicly guaranteed	..	..	..	..	..	..	..	..
Private nonguaranteed	..	..	..	..	..	..	..	2
Short-term	-6	-34	..	..	..	..	..	..
Net equity inflows								
Foreign direct investment	13	26	55	178	119	156	186	99
Portfolio equity	..	..	..	..	..	..	..	..
Major economic aggregates								
Gross national income (GNI)	..	4,387	6,597	6,645	7,555	7,945	8,485	8,725
Exports of goods, services & prim. income	504	605	1,065	1,049	1,356	1,400	1,608	..
Imports of goods, services & prim. income	1,378	1,888	2,823	4,298	4,437	4,199	4,435	..
Primary income on FDI	..	..	..	..	..	..	..	..
Personal transfers & comp. of employees	578	986	1,376	1,474	1,551	1,612	1,781	1,954
International reserves	182	218	1,052	1,891	1,880	2,164	2,448	1,916
Ratios								
External debt stocks to exports (%)	238.9	222.6	136.0	91.2	56.8	82.5	96.8	..
External debt stocks to GNI (%)	..	30.7	22.0	14.4	10.2	14.5	18.3	22.2
Debt service to exports (%)	9.2	9.5	4.2	12.5	0.4	0.3	0.7	..
Reserves to external debt stocks (%)	15.1	16.2	72.6	197.7	243.9	187.2	157.3	98.9

Notes:

Short-term debt before 2007 is based on data from the BIS. Data include the effects of Paris Club restructuring agreements signed in 2006 and 2009 and HIPC and MDRI debt relief.

HONDURAS

(US$ million, unless otherwise indicated)

	2000	2005	2009	2010	2011	2012	2013	2014
Summary external debt data								
External debt stocks	**5,474**	**5,135**	**3,806**	**3,977**	**4,388**	**5,055**	**6,831**	**7,331**
Long-term external debt	4,860	4,620	3,330	3,382	3,905	4,444	6,116	6,639
Short-term external debt	373	320	249	374	267	402	512	507
interest arrears on long-term	35	11	10	11	6	6	4	3
Use of IMF credit	241	195	226	220	215	209	203	185
Long-term external debt								
Debt outstanding and disbursed	**4,860**	**4,620**	**3,330**	**3,382**	**3,905**	**4,444**	**6,116**	**6,639**
Public and publicly guaranteed	4,300	4,111	2,451	2,803	3,186	3,646	5,170	5,527
Official creditors	4,198	4,073	2,364	2,719	3,106	3,544	3,983	4,232
Private creditors	102	38	87	84	81	102	1,187	1,295
of which: Bonds	0	0	50	50	50	50	1,051	1,051
Private nonguaranteed	560	509	880	579	719	798	946	1,112
of which: Bonds	..	..	..	..	..	..	..	..
Disbursements	**347**	**481**	**703**	**904**	**1,554**	**1,348**	**2,444**	**899**
Public and publicly guaranteed	163	302	246	452	558	513	1,602	581
Official creditors	159	297	196	452	558	493	521	455
Private creditors	4	4	50	0	0	20	1,082	125
of which: Bonds	0	0	50	0	0	0	1,001	0
Private nonguaranteed	184	179	457	452	996	835	841	318
of which: Bonds	..	..	..	..	..	..	..	..
Principal repayments	**259**	**265**	**341**	**452**	**922**	**824**	**783**	**492**
Public and publicly guaranteed	93	139	107	62	65	58	82	111
Official creditors	91	138	106	61	63	58	81	108
Private creditors	1	1	1	1	2	0	0	2
of which: Bonds	0	0	0	0	0	0	0	0
Private nonguaranteed	166	126	234	390	856	766	701	381
of which: Bonds	..	..	..	..	..	..	..	..
Interest payments	**108**	**83**	**68**	**56**	**77**	**89**	**130**	**198**
Public and publicly guaranteed	77	64	41	46	59	70	111	178
Official creditors	76	63	41	46	58	70	81	92
Private creditors	0	0	0	0	0	0	30	86
of which: Bonds	0	0	0	0	0	0	29	82
Private nonguaranteed	31	20	27	10	19	19	19	20
of which: Bonds	..	..	..	..	..	..	..	..
Net financial flows								
Net debt inflows	42	155	139	575	526	652	1,768	396
Official creditors (incl. IMF)	84	159	90	389	490	428	433	341
Private creditors	-42	-4	49	185	36	223	1,335	55
Long-term	20	57	272	62	138	89	1,222	60
Public and publicly guaranteed	3	4	49	-1	-2	20	1,081	123
Private nonguaranteed	18	54	223	62	140	69	141	-63
Short-term	-63	-61	-223	124	-102	134	113	-5
Net equity inflows								
Foreign direct investment	382	537	443	469	958	1,006	820	1,144
Portfolio equity	..	..	..	..	..	..	..	..
Major economic aggregates								
Gross national income (GNI)	6,885	9,219	14,299	15,110	16,769	17,247	17,134	18,062
Exports of goods, services & prim. income	4,001	3,817	4,318	4,993	6,290	6,747	6,433	..
Imports of goods, services & prim. income	5,047	6,016	7,514	8,557	10,836	11,568	11,431	..
Primary income on FDI	160	479	602	681	910	1,220	1,169	..
Personal transfers & comp. of employees	484	1,805	2,477	2,618	2,811	2,920	3,136	3,353
International reserves	1,313	2,327	2,086	2,671	2,750	2,495	2,982	3,432
Ratios								
External debt stocks to exports (%)	136.8	134.6	88.1	79.6	69.8	74.9	106.2	..
External debt stocks to GNI (%)	79.5	55.7	26.6	26.3	26.2	29.3	39.9	40.6
Debt service to exports (%)	9.9	10.0	9.6	10.3	16.0	13.7	14.4	..
Reserves to external debt stocks (%)	24.0	45.3	54.8	67.2	62.7	49.4	43.7	46.8

Notes:

Data include the effects of HIPC and MDRI debt relief.

INDIA

(US$ million, unless otherwise indicated)

	2000	2005	2009	2010	2011	2012	2013	2014
Summary external debt data								
External debt stocks	**101,130**	**121,195**	**256,312**	**291,651**	**336,845**	**395,071**	**429,742**	**463,230**
Long-term external debt	96,781	111,406	203,473	229,076	252,686	295,608	330,910	371,892
Short-term external debt	3,462	8,816	46,603	56,448	78,052	93,349	92,706	85,574
interest arrears on long-term	0	0	0	0	0	0	0	0
Use of IMF credit	888	974	6,237	6,127	6,108	6,114	6,127	5,764
Long-term external debt								
Debt outstanding and disbursed	**96,781**	**111,406**	**203,473**	**229,076**	**252,686**	**295,608**	**330,910**	**371,892**
Public and publicly guaranteed	81,195	54,726	85,293	101,786	110,372	135,652	135,826	164,122
Official creditors	51,729	50,058	65,971	73,956	78,355	80,984	80,764	75,444
Private creditors	29,466	4,668	19,322	27,830	32,017	54,668	55,062	88,678
of which: Bonds	10,240	1,360	9,521	14,700	16,517	24,007	21,910	50,811
Private nonguaranteed	15,586	56,680	118,180	127,290	142,314	159,956	195,084	207,770
of which: Bonds	1,515	5,761	15,326	13,217	10,861	7,848	8,286	6,731
Disbursements	**10,556**	**19,380**	**26,646**	**44,629**	**44,073**	**49,929**	**70,314**	**130,057**
Public and publicly guaranteed	10,256	6,630	10,396	25,560	14,865	17,269	14,108	47,051
Official creditors	3,270	3,824	5,971	9,780	7,924	5,170	6,673	6,205
Private creditors	6,986	2,805	4,425	15,781	6,941	12,099	7,435	40,846
of which: Bonds	5,520	1,714	1,765	11,050	2,032	7,478	2,045	29,116
Private nonguaranteed	300	12,751	16,250	19,069	29,207	32,661	56,206	83,006
of which: Bonds	..	2,920	2,473	1,288	737	665	1,224	819
Principal repayments	**6,425**	**19,384**	**10,990**	**19,018**	**22,227**	**21,202**	**28,931**	**80,937**
Public and publicly guaranteed	6,176	12,470	5,336	5,164	6,823	6,183	10,756	14,398
Official creditors	3,217	2,701	2,923	3,159	3,907	3,695	4,004	7,437
Private creditors	2,959	9,769	2,413	2,005	2,915	2,488	6,752	6,961
of which: Bonds	0	8,457	588	148	200	0	4,153	150
Private nonguaranteed	249	6,914	5,654	13,854	15,405	15,019	18,176	66,538
of which: Bonds	35	117	1,679	1,851	2,847	3,678	833	2,347
Interest payments	**3,993**	**4,196**	**4,942**	**4,675**	**6,258**	**8,136**	**8,741**	**11,078**
Public and publicly guaranteed	3,363	3,022	1,322	1,063	1,262	1,758	1,558	1,948
Official creditors	1,422	1,062	1,012	798	926	1,265	916	867
Private creditors	1,941	1,960	310	265	335	493	642	1,081
of which: Bonds	143	1,799	60	39	51	121	158	256
Private nonguaranteed	630	1,174	3,620	3,612	4,996	6,378	7,183	9,131
of which: Bonds	224	141	290	421	848	516	518	375
Net financial flows								
Net debt inflows	3,635	1,949	18,437	35,457	43,449	44,025	40,739	41,989
Official creditors (incl. IMF)	28	1,124	3,048	6,621	4,016	1,474	2,670	-1,232
Private creditors	3,607	825	15,389	28,836	39,433	42,550	38,070	43,221
Long-term	4,078	-1,127	12,607	18,991	17,829	27,253	38,713	50,353
Public and publicly guaranteed	4,026	-6,964	2,011	13,776	4,026	9,611	683	33,885
Private nonguaranteed	51	5,837	10,596	5,215	13,803	17,642	38,030	16,468
Short-term	-471	1,952	2,782	9,845	21,604	15,297	-643	-7,132
Net equity inflows								
Foreign direct investment	3,584	7,269	34,111	27,357	34,643	23,172	26,713	31,602
Portfolio equity	2,481	12,151	24,689	30,442	-4,048	22,809	19,892	12,369
Major economic aggregates								
Gross national income (GNI)	471,633	828,316	1,357,362	1,690,504	1,819,846	1,810,369	1,838,845	2,041,568
Exports of goods, services & prim. income	62,453	160,228	274,580	357,996	456,523	453,744	478,989	497,403
Imports of goods, services & prim. income	80,489	194,154	349,529	464,622	579,253	610,650	593,029	594,295
Primary income on FDI	..	5,244	12,279	21,763	23,760	16,389	12,555	17,767
Personal transfers & comp. of employees	12,883	22,125	49,204	53,480	62,499	68,821	69,970	70,389
International reserves	37,902	131,924	265,182	275,277	271,285	270,587	276,493	303,455
Ratios								
External debt stocks to exports (%)	161.9	75.6	93.3	81.5	73.8	87.1	89.7	93.1
External debt stocks to GNI (%)	21.4	14.6	18.9	17.3	18.5	21.8	23.4	22.7
Debt service to exports (%)	17.1	14.9	6.0	6.8	6.4	6.8	8.1	18.6
Reserves to external debt stocks (%)	37.5	108.9	103.5	94.4	80.5	68.5	64.3	65.5

Notes:

External debt data prior to 2003 are revised from fiscal year to calendar year. Long-term public and publicly guaranteed bonds include Foreign Institutional Investor debt (FII) as reported by the Reserve Bank of India.

INDONESIA

(US$ million, unless otherwise indicated)

	2000	2005	2009	2010	2011	2012	2013	2014
Summary external debt data								
External debt stocks	**143,655**	**141,820**	**179,395**	**198,268**	**219,619**	**252,555**	**266,134**	**293,397**
Long-term external debt	110,818	122,649	152,240	162,171	178,405	205,258	216,974	243,948
Short-term external debt	21,688	11,023	24,050	33,047	38,173	44,253	46,110	46,580
interest arrears on long-term	4,632	0	0	0	0	0	0	0
Use of IMF credit	11,149	8,148	3,105	3,050	3,041	3,044	3,050	2,869
Long-term external debt								
Debt outstanding and disbursed	**110,818**	**122,649**	**152,240**	**162,171**	**178,405**	**205,258**	**216,974**	**243,948**
Public and publicly guaranteed	69,649	77,405	97,447	103,388	108,786	128,044	129,249	143,068
Official creditors	54,883	59,945	63,259	66,487	66,502	61,518	55,741	50,722
Private creditors	14,766	17,460	34,188	36,901	42,283	66,526	73,508	92,346
of which: Bonds	971	7,192	25,833	29,348	35,501	60,551	67,720	83,838
Private nonguaranteed	41,169	45,244	54,793	58,783	69,620	77,214	87,725	100,880
of which: Bonds	6,337	7,858	7,856	7,787	14,112	9,337	11,121	12,556
Disbursements	**5,651**	**13,881**	**31,425**	**34,335**	**39,430**	**55,702**	**50,567**	**66,221**
Public and publicly guaranteed	3,301	5,015	12,729	14,345	9,820	18,942	13,330	21,284
Official creditors	3,038	2,581	6,142	6,587	3,782	3,202	3,883	3,183
Private creditors	263	2,434	6,587	7,758	6,038	15,740	9,447	18,101
of which: Bonds	0	2,095	3,893	5,640	5,775	15,536	8,647	14,219
Private nonguaranteed	2,350	8,866	18,695	19,990	29,609	36,761	37,237	44,938
of which: Bonds	350	194	1,808	195	295	1,470	2,590	1,170
Principal repayments	**9,268**	**15,746**	**20,432**	**23,975**	**25,165**	**29,527**	**32,166**	**37,582**
Public and publicly guaranteed	3,868	6,232	7,063	5,846	6,132	6,430	6,088	8,641
Official creditors	1,586	3,539	6,134	5,214	5,156	5,152	5,049	5,014
Private creditors	2,282	2,692	929	632	976	1,278	1,039	3,627
of which: Bonds	0	310	0	0	0	230	0	2,745
Private nonguaranteed	5,400	9,515	13,368	18,129	19,032	23,097	26,077	28,941
of which: Bonds	2,400	267	588	411	1,771	1,560	510	715
Interest payments	**5,673**	**2,933**	**4,301**	**4,944**	**5,532**	**5,951**	**7,967**	**8,140**
Public and publicly guaranteed	3,738	1,921	2,802	3,034	3,484	3,475	3,966	4,373
Official creditors	2,575	1,189	1,693	1,586	1,507	1,376	1,170	1,304
Private creditors	1,163	732	1,109	1,448	1,977	2,098	2,796	3,069
of which: Bonds	72	136	837	1,225	1,655	1,811	2,549	2,830
Private nonguaranteed	1,935	1,012	1,499	1,910	2,048	2,477	4,001	3,766
of which: Bonds	735	113	31	81	1,145	1,104	1,083	1,185
Net financial flows								
Net debt inflows	-1,967	-6,611	14,554	19,358	19,391	32,255	20,258	29,109
Official creditors (incl. IMF)	2,575	-2,103	8	1,373	-1,374	-1,950	-1,166	-1,831
Private creditors	-4,542	-4,508	14,546	17,985	20,765	34,205	21,424	30,940
Long-term	-5,069	-906	10,985	8,987	15,639	28,125	19,567	30,470
Public and publicly guaranteed	-2,019	-258	5,658	7,127	5,062	14,462	8,407	14,474
Private nonguaranteed	-3,050	-649	5,327	1,861	10,577	13,663	11,160	15,996
Short-term	527	-3,602	3,561	8,998	5,126	6,080	1,857	470
Net equity inflows								
Foreign direct investment	-4,550	7,812	4,982	12,447	16,278	18,615	20,004	22,108
Portfolio equity	-1,021	-165	787	2,132	-326	1,698	-1,856	3,259
Major economic aggregates								
Gross national income (GNI)	150,317	271,958	520,695	734,396	866,422	891,242	883,425	860,716
Exports of goods, services & prim. income	73,079	97,017	127,243	168,570	215,578	213,656	207,635	200,953
Imports of goods, services & prim. income	66,903	101,533	121,192	168,056	218,103	242,169	240,923	233,658
Primary income on FDI	3,574	9,525	8,848	12,844	17,975	18,166	17,395	19,422
Personal transfers & comp. of employees	1,190	5,420	6,793	6,916	6,924	7,212	7,614	8,551
International reserves	28,502	33,140	63,563	92,908	106,539	108,837	96,364	108,836
Ratios								
External debt stocks to exports (%)	196.6	146.2	141.0	117.6	101.9	118.2	128.2	146.0
External debt stocks to GNI (%)	95.6	52.1	34.5	27.0	25.3	28.3	30.1	34.1
Debt service to exports (%)	22.8	20.9	19.6	17.4	14.4	16.8	19.6	23.1
Reserves to external debt stocks (%)	19.8	23.4	35.4	46.9	48.5	43.1	36.2	37.1

IRAN, ISLAMIC REPUBLIC OF

(US$ million, unless otherwise indicated)

	2000	2005	2009	2010	2011	2012	2013	2014
Summary external debt data								
External debt stocks	**8,024**	**21,543**	**18,247**	**20,030**	**17,344**	**7,406**	**7,006**	**5,495**
Long-term external debt	4,709	10,506	7,295	6,156	4,815	4,271	4,025	3,042
Short-term external debt	3,008	10,686	8,787	11,613	10,320	943	777	486
interest arrears on long-term	0	0	0	0	0	0	0	0
Use of IMF credit	308	352	2,165	2,261	2,209	2,192	2,204	1,967
Long-term external debt								
Debt outstanding and disbursed	**4,709**	**10,506**	**7,295**	**6,156**	**4,815**	**4,271**	**4,025**	**3,042**
Public and publicly guaranteed	4,709	10,506	7,295	6,156	4,815	4,271	4,025	3,042
Official creditors	1,664	2,045	2,266	2,024	1,640	1,456	1,176	918
Private creditors	3,045	8,461	5,029	4,132	3,174	2,815	2,849	2,125
of which: Bonds	0	0	0	0	0	0	0	0
Private nonguaranteed	..	..	..	..	..	..	..	..
of which: Bonds	..	..	..	..	..	..	..	..
Disbursements	**1,469**	**2,740**	**400**	**252**	**216**	**18**	**22**	**0**
Public and publicly guaranteed	1,469	2,740	400	252	216	18	22	0
Official creditors	477	673	223	105	31	15	18	0
Private creditors	993	2,068	177	147	185	3	4	0
of which: Bonds	0	0	0	0	0	0	0	0
Private nonguaranteed	..	..	..	..	..	..	..	..
of which: Bonds	..	..	..	..	..	..	..	..
Principal repayments	**2,345**	**1,734**	**2,046**	**1,575**	**1,389**	**446**	**396**	**468**
Public and publicly guaranteed	2,345	1,734	2,046	1,575	1,389	446	396	468
Official creditors	1,785	329	379	321	420	183	263	225
Private creditors	561	1,405	1,667	1,255	970	263	133	243
of which: Bonds	0	0	0	0	0	0	0	0
Private nonguaranteed	..	..	..	..	..	..	..	..
of which: Bonds	..	..	..	..	..	..	..	..
Interest payments	**391**	**418**	**274**	**139**	**110**	**35**	**33**	**33**
Public and publicly guaranteed	391	418	274	139	110	35	33	33
Official creditors	190	103	73	53	46	17	24	26
Private creditors	202	316	201	86	64	19	8	7
of which: Bonds	0	0	0	0	0	0	0	0
Private nonguaranteed	..	..	..	..	..	..	..	..
of which: Bonds	..	..	..	..	..	..	..	..
Net financial flows								
Net debt inflows	-1,485	1,440	542	1,502	-2,466	-9,805	-540	-759
Official creditors (incl. IMF)	-1,308	344	-156	-216	-389	-168	-245	-225
Private creditors	-177	1,096	698	1,718	-2,077	-9,637	-295	-534
Long-term	432	663	-1,490	-1,108	-784	-260	-129	-243
Public and publicly guaranteed	432	663	-1,490	-1,108	-784	-260	-129	-243
Private nonguaranteed	..	..	..	..	..	..	..	..
Short-term	-609	433	2,188	2,826	-1,293	-9,377	-166	-291
Net equity inflows								
Foreign direct investment	39	2,889	2,983	3,649	4,277	4,662	3,050	2,105
Portfolio equity	..	..	..	..	..	..	..	..
Major economic aggregates								
Gross national income (GNI)	101,335	188,503	328,593	..	..	558,362	494,166	..
Exports of goods, services & prim. income	30,131	50,757	112,334	98,191	123,593	155,666	107,189	101,962
Imports of goods, services & prim. income	18,107	50,115	89,859	88,815	96,224	96,707	81,468	74,578
Primary income on FDI	..	..	..	..	..	..	..	..
Personal transfers & comp. of employees	536	1,032	1,072	1,181	1,330	1,330	1,330	1,382
International reserves	..	..	..	..	..	..	..	..
Ratios								
External debt stocks to exports (%)	26.6	42.4	16.2	20.4	14.0	4.8	6.5	5.4
External debt stocks to GNI (%)	7.9	11.4	5.6	..	..	1.3	1.4	..
Debt service to exports (%)	9.7	5.5	2.2	1.9	1.3	0.4	0.4	0.5
Reserves to external debt stocks (%)	..	..	..	..	..	..	..	..

Notes:

Fiscal year-end for external debt data is March. Short-term debt is based on Central Bank data.

JAMAICA

(US$ million, unless otherwise indicated)

	2000	2005	2009	2010	2011	2012	2013	2014
Summary external debt data								
External debt stocks	**4,716**	**6,466**	**11,026**	**14,085**	**14,250**	**14,223**	**12,923**	**14,046**
Long-term external debt	3,818	5,848	9,917	11,876	12,086	11,276	10,241	11,528
Short-term external debt	785	559	699	1,021	931	1,712	1,443	1,472
interest arrears on long-term	142	167	174	146	140	73	44	50
Use of IMF credit	113	58	410	1,188	1,234	1,235	1,239	1,046
Long-term external debt								
Debt outstanding and disbursed	**3,818**	**5,848**	**9,917**	**11,876**	**12,086**	**11,276**	**10,241**	**11,528**
Public and publicly guaranteed	3,715	5,458	6,676	7,569	7,743	7,366	7,421	7,957
Official creditors	2,396	2,078	2,387	3,243	3,201	3,164	3,318	3,397
Private creditors	1,320	3,380	4,289	4,326	4,541	4,202	4,103	4,559
of which: Bonds	1,004	3,043	3,890	3,786	4,027	3,724	3,686	4,181
Private nonguaranteed	103	390	3,241	4,307	4,343	3,910	2,820	3,571
of which: Bonds	..	300	3,215	4,290	4,290	3,840	2,750	2,750
Disbursements	**899**	**1,350**	**1,542**	**2,360**	**1,208**	**2,033**	**1,402**	**1,898**
Public and publicly guaranteed	899	1,043	457	1,285	1,170	265	401	1,145
Official creditors	306	91	353	1,075	418	225	375	293
Private creditors	593	953	103	210	753	39	26	852
of which: Bonds	553	875	0	0	694	0	0	800
Private nonguaranteed	..	307	1,085	1,075	37	1,768	1,001	752
of which: Bonds	..	300	1,085	1,075	..	1,750	1,000	..
Principal repayments	**420**	**540**	**727**	**339**	**713**	**1,077**	**347**	**497**
Public and publicly guaranteed	356	531	718	331	712	626	345	495
Official creditors	270	221	253	207	194	244	224	182
Private creditors	87	310	466	124	517	383	122	313
of which: Bonds	13	256	345	68	438	302	48	243
Private nonguaranteed	64	9	9	9	2	451	1	1
of which: Bonds	55	..	..	..	..	450	..	..
Interest payments	**205**	**386**	**746**	**828**	**899**	**687**	**561**	**611**
Public and publicly guaranteed	192	360	521	488	491	458	415	404
Official creditors	117	83	96	100	108	66	68	67
Private creditors	75	277	426	388	383	393	347	338
of which: Bonds	50	265	404	375	368	379	333	325
Private nonguaranteed	13	26	225	341	408	228	146	206
of which: Bonds	2	21	224	340	406	226	141	201
Net financial flows								
Net debt inflows	439	331	344	3,149	461	1,804	818	1,297
Official creditors (incl. IMF)	17	-131	101	1,647	274	-18	153	-15
Private creditors	421	462	243	1,502	187	1,822	664	1,313
Long-term	443	941	714	1,152	271	974	904	1,290
Public and publicly guaranteed	506	642	-362	86	235	-343	-96	539
Private nonguaranteed	-64	298	1,076	1,066	36	1,317	1,000	751
Short-term	-21	-479	-471	350	-84	848	-240	23
Net equity inflows								
Foreign direct investment	468	660	410	183	199	413	593	551
Portfolio equity	..	..	..	..	..	122	5	140
Major economic aggregates								
Gross national income (GNI)	8,662	10,561	11,457	12,736	13,896	14,360	13,708	..
Exports of goods, services & prim. income	3,782	4,322	4,273	4,248	4,508	4,906	4,644	4,677
Imports of goods, services & prim. income	4,970	6,972	7,259	7,192	8,567	8,396	8,178	8,081
Primary income on FDI	290	454	232	127	112	190	216	263
Personal transfers & comp. of employees	892	1,762	1,889	2,026	2,106	2,158	2,161	2,258
International reserves	1,054	2,170	2,076	2,501	2,282	1,996	1,818	2,473
Ratios								
External debt stocks to exports (%)	124.7	149.6	258.0	331.6	316.1	289.9	278.3	300.3
External debt stocks to GNI (%)	54.4	61.2	96.2	110.6	102.5	99.0	94.3	..
Debt service to exports (%)	18.5	22.2	34.7	27.9	36.3	36.6	25.9	33.0
Reserves to external debt stocks (%)	22.3	33.6	18.8	17.8	16.0	14.0	14.1	17.6

Notes:

Short-term debt is based on data from the BIS.

JORDAN

(US$ million, unless otherwise indicated)

	2000	2005	2009	2010	2011	2012	2013	2014
Summary external debt data								
External debt stocks	**11,063**	**12,904**	**14,427**	**17,073**	**17,669**	**18,484**	**23,173**	**24,256**
Long-term external debt	6,183	6,901	5,643	7,767	7,818	8,105	11,000	11,775
Short-term external debt	4,396	5,742	8,518	9,049	9,594	9,737	10,873	10,887
interest arrears on long-term	102	0	0	1	1	1	1	1
Use of IMF credit	484	260	266	257	257	642	1,300	1,593
Long-term external debt								
Debt outstanding and disbursed	**6,183**	**6,901**	**5,643**	**7,767**	**7,818**	**8,105**	**11,000**	**11,775**
Public and publicly guaranteed	6,183	6,878	5,445	6,502	6,317	6,302	8,855	9,688
Official creditors	5,243	6,483	5,137	5,452	5,291	5,308	5,494	5,352
Private creditors	940	395	308	1,050	1,026	994	3,361	4,335
of which: Bonds	583	145	145	881	866	852	3,237	4,223
Private nonguaranteed	..	24	198	1,265	1,501	1,803	2,145	2,087
of which: Bonds	..	..	..	..	..	..	..	..
Disbursements	**176**	**434**	**787**	**1,538**	**475**	**1,010**	**3,644**	**2,273**
Public and publicly guaranteed	176	434	762	1,388	325	711	3,308	1,979
Official creditors	176	269	756	626	325	711	908	979
Private creditors	0	165	6	762	0	0	2,400	1,000
of which: Bonds	0	145	0	750	0	0	2,400	1,000
Private nonguaranteed	..	..	25	150	150	299	336	294
of which: Bonds	..	..	..	..	..	..	..	..
Principal repayments	**308**	**366**	**425**	**513**	**599**	**615**	**606**	**910**
Public and publicly guaranteed	308	341	405	487	574	585	566	874
Official creditors	238	323	396	463	548	557	538	853
Private creditors	70	19	9	25	26	28	28	22
of which: Bonds	10	10	0	15	15	15	15	15
Private nonguaranteed	..	25	20	26	25	30	40	36
of which: Bonds	..	..	..	..	..	..	..	..
Interest payments	**239**	**161**	**155**	**162**	**191**	**190**	**206**	**287**
Public and publicly guaranteed	239	160	147	147	171	165	162	254
Official creditors	162	157	134	124	130	126	113	125
Private creditors	77	4	12	22	41	39	49	130
of which: Bonds	43	0	9	19	39	37	48	129
Private nonguaranteed	..	1	8	15	20	25	44	33
of which: Bonds	..	..	..	..	..	..	..	..
Net financial flows								
Net debt inflows	3,371	325	268	1,551	421	921	4,824	1,765
Official creditors (incl. IMF)	-73	-131	344	159	-223	537	1,020	515
Private creditors	3,445	456	-76	1,392	644	384	3,804	1,250
Long-term	-70	121	2	862	99	241	2,667	1,236
Public and publicly guaranteed	-70	146	-3	738	-26	-28	2,372	978
Private nonguaranteed	..	-25	5	124	125	269	296	258
Short-term	3,515	335	-78	530	545	143	1,136	14
Net equity inflows								
Foreign direct investment	913	1,984	2,413	1,651	1,474	1,497	1,747	1,760
Portfolio equity	-17	169	-30	-21	109	53	158	..
Major economic aggregates								
Gross national income (GNI)	8,558	12,925	24,326	26,218	28,576	30,549	33,255	35,410
Exports of goods, services & prim. income	4,207	7,426	12,022	13,639	14,454	14,997	15,062	16,387
Imports of goods, services & prim. income	6,363	12,314	17,044	19,343	22,276	24,053	25,088	26,093
Primary income on FDI	33	72	313	813	713	821	845	..
Personal transfers & comp. of employees	1,845	2,421	3,465	3,517	3,368	3,490	3,643	3,757
International reserves	3,331	5,250	11,689	13,057	11,467	8,090	13,224	15,299
Ratios								
External debt stocks to exports (%)	263.0	173.8	120.0	125.2	122.2	123.3	153.9	148.0
External debt stocks to GNI (%)	129.3	99.8	59.3	65.1	61.8	60.5	69.7	68.5
Debt service to exports (%)	20.1	11.9	6.0	5.8	6.6	6.5	6.6	8.5
Reserves to external debt stocks (%)	30.1	40.7	81.0	76.5	64.9	43.8	57.1	63.1

Notes:

Long-term private nonguaranteed debt data from 2001 are based on reports provided by the country. Short-term debt before 1999 is based on data from the BIS.

KAZAKHSTAN

(US$ million, unless otherwise indicated)

	2000	2005	2009	2010	2011	2012	2013	2014
Summary external debt data								
External debt stocks	**12,890**	**43,857**	**109,734**	**119,145**	**124,317**	**135,498**	**149,653**	**157,595**
Long-term external debt	11,481	35,263	102,210	109,751	115,033	125,883	139,627	147,111
Short-term external debt	961	8,102	6,985	8,864	8,756	9,086	9,497	9,986
interest arrears on long-term	0	0	0	0	0	0	0	67
Use of IMF credit	448	491	539	529	528	528	529	498
Long-term external debt								
Debt outstanding and disbursed	**11,481**	**35,263**	**102,210**	**109,751**	**115,033**	**125,883**	**139,627**	**147,111**
Public and publicly guaranteed	3,623	2,177	2,487	3,845	4,675	7,375	12,266	15,080
Official creditors	2,239	1,780	2,486	3,845	4,675	5,065	5,331	5,645
Private creditors	1,384	396	1	0	0	2,310	6,935	9,435
of which: Bonds	1,000	350	0	0	0	2,300	6,925	9,425
Private nonguaranteed	7,859	33,087	99,724	105,905	110,358	118,508	127,361	132,031
of which: Bonds	100	7,550	22,097	21,044	17,995	15,098	11,790	13,682
Disbursements	**3,063**	**17,207**	**30,471**	**45,054**	**32,740**	**31,396**	**45,774**	**39,152**
Public and publicly guaranteed	623	197	717	1,522	920	3,050	5,445	3,376
Official creditors	168	197	717	1,522	920	740	820	876
Private creditors	455	0	0	0	0	2,310	4,625	2,500
of which: Bonds	350	0	0	0	0	2,300	4,625	2,500
Private nonguaranteed	2,440	17,010	29,754	43,532	31,821	28,346	40,329	35,776
of which: Bonds	..	3,050	..	450	800	560	6,684	6,692
Principal repayments	**2,155**	**11,417**	**20,032**	**34,639**	**26,226**	**20,862**	**28,341**	**27,854**
Public and publicly guaranteed	216	1,090	131	278	134	254	409	459
Official creditors	133	1,018	130	278	134	254	409	459
Private creditors	83	72	2	1	0	0	0	0
of which: Bonds	0	0	0	0	0	0	0	0
Private nonguaranteed	1,939	10,327	19,901	34,360	26,092	20,607	27,932	27,395
of which: Bonds	..	..	2,108	1,503	3,789	3,457	4,210	3,092
Interest payments	**713**	**1,521**	**5,365**	**4,517**	**5,921**	**2,033**	**2,257**	**2,980**
Public and publicly guaranteed	235	146	58	54	61	75	147	405
Official creditors	124	102	58	54	61	75	68	57
Private creditors	112	44	0	0	0	0	79	348
of which: Bonds	90	39	0	0	0	0	78	347
Private nonguaranteed	478	1,376	5,307	4,463	5,860	1,957	2,110	2,575
of which: Bonds	11	543	1,706	1,525	1,343	1,115	655	1,115
Net financial flows								
Net debt inflows	1,061	9,950	7,937	12,295	6,406	10,865	17,844	11,720
Official creditors (incl. IMF)	-407	-820	587	1,244	786	486	411	417
Private creditors	1,469	10,770	7,350	11,050	5,620	10,379	17,432	11,303
Long-term	873	6,610	9,851	9,171	5,729	10,048	17,022	10,881
Public and publicly guaranteed	373	-72	-2	-1	..	2,310	4,625	2,500
Private nonguaranteed	501	6,683	9,853	9,172	5,729	7,738	12,397	8,381
Short-term	595	4,160	-2,502	1,879	-109	331	410	422
Net equity inflows								
Foreign direct investment	1,283	237	4,183	4,162	5,907	7,266	5,157	7,051
Portfolio equity	19	150	38	134	8	-418	65	..
Major economic aggregates								
Gross national income (GNI)	17,038	51,757	102,688	128,676	160,325	175,377	206,592	189,248
Exports of goods, services & prim. income	10,480	31,380	51,205	68,212	91,764	93,845	90,998	88,745
Imports of goods, services & prim. income	10,362	32,008	54,597	66,337	81,301	91,756	89,528	79,405
Primary income on FDI	1,046	4,805	10,961	17,997	25,213	24,740	22,722	..
Personal transfers & comp. of employees	122	62	198	226	180	171	207	209
International reserves	1,594	6,084	20,720	25,223	25,179	22,132	19,127	21,525
Ratios								
External debt stocks to exports (%)	123.0	139.8	214.3	174.7	135.5	144.4	164.5	177.6
External debt stocks to GNI (%)	75.7	84.7	106.9	92.6	77.5	77.3	72.4	83.3
Debt service to exports (%)	32.4	41.9	50.2	57.9	35.4	24.7	34.0	35.1
Reserves to external debt stocks (%)	12.4	13.9	18.9	21.2	20.3	16.3	12.8	13.7

KENYA

(US$ million, unless otherwise indicated)

	2000	2005	2009	2010	2011	2012	2013	2014
Summary external debt data								
External debt stocks	**6,189**	**6,496**	**8,600**	**8,812**	**10,492**	**11,759**	**13,655**	**16,179**
Long-term external debt	5,216	5,785	6,731	6,989	7,771	9,024	9,830	12,605
Short-term external debt	798	499	1,012	1,005	1,622	1,442	2,353	2,247
interest arrears on long-term	47	21	73	80	100	93	111	84
Use of IMF credit	175	212	858	817	1,100	1,293	1,471	1,328
Long-term external debt								
Debt outstanding and disbursed	**5,216**	**5,785**	**6,731**	**6,989**	**7,771**	**9,024**	**9,830**	**12,605**
Public and publicly guaranteed	5,041	5,785	6,731	6,989	7,771	9,024	9,830	12,605
Official creditors	4,559	5,421	6,379	6,679	7,451	8,086	8,885	10,301
Private creditors	482	363	352	311	320	938	946	2,303
of which: Bonds	0	0	0	0	0	0	0	2,000
Private nonguaranteed	175	..	..	..	..	..	..	..
of which: Bonds	..	..	..	..	..	..	..	..
Disbursements	**333**	**169**	**538**	**530**	**1,073**	**1,682**	**1,235**	**4,397**
Public and publicly guaranteed	333	169	538	530	1,073	1,682	1,235	4,397
Official creditors	248	140	510	519	1,050	1,005	1,221	2,391
Private creditors	85	28	27	12	23	677	14	2,006
of which: Bonds	0	0	0	0	0	0	0	2,000
Private nonguaranteed	..	..	..	..	..	..	..	..
of which: Bonds	..	..	..	..	..	..	..	..
Principal repayments	**407**	**439**	**259**	**260**	**290**	**357**	**338**	**952**
Public and publicly guaranteed	362	429	259	260	290	357	338	952
Official creditors	241	356	256	256	283	347	321	333
Private creditors	121	74	3	4	7	10	17	619
of which: Bonds	0	0	0	0	0	0	0	0
Private nonguaranteed	45	10	..	..	..	..	..	..
of which: Bonds	..	..	..	..	..	..	..	..
Interest payments	**100**	**73**	**85**	**90**	**93**	**171**	**225**	**197**
Public and publicly guaranteed	81	73	85	90	93	171	225	197
Official creditors	55	67	84	90	92	144	189	169
Private creditors	27	6	1	1	1	26	36	29
of which: Bonds	0	0	0	0	0	0	0	0
Private nonguaranteed	19	0	..	..	..	..	..	..
of which: Bonds	..	..	..	..	..	..	..	..
Net financial flows								
Net debt inflows	-31	-458	565	231	1,674	1,343	1,963	3,308
Official creditors (incl. IMF)	9	-149	446	237	1,060	848	1,074	2,000
Private creditors	-40	-310	119	-6	614	495	889	1,308
Long-term	-81	-56	24	8	17	668	-4	1,387
Public and publicly guaranteed	-36	-46	24	8	17	668	-4	1,387
Private nonguaranteed	-45	-10	..	..	..	..	..	..
Short-term	41	-254	95	-14	597	-173	893	-79
Net equity inflows								
Foreign direct investment	111	6	32	89	40	49	71	467
Portfolio equity	-6	3	3	22	20	26	260	954
Major economic aggregates								
Gross national income (GNI)	12,576	18,732	36,977	39,852	41,960	50,263	54,622	60,611
Exports of goods, services & prim. income	2,821	5,416	7,567	9,127	10,130	11,205	10,951	11,290
Imports of goods, services & prim. income	3,941	6,921	11,514	13,823	16,631	18,270	18,959	21,407
Primary income on FDI	29	35	60	60	105	111	124	214
Personal transfers & comp. of employees	538	425	631	686	934	1,211	1,304	1,441
International reserves	898	1,799	3,849	4,320	4,264	5,711	6,598	7,911
Ratios								
External debt stocks to exports (%)	219.4	119.9	113.7	96.5	103.6	104.9	124.7	143.3
External debt stocks to GNI (%)	49.2	34.7	23.3	22.1	25.0	23.4	25.0	26.7
Debt service to exports (%)	21.0	10.0	5.1	4.4	4.3	5.3	5.9	11.0
Reserves to external debt stocks (%)	14.5	27.7	44.8	49.0	40.6	48.6	48.3	48.9

Notes:

Short-term debt is based on data from the BIS.

KOSOVO

(US$ million, unless otherwise indicated)

	2000	2005	2009	2010	2011	2012	2013	2014
Summary external debt data								
External debt stocks	..	..	**1,726**	**1,456**	**1,700**	**2,002**	**2,221**	**2,242**
Long-term external debt	..	..	818	886	1,130	1,116	1,315	1,258
Short-term external debt	..	..	821	455	456	652	675	780
interest arrears on long-term	..	..	0	0	0	0	0	0
Use of IMF credit	..	..	87	114	114	234	231	204
Long-term external debt								
Debt outstanding and disbursed	..	..	**818**	**886**	**1,130**	**1,116**	**1,315**	**1,258**
Public and publicly guaranteed	..	..	359	319	299	295	300	273
Official creditors	..	..	359	319	299	295	300	271
Private creditors	..	..	0	0	0	0	0	2
of which: Bonds	..	..	0	0	0	0	0	0
Private nonguaranteed	..	..	459	567	830	822	1,015	985
of which: Bonds	..	..	..	..	..	..	..	..
Disbursements	..	..	**90**	**169**	**158**	**109**	**145**	**76**
Public and publicly guaranteed	..	..	0	0	7	5	8	22
Official creditors	..	..	0	0	7	5	8	19
Private creditors	..	..	0	0	0	0	0	3
of which: Bonds	..	..	0	0	0	0	0	0
Private nonguaranteed	..	..	90	169	152	105	136	54
of which: Bonds	..	..	..	..	..	..	..	..
Principal repayments	..	..	**269**	**76**	**85**	**94**	**101**	**93**
Public and publicly guaranteed	..	..	208	14	17	15	15	15
Official creditors	..	..	208	14	17	15	15	15
Private creditors	..	..	0	0	0	0	0	0
of which: Bonds	..	..	0	0	0	0	0	0
Private nonguaranteed	..	..	61	61	68	79	86	78
of which: Bonds	..	..	..	..	..	..	..	..
Interest payments	..	..	**44**	**34**	**38**	**33**	**42**	**44**
Public and publicly guaranteed	..	..	23	11	12	11	12	12
Official creditors	..	..	23	11	12	11	12	12
Private creditors	..	..	0	0	0	0	0	0
of which: Bonds	..	..	0	0	0	0	0	0
Private nonguaranteed	..	..	22	23	26	22	29	32
of which: Bonds	..	..	..	..	..	..	..	..
Net financial flows								
Net debt inflows	..	..	448	-244	75	331	63	74
Official creditors (incl. IMF)	..	..	-208	14	-10	109	-10	-10
Private creditors	..	..	656	-258	85	221	74	83
Long-term	..	..	29	108	84	25	51	-22
Public and publicly guaranteed	..	..	..	..	..	..	..	3
Private nonguaranteed	..	..	29	108	84	25	51	-24
Short-term	..	..	627	-366	1	196	23	105
Net equity inflows								
Foreign direct investment	..	..	376	439	478	260	223	154
Portfolio equity	..	..	..	..	..	1	-1	..
Major economic aggregates								
Gross national income (GNI)	..	..	5,740	5,919	6,854	6,698	7,235	7,415
Exports of goods, services & prim. income	..	..	1,170	1,333	1,670	1,477	1,520	1,731
Imports of goods, services & prim. income	..	..	3,101	3,377	4,018	3,495	3,596	3,861
Primary income on FDI	..	..	102	130	148	65	97	98
Personal transfers & comp. of employees	..	..	1,055	997	1,122	1,059	1,122	1,192
International reserves	..	..	830	846	742	1,108	1,103	906
Ratios								
External debt stocks to exports (%)	..	..	147.5	109.2	101.8	135.6	146.1	129.5
External debt stocks to GNI (%)	..	..	30.1	24.6	24.8	29.9	30.7	30.2
Debt service to exports (%)	..	..	26.8	8.3	7.4	8.6	9.7	8.8
Reserves to external debt stocks (%)	..	..	48.1	58.2	43.6	55.3	49.7	40.4

KYRGYZ REPUBLIC

(US$ million, unless otherwise indicated)

	2000	2005	2009	2010	2011	2012	2013	2014
Summary external debt data								
External debt stocks	**1,938**	**2,257**	**4,119**	**4,114**	**5,486**	**6,026**	**6,804**	**7,257**
Long-term external debt	1,510	1,825	3,395	3,612	4,986	5,492	6,163	6,636
Short-term external debt	129	132	424	195	188	214	308	313
interest arrears on long-term	10	3	2	12	3	4	1	1
Use of IMF credit	298	299	300	307	312	321	333	308
Long-term external debt								
Debt outstanding and disbursed	**1,510**	**1,825**	**3,395**	**3,612**	**4,986**	**5,492**	**6,163**	**6,636**
Public and publicly guaranteed	1,220	1,665	2,320	2,442	2,618	2,840	2,945	3,222
Official creditors	1,184	1,665	2,320	2,442	2,618	2,840	2,945	3,222
Private creditors	37	0	0	0	0	0	0	0
of which: Bonds	0	0	0	0	0	0	0	0
Private nonguaranteed	290	161	1,076	1,171	2,368	2,652	3,218	3,414
of which: Bonds	..	..	..	..	..	..	..	..
Disbursements	**161**	**132**	**635**	**668**	**746**	**853**	**916**	**927**
Public and publicly guaranteed	153	76	378	147	211	344	386	479
Official creditors	149	76	378	147	211	344	386	479
Private creditors	4	0	0	0	0	0	0	0
of which: Bonds	0	0	0	0	0	0	0	0
Private nonguaranteed	8	56	257	521	535	510	530	449
of which: Bonds	..	..	..	..	..	..	..	..
Principal repayments	**86**	**73**	**200**	**462**	**314**	**266**	**305**	**309**
Public and publicly guaranteed	17	16	38	38	44	41	44	57
Official creditors	13	16	38	38	44	41	44	57
Private creditors	4	0	0	0	0	0	0	0
of which: Bonds	0	0	0	0	0	0	0	0
Private nonguaranteed	69	57	162	424	270	226	261	252
of which: Bonds	..	..	..	..	..	..	..	..
Interest payments	**69**	**21**	**37**	**69**	**70**	**58**	**63**	**69**
Public and publicly guaranteed	23	12	19	23	40	32	34	41
Official creditors	20	12	19	23	40	32	34	41
Private creditors	2	0	0	0	0	0	0	0
of which: Bonds	0	0	0	0	0	0	0	0
Private nonguaranteed	47	9	18	46	29	25	29	28
of which: Bonds	..	..	..	..	..	..	..	..
Net financial flows								
Net debt inflows	152	-150	472	-20	439	620	719	617
Official creditors (incl. IMF)	143	47	339	121	173	311	354	416
Private creditors	9	-196	132	-141	266	309	365	201
Long-term	-60	-1	96	97	265	284	269	196
Public and publicly guaranteed	0	..	..	..	..	..	..	..
Private nonguaranteed	-60	-1	96	97	265	284	269	196
Short-term	69	-195	37	-238	1	25	97	5
Net equity inflows								
Foreign direct investment	-2	47	178	231	547	112	228	182
Portfolio equity	..	0	1	-18	5	0	-2	6
Major economic aggregates								
Gross national income (GNI)	1,288	2,372	4,509	4,489	5,539	6,436	7,045	7,177
Exports of goods, services & prim. income	590	963	2,354	2,408	3,159	2,951	3,131	2,829
Imports of goods, services & prim. income	753	1,501	3,763	4,117	5,591	6,687	7,053	6,793
Primary income on FDI	37	36	118	248	611	111	227	153
Personal transfers & comp. of employees	9	313	982	1,266	1,709	2,031	2,278	2,243
International reserves	239	570	1,494	1,604	1,703	1,903	2,099	1,805
Ratios								
External debt stocks to exports (%)	328.5	234.4	175.0	170.8	173.7	204.2	217.3	256.5
External debt stocks to GNI (%)	150.5	95.1	91.4	91.7	99.0	93.6	96.6	101.1
Debt service to exports (%)	30.2	14.8	11.4	23.1	13.0	11.8	12.4	14.2
Reserves to external debt stocks (%)	12.3	25.2	36.3	39.0	31.0	31.6	30.8	24.9

Notes:

Long-term private nonguaranteed debt data are World Bank staff estimates based on reports provided by the country. Short-term debt is based on data from the National Statistical Committee of Kyrgyz Republic.

LAO PEOPLE'S DEMOCRATIC REPUBLIC

(US$ million, unless otherwise indicated)

	2000	2005	2009	2010	2011	2012	2013	2014
Summary external debt data								
External debt stocks	**2,535**	**3,277**	**6,383**	**6,487**	**7,547**	**8,169**	**9,426**	**10,724**
Long-term external debt	2,474	3,179	6,089	6,381	7,402	8,042	8,545	9,780
Short-term external debt	6	55	199	18	62	47	803	871
interest arrears on long-term	0	0	0	0	0	0	0	0
Use of IMF credit	55	43	95	88	83	79	78	73
Long-term external debt								
Debt outstanding and disbursed	**2,474**	**3,179**	**6,089**	**6,381**	**7,402**	**8,042**	**8,545**	**9,780**
Public and publicly guaranteed	2,474	2,354	3,464	3,771	4,277	4,542	5,146	5,631
Official creditors	2,474	2,354	3,464	3,768	4,272	4,536	4,995	5,311
Private creditors	0	0	0	3	5	7	151	320
of which: Bonds	0	0	0	0	0	0	143	300
Private nonguaranteed	..	825	2,625	2,610	3,125	3,500	3,398	4,149
of which: Bonds	..	..	..	..	..	..	..	246
Disbursements	**82**	**544**	**743**	**427**	**1,086**	**867**	**1,613**	**1,610**
Public and publicly guaranteed	82	222	296	282	471	417	803	764
Official creditors	82	222	296	280	468	416	658	595
Private creditors	0	0	0	3	3	1	145	169
of which: Bonds	0	0	0	0	0	0	143	157
Private nonguaranteed	..	321	447	144	615	450	810	846
of which: Bonds	..	..	..	..	..	..	..	246
Principal repayments	**23**	**80**	**150**	**217**	**208**	**174**	**197**	**217**
Public and publicly guaranteed	23	40	61	59	108	99	106	122
Official creditors	23	40	61	59	108	99	106	122
Private creditors	0	0	0	0	0	0	0	0
of which: Bonds	0	0	0	0	0	0	0	0
Private nonguaranteed	..	40	89	159	100	75	92	95
of which: Bonds	..	..	..	..	..	..	..	..
Interest payments	**9**	**48**	**72**	**78**	**101**	**87**	**133**	**140**
Public and publicly guaranteed	9	15	29	28	51	57	75	94
Official creditors	9	15	29	28	51	57	74	89
Private creditors	0	0	0	0	0	0	1	5
of which: Bonds	0	0	0	0	0	0	1	5
Private nonguaranteed	..	32	43	50	50	30	58	47
of which: Bonds	..	..	..	..	..	..	..	..
Net financial flows								
Net debt inflows	58	513	621	23	917	675	2,170	1,461
Official creditors (incl. IMF)	52	177	230	216	355	314	551	473
Private creditors	6	336	391	-193	562	361	1,619	988
Long-term	..	281	358	-12	518	376	863	920
Public and publicly guaranteed	..	..	..	3	3	1	145	169
Private nonguaranteed	..	281	358	-14	515	375	718	751
Short-term	6	55	33	-181	44	-15	756	68
Net equity inflows								
Foreign direct investment	34	28	319	279	301	294	427	721
Portfolio equity	..	..	..	54	11	6	7	..
Major economic aggregates								
Gross national income (GNI)	1,660	2,670	5,668	6,713	7,690	8,751	10,553	11,186
Exports of goods, services & prim. income	513	762	1,492	2,308	2,452	2,917	3,118	..
Imports of goods, services & prim. income	638	1,003	1,685	2,457	2,881	3,582	3,731	..
Primary income on FDI	..	25	43	44	16	52	52	..
Personal transfers & comp. of employees	1	1	38	42	110	59	60	60
International reserves	139	234	609	703	741	799	722	875
Ratios								
External debt stocks to exports (%)	493.9	429.8	427.9	281.1	307.8	280.0	302.3	..
External debt stocks to GNI (%)	152.7	122.7	112.6	96.6	98.1	93.3	89.3	95.9
Debt service to exports (%)	8.0	17.6	15.3	13.0	12.8	9.1	10.6	..
Reserves to external debt stocks (%)	5.5	7.2	9.5	10.8	9.8	9.8	7.7	8.2

Notes:

Long-term private nonguaranteed debt data are World Bank staff estimates. Short-term debt is based on data from the BIS.

LEBANON

(US$ million, unless otherwise indicated)

	2000	2005	2009	2010	2011	2012	2013	2014
Summary external debt data								
External debt stocks	**10,248**	**23,334**	**24,803**	**24,591**	**24,767**	**28,951**	**30,947**	**30,608**
Long-term external debt	7,701	19,877	21,285	20,713	21,101	24,691	26,124	26,018
Short-term external debt	2,541	3,450	3,096	3,482	3,311	3,943	4,525	4,310
interest arrears on long-term	0	0	0	0	0	0	0	0
Use of IMF credit	6	6	422	395	355	317	298	280
Long-term external debt								
Debt outstanding and disbursed	**7,701**	**19,877**	**21,285**	**20,713**	**21,101**	**24,691**	**26,124**	**26,018**
Public and publicly guaranteed	6,965	18,866	20,615	20,213	20,601	23,991	25,424	25,318
Official creditors	1,288	2,172	2,356	2,226	2,088	1,997	1,734	1,458
Private creditors	5,677	16,694	18,259	17,987	18,513	21,994	23,690	23,860
of which: Bonds	5,260	16,142	17,704	17,422	17,966	21,489	23,298	23,529
Private nonguaranteed	736	1,011	670	500	500	700	700	700
of which: Bonds	736	1,011	670	500	500	700	700	700
Disbursements	**2,445**	**3,179**	**3,332**	**2,143**	**4,174**	**6,221**	**3,185**	**1,675**
Public and publicly guaranteed	2,330	2,649	3,132	2,143	4,174	5,721	3,185	1,675
Official creditors	238	106	223	199	206	226	136	91
Private creditors	2,092	2,543	2,909	1,943	3,968	5,495	3,049	1,584
of which: Bonds	2,031	2,500	2,894	1,925	3,954	5,478	2,992	1,575
Private nonguaranteed	115	530	200	..	..	500	..	..
of which: Bonds	115	530	200	..	..	500	..	..
Principal repayments	**884**	**2,172**	**3,096**	**2,632**	**3,743**	**2,642**	**1,801**	**1,583**
Public and publicly guaranteed	834	1,907	3,096	2,462	3,743	2,342	1,801	1,583
Official creditors	74	143	334	298	328	318	415	260
Private creditors	760	1,764	2,762	2,164	3,415	2,024	1,386	1,324
of which: Bonds	400	1,695	2,706	2,151	3,385	1,965	1,209	1,271
Private nonguaranteed	50	265	..	170	..	300	..	..
of which: Bonds	50	265	..	170	..	300	..	..
Interest payments	**475**	**1,287**	**1,475**	**1,454**	**1,491**	**1,484**	**1,618**	**1,665**
Public and publicly guaranteed	418	1,197	1,431	1,403	1,453	1,446	1,577	1,624
Official creditors	57	92	88	100	82	75	72	63
Private creditors	361	1,106	1,344	1,303	1,372	1,371	1,505	1,561
of which: Bonds	300	1,087	1,328	1,289	1,359	1,359	1,495	1,551
Private nonguaranteed	57	90	43	51	38	38	42	42
of which: Bonds	57	90	43	51	38	38	42	42
Net financial flows								
Net debt inflows	1,900	486	195	-122	220	4,173	1,947	-123
Official creditors (incl. IMF)	164	-37	-111	-117	-161	-130	-298	-169
Private creditors	1,735	524	305	-5	382	4,303	2,245	46
Long-term	1,397	1,045	347	-391	553	3,671	1,663	261
Public and publicly guaranteed	1,332	780	147	-221	553	3,471	1,663	261
Private nonguaranteed	65	265	200	-170	..	200	..	..
Short-term	339	-521	-42	386	-171	632	582	-215
Net equity inflows								
Foreign direct investment	..	2,624	4,804	4,280	3,490	3,540	3,029	3,070
Portfolio equity	..	1,436	929	154	-145	-239	-134	..
Major economic aggregates								
Gross national income (GNI)	17,581	21,101	34,912	37,501	40,194	43,242	44,021	45,009
Exports of goods, services & prim. income	..	14,958	23,137	22,177	26,687	23,343	21,004	19,883
Imports of goods, services & prim. income	..	18,768	31,705	32,179	34,071	33,681	34,245	33,486
Primary income on FDI	..	95	95	209	184	213	345	..
Personal transfers & comp. of employees	..	4,924	7,558	6,914	6,913	6,730	7,864	8,899
International reserves	5,944	11,887	29,103	31,514	33,741	37,186	36,748	39,547
Ratios								
External debt stocks to exports (%)	..	156.0	107.2	110.9	92.8	124.0	147.3	153.9
External debt stocks to GNI (%)	58.3	110.6	71.0	65.6	61.6	67.0	70.3	68.0
Debt service to exports (%)	..	24.3	19.9	18.7	20.0	18.1	16.7	16.6
Reserves to external debt stocks (%)	58.0	50.9	117.3	128.2	136.2	128.4	118.7	129.2

Notes:

Long-term private nonguaranteed debt only cover Bonds. Short-term debt is based on data from the BIS.

LESOTHO

(US$ million, unless otherwise indicated)

	2000	2005	2009	2010	2011	2012	2013	2014
Summary external debt data								
External debt stocks	**676.7**	**667.3**	**756.3**	**778.0**	**797.6**	**860.2**	**885.2**	**876.3**
Long-term external debt	656.7	618.9	680.6	699.2	717.2	745.1	755.0	755.2
Short-term external debt	4.0	8.0	0.0	0.0	0.0	0.0	0.0	0.1
interest arrears on long-term	0.0	0.0	0.0	0.0	0.0	0.0	0.0	0.1
Use of IMF credit	16.0	40.4	75.7	78.8	80.3	115.2	130.2	121.0
Long-term external debt								
Debt outstanding and disbursed	**656.7**	**618.9**	**680.6**	**699.2**	**717.2**	**745.1**	**755.0**	**755.2**
Public and publicly guaranteed	656.7	618.9	680.6	699.2	717.2	745.1	755.0	755.2
Official creditors	580.9	590.6	667.1	685.6	705.6	733.9	745.0	746.6
Private creditors	75.8	28.4	13.6	13.6	11.7	11.2	10.0	8.6
of which: Bonds	0.0	0.0	0.0	0.0	0.0	0.0	0.0	0.0
Private nonguaranteed	..	..	..	..	..	..	..	..
of which: Bonds	..	..	..	..	..	..	..	..
Disbursements	**69.4**	**21.1**	**37.4**	**42.1**	**44.0**	**54.8**	**39.7**	**74.2**
Public and publicly guaranteed	69.4	21.1	37.4	42.1	44.0	54.8	39.7	74.2
Official creditors	67.4	21.1	37.4	42.1	44.0	54.8	39.7	74.2
Private creditors	2.0	0.0	0.0	0.0	0.0	0.0	0.0	0.0
of which: Bonds	0.0	0.0	0.0	0.0	0.0	0.0	0.0	0.0
Private nonguaranteed	..	..	..	..	..	..	..	..
of which: Bonds	..	..	..	..	..	..	..	..
Principal repayments	**33.2**	**65.3**	**24.6**	**19.4**	**23.3**	**24.3**	**27.6**	**27.6**
Public and publicly guaranteed	33.2	65.3	24.6	19.4	23.3	24.3	27.6	27.6
Official creditors	26.4	32.0	23.9	19.1	23.0	24.0	27.3	27.3
Private creditors	6.8	33.3	0.7	0.3	0.3	0.3	0.3	0.3
of which: Bonds	0.0	0.0	0.0	0.0	0.0	0.0	0.0	0.0
Private nonguaranteed	..	..	..	..	..	..	..	..
of which: Bonds	..	..	..	..	..	..	..	..
Interest payments	**22.9**	**13.7**	**7.4**	**7.5**	**8.8**	**9.2**	**9.9**	**11.7**
Public and publicly guaranteed	22.9	13.7	7.4	7.5	8.8	9.2	9.9	11.7
Official creditors	16.0	7.7	6.9	6.4	7.8	8.3	9.1	11.0
Private creditors	7.0	6.0	0.5	1.0	1.0	0.9	0.7	0.7
of which: Bonds	0.0	0.0	0.0	0.0	0.0	0.0	0.0	0.0
Private nonguaranteed	..	..	..	..	..	..	..	..
of which: Bonds	..	..	..	..	..	..	..	..
Net financial flows								
Net debt inflows	31.0	-43.2	6.8	27.1	22.5	65.1	26.7	45.0
Official creditors (incl. IMF)	35.9	-10.9	7.5	27.4	22.8	65.3	27.0	45.2
Private creditors	-4.9	-32.3	-0.7	-0.3	-0.3	-0.3	-0.3	-0.3
Long-term	-4.9	-33.3	-0.7	-0.3	-0.3	-0.3	-0.3	-0.3
Public and publicly guaranteed	-4.9	-33.3	-0.7	-0.3	-0.3	-0.3	-0.3	-0.3
Private nonguaranteed	..	..	..	..	..			..
Short-term	..	1.0	..	..	..	..	..	..
Net equity inflows								
Foreign direct investment	32.4	71.1	171.2	170.2	192.3	89.3	58.8	46.4
Portfolio equity	..	0.0	..	..	..	..	..	..
Major economic aggregates								
Gross national income (GNI)	1,014.4	1,869.4	2,108.1	2,594.0	3,124.2	2,861.5	2,862.9	2,605.0
Exports of goods, services & prim. income	824.4	1,391.2	1,473.7	1,669.3	1,952.7	1,663.0	1,447.2	..
Imports of goods, services & prim. income	1,132.8	1,891.8	2,138.5	2,740.8	3,027.8	2,834.0	2,353.2	..
Primary income on FDI	68.3	196.2	116.6	317.8	386.4	118.2	84.4	..
Personal transfers & comp. of employees	478.1	599.4	547.9	610.1	649.3	554.0	462.5	456.5
International reserves	417.9	519.1	1,179.8	1,071.0	919.1	1,027.9	1,055.2	1,070.8
Ratios								
External debt stocks to exports (%)	82.1	48.0	51.3	46.6	40.8	51.7	61.2	..
External debt stocks to GNI (%)	66.7	35.7	35.9	30.0	25.5	30.1	30.9	33.6
Debt service to exports (%)	7.5	5.7	2.6	2.1	2.0	2.3	2.8	..
Reserves to external debt stocks (%)	61.8	77.8	156.0	137.6	115.2	119.5	119.2	122.2

Notes:

Large interest payment was made during 2007 to a creditor country to settle a long standing claim. Short-term debt is based on data from the BIS.

LIBERIA

(US$ million, unless otherwise indicated)

	2000	2005	2009	2010	2011	2012	2013	2014
Summary external debt data								
External debt stocks	**2,836.3**	**3,928.0**	**1,850.3**	**418.9**	**448.4**	**487.2**	**541.0**	**633.1**
Long-term external debt	1,104.0	1,156.5	673.1	183.1	188.0	208.5	239.7	305.9
Short-term external debt	1,412.6	2,421.8	91.6	0.4	12.2	12.0	11.4	0.0
interest arrears on long-term	1,412.6	2,421.8	91.6	0.4	12.2	12.0	11.4	0.0
Use of IMF credit	319.7	349.7	1,085.5	235.3	248.2	266.7	289.9	327.2
Long-term external debt								
Debt outstanding and disbursed	**1,104.0**	**1,156.5**	**673.1**	**183.1**	**188.0**	**208.5**	**239.7**	**305.9**
Public and publicly guaranteed	1,104.0	1,156.5	673.1	183.1	188.0	208.5	239.7	305.8
Official creditors	907.3	958.7	652.6	183.1	188.0	208.5	239.7	305.8
Private creditors	196.8	197.7	20.5	0.0	0.0	0.0	0.0	0.0
of which: Bonds	0.0	0.0	0.0	0.0	0.0	0.0	0.0	0.0
Private nonguaranteed	..	..	..	..	..	..	..	0.1
of which: Bonds	..	..	..	..	..	..	..	..
Disbursements	**0.0**	**0.0**	**0.0**	**0.0**	**20.3**	**23.1**	**35.1**	**81.2**
Public and publicly guaranteed	0.0	0.0	0.0	0.0	20.3	23.1	35.1	81.2
Official creditors	0.0	0.0	0.0	0.0	20.3	23.1	35.1	81.2
Private creditors	0.0	0.0	0.0	0.0	0.0	0.0	0.0	0.0
of which: Bonds	0.0	0.0	0.0	0.0	0.0	0.0	0.0	0.0
Private nonguaranteed	..	..	..	..	..	..	..	0.1
of which: Bonds	..	..	..	..	..	..	..	..
Principal repayments	**0.0**	**0.0**	**4.3**	**3.7**	**2.6**	**3.5**	**4.6**	**5.5**
Public and publicly guaranteed	0.0	0.0	4.3	3.7	2.6	3.5	4.6	5.5
Official creditors	0.0	0.0	4.3	3.7	2.6	3.5	4.6	5.5
Private creditors	0.0	0.0	0.0	0.0	0.0	0.0	0.0	0.0
of which: Bonds	0.0	0.0	0.0	0.0	0.0	0.0	0.0	0.0
Private nonguaranteed	..	..	..	..	..	..	..	..
of which: Bonds	..	..	..	..	..	..	..	..
Interest payments	**0.0**	**0.0**	**11.8**	**0.6**	**0.4**	**1.1**	**1.5**	**8.6**
Public and publicly guaranteed	0.0	0.0	11.8	0.6	0.4	1.1	1.5	8.6
Official creditors	0.0	0.0	11.8	0.6	0.4	1.1	1.5	8.6
Private creditors	0.0	0.0	0.0	0.0	0.0	0.0	0.0	0.0
of which: Bonds	0.0	0.0	0.0	0.0	0.0	0.0	0.0	0.0
Private nonguaranteed	..	..	..	..	..	..	..	..
of which: Bonds	..	..	..	..	..	..	..	..
Net financial flows								
Net debt inflows	-0.6	-0.1	13.3	9.8	31.8	37.7	53.0	132.8
Official creditors (incl. IMF)	-0.6	-0.1	13.3	9.8	31.8	37.7	53.0	132.8
Private creditors	..	..	..	..	..	..	..	0.1
Long-term	..	..	..	..	..	..	..	0.1
Public and publicly guaranteed	..	..	..	..	..	..	..	..
Private nonguaranteed	..	..	..	..	..	..	..	0.1
Short-term	..	..	..	..	..	..	..	..
Net equity inflows								
Foreign direct investment	20.8	3.5	2.9	0.0	30.5	646.6	700.3	302.0
Portfolio equity	..	..	..	..	..	..	..	..
Major economic aggregates								
Gross national income (GNI)	514.1	394.4	1,010.5	1,113.3	1,420.6	1,581.5	1,645.0	1,694.0
Exports of goods, services & prim. income	..	354.7	472.2	430.4	1,351.8	709.6	850.0	..
Imports of goods, services & prim. income	..	1,317.7	1,850.0	1,804.7	3,325.3	2,317.1	2,362.0	..
Primary income on FDI	..	7.1	5.8	0.1	11.7	232.2	252.9	..
Personal transfers & comp. of employees	..	31.9	25.1	31.4	360.0	515.8	383.4	528.2
International reserves	0.3	25.4	372.5	465.9	512.8	497.2	493.1	..
Ratios								
External debt stocks to exports (%)	..	1107.4	391.9	97.3	33.2	68.7	63.6	..
External debt stocks to GNI (%)	551.7	995.9	183.1	37.6	31.6	30.8	32.9	37.4
Debt service to exports (%)	..	0.5	5.8	1.4	0.2	0.6	0.7	..
Reserves to external debt stocks (%)	0.0	0.6	20.1	111.2	114.4	102.1	91.1	..

Notes:

Long-term public and publicly guaranteed debt data before 2011 are revised based on reports provided by the country. Data include the effects of Paris Club rescheduling agreement signed in 2008 and 2010, and HIPC and MDRI debt relief.

MACEDONIA, FYR

(US$ million, unless otherwise indicated)

	2000	2005	2009	2010	2011	2012	2013	2014
Summary external debt data								
External debt stocks	**1,480**	**2,981**	**5,247**	**5,159**	**6,131**	**6,469**	**6,737**	**7,241**
Long-term external debt	1,333	2,108	3,731	3,840	4,132	4,376	4,941	5,746
Short-term external debt	55	800	1,413	1,218	1,597	1,690	1,392	1,222
interest arrears on long-term	4	9	30	64	80	109	129	125
Use of IMF credit	92	74	103	101	403	404	404	273
Long-term external debt								
Debt outstanding and disbursed	**1,333**	**2,108**	**3,731**	**3,840**	**4,132**	**4,376**	**4,941**	**5,746**
Public and publicly guaranteed	1,206	1,637	1,874	1,880	2,110	2,270	2,572	3,140
Official creditors	921	1,202	1,321	1,369	1,392	1,453	1,596	1,691
Private creditors	284	435	552	512	717	817	976	1,449
of which: Bonds	0	177	468	434	421	429	207	789
Private nonguaranteed	127	471	1,858	1,959	2,022	2,106	2,368	2,606
of which: Bonds	..	..	..	..	..	..	..	..
Disbursements	**151**	**318**	**1,012**	**596**	**968**	**637**	**1,063**	**1,514**
Public and publicly guaranteed	98	293	347	197	414	303	694	1,099
Official creditors	96	104	103	190	155	176	305	436
Private creditors	1	189	244	7	259	127	389	663
of which: Bonds	0	187	244	0	0	0	0	660
Private nonguaranteed	54	25	665	399	555	334	369	415
of which: Bonds	..	..	..	..	..	..	..	..
Principal repayments	**74**	**171**	**375**	**443**	**739**	**479**	**734**	**661**
Public and publicly guaranteed	25	81	88	98	126	168	462	186
Official creditors	23	67	81	90	103	124	192	162
Private creditors	2	14	7	9	23	44	270	24
of which: Bonds	0	0	0	0	0	0	235	0
Private nonguaranteed	49	90	287	344	614	310	272	475
of which: Bonds	..	..	..	..	..	..	..	..
Interest payments	**37**	**54**	**93**	**128**	**129**	**125**	**117**	**151**
Public and publicly guaranteed	30	41	47	56	60	64	64	62
Official creditors	20	32	33	22	24	23	19	22
Private creditors	10	9	15	35	36	41	45	39
of which: Bonds	0	0	10	32	33	31	21	9
Private nonguaranteed	7	13	46	71	70	60	54	89
of which: Bonds	..	..	..	..	..	..	..	..
Net financial flows								
Net debt inflows	59	117	737	-75	902	222	12	575
Official creditors (incl. IMF)	58	42	22	101	362	51	113	162
Private creditors	2	75	715	-176	539	171	-101	413
Long-term	5	109	615	53	177	108	216	579
Public and publicly guaranteed	0	174	237	-2	236	83	119	639
Private nonguaranteed	5	-65	378	55	-59	24	97	-60
Short-term	-3	-34	100	-229	362	64	-317	-166
Net equity inflows								
Foreign direct investment	215	155	57	202	572	142	212	13
Portfolio equity	..	54	-14	-4	-8	-6	-1	-4
Major economic aggregates								
Gross national income (GNI)	3,703	6,149	9,335	9,276	10,307	9,555	10,486	11,026
Exports of goods, services & prim. income	1,679	2,190	3,175	3,801	5,019	4,535	4,883	5,549
Imports of goods, services & prim. income	2,391	3,393	5,378	5,789	7,347	6,918	7,112	7,843
Primary income on FDI	31	142	138	230	272	265	324	357
Personal transfers & comp. of employees	81	227	381	388	434	394	376	367
International reserves	429	1,229	2,051	1,970	2,331	2,528	2,485	2,701
Ratios								
External debt stocks to exports (%)	88.1	136.2	165.3	135.7	122.2	142.7	138.0	130.5
External debt stocks to GNI (%)	40.0	48.5	56.2	55.6	59.5	67.7	64.2	65.7
Debt service to exports (%)	8.3	12.5	16.9	16.4	18.8	15.0	18.7	17.6
Reserves to external debt stocks (%)	29.0	41.2	39.1	38.2	38.0	39.1	36.9	37.3

MADAGASCAR

(US$ million, unless otherwise indicated)

	2000	2005	2009	2010	2011	2012	2013	2014
Summary external debt data								
External debt stocks	**4,716**	**3,519**	**2,788**	**2,699**	**2,810**	**2,930**	**2,872**	**2,853**
Long-term external debt	4,286	3,180	1,855	1,997	2,106	2,200	2,271	2,300
Short-term external debt	301	99	649	425	430	463	345	286
interest arrears on long-term	203	72	189	188	188	192	52	43
Use of IMF credit	129	240	284	278	273	267	256	267
Long-term external debt								
Debt outstanding and disbursed	**4,286**	**3,180**	**1,855**	**1,997**	**2,106**	**2,200**	**2,271**	**2,300**
Public and publicly guaranteed	4,286	3,180	1,836	1,982	2,093	2,191	2,263	2,294
Official creditors	4,247	3,171	1,829	1,975	2,086	2,181	2,229	2,260
Private creditors	39	9	7	7	7	10	34	33
of which: Bonds	0	0	0	0	0	0	0	0
Private nonguaranteed	..	..	19	15	12	10	8	7
of which: Bonds	..	..	..	..	..	..	..	..
Disbursements	**150**	**249**	**126**	**198**	**137**	**138**	**149**	**189**
Public and publicly guaranteed	150	249	124	198	137	138	149	189
Official creditors	150	249	124	197	137	135	146	187
Private creditors	0	0	0	0	0	3	3	2
of which: Bonds	0	0	0	0	0	0	0	0
Private nonguaranteed	..	..	2	..	..	..	..	..
of which: Bonds	..	..	..	..	..	..	..	..
Principal repayments	**74**	**38**	**34**	**37**	**25**	**44**	**48**	**54**
Public and publicly guaranteed	74	38	32	36	24	42	48	53
Official creditors	73	37	32	36	24	42	48	53
Private creditors	0	1	0	0	0	0	0	0
of which: Bonds	0	0	0	0	0	0	0	0
Private nonguaranteed	..	..	1	1	1	2	1	1
of which: Bonds	..	..	..	..	..	..	..	..
Interest payments	**28**	**28**	**15**	**16**	**16**	**17**	**17**	**19**
Public and publicly guaranteed	28	28	15	16	16	17	17	18
Official creditors	28	28	15	16	16	17	17	18
Private creditors	0	0	0	0	0	0	0	0
of which: Bonds	0	0	0	0	0	0	0	0
Private nonguaranteed	..	..	0	0	0	0	0	0
of which: Bonds	..	..	..	..	..	..	..	..
Net financial flows								
Net debt inflows	45	244	127	-65	115	116	112	112
Official creditors (incl. IMF)	122	218	92	160	109	87	87	161
Private creditors	-77	26	35	-225	5	29	24	-49
Long-term	0	-1	0	-1	-1	1	2	1
Public and publicly guaranteed	0	-1	0	..	0	3	3	2
Private nonguaranteed	..	..	0	-1	-1	-2	-1	-1
Short-term	-76	27	35	-224	6	29	22	-50
Net equity inflows								
Foreign direct investment	83	53	72	65	41	41	32	..
Portfolio equity	..	..	..	0	..	..	..	..
Major economic aggregates								
Gross national income (GNI)	3,807	4,960	8,459	8,643	9,720	9,631	10,279	10,317
Exports of goods, services & prim. income	1,210	1,353	1,954	2,241	2,733	2,867	3,205	..
Imports of goods, services & prim. income	1,584	2,251	4,066	3,616	4,016	4,223	4,461	..
Primary income on FDI	4	65	105	120	162	276	249	..
Personal transfers & comp. of employees	11	115	338	547	398	397	427	432
International reserves	285	481	982	1,023	1,135	1,053	776	774
Ratios								
External debt stocks to exports (%)	389.7	260.2	142.7	120.5	102.8	102.2	89.6	..
External debt stocks to GNI (%)	123.9	70.9	33.0	31.2	28.9	30.4	27.9	27.6
Debt service to exports (%)	9.7	5.9	2.8	2.7	1.8	2.5	2.5	..
Reserves to external debt stocks (%)	6.0	13.7	35.2	37.9	40.4	35.9	27.0	27.1

Notes:

Data include the effects of HIPC and MDRI debt relief.

MALAWI

(US$ million, unless otherwise indicated)

	2000	2005	2009	2010	2011	2012	2013	2014
Summary external debt data								
External debt stocks	**2,719**	**3,196**	**1,144**	**1,039**	**1,205**	**1,316**	**1,554**	**1,637**
Long-term external debt	2,544	3,062	846	729	929	1,025	1,244	1,364
Short-term external debt	78	43	67	61	30	8	15	1
interest arrears on long-term	37	34	0	0	0	0	0	1
Use of IMF credit	97	91	231	248	247	283	295	273
Long-term external debt								
Debt outstanding and disbursed	**2,544**	**3,062**	**846**	**729**	**929**	**1,025**	**1,244**	**1,364**
Public and publicly guaranteed	2,544	3,062	846	729	929	1,025	1,244	1,364
Official creditors	2,526	3,043	841	724	923	1,019	1,238	1,362
Private creditors	18	18	6	5	5	5	6	2
of which: Bonds	0	0	0	0	0	0	0	0
Private nonguaranteed	..	..	..	..	..	..	..	..
of which: Bonds	..	..	..	..	..	..	..	..
Disbursements	**119**	**89**	**107**	**81**	**208**	**109**	**230**	**211**
Public and publicly guaranteed	119	89	107	81	208	109	230	211
Official creditors	119	89	107	81	208	109	230	211
Private creditors	0	0	0	0	0	0	0	0
of which: Bonds	0	0	0	0	0	0	0	0
Private nonguaranteed	..	..	..	..	..	..	..	..
of which: Bonds	..	..	..	..	..	..	..	..
Principal repayments	**33**	**38**	**22**	**13**	**14**	**15**	**22**	**24**
Public and publicly guaranteed	33	38	22	13	14	15	22	24
Official creditors	33	35	22	13	14	15	22	21
Private creditors	0	3	0	0	0	0	0	3
of which: Bonds	0	0	0	0	0	0	0	0
Private nonguaranteed	..	..	..	..	..	..	..	..
of which: Bonds	..	..	..	..	..	..	..	..
Interest payments	**18**	**22**	**15**	**7**	**7**	**9**	**14**	**16**
Public and publicly guaranteed	18	22	15	7	7	9	14	16
Official creditors	18	22	15	7	7	9	14	16
Private creditors	0	0	0	0	0	0	0	0
of which: Bonds	0	0	0	0	0	0	0	0
Private nonguaranteed	..	..	..	..	..	..	..	..
of which: Bonds	..	..	..	..	..	..	..	..
Net financial flows								
Net debt inflows	83	42	67	83	162	108	227	166
Official creditors (incl. IMF)	85	47	85	89	193	130	220	184
Private creditors	-2	-5	-18	-6	-31	-22	7	-18
Long-term	..	-3	..	..	..	..	..	-3
Public and publicly guaranteed	..	-3	..	..	..	..	..	-3
Private nonguaranteed	..	..	..	..	..	..	..	..
Short-term	-2	-2	-18	-6	-31	-22	7	-15
Net equity inflows								
Foreign direct investment	26	88	69	133	89	89	120	130
Portfolio equity	..	-4	0	1	1	1	0	0
Major economic aggregates								
Gross national income (GNI)	1,707	2,715	4,972	5,290	5,512	4,105	3,722	4,087
Exports of goods, services & prim. income	471	609	1,348	1,224	1,632	1,397	1,397	1,558
Imports of goods, services & prim. income	680	1,390	2,298	2,650	2,917	2,646	3,125	3,276
Primary income on FDI	15	52	103	173	92	93	..	..
Personal transfers & comp. of employees	1	23	17	22	25	28	..	..
International reserves	243	159	149	307	197	223	413	602
Ratios								
External debt stocks to exports (%)	577.7	524.5	84.9	84.9	73.9	94.2	111.3	105.1
External debt stocks to GNI (%)	159.3	117.7	23.0	19.6	21.9	32.1	41.8	40.1
Debt service to exports (%)	13.5	12.5	2.9	1.7	1.4	2.0	3.2	4.2
Reserves to external debt stocks (%)	8.9	5.0	13.1	29.6	16.4	17.0	26.6	36.8

Notes:

Short-term debt is based on data from the BIS. Data include the effects of Paris Club rescheduling agreement signed in 2006 and HIPC and MDRI debt relief.

MALAYSIA

(US$ million, unless otherwise indicated)

	2000	2005	2009	2010	2011	2012	2013	2014
Summary external debt data								
External debt stocks	**41,946**	**64,911**	**119,611**	**133,800**	**144,898**	**193,880**	**212,387**	**210,820**
Long-term external debt	37,192	51,537	73,806	80,450	78,128	99,201	107,502	105,037
Short-term external debt	4,573	13,176	43,695	51,276	64,704	92,610	102,812	103,833
interest arrears on long-term	0	0	0	0	0	0	0	0
Use of IMF credit	181	199	2,110	2,073	2,067	2,069	2,073	1,950
Long-term external debt								
Debt outstanding and disbursed	**37,192**	**51,537**	**73,806**	**80,450**	**78,128**	**99,201**	**107,502**	**105,037**
Public and publicly guaranteed	19,125	34,387	53,717	61,858	60,647	67,392	70,365	66,237
Official creditors	4,950	6,542	4,092	3,750	3,263	2,980	2,463	2,071
Private creditors	14,175	27,845	49,626	58,108	57,384	64,412	67,901	64,166
of which: Bonds	9,836	24,585	45,670	51,638	52,735	61,762	66,044	62,581
Private nonguaranteed	18,067	17,150	20,089	18,593	17,481	31,809	37,137	38,800
of which: Bonds	18,067	17,150	20,089	18,593	17,481	30,213	35,722	37,388
Disbursements	**5,921**	**10,378**	**12,554**	**9,938**	**12,354**	**24,260**	**18,484**	**11,115**
Public and publicly guaranteed	3,460	6,195	9,634	6,014	3,311	8,870	7,887	1,173
Official creditors	1,446	981	47	18	10	514	56	0
Private creditors	2,015	5,215	9,587	5,996	3,301	8,356	7,831	1,173
of which: Bonds	1,061	5,164	8,815	2,339	2,892	8,033	7,227	1,173
Private nonguaranteed	2,461	4,183	2,920	3,923	9,043	15,390	10,597	9,942
of which: Bonds	2,461	4,183	2,920	3,923	9,043	13,794	9,842	9,369
Principal repayments	**4,146**	**7,192**	**7,750**	**3,564**	**4,551**	**4,171**	**8,995**	**9,876**
Public and publicly guaranteed	2,017	4,752	5,351	1,863	3,608	3,304	1,681	2,547
Official creditors	840	1,218	1,053	688	625	604	300	269
Private creditors	1,176	3,534	4,298	1,176	2,983	2,701	1,381	2,277
of which: Bonds	200	2,036	2,959	0	750	380	9	2,009
Private nonguaranteed	2,129	2,440	2,399	1,701	943	867	7,313	7,329
of which: Bonds	2,129	2,440	2,399	1,701	943	867	6,376	6,754
Interest payments	**2,021**	**1,858**	**1,746**	**1,708**	**1,563**	**2,053**	**2,451**	**2,540**
Public and publicly guaranteed	1,159	1,208	876	1,024	1,017	1,293	1,251	1,233
Official creditors	259	314	124	97	86	79	69	72
Private creditors	900	894	752	927	931	1,214	1,182	1,161
of which: Bonds	599	746	652	771	853	1,084	1,117	1,136
Private nonguaranteed	862	650	870	684	545	760	1,200	1,307
of which: Bonds	862	650	870	684	545	760	1,187	1,288
Net financial flows								
Net debt inflows	337	4,929	9,698	13,955	21,231	47,995	19,692	2,261
Official creditors (incl. IMF)	606	-238	-1,006	-669	-614	-90	-245	-269
Private creditors	-269	5,167	10,705	14,625	21,846	48,085	19,936	2,530
Long-term	1,170	3,424	5,810	7,043	8,418	20,179	9,735	1,509
Public and publicly guaranteed	838	1,681	5,289	4,821	317	5,656	6,450	-1,104
Private nonguaranteed	331	1,743	521	2,223	8,101	14,523	3,284	2,613
Short-term	-1,439	1,744	4,895	7,581	13,428	27,906	10,202	1,021
Net equity inflows								
Foreign direct investment	3,788	4,232	706	11,090	14,827	8,900	11,171	10,465
Portfolio equity	..	-1,200	-449	..	..	..	..	..
Major economic aggregates								
Gross national income (GNI)	86,182	137,212	198,224	239,358	282,200	293,285	302,328	315,509
Exports of goods, services & prim. income	114,356	166,725	197,562	243,301	281,911	279,255	274,038	221,355
Imports of goods, services & prim. income	103,944	142,268	160,181	209,534	241,520	254,714	257,485	243,230
Primary income on FDI	7,173	8,330	11,119	15,298	18,105	18,385	18,408	..
Personal transfers & comp. of employees	342	1,117	1,131	1,103	1,211	1,320	1,396	1,565
International reserves	28,330	69,858	95,432	104,884	131,780	137,784	133,444	114,572
Ratios								
External debt stocks to exports (%)	36.7	38.9	60.5	40.8	39.5	69.4	77.5	95.2
External debt stocks to GNI (%)	48.7	47.3	60.3	41.5	39.5	66.1	70.3	66.8
Debt service to exports (%)	5.6	5.6	5.1	2.3	2.3	2.4	4.3	5.8
Reserves to external debt stocks (%)	67.5	107.6	79.8	105.6	118.3	71.1	62.8	54.3

Notes:

Long-term public and publicly guaranteed, long-term private nonguaranteed, and short-term debt data are World Bank staff estimates based on reports.

MALDIVES

(US$ million, unless otherwise indicated)

	2000	2005	2009	2010	2011	2012	2013	2014
Summary external debt data								
External debt stocks	**206.4**	**362.3**	**965.1**	**994.3**	**973.8**	**844.8**	**821.1**	**1,025.5**
Long-term external debt	184.7	299.8	758.5	743.1	717.1	721.1	748.6	861.7
Short-term external debt	21.4	56.3	185.6	223.6	229.2	96.1	50.4	149.0
interest arrears on long-term	0.0	0.3	1.0	2.9	1.3	3.0	5.6	6.0
Use of IMF credit	0.4	6.3	20.9	27.6	27.5	27.6	22.1	14.9
Long-term external debt								
Debt outstanding and disbursed	**184.7**	**299.8**	**758.5**	**743.1**	**717.1**	**721.1**	**748.6**	**861.7**
Public and publicly guaranteed	184.7	299.8	542.7	627.8	675.2	721.1	748.6	711.7
Official creditors	154.8	250.2	445.2	522.3	565.3	633.8	669.5	656.1
Private creditors	29.9	49.6	97.5	105.5	109.9	87.3	79.1	55.5
of which: Bonds	0.0	0.0	0.0	0.0	0.0	0.0	0.0	0.0
Private nonguaranteed	..	..	215.8	115.2	41.9	..	..	150.0
of which: Bonds	..	..	..	..	..	..	..	..
Disbursements	**13.6**	**45.9**	**156.8**	**168.5**	**124.5**	**113.3**	**77.0**	**204.3**
Public and publicly guaranteed	13.6	45.9	112.0	142.4	115.9	113.3	77.0	54.3
Official creditors	6.3	29.5	107.3	108.4	82.9	111.7	70.4	54.0
Private creditors	7.3	16.3	4.6	34.0	33.0	1.6	6.6	0.3
of which: Bonds	0.0	0.0	0.0	0.0	0.0	0.0	0.0	0.0
Private nonguaranteed	..	..	44.8	26.1	8.6	..	..	150.0
of which: Bonds	..	..	..	..	..	..	..	..
Principal repayments	**13.9**	**22.1**	**64.7**	**59.8**	**70.3**	**66.1**	**54.9**	**58.7**
Public and publicly guaranteed	13.9	22.1	44.4	50.9	66.3	66.1	54.9	58.7
Official creditors	6.7	13.1	21.5	27.1	40.9	40.8	37.2	41.6
Private creditors	7.3	9.0	22.9	23.9	25.4	25.2	17.7	17.0
of which: Bonds	0.0	0.0	0.0	0.0	0.0	0.0	0.0	0.0
Private nonguaranteed	..	..	20.3	8.9	3.9	..	..	..
of which: Bonds	..	..	..	..	..	..	..	..
Interest payments	**4.7**	**7.1**	**16.4**	**10.6**	**11.0**	**10.1**	**9.1**	**9.7**
Public and publicly guaranteed	4.7	7.1	12.1	9.2	10.4	10.1	9.1	9.7
Official creditors	2.6	4.8	6.8	5.4	6.2	6.9	7.4	8.9
Private creditors	2.2	2.2	5.3	3.7	4.2	3.2	1.7	0.8
of which: Bonds	0.0	0.0	0.0	0.0	0.0	0.0	0.0	0.0
Private nonguaranteed	..	..	4.2	1.5	0.5	..	..	..
of which: Bonds	..	..	..	..	..	..	..	..
Net financial flows								
Net debt inflows	-3.8	53.8	67.2	151.8	61.4	-87.5	-31.7	237.6
Official creditors (incl. IMF)	-0.4	22.5	90.6	88.3	42.0	70.9	27.7	6.1
Private creditors	-3.4	31.3	-23.4	63.5	19.4	-158.4	-59.4	231.5
Long-term	0.0	7.3	6.2	27.4	12.2	-23.6	-11.1	133.3
Public and publicly guaranteed	0.0	7.3	-18.2	10.2	7.6	-23.6	-11.1	-16.7
Private nonguaranteed	..	..	24.5	17.2	4.7	..	..	150.0
Short-term	-3.5	24.0	-29.6	36.1	7.2	-134.8	-48.3	98.2
Net equity inflows								
Foreign direct investment	22.3	53.0	158.0	216.5	423.5	228.0	360.8	363.3
Portfolio equity	..	..	-14.5	-10.4	2.3	-2.0	0.2	-1.2
Major economic aggregates								
Gross national income (GNI)	594.3	1,088.9	1,893.9	2,021.2	2,152.3	2,255.0	2,335.4	2,619.9
Exports of goods, services & prim. income	467.5	495.4	1,718.0	2,011.5	2,459.0	2,503.6	2,935.1	3,288.4
Imports of goods, services & prim. income	492.0	910.4	1,758.2	2,008.5	2,610.6	2,430.6	2,767.6	3,130.9
Primary income on FDI	34.4	31.0	235.9	271.9	266.5	234.5	333.9	350.3
Personal transfers & comp. of employees	2.2	2.3	4.5	3.2	3.0	3.1	3.3	3.5
International reserves	122.8	189.0	275.6	364.3	348.7	318.3	381.9	627.4
Ratios								
External debt stocks to exports (%)	44.1	73.1	56.2	49.4	39.6	33.7	28.0	31.2
External debt stocks to GNI (%)	34.7	33.3	51.0	49.2	45.2	37.5	35.2	39.1
Debt service to exports (%)	4.2	6.3	5.2	4.0	3.7	3.2	2.4	2.3
Reserves to external debt stocks (%)	59.5	52.2	28.6	36.6	35.8	37.7	46.5	61.2

Notes:

Long-term private nonguaranteed and short-term debt data from 2006 are World Bank staff estimates based on reports provided by the country. 2014 Short-term debt is based on data from the BIS.

MALI

(US$ million, unless otherwise indicated)

	2000	2005	2009	2010	2011	2012	2013	2014
Summary external debt data								
External debt stocks	**2,981**	**3,224**	**2,210**	**2,456**	**2,922**	**3,057**	**3,430**	**3,416**
Long-term external debt	2,671	3,036	2,002	2,263	2,499	2,781	3,087	3,090
Short-term external debt	114	55	25	6	193	39	67	62
interest arrears on long-term	42	6	1	0	18	26	29	33
Use of IMF credit	196	132	184	187	230	237	277	264
Long-term external debt								
Debt outstanding and disbursed	**2,671**	**3,036**	**2,002**	**2,263**	**2,499**	**2,781**	**3,087**	**3,090**
Public and publicly guaranteed	2,671	3,036	2,002	2,263	2,499	2,781	3,087	3,090
Official creditors	2,671	3,032	1,995	2,258	2,495	2,777	3,084	3,088
Private creditors	0	5	7	5	4	3	3	1
of which: Bonds	0	0	0	0	0	0	0	0
Private nonguaranteed	..	..	..	..	..	..	..	..
of which: Bonds	..	..	..	..	..	..	..	..
Disbursements	**100**	**280**	**494**	**304**	**292**	**277**	**346**	**265**
Public and publicly guaranteed	100	280	494	304	292	277	346	265
Official creditors	100	277	491	304	292	277	346	265
Private creditors	0	3	3	0	0	0	0	0
of which: Bonds	0	0	0	0	0	0	0	0
Private nonguaranteed	..	..	..	..	..	..	..	..
of which: Bonds	..	..	..	..	..	..	..	..
Principal repayments	**50**	**52**	**46**	**39**	**41**	**33**	**68**	**54**
Public and publicly guaranteed	50	52	46	39	41	33	68	54
Official creditors	50	52	45	38	39	32	66	53
Private creditors	0	0	1	1	1	0	1	1
of which: Bonds	0	0	0	0	0	0	0	0
Private nonguaranteed	..	..	..	..	..	..	..	..
of which: Bonds	..	..	..	..	..	..	..	..
Interest payments	**18**	**27**	**22**	**21**	**25**	**24**	**27**	**25**
Public and publicly guaranteed	18	27	22	21	25	24	27	25
Official creditors	18	27	21	21	25	24	27	25
Private creditors	0	0	0	0	0	0	0	0
of which: Bonds	0	0	0	0	0	0	0	0
Private nonguaranteed	..	..	..	..	..	..	..	..
of which: Bonds	..	..	..	..	..	..	..	..
Net financial flows								
Net debt inflows	-31	219	475	253	466	90	342	206
Official creditors (incl. IMF)	42	210	449	272	298	252	318	216
Private creditors	-73	8	25	-19	168	-162	24	-10
Long-term	..	3	1	-1	-1	0	-1	-1
Public and publicly guaranteed	..	3	1	-1	-1	0	-1	-1
Private nonguaranteed	..	..	..	..	..	..	..	..
Short-term	-73	5	24	-18	169	-162	25	-9
Net equity inflows								
Foreign direct investment	82	160	645	373	393	189	95	199
Portfolio equity	0	9	-3	1	2	-4	-1	..
Major economic aggregates								
Gross national income (GNI)	2,392	5,099	8,508	9,003	10,195	9,808	10,679	11,583
Exports of goods, services & prim. income	665	1,443	2,210	2,508	2,859	3,427	3,384	..
Imports of goods, services & prim. income	1,046	2,108	3,351	4,236	4,371	4,495	5,794	..
Primary income on FDI	76	190	459	402	407	445	393	..
Personal transfers & comp. of employees	73	177	454	473	784	827	895	923
International reserves	382	854	1,604	1,344	1,379	1,341	1,306	861
Ratios								
External debt stocks to exports (%)	448.5	223.4	100.0	97.9	102.2	89.2	101.4	..
External debt stocks to GNI (%)	124.6	63.2	26.0	27.3	28.7	31.2	32.1	29.5
Debt service to exports (%)	14.1	6.9	3.1	2.5	2.4	1.7	3.0	..
Reserves to external debt stocks (%)	12.8	26.5	72.6	54.7	47.2	43.9	38.1	25.2

Notes:

Short-term debt is based on data from the BIS. The data for Principal Arrears on long-term are revised from 2001. Data include the effects of HIPC and MDRI debt relief.

MAURITANIA

(US$ million, unless otherwise indicated)

	2000	2005	2009	2010	2011	2012	2013	2014
Summary external debt data								
External debt stocks	**2,390**	**2,321**	**2,289**	**2,683**	**2,815**	**3,308**	**3,529**	**3,522**
Long-term external debt	2,028	2,071	1,984	2,301	2,485	2,901	3,102	3,135
Short-term external debt	251	167	192	237	151	196	201	178
interest arrears on long-term	112	109	134	76	77	76	75	73
Use of IMF credit	111	83	113	145	178	211	226	210
Long-term external debt								
Debt outstanding and disbursed	**2,028**	**2,071**	**1,984**	**2,301**	**2,485**	**2,901**	**3,102**	**3,135**
Public and publicly guaranteed	2,028	2,071	1,984	2,301	2,485	2,901	3,102	3,135
Official creditors	2,009	2,048	1,972	2,300	2,485	2,901	3,102	3,135
Private creditors	19	23	12	1	0	0	0	0
of which: Bonds	0	0	0	0	0	0	0	0
Private nonguaranteed	..	..	..	..	..	..	..	..
of which: Bonds	..	..	..	..	..	..	..	..
Disbursements	**115**	**143**	**407**	**390**	**256**	**452**	**296**	**302**
Public and publicly guaranteed	115	143	407	390	256	452	296	302
Official creditors	115	128	407	390	256	452	296	302
Private creditors	0	15	0	0	0	0	0	0
of which: Bonds	0	0	0	0	0	0	0	0
Private nonguaranteed	..	..	..	..	..	..	..	..
of which: Bonds	..	..	..	..	..	..	..	..
Principal repayments	**46**	**33**	**53**	**76**	**79**	**85**	**106**	**154**
Public and publicly guaranteed	46	33	53	76	79	85	106	154
Official creditors	43	31	52	65	78	85	106	154
Private creditors	2	1	1	11	1	0	0	0
of which: Bonds	0	0	0	0	0	0	0	0
Private nonguaranteed	..	..	..	..	..	..	..	..
of which: Bonds	..	..	..	..	..	..	..	..
Interest payments	**20**	**20**	**23**	**35**	**41**	**55**	**54**	**62**
Public and publicly guaranteed	20	20	23	35	41	55	54	62
Official creditors	18	19	23	34	41	55	54	62
Private creditors	2	1	0	1	0	0	0	0
of which: Bonds	0	0	0	0	0	0	0	0
Private nonguaranteed	..	..	..	..	..	..	..	..
of which: Bonds	..	..	..	..	..	..	..	..
Net financial flows								
Net debt inflows	62	92	246	451	125	445	210	124
Official creditors (incl. IMF)	74	87	355	359	214	399	204	145
Private creditors	-11	5	-109	92	-88	46	6	-21
Long-term	-2	14	-1	-11	-1	..	..	..
Public and publicly guaranteed	-2	14	-1	-11	-1	..	..	..
Private nonguaranteed	..	..	..	..			..	..
Short-term	-9	-9	-108	103	-87	46	6	-21
Net equity inflows								
Foreign direct investment	40	812	-3	131	589	1,386	1,126	492
Portfolio equity	..	..	..	..	..	..	..	..
Major economic aggregates								
Gross national income (GNI)	1,307	2,249	3,594	4,256	4,967	4,654	4,863	4,801
Exports of goods, services & prim. income	..	..	1,641	2,306	3,124	2,911	2,957	..
Imports of goods, services & prim. income	..	..	2,176	2,787	3,522	4,448	4,360	..
Primary income on FDI	..	..	..	..	..	..	..	..
Personal transfers & comp. of employees	..	..	..	..	..	..	..	..
International reserves	46	64	225	272	485	949	..	..
Ratios								
External debt stocks to exports (%)	..	..	139.5	116.4	90.1	113.6	119.3	..
External debt stocks to GNI (%)	182.8	103.2	63.7	63.1	56.7	71.1	72.6	73.4
Debt service to exports (%)	..	..	4.7	4.9	3.9	4.9	5.6	..
Reserves to external debt stocks (%)	1.9	2.8	9.8	10.1	17.2	28.7	..	..

Notes:

Short-term debt is based on data from the BIS. Data include the effects of MDRI debt relief.

MAURITIUS

(US$ million, unless otherwise indicated)

	2000	2005	2009	2010	2011	2012	2013	2014
Summary external debt data								
External debt stocks	**967**	**805**	**2,265**	**2,734**	**9,574**	**10,218**	**10,916**	**11,288**
Long-term external debt	946	782	821	1,107	7,720	7,161	7,909	7,554
Short-term external debt	0	0	1,292	1,478	1,706	2,908	2,858	3,595
interest arrears on long-term	0	0	0	0	0	1	0	1
Use of IMF credit	21	23	152	149	149	149	149	140
Long-term external debt								
Debt outstanding and disbursed	**946**	**782**	**821**	**1,107**	**7,720**	**7,161**	**7,909**	**7,554**
Public and publicly guaranteed	828	716	740	1,007	1,215	1,409	1,774	1,842
Official creditors	494	504	655	888	1,098	1,298	1,679	1,771
Private creditors	334	213	85	119	116	110	95	71
of which: Bonds	0	0	0	0	0	0	0	0
Private nonguaranteed	118	66	81	100	6,505	5,752	6,135	5,712
of which: Bonds	..	..	..	..	..	..	..	..
Disbursements	**128**	**138**	**287**	**425**	**4,627**	**3,719**	**3,934**	**2,924**
Public and publicly guaranteed	119	126	218	356	298	250	406	291
Official creditors	43	62	199	293	269	239	406	291
Private creditors	76	64	19	63	29	11	0	0
of which: Bonds	0	0	0	0	0	0	0	0
Private nonguaranteed	9	11	69	69	4,329	3,469	3,528	2,633
of which: Bonds	..	..	..	..	..	..	..	..
Principal repayments	**401**	**197**	**122**	**118**	**3,341**	**3,030**	**3,276**	**3,170**
Public and publicly guaranteed	385	176	85	69	77	64	66	114
Official creditors	55	87	52	45	49	45	46	100
Private creditors	330	89	33	24	28	19	20	14
of which: Bonds	150	0	0	0	0	0	0	0
Private nonguaranteed	16	21	37	49	3,264	2,966	3,210	3,056
of which: Bonds	..	..	..	..	..	..	..	..
Interest payments	**52**	**30**	**21**	**18**	**78**	**73**	**76**	**298**
Public and publicly guaranteed	51	30	20	17	23	27	26	29
Official creditors	23	19	16	15	20	24	24	28
Private creditors	29	10	4	2	4	3	2	1
of which: Bonds	5	0	0	0	0	0	0	0
Private nonguaranteed	1	0	1	1	55	46	50	269
of which: Bonds	..	..	..	..	..	..	..	..
Net financial flows								
Net debt inflows	-273	-59	1,458	492	1,514	1,891	608	490
Official creditors (incl. IMF)	-12	-24	147	249	220	194	360	192
Private creditors	-261	-35	1,310	243	1,294	1,697	248	298
Long-term	-261	-35	18	58	1,066	495	297	-438
Public and publicly guaranteed	-254	-25	-14	38	1	-8	-20	-14
Private nonguaranteed	-6	-10	32	20	1,065	503	317	-423
Short-term	..	..	1,292	185	228	1,202	-49	736
Net equity inflows								
Foreign direct investment	266	42	257	430	433	589	259	418
Portfolio equity	-4	36	206	..	..	..	..	..
Major economic aggregates								
Gross national income (GNI)	4,553	6,276	8,793	9,835	11,282	11,479	11,942	12,419
Exports of goods, services & prim. income	2,671	3,899	4,635	10,189	6,983	8,048	12,268	13,089
Imports of goods, services & prim. income	2,772	4,284	5,514	11,378	8,664	9,017	12,926	13,578
Primary income on FDI	8	34	195	4,639	601	1,074	4,331	4,204
Personal transfers & comp. of employees	177	1	1	1	1	1	1	1
International reserves	897	1,340	2,179	2,442	2,583	2,837	3,340	3,615
Ratios								
External debt stocks to exports (%)	36.2	20.6	48.9	26.8	137.1	127.0	89.0	86.2
External debt stocks to GNI (%)	21.2	12.8	25.8	27.8	84.9	89.0	91.4	90.9
Debt service to exports (%)	17.0	5.8	3.4	1.5	49.3	39.1	27.7	26.8
Reserves to external debt stocks (%)	92.8	166.4	96.2	89.3	27.0	27.8	30.6	32.0

Notes:

Long-term private nonguaranteed debt data from 2009 are based on reports provided by the country and do not include offshore liabilities and 2011-2013 are World Bank staff estimates based on reports provided by the country. Short-term debt data are based on reports provided by the country and include offshore liabilities.

MEXICO

(US$ million, unless otherwise indicated)

	2000	2005	2009	2010	2011	2012	2013	2014
Summary external debt data								
External debt stocks	**152,260**	**170,520**	**193,343**	**245,906**	**291,833**	**348,945**	**406,042**	**432,602**
Long-term external debt	132,951	147,905	163,318	198,455	234,924	268,863	308,990	337,324
Short-term external debt	18,932	22,201	25,555	43,061	52,532	75,700	92,661	91,147
interest arrears on long-term	0	0	0	0	0	0	0	0
Use of IMF credit	378	415	4,470	4,391	4,377	4,382	4,391	4,131
Long-term external debt								
Debt outstanding and disbursed	**132,951**	**147,905**	**163,318**	**198,455**	**234,924**	**268,863**	**308,990**	**337,324**
Public and publicly guaranteed	82,470	115,246	118,878	145,925	164,252	195,795	219,687	238,410
Official creditors	20,892	18,789	21,085	25,975	28,162	29,850	31,082	31,529
Private creditors	61,577	96,457	97,793	119,950	136,090	165,945	188,604	206,881
of which: Bonds	53,693	75,294	78,522	97,656	115,543	147,704	158,176	175,735
Private nonguaranteed	50,481	32,658	44,440	52,529	70,672	73,067	89,303	98,914
of which: Bonds	20,644	16,943	21,444	32,898	47,393	54,967	80,400	84,752
Disbursements	**32,830**	**29,393**	**37,074**	**54,656**	**57,056**	**92,888**	**87,458**	**58,509**
Public and publicly guaranteed	11,483	18,588	26,995	41,812	31,408	42,307	39,657	32,898
Official creditors	2,855	2,309	8,572	6,166	4,518	3,099	2,875	2,465
Private creditors	8,628	16,278	18,423	35,646	26,890	39,207	36,783	30,434
of which: Bonds	7,368	13,541	16,114	26,489	24,189	36,167	17,413	26,099
Private nonguaranteed	21,346	10,806	10,079	12,844	25,649	50,582	47,801	25,610
of which: Bonds	3,346	6,669	5,067	11,298	18,065	31,005	43,355	17,759
Principal repayments	**38,967**	**25,101**	**22,318**	**21,683**	**28,708**	**35,413**	**20,200**	**29,391**
Public and publicly guaranteed	16,337	15,686	11,873	13,941	12,383	8,501	12,209	8,998
Official creditors	3,386	2,530	1,795	1,679	1,947	1,490	1,426	1,475
Private creditors	12,950	13,155	10,077	12,263	10,436	7,011	10,783	7,523
of which: Bonds	9,256	9,989	4,965	7,118	5,851	1,703	3,630	4,591
Private nonguaranteed	22,630	9,416	10,446	7,742	16,325	26,912	7,991	20,393
of which: Bonds	3,552	2,645	3,500	2,826	2,216	3,723	2,190	9,166
Interest payments	**12,174**	**9,398**	**8,792**	**8,345**	**10,887**	**32,204**	**16,659**	**18,178**
Public and publicly guaranteed	7,923	7,532	6,019	5,859	7,318	28,709	10,287	10,260
Official creditors	1,554	848	551	627	730	756	763	732
Private creditors	6,368	6,685	5,468	5,232	6,587	27,954	9,524	9,528
of which: Bonds	4,897	6,247	4,856	4,927	6,258	27,633	9,197	8,722
Private nonguaranteed	4,251	1,866	2,773	2,486	3,570	3,495	6,372	7,918
of which: Bonds	1,620	957	1,583	1,379	1,761	1,849	4,606	6,347
Net financial flows								
Net debt inflows	-15,566	6,181	16,133	50,480	37,819	80,643	84,219	27,603
Official creditors (incl. IMF)	-4,830	-221	6,777	4,487	2,570	1,609	1,448	990
Private creditors	-10,736	6,402	9,356	45,992	35,249	79,035	82,770	26,614
Long-term	-5,606	4,513	7,979	28,486	25,778	55,867	65,809	28,128
Public and publicly guaranteed	-4,322	3,123	8,346	23,384	16,454	32,197	25,999	22,911
Private nonguaranteed	-1,284	1,390	-367	5,103	9,324	23,670	39,810	5,217
Short-term	-5,130	1,889	1,377	17,506	9,471	23,168	16,961	-1,514
Net equity inflows								
Foreign direct investment	18,110	17,302	16,099	20,189	18,603	12,867	37,324	17,471
Portfolio equity	447	3,353	4,155	373	-6,566	9,877	-943	4,833
Major economic aggregates								
Gross national income (GNI)	668,631	850,654	879,995	1,046,859	1,150,164	1,161,265	1,224,887	1,248,338
Exports of goods, services & prim. income	185,853	235,187	251,597	324,906	376,155	400,742	412,165	427,894
Imports of goods, services & prim. income	211,589	266,281	281,511	351,466	412,434	439,177	463,853	477,259
Primary income on FDI	6,076	8,486	8,742	9,682	13,028	16,922	26,789	16,581
Personal transfers & comp. of employees	7,525	22,742	22,076	22,080	23,588	23,366	23,022	24,460
International reserves	35,509	74,054	99,589	120,265	143,991	160,413	175,432	190,923
Ratios								
External debt stocks to exports (%)	81.9	72.5	76.8	75.7	77.6	87.1	98.5	101.1
External debt stocks to GNI (%)	22.8	20.0	22.0	23.5	25.4	30.0	33.1	34.7
Debt service to exports (%)	31.6	15.5	12.6	10.1	11.2	17.7	10.1	12.2
Reserves to external debt stocks (%)	23.3	43.4	51.5	48.9	49.3	46.0	43.2	44.1

MOLDOVA

(US$ million, unless otherwise indicated)

	2000	2005	2009	2010	2011	2012	2013	2014
Summary external debt data								
External debt stocks	**1,843**	**2,219**	**3,715**	**4,725**	**5,209**	**5,760**	**6,491**	**6,463**
Long-term external debt	1,047	1,238	2,011	2,745	2,899	3,205	3,579	3,653
Short-term external debt	489	718	1,366	1,471	1,655	1,762	2,139	2,112
interest arrears on long-term	22	56	38	37	42	52	56	60
Use of IMF credit	308	264	338	509	655	793	773	699
Long-term external debt								
Debt outstanding and disbursed	**1,047**	**1,238**	**2,011**	**2,745**	**2,899**	**3,205**	**3,579**	**3,653**
Public and publicly guaranteed	850	698	809	839	857	942	973	1,003
Official creditors	743	664	790	823	836	913	944	979
Private creditors	107	34	19	16	21	29	29	24
of which: Bonds	75	25	0	0	0	0	0	0
Private nonguaranteed	197	540	1,203	1,906	2,042	2,263	2,606	2,650
of which: Bonds	..	..	..	..	..	..	..	..
Disbursements	**164**	**237**	**284**	**464**	**530**	**648**	**683**	**437**
Public and publicly guaranteed	54	26	54	94	94	142	109	161
Official creditors	52	26	41	89	80	121	94	156
Private creditors	2	0	13	5	14	21	15	5
of which: Bonds	0	0	0	0	0	0	0	0
Private nonguaranteed	110	211	230	370	436	505	574	276
of which: Bonds	..	..	..	..	..	..	..	..
Principal repayments	**57**	**163**	**303**	**306**	**368**	**467**	**543**	**456**
Public and publicly guaranteed	30	42	55	55	71	65	84	61
Official creditors	27	35	46	47	63	51	67	54
Private creditors	3	7	9	8	8	14	16	8
of which: Bonds	0	6	6	0	0	0	0	0
Private nonguaranteed	28	120	248	251	297	402	459	394
of which: Bonds	..	..	..	..	..	..	..	..
Interest payments	**46**	**42**	**54**	**49**	**58**	**54**	**65**	**63**
Public and publicly guaranteed	39	22	22	16	16	16	16	16
Official creditors	28	20	21	16	16	15	15	15
Private creditors	11	2	1	1	0	1	1	1
of which: Bonds	7	2	0	0	0	0	0	0
Private nonguaranteed	7	20	32	33	42	38	49	47
of which: Bonds	..	..	..	..	..	..	..	..
Net financial flows								
Net debt inflows	560	157	-42	439	494	414	492	-80
Official creditors (incl. IMF)	13	-31	-21	217	169	207	5	73
Private creditors	547	188	-21	223	325	207	487	-153
Long-term	82	84	-13	117	145	111	113	-121
Public and publicly guaranteed	0	-7	4	-3	6	7	-1	-3
Private nonguaranteed	82	91	-18	119	140	104	114	-119
Short-term	465	104	-8	106	180	96	373	-32
Net equity inflows								
Foreign direct investment	128	107	150	172	231	134	180	215
Portfolio equity	3	1	2	6	5	14	10	10
Major economic aggregates								
Gross national income (GNI)	1,310	3,347	5,746	6,297	7,580	8,127	8,850	8,740
Exports of goods, services & prim. income	780	1,871	2,308	2,725	3,636	3,781	4,200	4,011
Imports of goods, services & prim. income	1,089	2,673	3,975	4,463	5,903	5,882	6,306	6,192
Primary income on FDI	3	45	141	152	257	117	165	162
Personal transfers & comp. of employees	179	915	1,199	1,351	1,600	1,793	1,985	2,075
International reserves	222	597	1,480	1,718	1,965	2,511	2,818	2,154
Ratios								
External debt stocks to exports (%)	236.2	118.6	161.0	173.4	143.2	152.4	154.5	161.1
External debt stocks to GNI (%)	140.7	66.3	64.7	75.0	68.7	70.9	73.3	74.0
Debt service to exports (%)	20.0	13.6	16.9	14.5	12.8	15.2	16.0	14.7
Reserves to external debt stocks (%)	12.1	26.9	39.8	36.4	37.7	43.6	43.4	33.3

MONGOLIA

(US$ million, unless otherwise indicated)

	2000	2005	2009	2010	2011	2012	2013	2014
Summary external debt data								
External debt stocks	**960**	**1,396**	**2,986**	**5,928**	**9,627**	**15,385**	**18,893**	**20,826**
Long-term external debt	833	1,267	2,479	5,290	8,775	14,248	17,189	18,379
Short-term external debt	13	25	248	365	583	903	1,563	2,374
interest arrears on long-term	2	0	0	0	0	0	4	0
Use of IMF credit	114	105	258	273	268	234	140	73
Long-term external debt								
Debt outstanding and disbursed	**833**	**1,267**	**2,479**	**5,290**	**8,775**	**14,248**	**17,189**	**18,379**
Public and publicly guaranteed	833	1,267	1,817	1,782	1,826	3,243	3,540	3,498
Official creditors	831	1,266	1,733	1,775	1,814	1,734	2,035	1,995
Private creditors	3	0	84	7	12	1,508	1,505	1,503
of which: Bonds	0	0	75	0	0	1,500	1,500	1,500
Private nonguaranteed	..	..	662	3,508	6,949	11,006	13,650	14,881
of which: Bonds	..	..	..	..	..	900	900	919
Disbursements	**75**	**91**	**520**	**2,929**	**3,554**	**6,422**	**3,867**	**2,058**
Public and publicly guaranteed	75	91	212	66	87	1,558	425	180
Official creditors	75	91	212	66	83	58	425	180
Private creditors	0	0	0	0	5	1,500	0	0
of which: Bonds	0	0	0	0	0	1,500	0	0
Private nonguaranteed	..	..	308	2,863	3,466	4,864	3,442	1,878
of which: Bonds	..	..	..	..	..	900	..	19
Principal repayments	**22**	**17**	**70**	**139**	**78**	**898**	**885**	**871**
Public and publicly guaranteed	22	17	62	122	54	84	71	63
Official creditors	19	17	59	44	54	80	68	60
Private creditors	3	0	2	77	0	4	3	3
of which: Bonds	0	0	0	75	0	0	0	0
Private nonguaranteed	..	..	8	18	24	814	814	808
of which: Bonds	..	..	..	..	..	..	..	..
Interest payments	**9**	**15**	**41**	**89**	**155**	**258**	**396**	**389**
Public and publicly guaranteed	9	15	26	20	20	21	59	23
Official creditors	9	15	19	19	20	21	22	22
Private creditors	0	0	7	1	0	0	38	1
of which: Bonds	0	0	6	1	0	0	38	1
Private nonguaranteed	..	..	15	70	134	236	337	366
of which: Bonds	..	..	..	..	..	27	79	80
Net financial flows								
Net debt inflows	45	-73	787	2,925	3,689	5,808	3,546	1,940
Official creditors (incl. IMF)	58	69	312	40	24	-58	264	58
Private creditors	-12	-142	475	2,885	3,665	5,866	3,282	1,882
Long-term	-3	0	297	2,768	3,447	5,547	2,625	1,067
Public and publicly guaranteed	-3	0	-2	-77	5	1,496	-3	-3
Private nonguaranteed	..	..	299	2,845	3,442	4,050	2,628	1,070
Short-term	-9	-142	179	117	218	319	657	815
Net equity inflows								
Foreign direct investment	54	185	488	1,331	1,501	1,487	377	278
Portfolio equity	..	..	4	680	9	15	3	-1
Major economic aggregates								
Gross national income (GNI)	1,132	2,472	4,388	6,591	9,566	11,343	11,835	11,187
Exports of goods, services & prim. income	627	1,494	2,322	3,423	5,481	5,402	5,030	6,407
Imports of goods, services & prim. income	791	1,635	2,850	4,496	8,480	9,004	8,364	7,955
Primary income on FDI	9	41	121	464	632	594	282	..
Personal transfers & comp. of employees	12	180	200	266	279	320	256	255
International reserves	179	333	1,294	2,197	2,275	3,930	2,096	1,540
Ratios								
External debt stocks to exports (%)	153.2	93.5	128.6	173.2	175.6	284.8	375.6	325.1
External debt stocks to GNI (%)	84.8	56.5	68.0	89.9	100.6	135.6	159.6	186.2
Debt service to exports (%)	6.6	3.0	5.3	7.0	4.6	22.4	27.9	21.2
Reserves to external debt stocks (%)	18.6	23.9	43.4	37.1	23.6	25.5	11.1	7.4

Notes:

Long-term private nonguaranteed debt data from 2008 are World Bank staff estimates based on reports provided by the country. Short-term debt before 2008 is based on data from the BIS.

MONTENEGRO

(US$ million, unless otherwise indicated)

	2000	2005	2009	2010	2011	2012	2013	2014
Summary external debt data								
External debt stocks	..	..	**2,357**	**1,603**	**2,354**	**2,830**	**3,023**	**2,454**
Long-term external debt	..	..	1,109	1,378	1,859	2,252	2,442	2,365
Short-term external debt	..	..	1,207	186	455	538	541	52
interest arrears on long-term	..	..	0	0	0	0	0	0
Use of IMF credit	..	..	40	40	40	40	40	37
Long-term external debt								
Debt outstanding and disbursed	..	..	**1,109**	**1,378**	**1,859**	**2,252**	**2,442**	**2,365**
Public and publicly guaranteed	..	..	1,094	1,359	1,805	2,184	2,366	2,285
Official creditors	..	..	894	846	1,012	1,168	1,203	1,095
Private creditors	..	..	201	512	792	1,016	1,162	1,190
of which: Bonds	..	..	0	267	492	501	634	786
Private nonguaranteed	..	..	15	19	54	68	77	80
of which: Bonds	..	..	..	..	..	..	..	..
Disbursements	..	..	**248**	**395**	**659**	**526**	**364**	**493**
Public and publicly guaranteed	..	..	242	383	619	506	344	463
Official creditors	..	..	61	35	258	187	76	94
Private creditors	..	..	181	348	361	319	268	369
of which: Bonds	..	..	0	265	248	0	107	369
Private nonguaranteed	..	..	7	12	40	21	20	30
of which: Bonds	..	..	..	..	..	..	..	..
Principal repayments	..	..	**25**	**61**	**127**	**174**	**269**	**176**
Public and publicly guaranteed	..	..	23	60	124	166	254	159
Official creditors	..	..	22	33	43	48	85	81
Private creditors	..	..	1	27	81	118	170	78
of which: Bonds	..	..	0	0	0	0	0	12
Private nonguaranteed	..	..	2	2	2	8	14	16
of which: Bonds	..	..	..	..	..	..	..	..
Interest payments	..	..	**28**	**34**	**79**	**87**	**97**	**91**
Public and publicly guaranteed	..	..	28	33	78	86	96	90
Official creditors	..	..	26	20	24	24	31	23
Private creditors	..	..	2	13	55	63	65	67
of which: Bonds	..	..	0	0	22	37	39	40
Private nonguaranteed	..	..	0	1	1	1	1	1
of which: Bonds	..	..	..	..	..	..	..	..
Net financial flows								
Net debt inflows	..	..	829	-687	802	435	98	-172
Official creditors (incl. IMF)	..	..	38	2	214	139	-8	13
Private creditors	..	..	790	-689	587	297	106	-184
Long-term	..	..	185	332	318	214	103	305
Public and publicly guaranteed	..	..	180	322	280	201	98	291
Private nonguaranteed	..	..	5	11	38	13	5	13
Short-term	..	..	605	-1,021	269	83	3	-489
Net equity inflows								
Foreign direct investment	..	..	1,359	566	438	535	330	272
Portfolio equity	..	..	-5	-8	-15	0	14	16
Major economic aggregates								
Gross national income (GNI)	..	..	4,149	4,082	4,532	4,115	4,504	4,644
Exports of goods, services & prim. income	..	..	1,663	1,722	2,198	1,975	2,125	2,142
Imports of goods, services & prim. income	..	..	2,933	2,826	3,152	2,918	2,938	2,992
Primary income on FDI	..	..	91	99	45	33	28	71
Personal transfers & comp. of employees	..	..	303	301	343	333	423	431
International reserves	..	..	573	556	393	459	584	661
Ratios								
External debt stocks to exports (%)	..	..	141.7	93.1	107.1	143.3	142.3	114.6
External debt stocks to GNI (%)	..	..	56.8	39.3	51.9	68.8	67.1	52.9
Debt service to exports (%)	..	..	4.1	5.7	9.7	13.6	17.5	12.6
Reserves to external debt stocks (%)	..	..	24.3	34.7	16.7	16.2	19.3	26.9

Notes:

Long-term private nonguaranteed debt data (excluding bonds) only cover European Bank for Reconstruction and Development lending. Short-term debt is based on data from the BIS. Montenegro became independent in 2006 and started to report data in 2007.

MOROCCO

(US$ million, unless otherwise indicated)

	2000	2005	2009	2010	2011	2012	2013	2014
Summary external debt data								
External debt stocks	**20,618**	**16,254**	**24,662**	**27,250**	**29,903**	**33,815**	**39,243**	**42,772**
Long-term external debt	18,933	15,449	21,572	23,638	25,204	28,785	33,027	34,351
Short-term external debt	1,573	682	2,210	2,747	3,837	4,167	5,351	7,607
interest arrears on long-term	122	0	0	0	0	0	0	0
Use of IMF credit	112	122	880	865	862	863	865	813
Long-term external debt								
Debt outstanding and disbursed	**18,933**	**15,449**	**21,572**	**23,638**	**25,204**	**28,785**	**33,027**	**34,351**
Public and publicly guaranteed	17,071	12,398	19,218	21,049	22,371	25,086	28,260	29,780
Official creditors	12,679	10,075	16,713	17,269	18,628	19,814	21,927	20,894
Private creditors	4,392	2,323	2,504	3,780	3,743	5,271	6,333	8,885
of which: Bonds	152	472	0	1,336	1,294	2,819	3,629	5,314
Private nonguaranteed	1,862	3,051	2,354	2,589	2,833	3,699	4,768	4,572
of which: Bonds	..	..	..	..	..	..	..	..
Disbursements	**1,638**	**2,456**	**4,551**	**4,999**	**4,506**	**6,122**	**7,486**	**8,244**
Public and publicly guaranteed	980	1,658	3,468	3,882	3,285	4,114	4,407	6,157
Official creditors	631	1,562	2,868	2,258	2,995	2,477	3,241	2,788
Private creditors	349	97	600	1,625	290	1,636	1,166	3,369
of which: Bonds	0	0	0	1,327	0	1,500	750	1,850
Private nonguaranteed	658	798	1,083	1,116	1,222	2,008	3,079	2,087
of which: Bonds	..	..	..	..	..	..	..	..
Principal repayments	**1,632**	**2,139**	**2,709**	**2,428**	**2,436**	**2,769**	**3,998**	**3,733**
Public and publicly guaranteed	1,593	1,881	1,138	1,274	1,481	1,572	1,821	1,893
Official creditors	928	1,303	966	1,090	1,277	1,392	1,557	1,662
Private creditors	666	578	172	184	205	179	264	231
of which: Bonds	30	41	0	0	0	0	0	0
Private nonguaranteed	39	258	1,572	1,154	955	1,198	2,177	1,841
of which: Bonds	..	..	..	..	..	..	..	..
Interest payments	**949**	**569**	**678**	**850**	**757**	**785**	**1,014**	**962**
Public and publicly guaranteed	877	501	612	819	722	750	906	900
Official creditors	548	388	523	731	571	587	660	517
Private creditors	329	113	89	88	152	163	246	384
of which: Bonds	14	25	0	0	62	57	130	256
Private nonguaranteed	71	68	66	31	35	35	107	62
of which: Bonds	..	..	..	..	..	..	..	..
Net financial flows								
Net debt inflows	-449	831	2,421	3,108	3,160	3,683	4,672	6,767
Official creditors (incl. IMF)	-296	259	1,902	1,168	1,718	1,085	1,684	1,126
Private creditors	-153	573	519	1,940	1,442	2,598	2,988	5,641
Long-term	302	59	-61	1,403	352	2,268	1,804	3,385
Public and publicly guaranteed	-317	-481	428	1,441	85	1,457	902	3,138
Private nonguaranteed	619	540	-489	-37	267	810	902	246
Short-term	-455	514	579	537	1,090	330	1,183	2,256
Net equity inflows								
Foreign direct investment	221	899	2,456	1,369	2,076	2,092	3,213	3,582
Portfolio equity	18	64	-4	132	166	-108	43	..
Major economic aggregates								
Gross national income (GNI)	36,053	58,760	88,519	88,304	96,119	92,687	101,042	104,106
Exports of goods, services & prim. income	10,729	17,281	24,924	27,913	32,649	32,954	33,086	31,721
Imports of goods, services & prim. income	13,686	21,616	37,346	39,109	48,764	49,913	49,667	45,883
Primary income on FDI	268	594	1,753	1,445	2,086	2,092	1,279	..
Personal transfers & comp. of employees	2,161	4,589	6,269	6,423	7,256	6,508	6,882	6,962
International reserves	4,823	16,187	22,797	22,613	19,526	16,356	18,404	19,555
Ratios								
External debt stocks to exports (%)	192.2	94.1	98.9	97.6	91.6	102.6	118.6	134.8
External debt stocks to GNI (%)	57.2	27.7	27.9	30.9	31.1	36.5	38.8	41.1
Debt service to exports (%)	25.3	15.8	13.7	11.8	9.9	10.9	15.3	15.1
Reserves to external debt stocks (%)	23.4	99.6	92.4	83.0	65.3	48.4	46.9	45.7

Notes:

Short-term debt before 2009 is based on data from the BIS.

MOZAMBIQUE

(US$ million, unless otherwise indicated)

	2000	2005	2009	2010	2011	2012	2013	2014
Summary external debt data								
External debt stocks	**5,613**	**4,392**	**4,138**	**3,747**	**4,093**	**4,878**	**7,010**	**7,793**
Long-term external debt	4,693	3,366	3,165	2,909	3,604	4,324	6,229	7,107
Short-term external debt	560	714	632	480	134	201	430	359
interest arrears on long-term	404	525	465	381	5	31	41	54
Use of IMF credit	361	312	342	357	355	353	351	327
Long-term external debt								
Debt outstanding and disbursed	**4,693**	**3,366**	**3,165**	**2,909**	**3,604**	**4,324**	**6,229**	**7,107**
Public and publicly guaranteed	4,693	3,366	3,165	2,909	3,604	4,324	6,229	7,107
Official creditors	4,682	3,364	3,136	2,811	3,374	4,062	5,098	5,962
Private creditors	11	2	28	98	230	262	1,131	1,145
of which: Bonds	0	0	0	0	0	0	850	850
Private nonguaranteed	..	..	..	..	..	..	..	..
of which: Bonds	..	..	..	..	..	..	..	..
Disbursements	**131**	**326**	**446**	**373**	**497**	**745**	**1,961**	**1,210**
Public and publicly guaranteed	131	326	446	373	497	745	1,961	1,210
Official creditors	131	326	422	294	346	714	1,089	1,154
Private creditors	0	0	23	79	151	31	872	56
of which: Bonds	0	0	0	0	0	0	850	0
Private nonguaranteed	..	..	..	..	..	..	..	..
of which: Bonds	..	..	..	..	..	..	..	..
Principal repayments	**34**	**18**	**15**	**38**	**28**	**40**	**85**	**80**
Public and publicly guaranteed	34	18	15	38	28	40	85	80
Official creditors	33	18	12	30	22	36	70	68
Private creditors	1	0	3	8	6	4	14	12
of which: Bonds	0	0	0	0	0	0	0	0
Private nonguaranteed	..	..	..	..	..	..	..	..
of which: Bonds	..	..	..	..	..	..	..	..
Interest payments	**20**	**22**	**23**	**47**	**27**	**29**	**51**	**89**
Public and publicly guaranteed	20	22	23	47	27	29	51	89
Official creditors	20	22	23	46	27	29	49	59
Private creditors	0	0	0	0	0	0	2	30
of which: Bonds	0	0	0	0	0	0	0	27
Private nonguaranteed	..	..	..	..	..	..	..	..
of which: Bonds	..	..	..	..	..	..	..	..
Net financial flows								
Net debt inflows	83	125	620	289	497	744	2,093	1,043
Official creditors (incl. IMF)	157	297	564	286	322	676	1,016	1,083
Private creditors	-74	-172	56	3	174	68	1,077	-40
Long-term	-1	..	20	71	144	27	858	44
Public and publicly guaranteed	-1	..	20	71	144	27	858	44
Private nonguaranteed	..	..	..	..	..	..	..	..
Short-term	-73	-172	36	-68	30	41	219	-84
Net equity inflows								
Foreign direct investment	139	60	242	410	1,383	216	959	..
Portfolio equity	..	0	0	0	0	..	0	..
Major economic aggregates								
Gross national income (GNI)	4,075	6,219	10,458	9,834	13,055	14,936	15,576	16,369
Exports of goods, services & prim. income	769	2,186	2,909	3,102	4,027	5,105	5,442	..
Imports of goods, services & prim. income	1,763	3,350	4,893	5,245	7,891	12,305	12,653	..
Primary income on FDI	0	284	240	214	234	54	78	..
Personal transfers & comp. of employees	37	59	111	139	157	220	217	218
International reserves	723	1,054	2,099	2,159	2,469	2,770	3,142	3,010
Ratios								
External debt stocks to exports (%)	730.3	200.9	142.3	120.8	101.7	95.6	128.8	..
External debt stocks to GNI (%)	137.7	70.6	39.6	38.1	31.4	32.7	45.0	47.6
Debt service to exports (%)	9.4	3.2	1.4	2.8	1.5	1.4	2.6	..
Reserves to external debt stocks (%)	12.9	24.0	50.7	57.6	60.3	56.8	44.8	38.6

Notes:

Short-term debt is based on data from the BIS. Data include HIPC and MDRI debt relief.

MYANMAR

(US$ million, unless otherwise indicated)

	2000	2005	2009	2010	2011	2012	2013	2014
Summary external debt data								
External debt stocks	**5,875**	**6,674**	**8,104**	**8,217**	**8,192**	**7,840**	**7,251**	**6,351**
Long-term external debt	5,328	5,815	6,671	6,646	6,620	6,486	5,978	5,260
Short-term external debt	492	796	1,061	1,181	1,191	977	893	752
interest arrears on long-term	492	796	1,061	1,181	1,191	977	893	752
Use of IMF credit	55	63	373	390	381	378	380	339
Long-term external debt								
Debt outstanding and disbursed	**5,328**	**5,815**	**6,671**	**6,646**	**6,620**	**6,486**	**5,978**	**5,260**
Public and publicly guaranteed	5,328	5,815	6,671	6,646	6,620	6,486	5,978	5,175
Official creditors	4,283	4,721	5,539	6,034	6,014	5,895	5,399	4,650
Private creditors	1,045	1,094	1,132	612	605	591	579	525
of which: Bonds	0	0	0	0	0	0	0	0
Private nonguaranteed	..	..	..	..	..	..	..	85
of which: Bonds	..	..	..	..	..	..	..	..
Disbursements	**38**	**1**	**0**	**0**	**0**	**931**	**0**	**103**
Public and publicly guaranteed	38	1	0	0	0	931	0	18
Official creditors	35	1	0	0	0	931	0	18
Private creditors	3	0	0	0	0	0	0	0
of which: Bonds	0	0	0	0	0	0	0	0
Private nonguaranteed	..	..	..	..	..	..	..	85
of which: Bonds	..	..	..	..	..	..	..	..
Principal repayments	**6**	**3**	**4**	**2**	**1**	**764**	**54**	**49**
Public and publicly guaranteed	6	3	4	2	1	764	54	49
Official creditors	2	3	4	2	1	764	54	49
Private creditors	4	0	0	0	0	0	0	0
of which: Bonds	0	0	0	0	0	0	0	0
Private nonguaranteed	..	..	..	..	..	..	..	..
of which: Bonds	..	..	..	..	..	..	..	..
Interest payments	**1**	**0**	**1**	**1**	**1**	**179**	**13**	**13**
Public and publicly guaranteed	1	0	1	1	1	179	13	13
Official creditors	0	0	1	1	1	179	13	13
Private creditors	0	0	0	0	0	0	0	0
of which: Bonds	0	0	0	0	0	0	0	0
Private nonguaranteed	..	..	..	..	..	..	..	..
of which: Bonds	..	..	..	..	..	..	..	..
Net financial flows								
Net debt inflows	31	-2	-4	-2	-1	167	-54	54
Official creditors (incl. IMF)	33	-2	-4	-2	-1	167	-54	-31
Private creditors	-2	..	..	..	..	..	..	85
Long-term	-2	..	..	..	..	..	..	85
Public and publicly guaranteed	-2	..	..	..	..	..	..	..
Private nonguaranteed	..	..	..	..	..		..	85
Short-term	..	..	..	..	..	..	..	..
Net equity inflows								
Foreign direct investment	258	235	1,079	901	2,520	1,334	2,255	946
Portfolio equity	..	..	..	..	..	..	..	..
Major economic aggregates								
Gross national income (GNI)	..	..	..	..	..	73,934	57,366	62,194
Exports of goods, services & prim. income	2,145	3,838	6,347	7,851	8,658	9,745	11,530	..
Imports of goods, services & prim. income	2,627	3,429	5,794	6,516	10,614	11,555	13,472	..
Primary income on FDI	135	1,388	1,811	1,816	1,955	2,396	2,344	..
Personal transfers & comp. of employees	104	129	54	115	127	275	229	232
International reserves	223	771	5,252	5,717	7,004	6,964	..	..
Ratios								
External debt stocks to exports (%)	273.9	173.9	127.7	104.7	94.6	80.5	62.9	..
External debt stocks to GNI (%)	..	..	..	..	..	10.6	12.6	10.2
Debt service to exports (%)	0.4	0.1	0.1	0.0	0.0	9.7	0.6	..
Reserves to external debt stocks (%)	3.8	11.5	64.8	69.6	85.5	88.8	..	..

Notes:

Fiscal year-end for external debt data is March. Long-term public and publicly guaranteed and short-term debt data are World Bank staff estimates based on the original terms of the loans. Country is expected to resume DRS reporting in 2015.

NEPAL

(US$ million, unless otherwise indicated)

	2000	2005	2009	2010	2011	2012	2013	2014
Summary external debt data								
External debt stocks	**2,878**	**3,191**	**3,778**	**3,789**	**3,828**	**3,888**	**4,087**	**4,010**
Long-term external debt	2,826	3,112	3,552	3,509	3,530	3,571	3,649	3,512
Short-term external debt	29	47	44	61	84	113	250	333
interest arrears on long-term	0	0	0	0	0	0	0	0
Use of IMF credit	23	32	183	219	214	204	189	165
Long-term external debt								
Debt outstanding and disbursed	**2,826**	**3,112**	**3,552**	**3,509**	**3,530**	**3,571**	**3,649**	**3,512**
Public and publicly guaranteed	2,826	3,112	3,552	3,509	3,530	3,571	3,649	3,512
Official creditors	2,821	3,108	3,548	3,506	3,528	3,569	3,647	3,511
Private creditors	5	5	4	3	2	2	2	1
of which: Bonds	0	0	0	0	0	0	0	0
Private nonguaranteed	..	..	..	..	..	..	..	..
of which: Bonds	..	..	..	..	..	..	..	..
Disbursements	**154**	**196**	**115**	**126**	**174**	**235**	**265**	**238**
Public and publicly guaranteed	154	196	115	126	174	235	265	238
Official creditors	154	196	115	126	174	235	265	238
Private creditors	0	0	0	0	0	0	0	0
of which: Bonds	0	0	0	0	0	0	0	0
Private nonguaranteed	..	..	..	..	..	..	..	..
of which: Bonds	..	..	..	..	..	..	..	..
Principal repayments	**67**	**86**	**140**	**148**	**154**	**175**	**165**	**165**
Public and publicly guaranteed	67	86	140	148	154	175	165	165
Official creditors	60	85	139	148	153	175	164	165
Private creditors	7	1	1	0	1	0	1	0
of which: Bonds	0	0	0	0	0	0	0	0
Private nonguaranteed	..	..	..	..	..	..	..	..
of which: Bonds	..	..	..	..	..	..	..	..
Interest payments	**28**	**30**	**32**	**32**	**35**	**33**	**36**	**40**
Public and publicly guaranteed	28	30	32	32	35	33	36	40
Official creditors	27	30	32	32	35	33	36	40
Private creditors	1	0	0	0	0	0	0	0
of which: Bonds	0	0	0	0	0	0	0	0
Private nonguaranteed	..	..	..	..	..	..	..	..
of which: Bonds	..	..	..	..	..	..	..	..
Net financial flows								
Net debt inflows	69	121	-40	34	39	78	221	143
Official creditors (incl. IMF)	90	111	-27	17	16	50	85	61
Private creditors	-21	10	-14	17	22	29	136	83
Long-term	-7	-1	-1	0	-1	0	-1	0
Public and publicly guaranteed	-7	-1	-1	0	-1	0	-1	0
Private nonguaranteed	..	..	..	..	..	..	..	..
Short-term	-14	11	-13	17	23	29	137	83
Net equity inflows								
Foreign direct investment	0	2	38	88	94	92	74	6
Portfolio equity	..	..	..	..	..	..	..	..
Major economic aggregates								
Gross national income (GNI)	5,514	8,153	13,008	16,125	19,018	19,003	19,393	20,025
Exports of goods, services & prim. income	1,354	1,423	1,752	1,781	2,150	2,177	2,516	2,748
Imports of goods, services & prim. income	1,825	2,803	5,153	5,995	6,588	6,969	7,618	8,666
Primary income on FDI	..	57	9	50	59	34	25	25
Personal transfers & comp. of employees	111	1,212	2,983	3,464	4,217	4,793	5,589	5,770
International reserves	945	1,499	2,769	2,937	3,631	4,307	5,293	6,027
Ratios								
External debt stocks to exports (%)	212.5	224.2	215.7	212.7	178.0	178.6	162.5	145.9
External debt stocks to GNI (%)	52.2	39.1	29.0	23.5	20.1	20.5	21.1	20.0
Debt service to exports (%)	7.6	8.5	10.1	10.6	9.2	10.3	8.8	8.2
Reserves to external debt stocks (%)	32.9	47.0	73.3	77.5	94.8	110.8	129.5	150.3

Notes:

Short-term debt for 2013 and 2014 is based on QEDS data reported by the country.

NICARAGUA

(US$ million, unless otherwise indicated)

	2000	2005	2009	2010	2011	2012	2013	2014
Summary external debt data								
External debt stocks	**6,822**	**5,000**	**5,883**	**7,002**	**7,924**	**8,950**	**9,777**	**10,216**
Long-term external debt	5,716	4,231	4,545	5,251	6,108	6,895	7,743	8,408
Short-term external debt	912	540	993	1,392	1,443	1,695	1,690	1,505
interest arrears on long-term	790	364	484	495	506	518	528	537
Use of IMF credit	194	229	346	359	373	361	345	303
Long-term external debt								
Debt outstanding and disbursed	**5,716**	**4,231**	**4,545**	**5,251**	**6,108**	**6,895**	**7,743**	**8,408**
Public and publicly guaranteed	5,435	3,939	2,505	2,683	2,846	3,055	3,295	3,564
Official creditors	5,219	3,867	2,502	2,680	2,843	3,051	3,291	3,561
Private creditors	216	72	3	3	3	3	3	3
of which: Bonds	0	0	0	0	0	0	0	0
Private nonguaranteed	281	292	2,040	2,567	3,262	3,840	4,448	4,844
of which: Bonds	..	..	..	..	..	..	..	..
Disbursements	**511**	**287**	**868**	**1,186**	**1,399**	**1,219**	**1,246**	**1,191**
Public and publicly guaranteed	226	226	291	267	239	258	287	401
Official creditors	220	226	291	267	239	258	287	401
Private creditors	6	0	0	0	0	0	0	0
of which: Bonds	0	0	0	0	0	0	0	0
Private nonguaranteed	285	61	578	919	1,159	961	960	790
of which: Bonds	..	..	..	..	..	..	..	..
Principal repayments	**184**	**110**	**366**	**456**	**540**	**453**	**456**	**532**
Public and publicly guaranteed	71	64	62	56	63	53	54	63
Official creditors	62	64	62	56	63	53	53	63
Private creditors	8	0	0	0	0	0	0	0
of which: Bonds	0	0	0	0	0	0	0	0
Private nonguaranteed	114	47	303	400	477	400	403	469
of which: Bonds	..	..	..	..	..	..	..	..
Interest payments	**91**	**46**	**121**	**104**	**121**	**144**	**150**	**156**
Public and publicly guaranteed	79	44	37	33	39	39	45	56
Official creditors	76	44	37	33	39	39	45	56
Private creditors	3	0	0	0	0	0	0	0
of which: Bonds	0	0	0	0	0	0	0	0
Private nonguaranteed	12	2	84	70	82	105	106	100
of which: Bonds	..	..	..	..	..	..	..	..
Net financial flows								
Net debt inflows	350	210	367	1,138	914	992	759	444
Official creditors (incl. IMF)	179	153	265	230	191	192	217	316
Private creditors	172	57	101	907	722	800	542	127
Long-term	169	14	274	518	683	561	557	321
Public and publicly guaranteed	-2	0	0	0	0	0	0	0
Private nonguaranteed	171	14	274	519	683	561	557	321
Short-term	3	43	-173	389	40	240	-15	-194
Net equity inflows								
Foreign direct investment	267	241	434	490	936	768	816	840
Portfolio equity	..	..	..	..	..	0	..	..
Major economic aggregates								
Gross national income (GNI)	4,906	6,171	8,126	8,500	9,503	10,140	10,538	11,498
Exports of goods, services & prim. income	1,133	1,434	2,839	3,379	4,192	4,760	4,639	5,030
Imports of goods, services & prim. income	2,479	3,075	4,681	5,319	6,576	7,183	7,208	7,311
Primary income on FDI	69	82	121	135	146	177	169	160
Personal transfers & comp. of employees	320	616	770	825	914	1,016	1,081	1,140
International reserves	488	728	1,573	1,799	1,892	1,887	1,993	2,276
Ratios								
External debt stocks to exports (%)	602.4	348.7	207.3	207.3	189.1	188.0	210.7	203.1
External debt stocks to GNI (%)	139.1	81.0	72.4	82.4	83.4	88.3	92.8	88.8
Debt service to exports (%)	25.6	12.1	17.9	17.3	16.7	13.6	14.3	14.8
Reserves to external debt stocks (%)	7.2	14.6	26.7	25.7	23.9	21.1	20.4	22.3

Notes:

Short-term debt before 2006 is based on data from the BIS. Data include the effects of HIPC and MDRI debt relief.

NIGER

(US$ million, unless otherwise indicated)

	2000	2005	2009	2010	2011	2012	2013	2014
Summary external debt data								
External debt stocks	**1,694**	**1,963**	**1,258**	**1,550**	**2,237**	**2,320**	**2,602**	**2,585**
Long-term external debt	1,535	1,783	972	1,221	1,930	2,059	2,265	2,274
Short-term external debt	72	40	131	171	154	97	164	109
interest arrears on long-term	60	37	17	22	19	22	117	71
Use of IMF credit	86	141	155	158	153	164	173	202
Long-term external debt								
Debt outstanding and disbursed	**1,535**	**1,783**	**972**	**1,221**	**1,930**	**2,059**	**2,265**	**2,274**
Public and publicly guaranteed	1,467	1,750	965	1,221	1,930	2,059	2,265	2,274
Official creditors	1,467	1,750	965	1,221	1,930	2,059	2,265	2,274
Private creditors	0	0	0	0	0	0	0	0
of which: Bonds	0	0	0	0	0	0	0	0
Private nonguaranteed	68	33	7	..	..	..	..	..
of which: Bonds	..	..	..	..	..	..	..	..
Disbursements	**76**	**122**	**211**	**283**	**747**	**144**	**225**	**129**
Public and publicly guaranteed	76	122	211	283	747	144	225	129
Official creditors	76	122	211	283	747	144	225	129
Private creditors	0	0	0	0	0	0	0	0
of which: Bonds	0	0	0	0	0	0	0	0
Private nonguaranteed	..	..	..	..	..	..	..	..
of which: Bonds	..	..	..	..	..	..	..	..
Principal repayments	**14**	**22**	**29**	**14**	**18**	**19**	**26**	**30**
Public and publicly guaranteed	12	15	22	7	18	19	26	30
Official creditors	12	15	22	7	18	19	26	30
Private creditors	0	0	0	0	0	0	0	0
of which: Bonds	0	0	0	0	0	0	0	0
Private nonguaranteed	2	7	7	7	..	..	..	..
of which: Bonds	..	..	..	..	..	..	..	..
Interest payments	**8**	**13**	**8**	**8**	**10**	**10**	**11**	**18**
Public and publicly guaranteed	8	11	8	8	10	10	11	18
Official creditors	8	11	8	8	10	10	11	18
Private creditors	0	0	0	0	0	0	0	0
of which: Bonds	0	0	0	0	0	0	0	0
Private nonguaranteed	0	2	0	0	..	..	..	..
of which: Bonds	..	..	..	..	..	..	..	..
Net financial flows								
Net debt inflows	52	109	227	309	711	76	180	131
Official creditors (incl. IMF)	73	119	194	281	725	136	208	140
Private creditors	-22	-10	33	28	-14	-60	-28	-9
Long-term	-2	-7	-7	-7	..	..	..	..
Public and publicly guaranteed	..	..	..	..	..	..	..	..
Private nonguaranteed	-2	-7	-7	-7	..	..	..	..
Short-term	-20	-3	40	35	-14	-60	-28	-9
Net equity inflows								
Foreign direct investment	8	23	-6	0	1,062	526	446	769
Portfolio equity	0	1	9	6	-4	20	..	..
Major economic aggregates								
Gross national income (GNI)	1,782	3,396	5,362	5,674	6,362	6,807	7,498	8,040
Exports of goods, services & prim. income	334	602	1,186	1,332	1,433	1,665	1,820	..
Imports of goods, services & prim. income	485	1,095	2,657	2,916	3,208	3,015	3,265	..
Primary income on FDI	2	21	84	17	60	179	181	..
Personal transfers & comp. of employees	14	66	102	134	166	152	146	157
International reserves	81	251	656	760	673	1,015	1,167	1,281
Ratios								
External debt stocks to exports (%)	507.6	326.0	106.1	116.4	156.1	139.3	143.0	..
External debt stocks to GNI (%)	95.0	57.8	23.5	27.3	35.2	34.1	34.7	32.1
Debt service to exports (%)	8.0	6.8	3.2	1.8	2.4	2.1	2.5	..
Reserves to external debt stocks (%)	4.8	12.8	52.1	49.1	30.1	43.7	44.8	49.6

Notes:

Short-term debt is based on data from the BIS. Data include the effects of HIPC and MDRI debt relief.

NIGERIA

(US$ million, unless otherwise indicated)

	2000	2005	2009	2010	2011	2012	2013	2014
Summary external debt data								
External debt stocks	**32,374**	**25,755**	**15,859**	**15,420**	**17,416**	**18,810**	**21,616**	**26,858**
Long-term external debt	31,049	25,527	13,233	12,840	14,844	16,235	19,035	24,431
Short-term external debt	1,120	3	0	0	0	0	1	0
interest arrears on long-term	43	3	0	0	0	0	1	0
Use of IMF credit	205	225	2,626	2,580	2,572	2,575	2,580	2,427
Long-term external debt								
Debt outstanding and disbursed	**31,049**	**25,527**	**13,233**	**12,840**	**14,844**	**16,235**	**19,035**	**24,431**
Public and publicly guaranteed	30,042	20,248	4,139	4,627	5,891	6,634	8,286	9,133
Official creditors	26,596	18,039	4,052	4,627	5,391	6,134	7,286	8,133
Private creditors	3,446	2,209	87	0	500	500	1,000	1,000
of which: Bonds	2,051	1,442	0	0	500	500	1,000	1,000
Private nonguaranteed	1,007	5,279	9,094	8,213	8,954	9,601	10,749	15,297
of which: Bonds	..	..	..	..	500	850	2,125	4,475
Disbursements	**946**	**2,449**	**954**	**1,543**	**2,480**	**1,586**	**3,174**	**8,423**
Public and publicly guaranteed	153	379	519	1,057	1,587	833	1,870	1,378
Official creditors	153	345	519	1,057	1,087	833	1,370	1,378
Private creditors	0	34	0	0	500	0	500	0
of which: Bonds	0	0	0	0	500	0	500	0
Private nonguaranteed	792	2,070	434	486	892	752	1,304	7,045
of which: Bonds	..	..	..	..	500	350	1,275	2,350
Principal repayments	**1,092**	**3,863**	**648**	**796**	**408**	**263**	**353**	**435**
Public and publicly guaranteed	1,057	3,863	323	229	256	158	203	139
Official creditors	915	3,685	297	225	256	158	203	139
Private creditors	142	179	26	4	0	0	0	0
of which: Bonds	0	0	0	0	0	0	0	0
Private nonguaranteed	35	..	325	567	152	105	150	296
of which: Bonds	..	..	..	..	..	..	..	..
Interest payments	**690**	**4,937**	**79**	**55**	**93**	**144**	**265**	**267**
Public and publicly guaranteed	673	4,937	79	55	74	94	166	126
Official creditors	516	4,717	73	54	57	60	68	80
Private creditors	157	220	6	0	17	34	97	46
of which: Bonds	128	170	0	0	17	34	97	46
Private nonguaranteed	18	..	..	..	19	50	99	141
of which: Bonds	..	..	..	..	19	50	99	141
Net financial flows								
Net debt inflows	95	-1,414	305	746	2,072	1,323	2,821	7,988
Official creditors (incl. IMF)	-762	-3,340	222	831	831	675	1,167	1,239
Private creditors	857	1,925	83	-85	1,240	648	1,654	6,748
Long-term	616	1,925	83	-85	1,240	648	1,654	6,748
Public and publicly guaranteed	-142	-145	-26	-4	500	..	500	..
Private nonguaranteed	757	2,070	109	-81	740	648	1,154	6,748
Short-term	241	..	0	..	..	..	..	..
Net equity inflows								
Foreign direct investment	1,140	4,983	8,534	5,988	8,590	7,033	5,608	4,694
Portfolio equity	..	751	487	2,161	2,571	10,003	5,577	1,045
Major economic aggregates								
Gross national income (GNI)	40,238	98,881	154,918	349,388	388,771	438,746	492,501	549,342
Exports of goods, services & prim. income	21,183	57,149	59,321	81,976	100,653	99,048	101,122	86,010
Imports of goods, services & prim. income	15,383	35,773	64,815	88,299	109,908	100,602	103,900	106,850
Primary income on FDI	2,279	2,603	15,042	20,032	23,072	22,430	..	..
Personal transfers & comp. of employees	1,392	14,640	18,368	19,818	20,619	20,633	20,968	20,968
International reserves	9,911	28,280	44,763	34,919	35,212	46,405	45,427	36,669
Ratios								
External debt stocks to exports (%)	152.8	45.1	26.7	18.8	17.3	19.0	21.4	31.2
External debt stocks to GNI (%)	80.5	26.0	10.2	4.4	4.5	4.3	4.4	4.9
Debt service to exports (%)	8.8	15.4	1.2	1.0	0.5	0.4	0.6	0.8
Reserves to external debt stocks (%)	30.6	109.8	282.2	226.5	202.2	246.7	210.2	136.5

Notes:

Long-term private nonguaranteed debt data from 2005 are estimates based on Central Bank data. Short-term debt is revised from 2001 based on reports provided by the country.

PAKISTAN

(US$ million, unless otherwise indicated)

	2000	2005	2009	2010	2011	2012	2013	2014
Summary external debt data								
External debt stocks	**32,954**	**34,018**	**56,340**	**64,003**	**65,520**	**62,144**	**60,045**	**62,184**
Long-term external debt	29,684	31,053	45,829	49,412	51,494	50,658	49,428	51,646
Short-term external debt	1,519	1,230	1,466	4,333	4,065	3,802	5,505	5,538
interest arrears on long-term	0	0	0	0	0	0	0	0
Use of IMF credit	1,751	1,735	9,045	10,258	9,962	7,684	5,113	5,001
Long-term external debt								
Debt outstanding and disbursed	**29,684**	**31,053**	**45,829**	**49,412**	**51,494**	**50,658**	**49,428**	**51,646**
Public and publicly guaranteed	27,124	30,089	42,564	43,403	45,129	44,738	43,305	45,879
Official creditors	25,074	28,907	40,059	41,604	43,362	43,009	41,614	40,490
Private creditors	2,051	1,182	2,505	1,799	1,768	1,729	1,690	5,389
of which: Bonds	623	1,100	2,150	1,550	1,550	1,550	1,550	4,550
Private nonguaranteed	2,560	964	3,265	6,009	6,365	5,920	6,123	5,767
of which: Bonds	45	600	850	250	250	250	..	..
Disbursements	**1,647**	**2,831**	**4,416**	**5,474**	**3,210**	**2,312**	**4,151**	**7,859**
Public and publicly guaranteed	1,530	2,231	3,735	1,854	2,572	2,312	2,418	7,257
Official creditors	1,526	1,619	3,734	1,852	2,572	2,312	2,418	3,489
Private creditors	4	612	1	1	0	0	0	3,768
of which: Bonds	0	600	0	0	0	0	0	3,000
Private nonguaranteed	117	600	681	3,620	638	..	1,734	602
of which: Bonds	..	600	..	..	..	..	..	..
Principal repayments	**1,588**	**1,466**	**2,241**	**3,009**	**1,665**	**1,527**	**3,361**	**2,847**
Public and publicly guaranteed	1,143	1,139	1,635	2,133	1,383	1,395	1,830	1,889
Official creditors	1,106	996	1,053	1,425	1,351	1,356	1,791	1,817
Private creditors	37	143	582	707	32	39	39	72
of which: Bonds	0	108	500	600	0	0	0	0
Private nonguaranteed	445	327	606	876	282	132	1,531	958
of which: Bonds	..	..	..	600	..	..	250	..
Interest payments	**858**	**681**	**909**	**840**	**784**	**752**	**914**	**1,047**
Public and publicly guaranteed	642	605	804	781	711	686	666	779
Official creditors	528	554	635	649	594	583	582	587
Private creditors	114	50	169	131	117	103	84	192
of which: Bonds	61	47	156	120	111	99	81	155
Private nonguaranteed	217	76	105	59	73	65	248	269
of which: Bonds	2	3	50	30	22	22	11	..
Net financial flows								
Net debt inflows	-341	1,108	5,288	6,692	1,005	-1,752	-69	5,245
Official creditors (incl. IMF)	331	381	5,698	1,787	950	-1,319	-1,936	1,871
Private creditors	-672	727	-410	4,906	56	-433	1,867	3,373
Long-term	-361	742	-506	2,038	324	-171	164	3,341
Public and publicly guaranteed	-33	469	-581	-706	-32	-39	-39	3,697
Private nonguaranteed	-328	273	75	2,744	356	-132	203	-356
Short-term	-311	-15	96	2,867	-269	-263	1,703	33
Net equity inflows								
Foreign direct investment	308	2,201	2,338	2,016	1,309	958	1,536	1,812
Portfolio equity	35	451	-37	524	-37	178	111	772
Major economic aggregates								
Gross national income (GNI)	73,025	111,767	172,564	184,164	223,348	236,253	244,281	260,228
Exports of goods, services & prim. income	10,237	19,760	22,921	28,738	32,173	31,962	30,544	31,081
Imports of goods, services & prim. income	14,484	32,445	39,373	43,885	50,838	52,875	53,631	55,535
Primary income on FDI	429	1,871	2,548	2,140	2,102	2,372	2,908	3,118
Personal transfers & comp. of employees	1,075	4,280	8,717	9,690	12,263	14,006	14,629	17,066
International reserves	1,513	10,033	11,318	14,346	14,528	10,242	5,156	11,807
Ratios								
External debt stocks to exports (%)	321.9	172.2	245.8	222.7	203.6	194.4	196.6	200.1
External debt stocks to GNI (%)	45.1	30.4	32.6	34.8	29.3	26.3	24.6	23.9
Debt service to exports (%)	28.1	12.5	15.1	14.9	9.1	14.8	26.3	19.1
Reserves to external debt stocks (%)	4.6	29.5	20.1	22.4	22.2	16.5	8.6	19.0

Notes:

Long-term private nonguaranteed debt data from 2006 are World Bank staff estimates based on the reports provided by the country. Short-term debt before 2010 is based on data from the BIS and thereafter short-term debt is World Bank staff estimates based on Central Bank data.

PANAMA

(US$ million, unless otherwise indicated)

	2000	2005	2009	2010	2011	2012	2013	2014
Summary external debt data								
External debt stocks	**6,606**	**8,106**	**11,243**	**11,382**	**12,583**	**13,361**	**16,696**	**19,343**
Long-term external debt	6,481	8,044	10,934	11,078	12,281	13,058	16,392	19,057
Short-term external debt	1	0	0	0	0	0	0	0
interest arrears on long-term	1	0	0	0	0	0	0	0
Use of IMF credit	124	61	309	303	302	303	303	285
Long-term external debt								
Debt outstanding and disbursed	**6,481**	**8,044**	**10,934**	**11,078**	**12,281**	**13,058**	**16,392**	**19,057**
Public and publicly guaranteed	5,700	6,302	9,798	10,087	10,890	10,790	12,197	14,060
Official creditors	1,289	1,304	1,833	2,126	2,399	2,733	3,199	3,782
Private creditors	4,411	4,999	7,965	7,961	8,491	8,057	8,998	10,278
of which: Bonds	4,141	4,920	7,738	7,738	8,272	7,725	8,306	9,506
Private nonguaranteed	780	1,742	1,136	991	1,391	2,268	4,195	4,998
of which: Bonds	266	635	1,061	911	1,261	2,061	3,671	4,420
Disbursements	**724**	**1,595**	**1,890**	**445**	**1,377**	**1,567**	**2,916**	**3,530**
Public and publicly guaranteed	486	1,325	1,865	440	973	652	2,302	2,466
Official creditors	97	94	461	440	438	537	691	1,109
Private creditors	388	1,231	1,404	0	535	114	1,610	1,357
of which: Bonds	370	1,230	1,323	0	535	0	1,250	1,250
Private nonguaranteed	238	270	25	5	404	915	615	1,064
of which: Bonds	..	150	..	..	350	800	270	969
Principal repayments	**411**	**1,207**	**190**	**320**	**185**	**955**	**792**	**476**
Public and publicly guaranteed	386	955	190	170	178	917	764	215
Official creditors	109	139	154	165	175	174	179	188
Private creditors	277	817	36	5	3	742	584	27
of which: Bonds	120	799	0	0	0	741	584	0
Private nonguaranteed	25	251	..	150	7	38	28	261
of which: Bonds	..	..	..	150	..	..	..	220
Interest payments	**418**	**541**	**684**	**726**	**745**	**744**	**882**	**925**
Public and publicly guaranteed	365	454	596	638	668	697	669	690
Official creditors	79	59	72	75	76	77	85	93
Private creditors	286	394	524	563	592	620	585	597
of which: Bonds	264	390	514	560	589	606	567	558
Private nonguaranteed	53	87	88	87	77	47	213	235
of which: Bonds	24	44	83	83	73	42	205	226
Net financial flows								
Net debt inflows	261	378	1,700	125	1,192	612	2,125	3,054
Official creditors (incl. IMF)	-63	-55	307	275	263	363	512	921
Private creditors	324	433	1,393	-150	929	249	1,613	2,133
Long-term	324	433	1,393	-150	929	249	1,613	2,133
Public and publicly guaranteed	112	414	1,368	-5	531	-628	1,026	1,330
Private nonguaranteed	213	19	25	-145	397	877	587	803
Short-term	..	..	..	..	..	..	..	..
Net equity inflows								
Foreign direct investment	624	470	1,155	1,967	1,929	2,298	4,113	4,379
Portfolio equity	..	..	..	..	..	..	..	..
Major economic aggregates								
Gross national income (GNI)	11,007	14,340	27,326	30,229	31,301	35,175	42,387	44,078
Exports of goods, services & prim. income	9,408	11,619	19,024	20,534	26,889	30,032	29,288	28,237
Imports of goods, services & prim. income	10,258	12,882	19,314	23,748	32,148	33,647	34,270	33,615
Primary income on FDI	562	1,048	1,310	2,176	2,025	2,055	3,516	3,557
Personal transfers & comp. of employees	16	130	337	410	368	411	452	760
International reserves	723	1,211	3,028	2,714	2,304	2,466	2,848	4,032
Ratios								
External debt stocks to exports (%)	70.2	69.8	59.1	55.4	46.8	44.5	57.0	68.5
External debt stocks to GNI (%)	60.0	56.5	41.1	37.7	40.2	38.0	39.4	43.9
Debt service to exports (%)	9.4	15.1	4.6	5.1	3.5	5.7	5.7	5.0
Reserves to external debt stocks (%)	10.9	14.9	26.9	23.8	18.3	18.5	17.1	20.8

Notes:

Long-term private nonguaranteed debt data only cover Inter-American Development Bank and Bonds.

PAPUA NEW GUINEA

(US$ million, unless otherwise indicated)

	2000	2005	2009	2010	2011	2012	2013	2014
Summary external debt data								
External debt stocks	**2,305**	**1,896**	**1,787**	**5,965**	**12,584**	**14,945**	**21,605**	**20,920**
Long-term external debt	2,204	1,651	1,460	5,380	12,268	14,468	21,102	19,726
Short-term external debt	49	232	130	392	123	284	309	1,013
interest arrears on long-term	0	0	0	0	0	0	0	0
Use of IMF credit	51	13	197	193	193	193	193	182
Long-term external debt								
Debt outstanding and disbursed	**2,204**	**1,651**	**1,460**	**5,380**	**12,268**	**14,468**	**21,102**	**19,726**
Public and publicly guaranteed	1,454	1,264	1,045	1,042	1,069	1,130	1,256	1,656
Official creditors	1,394	1,213	1,008	1,009	1,043	1,114	1,248	1,654
Private creditors	60	51	36	33	26	16	8	1
of which: Bonds	0	0	0	0	0	0	0	0
Private nonguaranteed	750	387	415	4,337	11,199	13,338	19,847	18,070
of which: Bonds	..	..	..	..	..	..	..	..
Disbursements	**254**	**335**	**516**	**3,153**	**8,158**	**2,717**	**7,692**	**1,324**
Public and publicly guaranteed	219	45	33	37	94	161	231	541
Official creditors	206	44	33	37	94	161	231	541
Private creditors	13	1	0	0	0	0	0	0
of which: Bonds	0	0	0	0	0	0	0	0
Private nonguaranteed	35	290	483	3,116	8,064	2,556	7,461	784
of which: Bonds	..	..	..	..	..	..	..	..
Principal repayments	**196**	**183**	**513**	**758**	**1,076**	**349**	**1,028**	**822**
Public and publicly guaranteed	115	114	62	67	79	78	75	74
Official creditors	96	93	55	60	71	70	69	68
Private creditors	19	21	7	7	8	8	7	6
of which: Bonds	0	0	0	0	0	0	0	0
Private nonguaranteed	80	69	451	691	997	271	953	748
of which: Bonds	..	..	..	..	..	..	..	..
Interest payments	**85**	**54**	**28**	**50**	**104**	**131**	**231**	**337**
Public and publicly guaranteed	54	38	21	16	19	18	18	20
Official creditors	50	36	20	16	19	18	17	20
Private creditors	5	2	1	1	1	0	0	0
of which: Bonds	0	0	0	0	0	0	0	0
Private nonguaranteed	31	16	7	33	85	113	213	317
of which: Bonds	..	..	..	..	..	..	..	..
Net financial flows								
Net debt inflows	30	214	124	2,657	6,812	2,529	6,689	1,206
Official creditors (incl. IMF)	128	-110	-22	-23	23	91	162	473
Private creditors	-99	323	146	2,680	6,790	2,438	6,527	734
Long-term	-51	200	25	2,418	7,059	2,277	6,502	30
Public and publicly guaranteed	-5	-20	-7	-7	-8	-8	-7	-6
Private nonguaranteed	-45	221	32	2,426	7,067	2,285	6,509	36
Short-term	-48	123	121	262	-269	161	25	704
Net equity inflows								
Foreign direct investment	96	31	419	28	-309	-64	18	-30
Portfolio equity	..	..	..	..	..	..	..	..
Major economic aggregates								
Gross national income (GNI)	3,303	4,528	7,868	9,261	12,003	15,024	14,642	..
Exports of goods, services & prim. income	2,369	3,649	4,624	6,097	7,380	6,855	..	..
Imports of goods, services & prim. income	2,013	3,368	5,382	6,920	7,796	9,274	..	..
Primary income on FDI	198	511	537	466	350	588	..	..
Personal transfers & comp. of employees	7	7	5	3	17	14	..	..
International reserves	287	718	2,561	3,033	4,256	3,930	2,775	2,254
Ratios								
External debt stocks to exports (%)	97.3	52.0	38.6	97.8	170.5	218.0	..	..
External debt stocks to GNI (%)	69.8	41.9	22.7	64.4	104.8	99.5	147.6	..
Debt service to exports (%)	12.9	8.4	11.7	13.3	16.0	7.0	..	..
Reserves to external debt stocks (%)	12.4	37.9	143.3	50.8	33.8	26.3	12.8	10.8

Notes:

Short-term debt is based on data from the BIS.

PARAGUAY

(US$ million, unless otherwise indicated)

	2000	2005	2009	2010	2011	2012	2013	2014
Summary external debt data								
External debt stocks	**3,135**	**5,412**	**10,624**	**12,652**	**13,078**	**12,881**	**13,413**	**14,092**
Long-term external debt	2,537	4,879	9,723	11,358	11,029	11,216	11,239	11,942
Short-term external debt	580	513	752	1,147	1,903	1,518	2,027	2,012
interest arrears on long-term	11	0	0	0	0	0	0	0
Use of IMF credit	18	20	149	147	146	146	147	138
Long-term external debt								
Debt outstanding and disbursed	**2,537**	**4,879**	**9,723**	**11,358**	**11,029**	**11,216**	**11,239**	**11,942**
Public and publicly guaranteed	2,087	2,266	2,261	2,366	2,305	2,245	2,680	3,699
Official creditors	1,639	1,845	1,979	2,099	2,072	2,051	2,025	2,082
Private creditors	449	421	282	267	233	194	655	1,616
of which: Bonds	0	0	0	0	0	0	500	1,500
Private nonguaranteed	450	2,614	7,462	8,992	8,724	8,971	8,559	8,243
of which: Bonds	..	..	..	..	..	500	500	800
Disbursements	**192**	**1,292**	**1,571**	**1,912**	**512**	**1,670**	**1,632**	**3,193**
Public and publicly guaranteed	192	144	248	308	163	227	709	1,258
Official creditors	192	141	248	308	163	227	209	258
Private creditors	0	3	0	0	0	0	500	1,000
of which: Bonds	0	0	0	0	0	0	500	1,000
Private nonguaranteed	..	1,147	1,323	1,605	349	1,443	922	1,935
of which: Bonds	..	..	..	..	..	500	..	300
Principal repayments	**207**	**332**	**308**	**313**	**711**	**1,738**	**1,543**	**2,445**
Public and publicly guaranteed	114	205	262	239	244	240	208	195
Official creditors	107	176	221	224	211	201	169	156
Private creditors	7	29	41	15	34	39	39	39
of which: Bonds	0	0	0	0	0	0	0	0
Private nonguaranteed	93	126	46	75	467	1,497	1,334	2,251
of which: Bonds	..	..	..	..	..	..	..	..
Interest payments	**116**	**115**	**122**	**131**	**140**	**179**	**236**	**227**
Public and publicly guaranteed	100	94	97	65	66	59	65	77
Official creditors	70	77	83	63	61	55	51	51
Private creditors	30	17	14	2	4	4	15	26
of which: Bonds	0	0	0	0	0	0	12	23
Private nonguaranteed	16	21	25	66	75	120	170	149
of which: Bonds	..	..	..	..	..	38	38	50
Net financial flows								
Net debt inflows	-187	807	868	1,994	557	-453	598	733
Official creditors (incl. IMF)	85	-35	27	84	-47	26	40	102
Private creditors	-272	842	841	1,910	605	-479	558	630
Long-term	-100	995	1,235	1,515	-151	-94	49	645
Public and publicly guaranteed	-7	-26	-41	-15	-34	-39	461	961
Private nonguaranteed	-93	1,021	1,277	1,530	-118	-54	-412	-316
Short-term	-173	-153	-394	395	756	-385	509	-15
Net equity inflows								
Foreign direct investment	104	32	197	87	277	300	263	236
Portfolio equity	..	..	..	..	..	..	..	..
Major economic aggregates								
Gross national income (GNI)	7,085	7,360	14,733	18,635	23,821	22,935	27,213	29,443
Exports of goods, services & prim. income	3,185	5,182	8,386	11,135	13,336	12,384	14,408	..
Imports of goods, services & prim. income	3,524	5,473	8,423	11,749	13,940	13,374	14,475	..
Primary income on FDI	84	158	555	759	641	800	896	..
Personal transfers & comp. of employees	278	161	377	410	541	634	591	591
International reserves	763	1,297	3,839	4,137	4,950	4,557	5,556	6,669
Ratios								
External debt stocks to exports (%)	98.4	104.4	126.7	113.6	98.1	104.0	93.1	..
External debt stocks to GNI (%)	44.2	73.5	72.1	67.9	54.9	56.2	49.3	47.9
Debt service to exports (%)	11.2	9.2	5.3	4.1	6.5	15.7	12.9	..
Reserves to external debt stocks (%)	24.3	24.0	36.1	32.7	37.9	35.4	41.4	47.3

Notes:

Long-term private nonguaranteed debt data from 2002 are estimates based on Central Bank data. Short-term debt is based on data from the BIS.

PERU

(US$ million, unless otherwise indicated)

	2000	2005	2009	2010	2011	2012	2013	2014
Summary external debt data								
External debt stocks	**28,813**	**29,508**	**37,390**	**42,154**	**45,012**	**54,150**	**56,661**	**66,469**
Long-term external debt	24,208	26,109	31,649	34,822	37,751	44,680	49,272	58,607
Short-term external debt	3,928	3,212	4,784	6,393	6,325	8,532	6,450	6,978
interest arrears on long-term	14	4	1	1	0	0	0	0
Use of IMF credit	677	188	956	939	936	937	939	884
Long-term external debt								
Debt outstanding and disbursed	**24,208**	**26,109**	**31,649**	**34,822**	**37,751**	**44,680**	**49,272**	**58,607**
Public and publicly guaranteed	19,270	22,537	20,788	20,009	20,142	19,966	17,077	15,753
Official creditors	14,439	13,830	11,727	10,555	10,721	9,982	7,505	7,086
Private creditors	4,830	8,706	9,061	9,454	9,422	9,984	9,573	8,667
of which: Bonds	3,727	8,390	8,911	9,311	9,299	9,894	9,511	8,625
Private nonguaranteed	4,938	3,572	10,862	14,813	17,608	24,714	32,195	42,854
of which: Bonds	150	1,230	4,428	727	1,705	4,665	9,885	13,571
Disbursements	**2,066**	**3,721**	**4,772**	**5,425**	**3,386**	**6,865**	**5,787**	**13,347**
Public and publicly guaranteed	1,489	2,635	3,232	3,862	1,003	1,347	370	432
Official creditors	1,454	985	1,232	1,601	1,003	447	370	432
Private creditors	35	1,650	2,000	2,261	0	900	0	0
of which: Bonds	0	1,650	2,000	2,261	0	900	0	0
Private nonguaranteed	577	1,086	1,539	1,563	2,382	5,518	5,417	12,915
of which: Bonds	..	1,080	878	..	1,705	2,960	5,220	3,686
Principal repayments	**1,003**	**4,189**	**2,221**	**4,060**	**2,128**	**2,758**	**5,130**	**3,293**
Public and publicly guaranteed	986	3,033	1,833	3,490	892	1,348	2,846	1,018
Official creditors	840	2,918	1,808	2,971	867	1,013	2,431	621
Private creditors	146	114	25	518	25	335	415	397
of which: Bonds	0	90	0	497	0	312	400	383
Private nonguaranteed	17	1,156	389	570	1,236	1,410	2,284	2,275
of which: Bonds	..	..	50	..	727	..	..	..
Interest payments	**1,174**	**1,718**	**1,976**	**2,550**	**1,789**	**3,007**	**1,571**	**1,679**
Public and publicly guaranteed	1,105	1,403	1,084	1,096	1,001	969	940	856
Official creditors	917	807	452	346	288	275	233	133
Private creditors	188	596	632	750	712	694	708	723
of which: Bonds	179	568	623	742	705	688	704	720
Private nonguaranteed	69	314	892	1,454	788	2,038	630	824
of which: Bonds	11	56	223	284	463	176	392	589
Net financial flows								
Net debt inflows	283	-46	1,935	2,974	1,191	6,314	-1,425	10,582
Official creditors (incl. IMF)	473	-1,972	-575	-1,370	136	-566	-2,061	-189
Private creditors	-190	1,927	2,511	4,344	1,055	6,880	636	10,771
Long-term	448	1,465	3,126	2,735	1,121	4,673	2,718	10,243
Public and publicly guaranteed	-111	1,536	1,975	1,742	-25	565	-415	-397
Private nonguaranteed	560	-70	1,151	993	1,147	4,108	3,133	10,640
Short-term	-638	461	-615	1,608	-67	2,207	-2,082	528
Net equity inflows								
Foreign direct investment	810	2,579	7,213	7,762	5,548	12,426	6,223	7,607
Portfolio equity	123	769	47	87	147	-142	585	-79
Major economic aggregates								
Gross national income (GNI)	49,571	69,883	112,807	137,317	157,207	180,278	191,731	193,575
Exports of goods, services & prim. income	9,247	20,006	31,801	39,986	51,052	51,699	48,564	46,618
Imports of goods, services & prim. income	11,794	20,631	35,411	46,794	57,430	61,287	61,036	59,023
Primary income on FDI	344	4,030	8,172	10,714	12,511	11,402	9,301	..
Personal transfers & comp. of employees	718	1,440	2,409	2,534	2,697	2,788	2,707	2,639
International reserves	8,374	13,599	32,013	42,648	47,206	62,300	64,423	61,185
Ratios								
External debt stocks to exports (%)	311.6	147.5	117.6	105.4	88.2	104.7	116.7	142.6
External debt stocks to GNI (%)	58.1	42.2	33.1	30.7	28.6	30.0	29.6	34.3
Debt service to exports (%)	27.9	30.3	13.4	16.7	7.9	11.3	14.0	10.9
Reserves to external debt stocks (%)	29.1	46.1	85.6	101.2	104.9	115.1	113.7	92.1

Notes:

Long-term private nonguaranteed debt data are World Bank staff estimates based on reports provided by the country.

PHILIPPINES

(US$ million, unless otherwise indicated)

	2000	2005	2009	2010	2011	2012	2013	2014
Summary external debt data								
External debt stocks	**58,456**	**58,693**	**55,986**	**65,304**	**66,383**	**69,874**	**66,871**	**77,659**
Long-term external debt	50,777	51,742	50,670	53,502	53,046	52,134	48,671	60,197
Short-term external debt	5,495	6,395	4,002	10,512	12,050	16,452	16,909	16,248
interest arrears on long-term	0	0	0	0	0	0	0	0
Use of IMF credit	2,183	555	1,314	1,290	1,287	1,288	1,290	1,214
Long-term external debt								
Debt outstanding and disbursed	**50,777**	**51,742**	**50,670**	**53,502**	**53,046**	**52,134**	**48,671**	**60,197**
Public and publicly guaranteed	33,744	35,364	42,198	45,040	44,902	43,552	39,262	38,014
Official creditors	19,890	18,580	22,054	23,210	23,587	21,934	18,665	17,640
Private creditors	13,855	16,784	20,144	21,831	21,315	21,618	20,597	20,374
of which: Bonds	10,466	14,290	18,901	20,534	20,045	20,470	19,689	19,669
Private nonguaranteed	17,033	16,378	8,472	8,462	8,144	8,582	9,410	22,183
of which: Bonds	2,856	2,975	956	1,651	1,579	2,600	6,250	7,325
Disbursements	**5,747**	**5,544**	**8,767**	**10,928**	**7,954**	**5,761**	**4,755**	**16,579**
Public and publicly guaranteed	5,228	3,874	8,124	8,251	4,999	3,828	962	3,355
Official creditors	1,528	1,144	2,349	1,370	1,709	1,436	910	1,809
Private creditors	3,701	2,730	5,776	6,881	3,290	2,392	52	1,546
of which: Bonds	2,630	2,384	5,510	6,680	3,121	2,241	0	1,500
Private nonguaranteed	519	1,670	642	2,677	2,954	1,933	3,793	13,224
of which: Bonds	5	250	..	..	1,075	1,525	3,650	1,075
Principal repayments	**4,047**	**5,748**	**5,675**	**8,341**	**6,311**	**2,725**	**2,918**	**3,047**
Public and publicly guaranteed	2,515	3,353	3,841	6,813	4,887	2,629	2,767	2,596
Official creditors	1,572	1,788	1,722	1,818	2,007	1,756	2,184	1,552
Private creditors	943	1,566	2,120	4,996	2,880	873	583	1,044
of which: Bonds	395	1,209	1,644	4,807	2,669	655	366	888
Private nonguaranteed	1,533	2,395	1,833	1,527	1,424	96	151	451
of which: Bonds	445	333	339	174	158	..	..	..
Interest payments	**2,469**	**3,152**	**3,266**	**3,112**	**3,195**	**2,973**	**2,922**	**3,045**
Public and publicly guaranteed	1,882	2,409	2,841	2,977	2,850	2,844	2,660	2,538
Official creditors	841	584	542	498	489	431	342	294
Private creditors	1,041	1,825	2,299	2,479	2,361	2,414	2,319	2,244
of which: Bonds	880	1,725	2,257	2,441	2,323	2,379	2,289	2,220
Private nonguaranteed	586	743	425	135	345	129	261	506
of which: Bonds	479	283	88	25	147	107	243	385
Net financial flows								
Net debt inflows	2,551	828	93	9,097	3,181	7,437	2,293	12,871
Official creditors (incl. IMF)	261	-961	627	-447	-298	-320	-1,275	257
Private creditors	2,290	1,788	-534	9,544	3,479	7,758	3,568	12,614
Long-term	1,744	439	2,465	3,035	1,941	3,356	3,111	13,275
Public and publicly guaranteed	2,758	1,164	3,656	1,885	410	1,520	-531	502
Private nonguaranteed	1,014	-725	-1,191	1,149	1,530	1,836	3,642	12,773
Short-term	546	1,349	-2,998	6,509	1,539	4,402	457	-661
Net equity inflows								
Foreign direct investment	2,240	1,321	1,886	-214	1,531	2,824	1,084	2,854
Portfolio equity	-202	420	308	833	1,040	1,753	-34	1,196
Major economic aggregates								
Gross national income (GNI)	94,969	129,804	223,417	265,931	268,494	299,115	326,317	341,481
Exports of goods, services & prim. income	44,060	38,514	49,632	61,241	64,792	75,080	76,206	81,641
Imports of goods, services & prim. income	51,931	48,158	57,753	71,658	77,716	87,631	85,896	91,546
Primary income on FDI	230	1,382	2,202	2,417	2,910	3,955	3,518	4,211
Personal transfers & comp. of employees	6,961	13,733	19,960	21,557	23,054	24,610	26,717	28,403
International reserves	13,090	15,926	38,783	55,363	67,290	73,478	75,689	72,057
Ratios								
External debt stocks to exports (%)	132.7	152.4	112.8	106.6	102.5	93.1	87.7	95.1
External debt stocks to GNI (%)	61.6	45.2	25.1	24.6	24.7	23.4	20.5	22.7
Debt service to exports (%)	16.0	24.7	18.1	18.7	14.7	7.6	7.7	7.5
Reserves to external debt stocks (%)	22.4	27.1	69.3	84.8	101.4	105.2	113.2	92.8

Notes:

Long-term private nonguaranteed debt data no longer include unregistered debt and are revised from 2005 based on the reports provided by the country.

ROMANIA

(US$ million, unless otherwise indicated)

	2000	2005	2009	2010	2011	2012	2013	2014
Summary external debt data								
External debt stocks	**11,252**	**38,626**	**113,389**	**115,170**	**119,379**	**120,709**	**123,955**	**111,290**
Long-term external debt	9,937	30,844	86,319	81,404	82,142	88,638	98,872	95,611
Short-term external debt	762	7,412	15,983	17,157	19,498	16,323	15,544	12,326
interest arrears on long-term	12	13	1	1	1	1	0	0
Use of IMF credit	552	369	11,088	16,609	17,738	15,748	9,540	3,352
Long-term external debt								
Debt outstanding and disbursed	**9,937**	**30,844**	**86,319**	**81,404**	**82,142**	**88,638**	**98,872**	**95,611**
Public and publicly guaranteed	6,575	13,071	18,022	20,578	24,646	29,378	35,576	36,794
Official creditors	4,149	5,930	11,099	14,058	16,665	17,284	19,178	16,863
Private creditors	2,426	7,141	6,922	6,520	7,981	12,095	16,397	19,931
of which: Bonds	736	2,123	2,809	3,006	4,852	10,166	14,783	18,802
Private nonguaranteed	3,362	17,773	68,297	60,826	57,496	59,260	63,296	58,818
of which: Bonds	..	..	..	..	117	288	4,707	311
Disbursements	**3,144**	**12,908**	**23,270**	**17,434**	**17,847**	**20,955**	**21,721**	**19,341**
Public and publicly guaranteed	1,937	2,637	3,937	5,622	6,177	6,504	6,379	6,355
Official creditors	1,083	1,016	3,735	4,128	3,900	1,263	2,154	719
Private creditors	854	1,620	202	1,494	2,277	5,241	4,225	5,635
of which: Bonds	139	623	0	1,327	2,070	5,117	4,186	5,627
Private nonguaranteed	1,207	10,272	19,332	11,812	11,670	14,451	15,342	12,986
of which: Bonds	..	..	..	..	83	38	135	382
Principal repayments	**1,705**	**5,159**	**13,161**	**15,779**	**15,729**	**15,889**	**19,560**	**16,161**
Public and publicly guaranteed	984	1,686	1,414	2,146	1,274	2,080	1,223	1,200
Official creditors	493	590	671	668	767	742	824	854
Private creditors	490	1,096	743	1,478	507	1,338	399	347
of which: Bonds	0	374	0	929	0	0	0	0
Private nonguaranteed	721	3,473	11,746	13,633	14,454	13,808	18,338	14,961
of which: Bonds	75	..	..	..	..	4	..	364
Interest payments	**631**	**1,245**	**2,775**	**2,180**	**2,454**	**2,313**	**2,230**	**2,267**
Public and publicly guaranteed	438	670	740	617	751	971	1,155	1,347
Official creditors	269	229	328	297	421	471	464	472
Private creditors	170	442	412	320	330	500	691	876
of which: Bonds	45	184	156	156	171	362	648	846
Private nonguaranteed	193	575	2,034	1,563	1,703	1,342	1,076	919
of which: Bonds	7	..	..	..	3	6	6	7
Net financial flows								
Net debt inflows	1,843	10,629	9,915	8,493	5,672	-106	-4,799	-5,935
Official creditors (incl. IMF)	608	275	12,454	9,124	4,346	-1,476	-4,851	-6,031
Private creditors	1,235	10,354	-2,539	-631	1,327	1,370	52	96
Long-term	850	7,322	7,046	-1,805	-1,015	4,545	831	3,314
Public and publicly guaranteed	364	524	-540	16	1,770	3,903	3,827	5,289
Private nonguaranteed	486	6,799	7,586	-1,821	-2,784	643	-2,996	-1,974
Short-term	386	3,032	-9,585	1,174	2,341	-3,175	-779	-3,218
Net equity inflows								
Foreign direct investment	1,037	4,790	2,402	2,419	2,100	1,022	3,236	3,039
Portfolio equity	58	229	7	4	-37	403	1,054	465
Major economic aggregates								
Gross national income (GNI)	37,024	96,279	161,693	162,255	179,539	165,510	183,822	195,235
Exports of goods, services & prim. income	12,438	25,693	47,150	54,951	69,695	65,765	79,462	85,585
Imports of goods, services & prim. income	14,653	38,645	59,813	66,966	82,665	77,678	84,636	88,889
Primary income on FDI	72	2,926	1,212	717	674	1,687	3,837	4,205
Personal transfers & comp. of employees	96	4,708	4,881	3,879	3,889	3,674	3,519	3,369
International reserves	2,470	19,872	40,757	43,361	42,939	41,162	44,811	39,165
Ratios								
External debt stocks to exports (%)	90.5	150.3	240.5	209.6	171.3	183.5	156.0	127.8
External debt stocks to GNI (%)	30.4	40.1	70.1	71.0	66.5	72.9	67.4	56.0
Debt service to exports (%)	20.1	26.8	34.4	33.6	27.2	31.7	36.1	21.8
Reserves to external debt stocks (%)	21.9	51.4	35.9	37.6	36.0	34.1	36.2	35.8

RWANDA

(US$ million, unless otherwise indicated)

	2000	2005	2009	2010	2011	2012	2013	2014
Summary external debt data								
External debt stocks	**1,289**	**1,528**	**861**	**906**	**1,216**	**1,266**	**1,691**	**2,022**
Long-term external debt	1,148	1,415	716	759	971	1,045	1,553	1,877
Short-term external debt	38	17	10	14	112	89	8	25
interest arrears on long-term	16	13	0	0	0	0	0	0
Use of IMF credit	104	97	136	133	132	131	130	119
Long-term external debt								
Debt outstanding and disbursed	**1,148**	**1,415**	**716**	**759**	**971**	**1,045**	**1,553**	**1,877**
Public and publicly guaranteed	1,148	1,415	716	759	971	1,045	1,553	1,877
Official creditors	1,147	1,415	716	759	971	1,045	1,153	1,355
Private creditors	1	0	0	0	0	0	400	522
of which: Bonds	0	0	0	0	0	0	400	400
Private nonguaranteed	..	..	..	..	..	..	..	..
of which: Bonds	..	..	..	..	..	..	..	..
Disbursements	**40**	**85**	**73**	**63**	**230**	**94**	**527**	**409**
Public and publicly guaranteed	40	85	73	63	230	94	527	409
Official creditors	40	85	73	63	230	94	127	287
Private creditors	0	0	0	0	0	0	400	122
of which: Bonds	0	0	0	0	0	0	400	0
Private nonguaranteed	..	..	..	..	..	..	..	..
of which: Bonds	..	..	..	..	..	..	..	..
Principal repayments	**13**	**13**	**5**	**8**	**12**	**13**	**14**	**15**
Public and publicly guaranteed	13	13	5	8	12	13	14	15
Official creditors	13	13	5	8	12	13	14	15
Private creditors	0	0	0	0	0	0	0	0
of which: Bonds	0	0	0	0	0	0	0	0
Private nonguaranteed	..	..	..	..	..	..	..	..
of which: Bonds	..	..	..	..	..	..	..	..
Interest payments	**8**	**10**	**6**	**6**	**7**	**8**	**24**	**38**
Public and publicly guaranteed	8	10	6	6	7	8	24	38
Official creditors	8	10	6	6	7	8	10	11
Private creditors	0	0	0	0	0	0	14	27
of which: Bonds	0	0	0	0	0	0	14	27
Private nonguaranteed	..	..	..	..	..	..	..	..
of which: Bonds	..	..	..	..	..	..	..	..
Net financial flows								
Net debt inflows	24	67	76	58	315	57	430	408
Official creditors (incl. IMF)	41	70	71	54	217	80	111	269
Private creditors	-16	-3	5	4	98	-23	319	139
Long-term	..	..	..	..	..	..	400	122
Public and publicly guaranteed	..	..	..	..	..	..	400	122
Private nonguaranteed	..	..	..	..	..	..	..	..
Short-term	-16	-3	5	4	98	23	-81	17
Net equity inflows								
Foreign direct investment	8	8	119	42	106	160	111	268
Portfolio equity	..	..	..	21	31	7	0	..
Major economic aggregates								
Gross national income (GNI)	1,719	2,554	5,273	5,656	6,348	7,125	7,387	7,751
Exports of goods, services & prim. income	142	260	611	639	933	1,027	1,217	..
Imports of goods, services & prim. income	452	693	1,594	1,710	2,291	2,570	2,615	..
Primary income on FDI	3	5	5	4	12	1	..	..
Personal transfers & comp. of employees	7	9	93	106	174	182	170	179
International reserves	191	406	743	813	1,050	848	1,070	..
Ratios								
External debt stocks to exports (%)	911.2	587.3	140.9	141.9	130.3	123.2	138.9	..
External debt stocks to GNI (%)	75.0	59.8	16.3	16.0	19.1	17.8	22.9	26.1
Debt service to exports (%)	25.7	10.8	1.9	2.3	2.1	2.2	3.4	..
Reserves to external debt stocks (%)	14.8	26.5	86.2	89.7	86.4	67.0	63.3	..

Notes:

Short-term debt is based on data from the BIS. Data include the effects of HIPC and MDRI debt relief.

SAMOA

(US$ million, unless otherwise indicated)

	2000	2005	2009	2010	2011	2012	2013	2014
Summary external debt data								
External debt stocks	**139.2**	**169.1**	**252.9**	**325.1**	**368.3**	**422.9**	**447.2**	**450.2**
Long-term external debt	137.7	167.5	226.4	299.1	342.4	396.9	412.3	417.3
Short-term external debt	0.0	0.0	0.0	0.0	0.0	0.0	0.0	0.0
interest arrears on long-term	0.0	0.0	0.0	0.0	0.0	0.0	0.0	0.0
Use of IMF credit	1.5	1.6	26.5	26.0	25.9	26.0	34.9	32.9
Long-term external debt								
Debt outstanding and disbursed	**137.7**	**167.5**	**226.4**	**299.1**	**342.4**	**396.9**	**412.3**	**417.3**
Public and publicly guaranteed	137.7	167.5	226.4	299.1	342.4	396.9	412.3	417.3
Official creditors	137.7	167.5	226.4	299.1	342.4	396.9	412.3	417.3
Private creditors	0.0	0.0	0.0	0.0	0.0	0.0	0.0	0.0
of which: Bonds	0.0	0.0	0.0	0.0	0.0	0.0	0.0	0.0
Private nonguaranteed	..	..	..	..	..	..	..	..
of which: Bonds	..	..	..	..	..	..	..	..
Disbursements	**6.7**	**10.4**	**25.2**	**78.9**	**47.6**	**64.3**	**26.0**	**36.5**
Public and publicly guaranteed	6.7	10.4	25.2	78.9	47.6	64.3	26.0	36.5
Official creditors	6.7	10.4	25.2	78.9	47.6	64.3	26.0	36.5
Private creditors	0.0	0.0	0.0	0.0	0.0	0.0	0.0	0.0
of which: Bonds	0.0	0.0	0.0	0.0	0.0	0.0	0.0	0.0
Private nonguaranteed	..	..	..	..	..	..	..	..
of which: Bonds	..	..	..	..	..	..	..	..
Principal repayments	**4.2**	**4.3**	**6.0**	**7.2**	**7.7**	**8.6**	**9.7**	**13.4**
Public and publicly guaranteed	4.2	4.3	6.0	7.2	7.7	8.6	9.7	13.4
Official creditors	4.2	4.3	6.0	7.2	7.7	8.6	9.7	13.4
Private creditors	0.0	0.0	0.0	0.0	0.0	0.0	0.0	0.0
of which: Bonds	0.0	0.0	0.0	0.0	0.0	0.0	0.0	0.0
Private nonguaranteed	..	..	..	..	..	..	..	..
of which: Bonds	..	..	..	..	..	..	..	..
Interest payments	**1.3**	**1.5**	**2.5**	**3.3**	**4.1**	**4.7**	**5.2**	**5.7**
Public and publicly guaranteed	1.3	1.5	2.5	3.3	4.1	4.7	5.2	5.7
Official creditors	1.3	1.5	2.5	3.3	4.1	4.7	5.2	5.7
Private creditors	0.0	0.0	0.0	0.0	0.0	0.0	0.0	0.0
of which: Bonds	0.0	0.0	0.0	0.0	0.0	0.0	0.0	0.0
Private nonguaranteed	..	..	..	..	..	..	..	..
of which: Bonds	..	..	..	..	..	..	..	..
Net financial flows								
Net debt inflows	2.5	6.1	28.1	71.6	39.8	55.7	25.2	23.1
Official creditors (incl. IMF)	2.5	6.1	28.1	71.6	39.8	55.7	25.2	23.1
Private creditors	..	..	..	..	..	..	..	..
Long-term	..	..	..	..	..	..	..	..
Public and publicly guaranteed	..	..	..	..	..	..	..	..
Private nonguaranteed	..	..	..	..	..	..	..	..
Short-term	..	..	..	..	..	..	..	..
Net equity inflows								
Foreign direct investment	-1.5	3.8	9.9	1.0	15.2	20.9	24.2	22.5
Portfolio equity	..	..	..	..	..	..	..	..
Major economic aggregates								
Gross national income (GNI)	269.0	441.4	554.1	635.7	734.9	767.4	763.1	774.5
Exports of goods, services & prim. income	..	147.3	181.4	210.4	217.6	250.7	244.2	241.3
Imports of goods, services & prim. income	..	300.2	319.8	386.4	434.2	454.0	464.2	455.9
Primary income on FDI	..	30.0	27.4	17.8	29.2	33.3	32.2	..
Personal transfers & comp. of employees	45.0	81.6	119.5	122.1	139.1	157.8	158.0	140.4
International reserves	63.7	81.8	165.8	209.4	166.8	168.7	170.7	140.7
Ratios								
External debt stocks to exports (%)	..	114.8	139.4	154.5	169.3	168.7	183.1	186.6
External debt stocks to GNI (%)	51.7	38.3	45.6	51.1	50.1	55.1	58.6	58.1
Debt service to exports (%)	..	3.9	4.7	5.0	5.5	5.3	6.1	7.9
Reserves to external debt stocks (%)	45.7	48.4	65.6	64.4	45.3	39.9	38.2	31.2

Notes:

Short-term debt data are excluded since BIS data include debt liabilities of offshore centers located in the country. BIS short-term debt data for 2012, 2013, and 2014 are $3 billion, $3.3 billion and $4.6 billion respectively.

SÃO TOMÉ AND PRÍNCIPE

(US$ million, unless otherwise indicated)

	2000	2005	2009	2010	2011	2012	2013	2014
Summary external debt data								
External debt stocks	**303.8**	**335.0**	**156.7**	**180.9**	**230.8**	**201.6**	**214.4**	**211.9**
Long-term external debt	277.3	316.5	124.7	145.1	189.1	169.3	183.3	185.4
Short-term external debt	23.3	14.4	16.4	19.9	25.9	15.9	14.1	11.6
interest arrears on long-term	11.3	14.4	5.4	5.9	5.9	7.9	8.1	6.6
Use of IMF credit	3.3	4.1	15.6	15.9	15.8	16.4	17.0	14.9
Long-term external debt								
Debt outstanding and disbursed	**277.3**	**316.5**	**124.7**	**145.1**	**189.1**	**169.3**	**183.3**	**185.4**
Public and publicly guaranteed	277.3	316.5	124.7	145.1	189.1	169.3	183.3	185.4
Official creditors	277.3	316.5	124.7	145.1	189.1	169.3	183.3	185.4
Private creditors	0.0	0.0	0.0	0.0	0.0	0.0	0.0	0.0
of which: Bonds	0.0	0.0	0.0	0.0	0.0	0.0	0.0	0.0
Private nonguaranteed	..	..	..	..	..	..	..	..
of which: Bonds	..	..	..	..	..	..	..	..
Disbursements	**9.4**	**5.4**	**18.8**	**19.8**	**47.6**	**3.1**	**16.0**	**26.3**
Public and publicly guaranteed	9.4	5.4	18.8	19.8	47.6	3.1	16.0	26.3
Official creditors	9.4	5.4	18.8	19.8	47.6	3.1	16.0	26.3
Private creditors	0.0	0.0	0.0	0.0	0.0	0.0	0.0	0.0
of which: Bonds	0.0	0.0	0.0	0.0	0.0	0.0	0.0	0.0
Private nonguaranteed	..	..	..	..	..	..	..	..
of which: Bonds	..	..	..	..	..	..	..	..
Principal repayments	**2.2**	**4.3**	**1.7**	**1.1**	**1.0**	**10.6**	**4.8**	**11.4**
Public and publicly guaranteed	2.2	4.3	1.7	1.1	1.0	10.6	4.8	11.4
Official creditors	2.2	4.3	1.7	1.1	1.0	10.6	4.8	11.4
Private creditors	0.0	0.0	0.0	0.0	0.0	0.0	0.0	0.0
of which: Bonds	0.0	0.0	0.0	0.0	0.0	0.0	0.0	0.0
Private nonguaranteed	..	..	..	..	..	..	..	..
of which: Bonds	..	..	..	..	..	..	..	..
Interest payments	**1.2**	**2.0**	**0.3**	**0.3**	**0.3**	**0.5**	**0.5**	**1.1**
Public and publicly guaranteed	1.2	2.0	0.3	0.3	0.3	0.5	0.5	1.1
Official creditors	1.2	2.0	0.3	0.3	0.3	0.5	0.5	1.1
Private creditors	0.0	0.0	0.0	0.0	0.0	0.0	0.0	0.0
of which: Bonds	0.0	0.0	0.0	0.0	0.0	0.0	0.0	0.0
Private nonguaranteed	..	..	..	..	..	..	..	..
of which: Bonds	..	..	..	..	..	..	..	..
Net financial flows								
Net debt inflows	9.7	1.6	18.7	22.2	52.6	-19.0	9.8	12.8
Official creditors (incl. IMF)	9.7	1.6	17.7	19.2	46.6	-7.0	11.8	13.8
Private creditors	..	..	1.0	3.0	6.0	-12.0	-2.0	-1.0
Long-term	..	..	..	..	..	..	..	..
Public and publicly guaranteed	..	..	..	..	..	..	..	..
Private nonguaranteed	..	..	..	..	..	..	..	..
Short-term	..	..	1.0	3.0	6.0	-12.0	-2.0	-1.0
Net equity inflows								
Foreign direct investment	3.8	15.7	15.5	50.6	32.2	22.5	7.5	11.7
Portfolio equity	..	..	..	..	..	..	0.0	..
Major economic aggregates								
Gross national income (GNI)	..	120.3	196.2	200.7	247.9	261.1	308.2	331.6
Exports of goods, services & prim. income	17.1	17.9	21.3	26.2	31.2	34.0	54.2	90.2
Imports of goods, services & prim. income	42.0	57.6	104.7	122.8	149.4	147.0	176.5	221.9
Primary income on FDI	..	..	..	..	..	..	..	0.3
Personal transfers & comp. of employees	0.5	1.5	2.0	6.4	6.9	6.4	26.5	29.1
International reserves	11.6	26.7	66.7	48.2	52.3	51.6	63.8	63.4
Ratios								
External debt stocks to exports (%)	1772.0	1870.2	737.3	690.1	739.7	593.7	395.6	235.0
External debt stocks to GNI (%)	..	278.4	79.9	90.1	93.1	77.2	69.6	63.9
Debt service to exports (%)	25.4	36.6	9.4	6.0	5.0	33.1	11.0	15.1
Reserves to external debt stocks (%)	3.8	8.0	42.5	26.6	22.7	25.6	29.8	29.9

Notes:

Short-term debt is based on data from the BIS. Data include HIPC and MDRI debt relief.

SENEGAL

(US$ million, unless otherwise indicated)

	2000	2005	2009	2010	2011	2012	2013	2014
Summary external debt data								
External debt stocks	**3,653**	**3,862**	**3,721**	**3,908**	**4,324**	**4,905**	**5,224**	**5,655**
Long-term external debt	3,221	3,643	3,312	3,457	3,878	4,463	4,787	5,260
Short-term external debt	146	36	0	0	0	0	0	0
interest arrears on long-term	1	0	0	0	0	0	0	0
Use of IMF credit	286	183	409	451	447	442	438	395
Long-term external debt								
Debt outstanding and disbursed	**3,221**	**3,643**	**3,312**	**3,457**	**3,878**	**4,463**	**4,787**	**5,260**
Public and publicly guaranteed	3,208	3,501	2,954	3,149	3,613	4,197	4,516	4,952
Official creditors	3,203	3,492	2,752	2,949	3,113	3,695	4,014	4,010
Private creditors	5	9	202	200	500	502	502	942
of which: Bonds	0	0	200	200	500	500	500	931
Private nonguaranteed	13	141	357	308	265	266	271	308
of which: Bonds	..	..	..	..	..	..	..	..
Disbursements	**137**	**382**	**837**	**434**	**1,009**	**747**	**535**	**995**
Public and publicly guaranteed	136	333	628	352	928	672	409	874
Official creditors	131	333	428	352	428	670	409	363
Private creditors	5	0	200	0	500	2	0	511
of which: Bonds	0	0	200	0	500	0	0	500
Private nonguaranteed	1	49	208	83	81	74	126	122
of which: Bonds	..	..	..	..	..	..	..	..
Principal repayments	**127**	**112**	**146**	**229**	**236**	**211**	**268**	**214**
Public and publicly guaranteed	125	83	97	84	139	138	147	117
Official creditors	124	81	94	83	139	138	147	107
Private creditors	0	2	3	2	0	0	0	10
of which: Bonds	0	0	0	0	0	0	0	10
Private nonguaranteed	3	29	49	144	96	73	121	97
of which: Bonds	..	..	..	..	..	..	..	..
Interest payments	**58**	**55**	**50**	**75**	**122**	**102**	**128**	**128**
Public and publicly guaranteed	58	45	41	64	108	85	107	111
Official creditors	58	44	41	46	57	48	61	64
Private creditors	0	1	0	18	51	37	46	46
of which: Bonds	0	0	0	18	51	37	46	46
Private nonguaranteed	0	10	9	11	15	17	21	17
of which: Bonds	..	..	..	..	..	..	..	..
Net financial flows								
Net debt inflows	-153	242	594	254	770	530	262	764
Official creditors (incl. IMF)	5	224	434	318	286	527	256	239
Private creditors	-158	18	160	-63	485	3	5	524
Long-term	3	18	357	-63	485	3	5	524
Public and publicly guaranteed	5	-2	197	-2	500	2	..	500
Private nonguaranteed	-1	20	159	-62	-15	2	5	24
Short-term	-161	..	-197	..	..	..	..	..
Net equity inflows								
Foreign direct investment	63	152	244	267	296	276	311	343
Portfolio equity	-2	-6	-2	23	14	..	..	..
Major economic aggregates								
Gross national income (GNI)	4,589	8,551	12,634	12,799	14,274	13,865	14,606	15,459
Exports of goods, services & prim. income	1,383	2,562	3,286	3,418	4,055	4,323	4,494	..
Imports of goods, services & prim. income	1,929	3,991	5,613	5,557	6,969	7,697	7,909	..
Primary income on FDI	75	173	147	135	209	..	..	..
Personal transfers & comp. of employees	233	789	1,350	1,478	1,614	..	..	..
International reserves	388	1,186	2,123	2,047	1,946	2,082	2,253	2,038
Ratios								
External debt stocks to exports (%)	264.2	150.8	113.2	114.3	106.6	113.5	116.2	..
External debt stocks to GNI (%)	79.6	45.2	29.5	30.5	30.3	35.4	35.8	36.6
Debt service to exports (%)	16.3	7.9	6.0	8.9	8.9	7.4	8.9	..
Reserves to external debt stocks (%)	10.6	30.7	57.1	52.4	45.0	42.4	43.1	36.0

Notes:

Short-term debt before 2009 is based on data from the BIS.

SERBIA

(US$ million, unless otherwise indicated)

	2000	2005	2009	2010	2011	2012	2013	2014
Summary external debt data								
External debt stocks	**11,573**	**16,159**	**33,814**	**32,935**	**31,724**	**34,444**	**36,397**	**33,103**
Long-term external debt	6,789	12,970	27,915	27,417	27,779	30,910	34,180	31,740
Short-term external debt	4,558	2,242	3,600	2,798	1,162	1,018	571	533
interest arrears on long-term	3,668	728	712	352	324	367	279	419
Use of IMF credit	226	947	2,299	2,720	2,783	2,517	1,647	830
Long-term external debt								
Debt outstanding and disbursed	**6,789**	**12,970**	**27,915**	**27,417**	**27,779**	**30,910**	**34,180**	**31,740**
Public and publicly guaranteed	6,178	7,756	8,839	9,504	11,339	13,701	16,722	16,598
Official creditors	4,243	6,679	7,664	8,172	8,738	9,324	10,085	9,204
Private creditors	1,935	1,077	1,175	1,332	2,601	4,378	6,637	7,394
of which: Bonds	0	0	0	0	1,000	2,750	5,250	6,250
Private nonguaranteed	611	5,214	19,076	17,912	16,440	17,208	17,457	15,142
of which: Bonds	..	..	165	165	165	..	641	878
Disbursements	**222**	**2,904**	**4,533**	**4,617**	**6,280**	**6,382**	**8,973**	**4,973**
Public and publicly guaranteed	222	311	971	1,388	2,541	2,854	3,789	1,890
Official creditors	187	311	971	1,149	1,137	965	999	822
Private creditors	35	0	0	239	1,404	1,889	2,789	1,068
of which: Bonds	0	0	0	0	1,000	1,750	2,500	1,000
Private nonguaranteed	..	2,593	3,562	3,230	3,739	3,528	5,184	3,083
of which: Bonds	..	..	..	..	..	..	641	237
Principal repayments	**0**	**570**	**3,613**	**3,431**	**4,257**	**4,756**	**6,296**	**6,295**
Public and publicly guaranteed	0	48	158	351	451	623	1,149	879
Official creditors	0	48	154	275	350	494	580	677
Private creditors	0	0	4	76	101	129	568	202
of which: Bonds	0	0	0	0	0	0	0	0
Private nonguaranteed	..	522	3,454	3,081	3,806	4,133	5,147	5,417
of which: Bonds	..	..	..	..	..	165	..	..
Interest payments	**0**	**367**	**916**	**759**	**905**	**978**	**1,269**	**1,237**
Public and publicly guaranteed	0	237	348	321	348	430	617	618
Official creditors	0	194	303	241	257	268	313	232
Private creditors	0	44	45	80	91	162	303	387
of which: Bonds	0	0	0	0	0	73	221	318
Private nonguaranteed	..	129	568	438	557	548	652	619
of which: Bonds	..	..	10	10	10	5	..	51
Net financial flows								
Net debt inflows	51	2,827	2,401	1,201	489	1,171	1,452	-2,255
Official creditors (incl. IMF)	268	241	2,392	1,332	861	204	-448	-609
Private creditors	-217	2,586	9	-130	-372	968	1,900	-1,646
Long-term	35	2,071	104	312	1,235	1,155	2,258	-1,468
Public and publicly guaranteed	35	0	-4	163	1,303	1,760	2,221	866
Private nonguaranteed	..	2,071	108	149	-68	-605	37	-2,334
Short-term	-252	515	-95	-442	-1,607	188	-358	-178
Net equity inflows								
Foreign direct investment	52	..	1,397	815	2,213	-157	1,272	2,196
Portfolio equity	..	..	22	84	69	-24	-41	..
Major economic aggregates								
Gross national income (GNI)	6,540	25,929	41,917	38,569	45,412	39,335	43,643	42,084
Exports of goods, services & prim. income	..	..	12,544	13,916	16,561	15,621	19,381	20,051
Imports of goods, services & prim. income	..	..	20,348	20,884	24,773	24,105	26,356	26,688
Primary income on FDI	..	..	451	552	531	1,253	1,548	..
Personal transfers & comp. of employees	..	..	3,933	3,349	3,271	3,545	4,023	3,656
International reserves	392	5,628	14,769	12,715	14,877	13,585	14,803	11,372
Ratios								
External debt stocks to exports (%)	..	..	269.6	236.7	191.6	220.5	187.8	165.1
External debt stocks to GNI (%)	177.0	62.3	80.7	85.4	69.9	87.6	83.4	78.7
Debt service to exports (%)	..	..	37.0	30.9	31.5	38.6	43.6	41.4
Reserves to external debt stocks (%)	3.4	34.8	43.7	38.6	46.9	39.4	40.7	34.4

Notes:

Beginning 2006, the data for Serbia exclude Montenegro. Short-term debt is World Bank staff estimates based on Central Bank data.

SIERRA LEONE

(US$ million, unless otherwise indicated)

	2000	2005	2009	2010	2011	2012	2013	2014
Summary external debt data								
External debt stocks	**1,213**	**1,776**	**857**	**931**	**1,050**	**1,126**	**1,396**	**1,238**
Long-term external debt	973	1,539	605	661	741	837	901	910
Short-term external debt	44	21	23	4	35	14	214	25
interest arrears on long-term	36	11	0	0	0	0	0	1
Use of IMF credit	196	217	229	266	274	274	281	303
Long-term external debt								
Debt outstanding and disbursed	**973**	**1,539**	**605**	**661**	**741**	**837**	**901**	**910**
Public and publicly guaranteed	973	1,539	605	661	741	837	901	910
Official creditors	967	1,326	394	450	533	628	705	715
Private creditors	5	213	211	211	208	210	195	195
of which: Bonds	0	0	0	0	0	0	0	0
Private nonguaranteed	..	..	..	..	..	..	..	..
of which: Bonds	..	..	..	..	..	..	..	..
Disbursements	**77**	**51**	**62**	**66**	**95**	**106**	**89**	**53**
Public and publicly guaranteed	77	51	62	66	95	106	89	53
Official creditors	77	51	62	66	95	106	89	53
Private creditors	0	0	0	0	0	0	0	0
of which: Bonds	0	0	0	0	0	0	0	0
Private nonguaranteed	..	..	..	..	..	..	..	..
of which: Bonds	..	..	..	..	..	..	..	..
Principal repayments	**10**	**5**	**3**	**5**	**7**	**8**	**10**	**14**
Public and publicly guaranteed	10	5	3	5	7	8	10	14
Official creditors	10	5	3	5	7	8	10	14
Private creditors	0	0	0	0	0	0	0	0
of which: Bonds	0	0	0	0	0	0	0	0
Private nonguaranteed	..	..	..	..	..	..	..	..
of which: Bonds	..	..	..	..	..	..	..	..
Interest payments	**9**	**9**	**4**	**4**	**6**	**6**	**7**	**8**
Public and publicly guaranteed	9	9	4	4	6	6	7	8
Official creditors	9	9	4	4	6	6	7	8
Private creditors	0	0	0	0	0	0	0	0
of which: Bonds	0	0	0	0	0	0	0	0
Private nonguaranteed	..	..	..	..	..	..	..	..
of which: Bonds	..	..	..	..	..	..	..	..
Net financial flows								
Net debt inflows	57	54	92	83	128	77	285	-111
Official creditors (incl. IMF)	55	64	78	102	97	98	85	79
Private creditors	1	-10	14	-19	31	-21	200	-190
Long-term	..	..	..	..	..	..	..	..
Public and publicly guaranteed	..	..	..	..	..	..	..	..
Private nonguaranteed	..	..	..	..	..	..	..	..
Short-term	1	-10	14	-19	31	-21	200	-190
Net equity inflows								
Foreign direct investment	39	53	85	225	770	164	209	440
Portfolio equity	..	..	6	0	0	7	9	..
Major economic aggregates								
Gross national income (GNI)	616	1,590	2,665	2,607	3,039	3,439	4,516	4,366
Exports of goods, services & prim. income	62	267	380	427	548	1,350	2,210	..
Imports of goods, services & prim. income	262	509	797	1,191	2,711	2,421	2,808	..
Primary income on FDI	2	41	39	46	219	130	135	..
Personal transfers & comp. of employees	7	2	36	44	59	61	68	104
International reserves	49	171	405	409	439	478	533	601
Ratios								
External debt stocks to exports (%)	1,941.0	664.9	225.7	218.3	191.8	83.4	63.1	..
External debt stocks to GNI (%)	196.8	111.7	32.2	35.7	34.6	32.7	30.9	28.4
Debt service to exports (%)	76.4	6.9	2.1	2.7	3.4	1.5	1.2	..
Reserves to external debt stocks (%)	4.1	9.6	47.3	43.9	41.8	42.5	38.2	48.5

Notes:

Short-term debt before is based on data from the BIS.

SOLOMON ISLANDS

(US$ million, unless otherwise indicated)

	2000	2005	2009	2010	2011	2012	2013	2014
Summary external debt data								
External debt stocks	**156.2**	**167.3**	**172.4**	**230.8**	**257.5**	**228.1**	**204.0**	**187.3**
Long-term external debt	152.1	151.2	154.4	201.9	210.3	191.5	166.0	140.7
Short-term external debt	3.2	15.2	2.5	4.0	12.9	2.0	3.0	14.8
interest arrears on long-term	1.8	12.2	1.5	4.0	8.9	0.0	0.0	0.0
Use of IMF credit	0.9	0.9	15.5	24.9	34.4	34.6	34.9	31.8
Long-term external debt								
Debt outstanding and disbursed	**152.1**	**151.2**	**154.4**	**201.9**	**210.3**	**191.5**	**166.0**	**140.7**
Public and publicly guaranteed	120.7	144.2	132.9	125.3	117.8	110.2	101.1	89.6
Official creditors	117.3	143.8	132.7	125.2	117.8	110.2	101.1	89.6
Private creditors	3.4	0.4	0.2	0.1	0.0	0.0	0.0	0.0
of which: Bonds	0.0	0.0	0.0	0.0	0.0	0.0	0.0	0.0
Private nonguaranteed	31.5	7.0	21.5	76.6	92.4	81.3	64.9	51.1
of which: Bonds	..	..	..	..	..	..	..	..
Disbursements	**3.4**	**5.7**	**13.7**	**36.8**	**27.3**	**2.2**	**5.5**	**13.4**
Public and publicly guaranteed	3.4	5.7	0.0	0.0	0.0	0.0	0.0	0.0
Official creditors	3.4	5.3	0.0	0.0	0.0	0.0	0.0	0.0
Private creditors	0.0	0.4	0.0	0.0	0.0	0.0	0.0	0.0
of which: Bonds	0.0	0.0	0.0	0.0	0.0	0.0	0.0	0.0
Private nonguaranteed	..	..	13.7	36.8	27.3	2.2	5.5	13.4
of which: Bonds	..	..	..	..	..	..	..	..
Principal repayments	**6.2**	**10.0**	**7.6**	**17.5**	**12.6**	**21.8**	**38.9**	**13.5**
Public and publicly guaranteed	2.7	5.8	6.5	8.6	6.6	6.5	6.4	6.5
Official creditors	2.7	3.2	6.3	8.4	6.5	6.5	6.4	6.5
Private creditors	0.0	2.6	0.2	0.2	0.1	0.0	0.0	0.0
of which: Bonds	0.0	0.0	0.0	0.0	0.0	0.0	0.0	0.0
Private nonguaranteed	3.5	4.2	1.1	8.9	6.0	15.3	32.5	7.0
of which: Bonds	..	..	..	..	..	..	..	..
Interest payments	**2.7**	**3.9**	**2.4**	**3.2**	**2.6**	**8.1**	**5.3**	**2.2**
Public and publicly guaranteed	0.8	1.7	1.8	1.7	1.7	1.5	1.4	1.4
Official creditors	0.8	1.7	1.8	1.7	1.7	1.5	1.4	1.4
Private creditors	0.0	0.0	0.0	0.0	0.0	0.0	0.0	0.0
of which: Bonds	0.0	0.0	0.0	0.0	0.0	0.0	0.0	0.0
Private nonguaranteed	1.9	2.3	0.5	1.5	0.9	6.5	3.9	0.8
of which: Bonds	..	..	..	..	..	..	..	..
Net financial flows								
Net debt inflows	-4.4	-2.3	7.1	27.9	28.5	-21.3	-32.2	10.5
Official creditors (incl. IMF)	0.6	2.1	-6.3	1.1	3.3	-6.3	-6.1	-7.6
Private creditors	-5.0	-4.4	13.4	26.8	25.2	-15.1	-26.0	18.2
Long-term	-3.5	-6.4	12.4	27.8	21.2	-13.1	-27.0	6.4
Public and publicly guaranteed	..	-2.1	-0.2	-0.2	-0.1	..	..	..
Private nonguaranteed	-3.5	-4.2	12.6	28.0	21.3	-13.1	-27.0	6.4
Short-term	-1.5	2.0	1.0	-1.0	4.0	-2.0	1.0	11.8
Net equity inflows								
Foreign direct investment	13.0	0.3	114.2	229.4	143.6	54.9	-29.0	20.7
Portfolio equity	..	..	..	..	..	..	..	..
Major economic aggregates								
Gross national income (GNI)	435.5	415.5	432.9	496.5	672.5	931.4	1,051.4	1,099.6
Exports of goods, services & prim. income	128.8	154.9	237.5	333.4	563.7	648.9	600.2	612.8
Imports of goods, services & prim. income	176.4	250.1	492.3	690.3	770.1	738.1	747.3	744.9
Primary income on FDI	8.3	5.3	135.5	127.0	133.5	74.5	12.2	..
Personal transfers & comp. of employees	4.3	7.2	12.5	12.7	14.3	17.2	16.5	16.3
International reserves	32.0	94.8	146.0	265.8	412.3	469.5	491.5	466.9
Ratios								
External debt stocks to exports (%)	121.3	108.0	72.6	69.2	45.7	35.2	34.0	30.6
External debt stocks to GNI (%)	35.9	40.3	39.8	46.5	38.3	24.5	19.4	17.0
Debt service to exports (%)	7.1	9.1	4.2	6.2	2.7	4.6	7.4	2.8
Reserves to external debt stocks (%)	20.5	56.7	84.7	115.2	160.1	205.8	241.0	249.3

Notes:

Long-term public and publicly guaranteed debt data for 2014 are World Bank staff estimates based on the original terms of the loans.

SOMALIA

(US$ million, unless otherwise indicated)

	2000	2005	2009	2010	2011	2012	2013	2014
Summary external debt data								
External debt stocks	**2,579**	**2,770**	**3,046**	**3,045**	**3,053**	**3,055**	**3,056**	**2,920**
Long-term external debt	1,825	1,882	1,987	1,990	1,992	1,985	1,977	1,913
Short-term external debt	591	709	810	811	818	827	835	777
interest arrears on long-term	569	709	810	811	818	827	835	777
Use of IMF credit	164	180	248	244	243	243	243	229
Long-term external debt								
Debt outstanding and disbursed	**1,825**	**1,882**	**1,987**	**1,990**	**1,992**	**1,985**	**1,977**	**1,913**
Public and publicly guaranteed	1,825	1,882	1,987	1,990	1,992	1,985	1,977	1,913
Official creditors	1,792	1,846	1,950	1,954	1,955	1,948	1,940	1,878
Private creditors	33	35	38	37	36	36	37	35
of which: Bonds	0	0	0	0	0	0	0	0
Private nonguaranteed	..	..	..	..	..	..	..	..
of which: Bonds	..	..	..	..	..	..	..	..
Disbursements	**0**	**0**	**0**	**0**	**0**	**0**	**0**	**0**
Public and publicly guaranteed	0	0	0	0	0	0	0	0
Official creditors	0	0	0	0	0	0	0	0
Private creditors	0	0	0	0	0	0	0	0
of which: Bonds	0	0	0	0	0	0	0	0
Private nonguaranteed	..	..	..	..	..	..	..	..
of which: Bonds	..	..	..	..	..	..	..	..
Principal repayments	**0**	**0**	**0**	**0**	**0**	**0**	**0**	**0**
Public and publicly guaranteed	0	0	0	0	0	0	0	0
Official creditors	0	0	0	0	0	0	0	0
Private creditors	0	0	0	0	0	0	0	0
of which: Bonds	0	0	0	0	0	0	0	0
Private nonguaranteed	..	..	..	..	..	..	..	..
of which: Bonds	..	..	..	..	..	..	..	..
Interest payments	**0**	**0**	**0**	**0**	**0**	**0**	**0**	**0**
Public and publicly guaranteed	0	0	0	0	0	0	0	0
Official creditors	0	0	0	0	0	0	0	0
Private creditors	0	0	0	0	0	0	0	0
of which: Bonds	0	0	0	0	0	0	0	0
Private nonguaranteed	..	..	..	..	..	..	..	..
of which: Bonds	..	..	..	..	..	..	..	..
Net financial flows								
Net debt inflows	-7	..	..	..	..	0	0	..
Official creditors (incl. IMF)	..	..	..	..	..	0	0	..
Private creditors	-7	..	..	..	..	..	..	..
Long-term	..	..	..	..	..	..	..	..
Public and publicly guaranteed	..	..	..	..	..	..	..	..
Private nonguaranteed	..	..	..	..	..	..	..	..
Short-term	-7	..	..	..	..	..	..	..
Net equity inflows								
Foreign direct investment	0	24	108	112	102	107	107	106
Portfolio equity	..	..	..	..	..	..	..	..
Major economic aggregates								
Gross national income (GNI)	..	..	..	..	..	..	..	..
Exports of goods, services & prim. income	..	..	..	..	..	..	..	..
Imports of goods, services & prim. income	..	..	..	..	..	..	..	..
Primary income on FDI	..	..	..	..	..	..	..	..
Personal transfers & comp. of employees	..	..	..	..	..	..	..	..
International reserves	..	..	..	..	..	..	..	..
Ratios								
External debt stocks to exports (%)	..	..	..	..	..	..	..	..
External debt stocks to GNI (%)	..	..	..	..	..	..	..	..
Debt service to exports (%)	..	..	..	..	..	..	..	..
Reserves to external debt stocks (%)	..	..	..	..	..	..	..	..

Notes:

Long-term public and publicly guaranteed debt data are World Bank staff estimates based on the original terms of the loans.

SOUTH AFRICA

(US$ million, unless otherwise indicated)

	2000	2005	2009	2010	2011	2012	2013	2014
Summary external debt data								
External debt stocks	**25,435**	**44,737**	**79,017**	**108,392**	**116,929**	**144,959**	**139,245**	**144,006**
Long-term external debt	15,595	30,146	54,932	83,912	93,654	114,347	109,246	106,377
Short-term external debt	9,553	14,276	21,286	21,730	20,534	27,868	27,249	35,042
interest arrears on long-term	0	0	0	0	0	0	0	0
Use of IMF credit	287	315	2,799	2,750	2,741	2,744	2,750	2,587
Long-term external debt								
Debt outstanding and disbursed	**15,595**	**30,146**	**54,932**	**83,912**	**93,654**	**114,347**	**109,246**	**106,377**
Public and publicly guaranteed	9,088	20,743	22,315	36,274	41,551	56,502	54,041	57,870
Official creditors	145	286	227	1,139	1,449	2,782	3,046	3,601
Private creditors	8,943	20,457	22,088	35,135	40,102	53,720	50,995	54,268
of which: Bonds	4,749	12,242	18,508	32,329	38,548	53,133	50,242	52,948
Private nonguaranteed	6,507	9,403	32,617	47,638	52,103	57,845	55,205	48,507
of which: Bonds	1,110	3,196	8,485	8,786	12,638	14,069	12,152	10,366
Disbursements	**3,611**	**2,678**	**4,202**	**7,001**	**9,995**	**7,842**	**9,111**	**9,757**
Public and publicly guaranteed	1,597	2,678	2,032	3,777	3,990	3,915	3,909	6,048
Official creditors	91	58	32	913	490	1,415	526	1,397
Private creditors	1,506	2,620	2,000	2,864	3,500	2,500	3,382	4,652
of which: Bonds	765	0	2,000	2,000	3,500	2,500	3,000	3,855
Private nonguaranteed	2,014	..	2,170	3,224	6,005	3,928	5,202	3,709
of which: Bonds	712	..	163	1,135	3,852	2,738	3,543	1,209
Principal repayments	**2,631**	**2,870**	**2,773**	**3,470**	**2,737**	**5,293**	**4,978**	**5,354**
Public and publicly guaranteed	1,649	2,870	2,065	1,678	1,520	2,674	1,779	1,240
Official creditors	0	27	38	40	42	37	25	22
Private creditors	1,649	2,844	2,028	1,638	1,478	2,638	1,754	1,219
of which: Bonds	306	1,091	250	0	104	1,670	1,535	1,000
Private nonguaranteed	982	..	708	1,792	1,217	2,618	3,199	4,113
of which: Bonds	..	..	..	834	..	1,307	2,083	2,104
Interest payments	**746**	**1,269**	**1,692**	**2,191**	**2,975**	**3,560**	**3,222**	**3,746**
Public and publicly guaranteed	549	1,058	1,041	1,573	2,061	2,612	2,352	2,452
Official creditors	1	12	10	20	40	62	70	131
Private creditors	548	1,046	1,030	1,553	2,021	2,550	2,282	2,320
of which: Bonds	278	771	953	1,488	1,968	2,475	2,278	2,311
Private nonguaranteed	196	212	652	618	914	948	869	1,294
of which: Bonds	27	212	432	460	664	776	602	968
Net financial flows								
Net debt inflows	-282	2,888	-2,747	3,975	6,062	9,884	3,514	12,196
Official creditors (incl. IMF)	91	31	-6	873	448	1,378	502	1,375
Private creditors	-373	2,857	-2,742	3,102	5,614	8,506	3,012	10,821
Long-term	889	-224	1,434	2,658	6,810	1,172	3,631	3,028
Public and publicly guaranteed	-143	-224	-28	1,226	2,022	-138	1,628	3,433
Private nonguaranteed	1,032	..	1,462	1,431	4,788	1,309	2,003	-405
Short-term	-1,262	3,081	-4,176	444	-1,196	7,334	-619	7,793
Net equity inflows								
Foreign direct investment	969	6,192	4,957	-4,194	2,903	1,671	2,699	1,292
Portfolio equity	4,169	7,230	9,364	5,826	-3,769	-679	1,011	2,551
Major economic aggregates								
Gross national income (GNI)	133,188	252,830	289,309	367,345	405,947	386,627	356,448	340,461
Exports of goods, services & prim. income	39,507	72,730	87,745	112,387	132,157	124,104	120,022	116,899
Imports of goods, services & prim. income	38,771	78,292	92,967	115,601	139,258	139,981	138,020	132,810
Primary income on FDI	2,329	4,320	5,279	6,165	8,375	8,486	8,053	8,707
Personal transfers & comp. of employees	344	614	862	1,070	1,158	1,085	971	913
International reserves	6,083	18,579	35,237	38,175	42,595	43,995	44,864	44,267
Ratios								
External debt stocks to exports (%)	64.4	61.5	90.1	96.4	88.5	116.8	116.0	123.2
External debt stocks to GNI (%)	19.1	17.7	27.3	29.5	28.8	37.5	39.1	42.3
Debt service to exports (%)	9.9	6.4	6.0	5.6	4.8	7.8	7.5	8.6
Reserves to external debt stocks (%)	23.9	41.5	44.6	35.2	36.4	30.4	32.2	30.7

Notes:

Long-term public and publicly guaranteed and long-term private nonguaranteed debt data are World Bank staff estimates based on reports provided by the country.

SRI LANKA

(US$ million, unless otherwise indicated)

	2000	2005	2009	2010	2011	2012	2013	2014
Summary external debt data								
External debt stocks	**9,241**	**11,297**	**19,567**	**21,762**	**25,887**	**35,792**	**40,257**	**43,609**
Long-term external debt	8,304	10,043	14,671	17,426	19,986	26,181	30,720	34,380
Short-term external debt	685	772	3,554	2,416	3,577	6,493	6,873	7,408
interest arrears on long-term	112	0	1	1	1	1	7	79
Use of IMF credit	253	483	1,341	1,920	2,325	3,118	2,665	1,821
Long-term external debt								
Debt outstanding and disbursed	**8,304**	**10,043**	**14,671**	**17,426**	**19,986**	**26,181**	**30,720**	**34,380**
Public and publicly guaranteed	7,936	9,655	13,704	16,507	18,773	22,978	26,517	29,502
Official creditors	6,928	8,982	11,938	13,613	14,808	15,895	16,638	17,028
Private creditors	1,008	673	1,766	2,893	3,965	7,083	9,879	12,475
of which: Bonds	65	65	1,000	2,000	3,000	3,500	4,750	6,500
Private nonguaranteed	368	388	967	919	1,213	3,203	4,203	4,878
of which: Bonds	..	100	..	..	..	..	100	275
Disbursements	**754**	**929**	**2,214**	**3,091**	**3,196**	**7,833**	**6,179**	**5,719**
Public and publicly guaranteed	585	818	1,827	2,994	2,751	5,877	4,994	4,821
Official creditors	348	670	1,165	1,810	1,613	2,145	2,065	2,026
Private creditors	237	149	662	1,183	1,138	3,732	2,930	2,795
of which: Bonds	0	0	500	1,000	1,000	1,000	1,250	1,750
Private nonguaranteed	169	111	387	97	445	1,955	1,185	898
of which: Bonds	..	..	..	..	..	..	100	175
Principal repayments	**453**	**246**	**967**	**715**	**805**	**1,365**	**911**	**1,055**
Public and publicly guaranteed	439	227	812	570	651	1,199	728	832
Official creditors	216	123	555	507	587	604	613	719
Private creditors	223	104	257	64	64	595	116	113
of which: Bonds	50	0	0	0	0	500	0	0
Private nonguaranteed	14	19	154	145	154	165	183	223
of which: Bonds	..	..	100	..	..	..	..	..
Interest payments	**213**	**106**	**325**	**616**	**448**	**550**	**618**	**694**
Public and publicly guaranteed	178	84	285	596	405	515	568	644
Official creditors	125	65	227	308	268	292	326	310
Private creditors	54	19	58	288	137	223	241	334
of which: Bonds	6	4	43	72	124	207	220	311
Private nonguaranteed	35	22	40	20	43	35	50	50
of which: Bonds	..	7	7	..	..	..	..	5
Net financial flows								
Net debt inflows	-3	539	2,616	1,834	3,973	10,169	5,188	4,407
Official creditors (incl. IMF)	45	661	1,150	1,900	1,448	2,327	997	587
Private creditors	-48	-122	1,466	-66	2,526	7,843	4,191	3,820
Long-term	170	137	637	1,072	1,366	4,927	3,816	3,357
Public and publicly guaranteed	15	45	405	1,120	1,075	3,137	2,814	2,682
Private nonguaranteed	155	92	233	-48	291	1,790	1,003	675
Short-term	-218	-259	828	-1,138	1,160	2,916	374	463
Net equity inflows								
Foreign direct investment	173	272	173	240	251	360	410	518
Portfolio equity	..	-216	-382	-1,049	-171	272	226	184
Major economic aggregates								
Gross national income (GNI)	16,016	24,107	41,581	48,948	58,529	58,178	65,454	73,103
Exports of goods, services & prim. income	6,527	7,963	9,099	11,423	14,109	13,716	15,211	16,889
Imports of goods, services & prim. income	8,554	10,441	12,318	16,159	23,368	23,117	23,391	25,134
Primary income on FDI	109	115	230	303	385	449	737	698
Personal transfers & comp. of employees	1,166	1,976	3,337	4,123	5,153	6,000	6,422	7,036
International reserves	1,039	2,650	4,616	6,710	6,248	6,378	6,611	7,316
Ratios								
External debt stocks to exports (%)	141.6	141.9	215.1	190.5	183.5	261.0	264.7	258.2
External debt stocks to GNI (%)	57.7	46.9	47.1	44.5	44.2	61.5	61.5	59.7
Debt service to exports (%)	12.1	5.5	15.5	12.2	9.2	14.6	13.3	14.7
Reserves to external debt stocks (%)	11.2	23.5	23.6	30.8	24.1	17.8	16.4	16.8

Notes:

Long-term private nonguaranteed debt data from 2012 are World Bank staff estimates based on reports provided by the country. Short-term debt before 2009 is based on data from the BIS.

ST. LUCIA

(US$ million, unless otherwise indicated)

	2000	2005	2009	2010	2011	2012	2013	2014
Summary external debt data								
External debt stocks	**222.2**	**415.7**	**433.1**	**579.6**	**451.2**	**429.8**	**474.0**	**527.5**
Long-term external debt	153.5	238.6	314.9	321.3	310.1	342.9	358.2	371.3
Short-term external debt	67.8	176.0	84.6	225.3	99.9	45.7	74.5	118.2
interest arrears on long-term	0.0	0.0	2.6	5.3	3.9	1.6	2.2	2.2
Use of IMF credit	1.0	1.1	33.6	33.0	41.2	41.2	41.3	38.0
Long-term external debt								
Debt outstanding and disbursed	**153.5**	**238.6**	**314.9**	**321.3**	**310.1**	**342.9**	**358.2**	**371.3**
Public and publicly guaranteed	153.5	238.6	314.9	321.3	310.1	342.9	358.2	371.3
Official creditors	120.7	164.6	239.8	258.0	258.7	249.5	246.5	249.5
Private creditors	32.8	74.0	75.1	63.3	51.4	93.4	111.7	121.8
of which: Bonds	23.5	70.9	75.1	63.3	51.4	93.4	111.7	121.8
Private nonguaranteed	..	..	..	..	..	..	..	..
of which: Bonds	..	..	..	..	..	..	..	..
Disbursements	**48.7**	**12.6**	**25.8**	**36.4**	**20.0**	**6.9**	**12.0**	**25.2**
Public and publicly guaranteed	48.7	12.6	25.8	36.4	20.0	6.9	12.0	25.2
Official creditors	16.8	12.6	22.4	36.4	20.0	6.9	12.0	25.2
Private creditors	31.9	0.0	3.4	0.0	0.0	0.0	0.0	0.0
of which: Bonds	23.5	0.0	3.4	0.0	0.0	0.0	0.0	0.0
Private nonguaranteed	..	..	..	..	..	..	..	..
of which: Bonds	..	..	..	..	..	..	..	..
Principal repayments	**20.9**	**14.2**	**27.8**	**29.9**	**31.3**	**28.2**	**20.5**	**17.0**
Public and publicly guaranteed	20.9	14.2	27.8	29.9	31.3	28.2	20.5	17.0
Official creditors	11.7	9.5	16.0	18.0	19.4	16.3	15.6	15.9
Private creditors	9.2	4.7	11.9	11.9	11.9	11.9	4.9	1.0
of which: Bonds	0.0	4.7	11.9	11.9	11.9	11.9	4.9	1.0
Private nonguaranteed	..	..	..	..	..	..	..	..
of which: Bonds	..	..	..	..	..	..	..	..
Interest payments	**6.4**	**12.8**	**13.4**	**10.6**	**11.3**	**14.4**	**13.6**	**16.4**
Public and publicly guaranteed	6.4	12.8	13.4	10.6	11.3	14.4	13.6	16.4
Official creditors	5.2	6.3	7.4	7.4	6.7	6.4	6.1	5.9
Private creditors	1.2	6.5	6.1	3.2	4.6	8.0	7.5	10.5
of which: Bonds	1.0	6.3	6.1	3.2	4.6	8.0	7.5	10.5
Private nonguaranteed	..	..	..	..	..	..	..	..
of which: Bonds	..	..	..	..	..	..	..	..
Net financial flows								
Net debt inflows	40.3	65.4	-423.4	144.5	-126.8	-73.1	19.7	51.1
Official creditors (incl. IMF)	5.1	3.1	17.1	18.4	9.1	-9.4	-3.5	8.4
Private creditors	35.2	62.3	-440.5	126.1	-135.9	-63.8	23.3	42.7
Long-term	22.7	-4.7	-8.5	-11.9	-11.9	-11.9	-4.9	-1.0
Public and publicly guaranteed	22.7	-4.7	-8.5	-11.9	-11.9	-11.9	-4.9	-1.0
Private nonguaranteed	..	..	..	..	..	..	..	..
Short-term	12.5	67.0	-432.0	138.0	-124.0	-51.9	28.2	43.7
Net equity inflows								
Foreign direct investment	53.7	75.3	72.6	67.9	44.8	45.2	52.4	75.2
Portfolio equity	..	..	..	..	..	..	..	..
Major economic aggregates								
Gross national income (GNI)	736.3	863.0	1,131.4	1,204.7	1,269.7	1,267.4	1,310.3	1,344.4
Exports of goods, services & prim. income	380.6	533.0	560.5	626.6	589.1	621.7	631.7	..
Imports of goods, services & prim. income	494.2	675.5	709.6	844.7	852.3	811.7	739.3	..
Primary income on FDI	33.4	51.1	35.3	31.7	12.0	23.3	19.8	..
Personal transfers & comp. of employees	26.4	27.1	28.0	29.0	29.4	29.8	30.1	30.1
International reserves	78.8	116.4	174.8	206.3	213.4	232.0	192.2	257.7
Ratios								
External debt stocks to exports (%)	58.4	78.0	77.3	92.5	76.6	69.1	75.0	..
External debt stocks to GNI (%)	30.2	48.2	38.3	48.1	35.5	33.9	36.2	39.2
Debt service to exports (%)	7.9	6.0	7.7	7.4	7.6	7.0	5.7	..
Reserves to external debt stocks (%)	35.5	28.0	40.4	35.6	47.3	54.0	40.6	48.8

Notes:

Short-term debt before 2012 is based on data from the BIS.

ST. VINCENT AND THE GRENADINES

(US$ million, unless otherwise indicated)

	2000	2005	2009	2010	2011	2012	2013	2014
Summary external debt data								
External debt stocks	**195.1**	**252.6**	**245.8**	**295.5**	**303.4**	**287.1**	**310.6**	**338.9**
Long-term external debt	163.3	247.8	227.0	277.5	280.4	264.1	287.5	311.7
Short-term external debt	31.4	4.3	0.5	0.0	0.0	0.0	0.0	0.0
interest arrears on long-term	0.4	4.3	0.5	0.0	0.0	0.0	0.0	0.0
Use of IMF credit	0.5	0.5	18.3	17.9	23.0	23.0	23.0	27.2
Long-term external debt								
Debt outstanding and disbursed	**163.3**	**247.8**	**227.0**	**277.5**	**280.4**	**264.1**	**287.5**	**311.7**
Public and publicly guaranteed	163.3	247.8	227.0	277.5	280.4	264.1	287.5	311.7
Official creditors	104.8	114.8	167.2	228.8	242.6	238.7	270.0	294.6
Private creditors	58.5	133.0	59.8	48.7	37.8	25.4	17.5	17.1
of which: Bonds	0.0	0.0	0.0	0.0	0.0	0.0	0.0	0.0
Private nonguaranteed	..	..	..	..	..	..	..	..
of which: Bonds	..	..	..	..	..	..	..	..
Disbursements	**8.5**	**42.4**	**20.2**	**78.1**	**28.3**	**12.0**	**47.1**	**49.4**
Public and publicly guaranteed	8.5	42.4	20.2	78.1	28.3	12.0	47.1	49.4
Official creditors	8.5	12.4	20.2	78.1	28.3	12.0	46.2	41.4
Private creditors	0.0	30.0	0.0	0.0	0.0	0.0	1.0	8.0
of which: Bonds	0.0	0.0	0.0	0.0	0.0	0.0	0.0	0.0
Private nonguaranteed	..	..	..	..	..	..	..	..
of which: Bonds	..	..	..	..	..	..	..	..
Principal repayments	**6.1**	**15.5**	**25.1**	**26.5**	**25.2**	**28.4**	**24.8**	**22.9**
Public and publicly guaranteed	6.1	15.5	25.1	26.5	25.2	28.4	24.8	22.9
Official creditors	5.7	7.7	14.4	15.4	14.3	16.0	15.9	14.6
Private creditors	0.4	7.7	10.7	11.1	10.9	12.4	8.9	8.4
of which: Bonds	0.0	0.0	0.0	0.0	0.0	0.0	0.0	0.0
Private nonguaranteed	..	..	..	..	..	..	..	..
of which: Bonds	..	..	..	..	..	..	..	..
Interest payments	**5.1**	**8.2**	**11.2**	**10.0**	**10.1**	**8.4**	**8.1**	**7.7**
Public and publicly guaranteed	5.1	8.2	11.2	10.0	10.1	8.4	8.1	7.7
Official creditors	3.3	3.5	5.9	5.7	6.6	5.6	6.2	6.6
Private creditors	1.8	4.7	5.4	4.3	3.4	2.8	1.9	1.1
of which: Bonds	0.0	0.0	0.0	0.0	0.0	0.0	0.0	0.0
Private nonguaranteed	..	..	..	..	..	..	..	..
of which: Bonds	..	..	..	..	..	..	..	..
Net financial flows								
Net debt inflows	1.6	26.9	0.9	51.7	8.3	-16.5	22.4	32.2
Official creditors (incl. IMF)	2.8	4.6	11.6	62.8	19.2	-4.0	30.3	32.6
Private creditors	-1.2	22.3	-10.7	-11.1	-10.9	-12.4	-7.9	-0.4
Long-term	-0.4	22.3	-10.7	-11.1	-10.9	-12.4	-7.9	-0.4
Public and publicly guaranteed	-0.4	22.3	-10.7	-11.1	-10.9	-12.4	-7.9	-0.4
Private nonguaranteed	..	..	..	..	..	..	..	..
Short-term	-0.8	..	..	..	..	..	..	..
Net equity inflows								
Foreign direct investment	37.7	23.7	60.2	63.1	74.6	88.3	89.5	138.6
Portfolio equity	..	..	..	..	..	..	..	...
Major economic aggregates								
Gross national income (GNI)	377.1	521.1	661.9	669.1	664.1	690.6	719.0	728.3
Exports of goods, services & prim. income	182.6	208.9	206.0	195.9	192.3	202.4	208.6	..
Imports of goods, services & prim. income	222.8	329.2	414.7	414.1	399.1	420.1	443.1	..
Primary income on FDI	12.7	22.1	12.4	11.0	7.4	5.6	5.8	..
Personal transfers & comp. of employees	22.5	22.4	29.1	29.1	29.2	31.1	31.6	32.6
International reserves	55.2	69.5	87.8	112.7	89.6	111.0	135.1	157.4
Ratios								
External debt stocks to exports (%)	106.9	120.9	119.3	150.9	157.7	141.9	148.9	..
External debt stocks to GNI (%)	51.7	48.5	37.1	44.2	45.7	41.6	43.2	46.5
Debt service to exports (%)	7.2	11.3	17.7	18.6	18.4	18.2	15.8	..
Reserves to external debt stocks (%)	28.3	27.5	35.7	38.1	29.5	38.7	43.5	46.4

Notes:

Short-term debt data are excluded since BIS data include debt liabilities of offshore centers located in the country. BIS short-term debt data for 2011, 2012, 2013 and 2014 are $393 million, $361 million, $464 million, $1237 million respectively.

SUDAN

(US$ million, unless otherwise indicated)

	2000	2005	2009	2010	2011	2012	2013	2014
Summary external debt data								
External debt stocks	**15,771**	**17,613**	**21,128**	**22,233**	**21,146**	**21,793**	**22,469**	**21,759**
Long-term external debt	10,381	11,232	13,707	14,444	15,093	15,697	16,402	15,922
Short-term external debt	4,697	5,788	6,740	7,126	5,402	5,452	5,428	5,246
interest arrears on long-term	4,426	5,377	6,523	6,772	4,891	5,090	5,180	5,102
Use of IMF credit	693	593	682	664	651	645	639	591
Long-term external debt								
Debt outstanding and disbursed	**10,381**	**11,232**	**13,707**	**14,444**	**15,093**	**15,697**	**16,402**	**15,922**
Public and publicly guaranteed	9,885	11,232	13,707	14,444	15,093	15,697	16,402	15,922
Official creditors	8,128	9,145	11,258	11,815	11,350	11,366	11,618	11,350
Private creditors	1,758	2,087	2,449	2,629	3,743	4,331	4,785	4,572
of which: Bonds	0	0	0	0	0	0	0	0
Private nonguaranteed	496	..	..	..	..	..	..	..
of which: Bonds	..	..	..	..	..	..	..	..
Disbursements	**861**	**387**	**971**	**935**	**793**	**319**	**422**	**283**
Public and publicly guaranteed	861	387	971	935	793	319	422	283
Official creditors	318	387	971	935	793	319	422	283
Private creditors	543	0	0	0	0	0	0	0
of which: Bonds	0	0	0	0	0	0	0	0
Private nonguaranteed	..	..	..	..	..	..	..	..
of which: Bonds	..	..	..	..	..	..	..	..
Principal repayments	**143**	**291**	**362**	**397**	**416**	**274**	**211**	**179**
Public and publicly guaranteed	143	291	362	397	416	274	211	179
Official creditors	143	291	362	397	416	274	211	179
Private creditors	0	0	0	0	0	0	0	0
of which: Bonds	0	0	0	0	0	0	0	0
Private nonguaranteed	..	..	..	..	..	..	..	..
of which: Bonds	..	..	..	..	..	..	..	..
Interest payments	**42**	**67**	**111**	**83**	**100**	**76**	**73**	**69**
Public and publicly guaranteed	42	67	111	83	100	76	73	69
Official creditors	42	67	111	83	100	76	73	69
Private creditors	0	0	0	0	0	0	0	0
of which: Bonds	0	0	0	0	0	0	0	0
Private nonguaranteed	..	..	..	..	..	..	..	..
of which: Bonds	..	..	..	..	..	..	..	..
Net financial flows								
Net debt inflows	625	76	339	669	524	-111	90	-11
Official creditors (incl. IMF)	121	67	598	532	367	38	204	93
Private creditors	504	9	-259	137	157	-149	-114	-104
Long-term	543	..	..	..	..	..	..	..
Public and publicly guaranteed	543		..	..	..	..	..	..
Private nonguaranteed	..	..	..	..	..	..	..	..
Short-term	-39	9	-259	137	157	-149	-114	104
Net equity inflows								
Foreign direct investment	392	-676	-846	-831	-378	-280	-232	-275
Portfolio equity	..	78	0	7	13	2	0	2
Major economic aggregates								
Gross national income (GNI)	11,548	24,581	49,160	60,507	64,564	60,268	63,708	71,181
Exports of goods, services & prim. income	1,839	5,019	8,618	11,785	10,502	5,551	6,057	5,894
Imports of goods, services & prim. income	2,594	8,899	14,761	15,677	12,973	12,559	13,171	12,152
Primary income on FDI	..	699	2,112	2,393	1,011	671	1,144	657
Personal transfers & comp. of employees	641	704	1,394	1,100	442	401	424	343
International reserves	138	1,869	1,094	1,036	193	193	193	181
Ratios								
External debt stocks to exports (%)	857.7	350.9	245.2	188.7	201.4	392.6	371.0	369.2
External debt stocks to GNI (%)	136.6	71.7	43.0	36.7	32.8	36.2	35.3	30.6
Debt service to exports (%)	13.5	8.0	5.7	4.2	5.1	6.5	4.9	4.4
Reserves to external debt stocks (%)	0.9	10.6	5.2	4.7	0.9	0.9	0.9	0.8

Notes:

Long-term public and publicly guaranteed debt data exclude penalty interest. Short-term debt is based on data from the BIS.

SWAZILAND

(US$ million, unless otherwise indicated)

	2000	2005	2009	2010	2011	2012	2013	2014
Summary external debt data								
External debt stocks	**259.9**	**459.2**	**507.9**	**707.1**	**653.7**	**481.8**	**463.5**	**438.4**
Long-term external debt	249.7	370.0	405.3	402.1	378.6	340.2	316.5	297.9
Short-term external debt	1.8	80.1	27.0	230.7	201.0	67.3	72.6	70.5
interest arrears on long-term	0.0	15.1	25.0	35.7	48.0	42.3	41.6	40.5
Use of IMF credit	8.4	9.2	75.7	74.4	74.1	74.2	74.4	70.0
Long-term external debt								
Debt outstanding and disbursed	**249.7**	**370.0**	**405.3**	**402.1**	**378.6**	**340.2**	**316.5**	**297.9**
Public and publicly guaranteed	249.7	370.0	405.3	402.1	378.6	340.2	316.5	297.9
Official creditors	229.9	338.6	380.8	375.5	357.5	320.5	300.7	284.0
Private creditors	19.8	31.4	24.5	26.6	21.1	19.7	15.8	13.9
of which: Bonds	0.0	0.0	0.0	0.0	0.0	0.0	0.0	0.0
Private nonguaranteed	..	..	..	..	..	..	..	..
of which: Bonds	..	..	..	..	..	..	..	..
Disbursements	**15.8**	**51.7**	**36.5**	**11.5**	**32.1**	**5.2**	**18.2**	**19.4**
Public and publicly guaranteed	15.8	51.7	36.5	11.5	32.1	5.2	18.2	19.4
Official creditors	15.8	51.1	36.5	11.5	32.1	5.2	18.2	19.4
Private creditors	0.0	0.6	0.0	0.0	0.0	0.0	0.0	0.0
of which: Bonds	0.0	0.0	0.0	0.0	0.0	0.0	0.0	0.0
Private nonguaranteed	..	..	..	..	..	..	..	..
of which: Bonds	..	..	..	..	..	..	..	..
Principal repayments	**12.4**	**18.8**	**28.9**	**27.9**	**26.7**	**35.4**	**19.4**	**18.4**
Public and publicly guaranteed	12.4	18.8	28.9	27.9	26.7	35.4	19.4	18.4
Official creditors	12.4	18.1	28.4	27.3	26.1	34.9	19.2	18.0
Private creditors	0.0	0.7	0.5	0.6	0.6	0.5	0.2	0.4
of which: Bonds	0.0	0.0	0.0	0.0	0.0	0.0	0.0	0.0
Private nonguaranteed	..	..	..	..	..	..	..	..
of which: Bonds	..	..	..	..	..	..	..	..
Interest payments	**16.1**	**14.7**	**16.4**	**13.5**	**14.4**	**15.7**	**10.2**	**11.2**
Public and publicly guaranteed	16.1	14.7	16.4	13.5	14.4	15.7	10.2	11.2
Official creditors	10.2	10.5	14.6	13.0	14.0	13.0	9.0	8.3
Private creditors	5.9	4.2	1.7	0.5	0.4	2.7	1.2	2.9
of which: Bonds	0.0	0.0	0.0	0.0	0.0	0.0	0.0	0.0
Private nonguaranteed	..	..	..	..	..	..	..	..
of which: Bonds	..	..	..	..	..	..	..	..
Net financial flows								
Net debt inflows	-47.5	54.0	-47.4	176.6	-36.6	-158.2	4.8	0.0
Official creditors (incl. IMF)	3.4	33.1	8.2	-15.7	6.0	-29.7	-0.9	1.4
Private creditors	-50.9	20.9	-55.5	192.4	-42.6	-128.5	5.8	-1.4
Long-term	..	-0.1	-0.5	-0.6	-0.6	-0.5	-0.2	-0.4
Public and publicly guaranteed	..	-0.1	-0.5	-0.6	-0.6	-0.5	-0.2	-0.4
Private nonguaranteed	..	..	..	..	..	..	..	..
Short-term	-50.9	21.0	-55.0	193.0	-42.0	-128.0	6.0	-1.0
Net equity inflows								
Foreign direct investment	90.7	-15.8	53.1	49.3	50.3	2.7	29.8	55.1
Portfolio equity	1.4	0.8	-6.6	4.7	..	..	..	..
Major economic aggregates								
Gross national income (GNI)	1,558.7	2,762.4	3,069.1	3,301.6	3,551.1	3,459.3	3,169.2	3,181.8
Exports of goods, services & prim. income	1,376.4	2,075.9	2,066.2	2,275.3	2,397.6	2,368.2	2,280.8	2,334.6
Imports of goods, services & prim. income	1,522.9	2,276.0	2,672.4	3,063.4	3,265.8	3,188.6	2,948.9	2,971.7
Primary income on FDI	65.9	44.0	352.5	401.6	397.6	466.1	524.8	602.6
Personal transfers & comp. of employees	56.9	95.4	93.5	54.7	38.1	31.3	26.3	19.8
International reserves	351.8	243.9	958.9	756.3	600.5	741.0	762.5	690.8
Ratios								
External debt stocks to exports (%)	18.9	22.1	24.6	31.1	27.3	20.3	20.3	18.8
External debt stocks to GNI (%)	16.7	16.6	16.6	21.4	18.4	13.9	14.6	13.8
Debt service to exports (%)	2.2	1.8	2.2	1.9	1.8	2.2	1.3	1.3
Reserves to external debt stocks (%)	135.3	53.1	188.8	107.0	91.9	153.8	164.5	157.6

SYRIAN ARAB REPUBLIC

(US$ million, unless otherwise indicated)

	2000	2005	2009	2010	2011	2012	2013	2014
Summary external debt data								
External debt stocks	**22,236**	**5,594**	**5,674**	**5,263**	**4,968**	**4,736**	**4,753**	**4,597**
Long-term external debt	16,480	5,031	4,480	4,276	3,998	3,948	3,898	3,664
Short-term external debt	5,708	511	756	558	542	359	425	528
interest arrears on long-term	2,388	198	206	217	218	316	401	457
Use of IMF credit	48	52	438	430	429	429	430	404
Long-term external debt								
Debt outstanding and disbursed	**16,480**	**5,031**	**4,480**	**4,276**	**3,998**	**3,948**	**3,898**	**3,664**
Public and publicly guaranteed	16,480	5,031	4,480	4,276	3,998	3,948	3,898	3,664
Official creditors	15,512	5,031	4,480	4,276	3,998	3,948	3,898	3,664
Private creditors	968	0	0	0	0	0	0	0
of which: Bonds	0	0	0	0	0	0	0	0
Private nonguaranteed	..	..	..	..	..	..	..	..
of which: Bonds	..	..	..	..	..	..	..	..
Disbursements	**18**	**189**	**281**	**286**	**222**	**0**	**0**	**0**
Public and publicly guaranteed	18	189	281	286	222	0	0	0
Official creditors	18	189	281	286	222	0	0	0
Private creditors	0	0	0	0	0	0	0	0
of which: Bonds	0	0	0	0	0	0	0	0
Private nonguaranteed	..	..	..	..	..	..	..	..
of which: Bonds	..	..	..	..	..	..	..	..
Principal repayments	**239**	**439**	**499**	**508**	**509**	**0**	**0**	**0**
Public and publicly guaranteed	239	439	499	508	509	0	0	0
Official creditors	224	428	499	508	509	0	0	0
Private creditors	16	11	0	0	0	0	0	0
of which: Bonds	0	0	0	0	0	0	0	0
Private nonguaranteed	..	..	..	..	..	..	..	..
of which: Bonds	..	..	..	..	..	..	..	..
Interest payments	**127**	**110**	**119**	**111**	**109**	**0**	**0**	**0**
Public and publicly guaranteed	127	110	119	111	109	0	0	0
Official creditors	126	110	119	111	109	0	0	0
Private creditors	1	0	0	0	0	0	0	0
of which: Bonds	0	0	0	0	0	0	0	0
Private nonguaranteed	..	..	..	..	..	..	..	..
of which: Bonds	..	..	..	..	..	..	..	..
Net financial flows								
Net debt inflows	-826	-357	-104	-430	-304	-281	-19	47
Official creditors (incl. IMF)	-206	-239	-218	-221	-287	..	..	..
Private creditors	-621	-118	114	-209	-17	-281	-19	47
Long-term	-16	-11	..	..	..	..	..	..
Public and publicly guaranteed	-16	-11	..	..	..	..	..	..
Private nonguaranteed	..	..	..	..	..	..	..	..
Short-term	-605	-107	114	-209	-17	-281	-19	47
Net equity inflows								
Foreign direct investment	270	500	2,570	1,469	804	..	..	..
Portfolio equity	..	..	..	..	..	..	..	..
Major economic aggregates								
Gross national income (GNI)	18,446	27,980	..	..	..	..	..	..
Exports of goods, services & prim. income	7,190	11,907	16,026	19,919	..	..	..	..
Imports of goods, services & prim. income	6,614	12,359	18,118	21,235	..	..	..	..
Primary income on FDI	..	1,220	1,301	1,684	..	..	..	..
Personal transfers & comp. of employees	180	823	1,350	1,623	..	..	..	..
International reserves	..	17,347	17,398	19,465	..	..	..	..
Ratios								
External debt stocks to exports (%)	309.3	47.0	35.4	26.4	..	..	..	..
External debt stocks to GNI (%)	120.5	20.0	..	..	..	..	..	..
Debt service to exports (%)	6.8	4.8	3.9	3.1	..	..	..	..
Reserves to external debt stocks (%)	..	310.1	306.6	369.8	..	..	..	..

Notes:

Long-term public and publicly guaranteed debt data are World Bank staff estimates. Short-term debt is based on data from the BIS.

TAJIKISTAN

(US$ million, unless otherwise indicated)

	2000	2005	2009	2010	2011	2012	2013	2014
Summary external debt data								
External debt stocks	**1,141**	**1,121**	**2,666**	**3,082**	**3,322**	**3,733**	**3,847**	**4,047**
Long-term external debt	846	850	2,423	2,734	2,946	3,340	3,451	3,758
Short-term external debt	77	27	74	122	129	106	109	22
interest arrears on long-term	45	2	0	0	0	16	1	0
Use of IMF credit	218	244	170	227	246	287	287	266
Long-term external debt								
Debt outstanding and disbursed	**846**	**850**	**2,423**	**2,734**	**2,946**	**3,340**	**3,451**	**3,758**
Public and publicly guaranteed	755	826	1,606	1,806	1,968	2,001	2,016	2,049
Official creditors	704	817	1,606	1,806	1,968	2,001	2,016	2,049
Private creditors	51	8	0	0	0	0	0	0
of which: Bonds	0	0	0	0	0	0	0	0
Private nonguaranteed	91	24	816	927	979	1,339	1,435	1,709
of which: Bonds	..	..	..	..	..	..	..	..
Disbursements	**37**	**108**	**518**	**924**	**723**	**556**	**431**	**677**
Public and publicly guaranteed	36	105	211	251	200	105	105	189
Official creditors	36	105	211	251	200	105	105	189
Private creditors	0	0	0	0	0	0	0	0
of which: Bonds	0	0	0	0	0	0	0	0
Private nonguaranteed	1	2	307	673	523	451	325	487
of which: Bonds	..	..	..	..	..	..	..	..
Principal repayments	**28**	**42**	**409**	**630**	**513**	**334**	**320**	**322**
Public and publicly guaranteed	15	37	35	37	34	74	93	108
Official creditors	15	37	35	37	34	74	93	108
Private creditors	0	0	0	0	0	0	0	0
of which: Bonds	0	0	0	0	0	0	0	0
Private nonguaranteed	12	5	374	593	479	261	227	213
of which: Bonds	..	..	..	..	..	..	..	..
Interest payments	**21**	**10**	**41**	**54**	**64**	**94**	**104**	**91**
Public and publicly guaranteed	7	9	24	23	28	30	30	31
Official creditors	4	9	24	23	28	30	30	31
Private creditors	4	0	0	0	0	0	0	0
of which: Bonds	0	0	0	0	0	0	0	0
Private nonguaranteed	14	1	17	31	36	63	74	60
of which: Bonds	..	..	..	..	..	..	..	..
Net financial flows								
Net debt inflows	-4	23	119	401	238	222	128	265
Official creditors (incl. IMF)	36	84	202	274	187	71	12	77
Private creditors	-40	-61	-83	127	52	151	116	188
Long-term	-11	-3	-67	80	44	190	98	274
Public and publicly guaranteed	..	..	..	..	..	..	..	..
Private nonguaranteed	-11	-3	-67	80	44	190	98	274
Short-term	-29	-58	-16	47	7	-39	18	-86
Net equity inflows								
Foreign direct investment	24	54	16	29	20	41	0	117
Portfolio equity	..	..	..	..	..	..	..	1
Major economic aggregates								
Gross national income (GNI)	824	2,234	4,908	5,563	6,483	7,581	8,456	9,145
Exports of goods, services & prim. income	..	1,264	1,225	899	1,198	1,684	1,232	1,096
Imports of goods, services & prim. income	..	1,733	3,141	3,458	4,319	5,383	5,507	5,455
Primary income on FDI	..	2	5	9	7	33	24	42
Personal transfers & comp. of employees	..	467	1,748	2,306	3,060	3,626	4,219	3,854
International reserves	93	168	175	324	289	298	461	169
Ratios								
External debt stocks to exports (%)	..	88.7	217.6	342.8	277.3	221.6	312.2	369.4
External debt stocks to GNI (%)	138.4	50.2	54.3	55.4	51.2	49.2	45.5	44.3
Debt service to exports (%)	..	5.8	38.0	76.3	48.3	25.5	34.6	38.2
Reserves to external debt stocks (%)	8.1	15.0	6.5	10.5	8.7	8.0	12.0	4.2

Notes:

Long-term private nonguaranteed debt data from 2013 are World Bank staff estimates based on reports provided by the country. Short-term debt is based on data from the BIS. Data include MDRI debt relief.

TANZANIA

(US$ million, unless otherwise indicated)

	2000	2005	2009	2010	2011	2012	2013	2014
Summary external debt data								
External debt stocks	**7,183**	**8,400**	**7,624**	**8,987**	**9,940**	**11,581**	**13,025**	**14,436**
Long-term external debt	5,969	7,006	5,656	6,825	7,686	8,830	10,624	11,765
Short-term external debt	849	1,006	1,341	1,515	1,611	2,110	1,647	1,989
interest arrears on long-term	647	615	836	908	989	1,054	1,108	1,122
Use of IMF credit	364	387	628	647	643	641	753	682
Long-term external debt								
Debt outstanding and disbursed	**5,969**	**7,006**	**5,656**	**6,825**	**7,686**	**8,830**	**10,624**	**11,765**
Public and publicly guaranteed	5,969	6,446	4,640	5,601	6,438	7,366	9,107	9,906
Official creditors	5,776	6,341	4,522	5,488	6,030	6,761	7,739	8,498
Private creditors	194	105	118	113	408	604	1,368	1,408
of which: Bonds	0	0	0	0	0	0	600	600
Private nonguaranteed	..	560	1,016	1,224	1,248	1,465	1,517	1,859
of which: Bonds	..	..	..	..	..	..	..	..
Disbursements	**211**	**466**	**1,065**	**1,254**	**1,179**	**978**	**2,007**	**1,580**
Public and publicly guaranteed	211	466	919	1,038	872	794	1,854	1,296
Official creditors	206	447	889	1,021	568	791	1,032	1,209
Private creditors	5	19	30	17	304	2	821	87
of which: Bonds	0	0	0	0	0	0	600	0
Private nonguaranteed	..	..	146	216	307	184	153	284
of which: Bonds	..	..	..	..	..	..	..	..
Principal repayments	**94**	**31**	**105**	**131**	**76**	**78**	**80**	**118**
Public and publicly guaranteed	94	31	26	52	33	35	61	54
Official creditors	77	31	13	35	26	27	29	27
Private creditors	17	0	13	17	7	7	32	27
of which: Bonds	0	0	0	0	0	0	0	0
Private nonguaranteed	..	..	79	79	44	43	19	64
of which: Bonds	..	..	..	..	..	..	..	..
Interest payments	**51**	**44**	**45**	**50**	**53**	**60**	**62**	**83**
Public and publicly guaranteed	51	42	27	32	39	43	58	76
Official creditors	49	42	24	31	36	39	46	52
Private creditors	2	0	3	2	3	4	13	24
of which: Bonds	0	0	0	0	0	0	0	0
Private nonguaranteed	..	2	18	17	14	17	3	7
of which: Bonds	..	..	..	..	..	..	..	..
Net financial flows								
Net debt inflows	205	459	1,188	1,255	1,116	1,331	1,520	1,763
Official creditors (incl. IMF)	172	378	1,182	1,016	540	761	1,114	1,155
Private creditors	33	81	6	239	576	569	406	608
Long-term	-12	19	84	137	561	135	923	280
Public and publicly guaranteed	-12	19	17	0	297	-5	789	60
Private nonguaranteed	..	..	67	137	264	140	134	220
Short-term	44	62	-78	102	15	434	-517	328
Net equity inflows								
Foreign direct investment	463	439	664	1,192	879	1,399	1,373	2,049
Portfolio equity	..	3	3	3	3	4	4	..
Major economic aggregates								
Gross national income (GNI)	10,114	13,836	27,323	29,942	32,197	37,313	42,822	47,972
Exports of goods, services & prim. income	1,411	3,053	5,314	6,530	7,582	8,807	8,581	..
Imports of goods, services & prim. income	2,230	4,641	8,015	9,541	12,477	13,383	14,059	..
Primary income on FDI	13	319	342	365	309	560	322	..
Personal transfers & comp. of employees	8	19	40	55	78	67	59	64
International reserves	974	2,049	3,470	3,905	3,726	4,052	4,674	4,390
Ratios								
External debt stocks to exports (%)	508.9	275.2	143.5	137.6	131.1	131.5	151.8	..
External debt stocks to GNI (%)	71.0	60.7	27.9	30.0	30.9	31.0	30.4	30.1
Debt service to exports (%)	11.9	4.4	3.1	3.0	1.9	1.9	1.9	..
Reserves to external debt stocks (%)	13.6	24.4	45.5	43.4	37.5	35.0	35.9	30.4

Notes:

Long-term public and publicly guaranteed debt data include debt liabilities of Zanzibar. Long-term private nonguaranteed debt data from 2004 to 2007 are World Bank staff estimates and from 2008 are reported by Central Bank. Short-term debt is based on data from the BIS. Data include the effects of HIPC and MDRI debt relief.

THAILAND

(US$ million, unless otherwise indicated)

	2000	2005	2009	2010	2011	2012	2013	2014
Summary external debt data								
External debt stocks	**79,830**	**58,464**	**80,787**	**106,323**	**109,910**	**134,222**	**137,317**	**135,799**
Long-term external debt	61,778	42,329	45,981	54,172	61,132	74,551	73,927	77,770
Short-term external debt	14,880	16,014	33,284	50,657	47,288	58,181	61,896	56,624
interest arrears on long-term	0	0	8	2	5	2	0	0
Use of IMF credit	3,172	121	1,521	1,494	1,490	1,491	1,494	1,406
Long-term external debt								
Debt outstanding and disbursed	**61,778**	**42,329**	**45,981**	**54,172**	**61,132**	**74,551**	**73,927**	**77,770**
Public and publicly guaranteed	29,462	17,449	14,707	21,172	26,445	34,731	34,014	33,420
Official creditors	20,820	7,862	6,468	6,843	6,865	6,327	6,001	5,527
Private creditors	8,643	9,587	8,239	14,329	19,580	28,403	28,013	27,893
of which: Bonds	2,630	3,836	3,074	8,004	12,894	21,894	21,854	21,754
Private nonguaranteed	32,316	24,880	31,274	33,000	34,687	39,820	39,913	44,350
of which: Bonds	8,414	4,685	5,125	4,265	3,618	6,040	5,575	9,720
Disbursements	**4,031**	**17,083**	**12,989**	**16,838**	**17,452**	**29,509**	**19,846**	**19,437**
Public and publicly guaranteed	3,031	2,521	1,716	6,442	6,128	9,735	1,552	479
Official creditors	2,156	434	76	160	493	735	1,552	479
Private creditors	876	2,086	1,640	6,282	5,635	9,000	0	0
of which: Bonds	0	936	970	5,080	4,890	9,000	0	0
Private nonguaranteed	1,000	14,562	11,273	10,396	11,324	19,775	18,294	18,958
of which: Bonds	..	1,600	198	..	700	1,500	..	4,370
Principal repayments	**8,945**	**16,464**	**11,313**	**9,386**	**8,815**	**13,316**	**11,054**	**12,937**
Public and publicly guaranteed	3,010	2,709	1,590	803	1,197	757	1,211	454
Official creditors	1,666	2,321	468	534	779	619	871	348
Private creditors	1,344	388	1,122	269	418	137	340	106
of which: Bonds	174	172	200	150	0	0	40	100
Private nonguaranteed	5,935	13,755	9,723	8,582	7,618	12,560	9,842	12,483
of which: Bonds	1,044	908	141	460	180	550	465	625
Interest payments	**3,776**	**1,074**	**1,085**	**1,075**	**1,176**	**1,354**	**1,213**	**1,473**
Public and publicly guaranteed	1,577	437	231	230	263	409	333	363
Official creditors	1,008	234	112	113	114	111	80	75
Private creditors	569	202	119	118	149	298	253	288
of which: Bonds	193	135	58	56	88	255	213	251
Private nonguaranteed	2,199	637	855	845	913	944	880	1,109
of which: Bonds	476	286	251	234	311	339	353	429
Net financial flows								
Net debt inflows	-13,649	5,145	14,501	24,831	5,266	27,088	12,510	1,227
Official creditors (incl. IMF)	292	-1,886	-392	-374	-285	115	681	131
Private creditors	-13,942	7,031	14,893	25,205	5,552	26,972	11,829	1,096
Long-term	-5,404	2,505	2,068	7,826	8,923	16,078	8,111	6,368
Public and publicly guaranteed	-469	1,698	518	6,012	5,217	8,863	-340	-106
Private nonguaranteed	-4,935	807	1,550	1,813	3,706	7,215	8,452	6,475
Short-term	-8,538	4,526	12,825	17,379	-3,371	10,895	3,718	-5,272
Net equity inflows								
Foreign direct investment	3,366	7,000	5,634	9,839	2,150	10,809	8,695	11,632
Portfolio equity	900	5,121	1,695	3,215	19	58	-3,352	-5,824
Major economic aggregates								
Gross national income (GNI)	120,809	167,799	253,430	305,181	333,324	351,389	361,246	355,637
Exports of goods, services & prim. income	85,997	131,744	186,028	231,029	267,633	282,957	290,488	286,999
Imports of goods, services & prim. income	77,269	143,591	169,485	227,130	269,537	296,631	304,761	282,426
Primary income on FDI	..	10,812	13,283	18,845	13,864	23,171	29,534	27,391
Personal transfers & comp. of employees	1,697	1,187	2,776	3,580	4,554	4,713	5,690	5,655
International reserves	32,016	50,691	135,483	167,530	167,389	173,328	161,328	151,253
Ratios								
External debt stocks to exports (%)	92.8	44.4	43.4	46.0	41.1	47.4	47.3	47.3
External debt stocks to GNI (%)	66.1	34.8	31.9	34.8	33.0	38.2	38.0	38.2
Debt service to exports (%)	16.3	13.7	6.8	4.7	3.9	5.4	4.4	5.2
Reserves to external debt stocks (%)	40.1	86.7	167.7	157.6	152.3	129.1	117.5	111.4

TOGO

(US$ million, unless otherwise indicated)

	2000	2005	2009	2010	2011	2012	2013	2014
Summary external debt data								
External debt stocks	**1,446.0**	**1,686.9**	**1,730.1**	**1,284.6**	**629.4**	**754.1**	**903.3**	**995.1**
Long-term external debt	1,229.6	1,439.5	1,481.9	1,004.2	369.4	450.0	563.2	679.4
Short-term external debt	132.5	217.7	47.0	38.9	5.8	49.6	86.9	89.2
interest arrears on long-term	62.6	166.7	30.0	9.9	2.8	3.6	2.9	1.2
Use of IMF credit	83.8	29.7	201.2	241.5	254.2	254.5	253.2	226.6
Long-term external debt								
Debt outstanding and disbursed	**1,229.6**	**1,439.5**	**1,481.9**	**1,004.2**	**369.4**	**450.0**	**563.2**	**679.4**
Public and publicly guaranteed	1,229.6	1,439.5	1,481.9	1,004.2	369.4	450.0	563.2	679.4
Official creditors	1,229.6	1,439.5	1,481.9	1,004.2	369.4	450.0	513.6	646.6
Private creditors	0.0	0.0	0.0	0.0	0.0	0.0	49.6	32.8
of which: Bonds	0.0	0.0	0.0	0.0	0.0	0.0	0.0	0.0
Private nonguaranteed	..	..	..	..	..	..	..	..
of which: Bonds	..	..	..	..	..	..	..	..
Disbursements	**24.4**	**9.9**	**34.6**	**82.8**	**30.0**	**126.6**	**183.7**	**177.8**
Public and publicly guaranteed	24.4	9.9	34.6	82.8	30.0	126.6	183.7	177.8
Official creditors	24.4	9.9	34.6	82.8	30.0	126.6	123.2	177.8
Private creditors	0.0	0.0	0.0	0.0	0.0	0.0	60.4	0.0
of which: Bonds	0.0	0.0	0.0	0.0	0.0	0.0	0.0	0.0
Private nonguaranteed	..	..	..	..	..	..	..	..
of which: Bonds	..	..	..	..	..	..	..	..
Principal repayments	**9.9**	**7.9**	**39.5**	**28.3**	**10.0**	**13.0**	**37.8**	**30.2**
Public and publicly guaranteed	9.9	7.9	39.5	28.3	10.0	13.0	37.8	30.2
Official creditors	9.9	7.9	39.5	28.3	10.0	13.0	25.7	18.3
Private creditors	0.0	0.0	0.0	0.0	0.0	0.0	12.1	11.9
of which: Bonds	0.0	0.0	0.0	0.0	0.0	0.0	0.0	0.0
Private nonguaranteed	..	..	..	..	..	..	..	..
of which: Bonds	..	..	..	..	..	..	..	..
Interest payments	**4.6**	**0.3**	**13.1**	**8.0**	**4.6**	**9.3**	**11.4**	**15.9**
Public and publicly guaranteed	4.6	0.3	13.1	8.0	4.6	9.3	11.4	15.9
Official creditors	4.6	0.3	13.1	8.0	4.6	9.3	11.4	15.9
Private creditors	0.0	0.0	0.0	0.0	0.0	0.0	0.0	0.0
of which: Bonds	0.0	0.0	0.0	0.0	0.0	0.0	0.0	0.0
Private nonguaranteed	..	..	..	..	..	..	..	..
of which: Bonds	..	..	..	..	..	..	..	..
Net financial flows								
Net debt inflows	-44.3	15.8	-30.6	110.2	7.9	156.7	182.1	139.3
Official creditors (incl. IMF)	5.1	-9.2	36.4	98.2	33.9	113.7	95.8	147.2
Private creditors	-49.4	25.0	-67.0	12.0	-26.0	43.0	86.3	-7.9
Long-term	..	..	..	..	..	..	48.3	-11.9
Public and publicly guaranteed	..		..	..	..	..	48.3	-11.9
Private nonguaranteed	..	..	..	..	..	..	..	..
Short-term	-49.4	25.0	-67.0	12.0	-26.0	43.0	38.0	4.0
Net equity inflows								
Foreign direct investment	41.9	54.4	32.6	78.0	44.6	109.4	183.5	292.1
Portfolio equity	6.1	16.0	2.1	4.5	0.0	..	..	..
Major economic aggregates								
Gross national income (GNI)	1,265.3	2,079.9	2,803.4	2,761.6	3,197.5	3,331.3	3,696.3	4,067.9
Exports of goods, services & prim. income	456.5	857.3	1,265.0	1,395.8	2,079.0	2,004.9	2,338.2	..
Imports of goods, services & prim. income	664.1	1,249.0	1,777.3	1,951.3	2,651.3	2,541.2	3,176.0	..
Primary income on FDI	17.2	47.2	41.5	67.0	120.2	180.4	..	..
Personal transfers & comp. of employees	34.2	192.5	334.5	336.6	244.1	344.8	..	..
International reserves	140.9	191.5	703.2	714.9	774.3	441.6	507.1	507.0
Ratios								
External debt stocks to exports (%)	316.7	196.8	136.8	92.0	30.3	37.6	38.6	..
External debt stocks to GNI (%)	114.3	81.1	61.7	46.5	19.7	22.6	24.4	24.5
Debt service to exports (%)	6.6	2.5	4.3	2.6	0.7	1.1	2.2	..
Reserves to external debt stocks (%)	9.7	11.4	40.6	55.7	123.0	58.6	56.1	50.9

Notes:
Short-term debt is based on data from the BIS. Data include the effects of Paris Club debt restructuring agreement and HIPC and MDRI debt relief.

TONGA

(US$ million, unless otherwise indicated)

	2000	2005	2009	2010	2011	2012	2013	2014
Summary external debt data								
External debt stocks	**73.8**	**89.0**	**114.9**	**153.7**	**190.6**	**197.4**	**199.1**	**195.8**
Long-term external debt	65.0	79.5	104.6	143.5	180.5	187.2	188.9	186.3
Short-term external debt	0.2	0.1	0.0	0.0	0.0	0.0	0.0	0.0
interest arrears on long-term	0.2	0.1	0.0	0.0	0.0	0.0	0.0	0.0
Use of IMF credit	8.6	9.4	10.3	10.1	10.1	10.1	10.1	9.5
Long-term external debt								
Debt outstanding and disbursed	**65.0**	**79.5**	**104.6**	**143.5**	**180.5**	**187.2**	**188.9**	**186.3**
Public and publicly guaranteed	65.0	79.5	104.6	143.5	180.5	187.2	188.9	186.3
Official creditors	65.0	79.5	103.7	142.4	180.0	187.0	188.8	186.1
Private creditors	0.0	0.0	0.9	1.1	0.4	0.3	0.2	0.1
of which: Bonds	0.0	0.0	0.0	0.0	0.0	0.0	0.0	0.0
Private nonguaranteed	..	..	..	..	..	..	..	..
of which: Bonds	..	..	..	..	..	..	..	..
Disbursements	**5.4**	**4.5**	**17.4**	**40.9**	**36.9**	**9.9**	**1.3**	**5.1**
Public and publicly guaranteed	5.4	4.5	17.4	40.9	36.9	9.9	1.3	5.1
Official creditors	5.4	4.5	16.5	40.7	36.9	9.9	1.3	5.1
Private creditors	0.0	0.0	0.8	0.2	0.0	0.0	0.0	0.0
of which: Bonds	0.0	0.0	0.0	0.0	0.0	0.0	0.0	0.0
Private nonguaranteed	..	..	..	..	..	..	..	..
of which: Bonds	..	..	..	..	..	..	..	..
Principal repayments	**3.7**	**3.7**	**2.4**	**2.7**	**3.3**	**3.4**	**3.4**	**3.6**
Public and publicly guaranteed	3.7	3.7	2.4	2.7	3.3	3.4	3.4	3.6
Official creditors	2.4	3.7	2.4	2.6	3.3	3.3	3.3	3.6
Private creditors	1.3	0.0	0.0	0.1	0.0	0.2	0.1	0.0
of which: Bonds	0.0	0.0	0.0	0.0	0.0	0.0	0.0	0.0
Private nonguaranteed	..	..	..	..	..	..	..	..
of which: Bonds	..	..	..	..	..	..	..	..
Interest payments	**0.9**	**1.2**	**1.4**	**2.4**	**2.6**	**2.9**	**3.1**	**3.0**
Public and publicly guaranteed	0.9	1.2	1.4	2.4	2.6	2.9	3.1	3.0
Official creditors	0.8	1.2	1.4	2.3	2.6	2.9	3.1	3.0
Private creditors	0.1	0.0	0.0	0.1	0.0	0.0	0.0	0.0
of which: Bonds	0.0	0.0	0.0	0.0	0.0	0.0	0.0	0.0
Private nonguaranteed	..	..	..	..	..	..	..	..
of which: Bonds	..	..	..	..	..	..	..	..
Net financial flows								
Net debt inflows	1.8	0.9	14.9	38.2	33.6	6.5	-2.1	1.5
Official creditors (incl. IMF)	3.0	0.9	14.2	38.1	33.7	6.6	-2.0	1.5
Private creditors	-1.3	..	0.8	0.1	0.0	-0.2	-0.1	0.0
Long-term	-1.3	..	0.8	0.1	0.0	-0.2	-0.1	0.0
Public and publicly guaranteed	-1.3	..	0.8	0.1	0.0	-0.2	-0.1	0.0
Private nonguaranteed	..	..	..	..	..	..	..	..
Short-term	..	..	..	..	..	..	..	..
Net equity inflows								
Foreign direct investment	4.8	7.2	0.0	7.3	3.2	1.5	51.4	56.0
Portfolio equity	..	..	..	..	..	..	..	..
Major economic aggregates								
Gross national income (GNI)	191.0	258.6	327.9	373.8	450.7	470.8	445.3	442.7
Exports of goods, services & prim. income	..	59.0	53.6	69.7	99.1	113.9	..	..
Imports of goods, services & prim. income	..	156.8	245.4	232.6	287.2	284.6	..	..
Primary income on FDI	..	..	0.0	..	5.0	7.7	..	..
Personal transfers & comp. of employees	..	68.6	72.1	76.0	69.9	112.3	..	..
International reserves	24.6	46.9	95.7	104.5	143.3	152.4	155.5	158.8
Ratios								
External debt stocks to exports (%)	..	151.0	214.5	220.6	192.2	173.3	..	..
External debt stocks to GNI (%)	38.6	34.4	35.0	41.1	42.3	41.9	44.7	44.2
Debt service to exports (%)	..	8.8	7.2	7.2	5.9	5.6	..	..
Reserves to external debt stocks (%)	33.4	52.6	83.3	68.0	75.2	77.2	78.1	81.1

TUNISIA

(US$ million, unless otherwise indicated)

	2000	2005	2009	2010	2011	2012	2013	2014
Summary external debt data								
External debt stocks	**11,355**	**17,922**	**22,722**	**22,472**	**22,642**	**25,261**	**25,661**	**26,405**
Long-term external debt	9,688	14,738	17,459	17,073	17,274	18,613	18,517	18,022
Short-term external debt	1,590	3,135	4,835	4,979	4,949	6,230	6,572	6,846
interest arrears on long-term	0	0	0	0	0	0	0	0
Use of IMF credit	77	49	428	420	419	419	572	1,537
Long-term external debt								
Debt outstanding and disbursed	**9,688**	**14,738**	**17,459**	**17,073**	**17,274**	**18,613**	**18,517**	**18,022**
Public and publicly guaranteed	8,888	12,997	14,852	14,671	14,931	16,569	16,879	16,508
Official creditors	6,093	8,417	9,979	10,220	11,295	12,500	13,336	12,715
Private creditors	2,795	4,580	4,873	4,451	3,636	4,068	3,543	3,793
of which: Bonds	1,327	3,510	3,776	3,819	3,063	3,571	3,110	3,364
Private nonguaranteed	800	1,741	2,607	2,402	2,343	2,044	1,638	1,514
of which: Bonds	..	..	..	..	..	..	..	..
Disbursements	**1,542**	**1,256**	**1,548**	**1,642**	**2,244**	**3,417**	**1,509**	**2,484**
Public and publicly guaranteed	1,242	1,126	1,371	1,545	2,157	3,361	1,489	2,484
Official creditors	709	843	1,315	1,507	2,131	2,047	1,255	1,849
Private creditors	533	283	56	39	26	1,314	234	635
of which: Bonds	0	249	0	0	0	1,298	225	500
Private nonguaranteed	300	130	177	97	87	56	20	..
of which: Bonds	..	..	..	..	..	..	..	..
Principal repayments	**1,296**	**1,187**	**1,350**	**1,617**	**1,905**	**1,899**	**1,800**	**1,316**
Public and publicly guaranteed	1,264	1,129	1,233	1,397	1,759	1,609	1,374	1,192
Official creditors	662	873	837	887	860	880	875	1,110
Private creditors	602	255	396	510	899	729	499	82
of which: Bonds	371	136	313	0	814	650	443	0
Private nonguaranteed	32	58	117	220	146	290	426	124
of which: Bonds	..	..	..	..	..	..	..	..
Interest payments	**489**	**686**	**700**	**670**	**678**	**610**	**572**	**458**
Public and publicly guaranteed	479	584	598	546	559	500	489	458
Official creditors	297	334	335	309	330	342	318	345
Private creditors	182	249	263	237	230	158	171	113
of which: Bonds	99	200	217	193	203	135	155	97
Private nonguaranteed	10	102	102	124	119	110	83	..
of which: Bonds	..	..	..	..	..	..	..	..
Net financial flows								
Net debt inflows	258	-141	703	169	310	2,797	203	2,489
Official creditors (incl. IMF)	7	-31	478	619	1,270	1,167	531	1,786
Private creditors	251	-111	226	-451	-961	1,631	-328	703
Long-term	199	99	-280	-594	-931	351	-670	429
Public and publicly guaranteed	-69	27	-340	-471	-872	585	-264	553
Private nonguaranteed	268	72	60	-123	-59	-234	-406	-124
Short-term	52	-210	505	144	-29	1,280	342	274
Net equity inflows								
Foreign direct investment	752	716	1,529	1,339	439	1,560	1,071	1,007
Portfolio equity	-18	12	-89	-26	-44	-15	80	72
Major economic aggregates								
Gross national income (GNI)	20,525	30,635	41,371	42,170	43,634	43,172	44,801	..
Exports of goods, services & prim. income	8,701	14,884	20,133	22,556	22,950	22,600	22,513	22,103
Imports of goods, services & prim. income	10,347	16,495	23,318	26,595	28,235	28,471	28,642	28,721
Primary income on FDI	468	962	1,588	1,658	1,716	1,533	1,756	1,362
Personal transfers & comp. of employees	796	1,393	1,964	2,063	2,004	2,266	2,291	2,347
International reserves	1,811	4,437	11,057	9,459	7,454	8,357	7,287	7,235
Ratios								
External debt stocks to exports (%)	130.5	120.4	112.9	99.6	98.7	111.8	114.0	119.5
External debt stocks to GNI (%)	55.3	58.5	54.9	53.3	51.9	58.5	57.3	..
Debt service to exports (%)	21.9	13.7	10.5	10.4	11.5	11.5	11.8	8.7
Reserves to external debt stocks (%)	15.9	24.8	48.7	42.1	32.9	33.1	28.4	27.4

Notes:

Long-term private nonguaranteed debt data from 2008 are World Bank staff estimates based on reports provided by the country.

TURKEY

(US$ million, unless otherwise indicated)

	2000	2005	2009	2010	2011	2012	2013	2014
Summary external debt data								
External debt stocks	**116,793**	**172,143**	**277,280**	**299,113**	**305,135**	**336,961**	**389,386**	**408,203**
Long-term external debt	83,558	118,420	218,649	214,589	219,034	234,256	257,311	273,792
Short-term external debt	28,912	38,916	48,993	77,247	81,580	100,195	130,425	132,859
interest arrears on long-term	0	0	0	0	0	0	0	0
Use of IMF credit	4,323	14,807	9,638	7,277	4,521	2,510	1,650	1,552
Long-term external debt								
Debt outstanding and disbursed	**83,558**	**118,420**	**218,649**	**214,589**	**219,034**	**234,256**	**257,311**	**273,792**
Public and publicly guaranteed	55,730	62,977	85,619	91,510	94,767	99,028	105,181	104,312
Official creditors	12,537	12,435	23,109	26,427	28,221	29,569	31,957	30,838
Private creditors	43,193	50,542	62,510	65,083	66,546	69,459	73,224	73,474
of which: Bonds	20,392	27,909	40,932	44,274	47,020	52,446	58,427	62,694
Private nonguaranteed	27,828	55,443	133,030	123,080	124,267	135,228	152,130	169,480
of which: Bonds	1,784	4,025	6,606	6,202	4,003	11,835	20,885	28,781
Disbursements	**22,955**	**41,260**	**39,688**	**48,617**	**54,358**	**64,575**	**77,937**	**75,172**
Public and publicly guaranteed	14,075	7,756	9,842	14,578	11,049	12,465	12,609	14,001
Official creditors	2,393	1,001	4,749	5,561	4,008	3,088	3,866	4,105
Private creditors	11,682	6,755	5,093	9,017	7,042	9,378	8,743	9,897
of which: Bonds	6,980	5,230	3,739	6,665	4,820	7,927	7,613	9,034
Private nonguaranteed	8,881	33,504	29,846	34,039	43,308	52,110	65,329	61,171
of which: Bonds	454	3,125	150	2,300	2,085	6,965	8,635	8,392
Principal repayments	**13,744**	**24,650**	**49,657**	**45,490**	**38,665**	**41,307**	**46,915**	**41,372**
Public and publicly guaranteed	6,268	7,957	6,470	6,014	5,011	5,672	5,069	7,035
Official creditors	1,745	1,653	1,650	1,788	1,714	1,739	1,795	2,030
Private creditors	4,523	6,304	4,820	4,226	3,297	3,933	3,274	5,006
of which: Bonds	1,858	3,886	2,275	2,575	1,785	2,274	1,500	3,069
Private nonguaranteed	7,476	16,693	43,188	39,476	33,654	35,635	41,846	34,337
of which: Bonds	..	1,150	350	420	523	404	1,965	915
Interest payments	**5,000**	**6,397**	**10,421**	**8,703**	**12,006**	**8,541**	**9,345**	**9,899**
Public and publicly guaranteed	3,467	4,472	4,786	4,526	4,594	4,752	4,507	4,573
Official creditors	659	596	650	488	580	611	536	552
Private creditors	2,807	3,876	4,135	4,038	4,015	4,141	3,972	4,022
of which: Bonds	1,479	2,673	3,100	3,203	3,268	3,507	3,443	3,637
Private nonguaranteed	1,533	1,925	5,635	4,177	7,412	3,789	4,837	5,325
of which: Bonds	126	338	288	228	385	266	813	1,158
Net financial flows								
Net debt inflows	18,023	19,346	-14,204	29,210	17,219	39,880	60,395	36,234
Official creditors (incl. IMF)	4,020	-5,972	2,392	1,602	-513	-655	1,213	2,075
Private creditors	14,003	25,317	-16,597	27,608	17,732	40,535	59,182	34,159
Long-term	8,563	17,262	-13,068	-646	13,399	21,920	28,952	31,725
Public and publicly guaranteed	7,158	451	274	4,791	3,745	5,445	5,469	4,891
Private nonguaranteed	1,405	16,811	-13,342	-5,437	9,654	16,475	23,483	26,834
Short-term	5,440	8,055	-3,529	28,254	4,333	18,615	30,230	2,434
Net equity inflows								
Foreign direct investment	982	9,975	7,966	8,715	16,159	12,762	12,347	12,775
Portfolio equity	489	5,669	2,827	3,468	-985	6,276	842	2,559
Major economic aggregates								
Gross national income (GNI)	262,146	477,159	606,200	723,958	766,977	781,700	814,320	790,802
Exports of goods, services & prim. income	53,189	109,975	150,711	161,923	187,602	210,548	213,452	223,761
Imports of goods, services & prim. income	67,873	132,878	165,245	208,866	264,497	260,651	279,501	271,384
Primary income on FDI	279	1,051	2,933	2,871	2,931	2,641	3,657	2,639
Personal transfers & comp. of employees	4,560	887	1,165	1,100	1,210	1,153	1,135	1,128
International reserves	22,488	50,579	70,874	80,713	78,322	99,943	110,927	106,906
Ratios								
External debt stocks to exports (%)	219.6	156.5	184.0	184.7	162.7	160.0	182.4	182.4
External debt stocks to GNI (%)	44.6	36.1	45.7	41.3	39.8	43.1	47.8	51.6
Debt service to exports (%)	38.9	37.4	41.6	36.6	30.1	26.3	28.9	25.0
Reserves to external debt stocks (%)	19.3	29.4	25.6	27.0	25.7	29.7	28.5	26.2

Notes:

Long-term public and publicly guaranteed debt data include nonresident deposits made under the Dresdner Bank scheme, amounting to $2.1 billion at end-2014.

TURKMENISTAN

(US$ million, unless otherwise indicated)

	2000	2005	2009	2010	2011	2012	2013	2014
Summary external debt data								
External debt stocks	**2,509.4**	**1,157.8**	**661.5**	**529.1**	**454.3**	**508.9**	**502.9**	**441.2**
Long-term external debt	2,188.2	911.0	477.2	366.8	299.3	309.8	328.6	309.3
Short-term external debt	230.3	147.0	74.8	54.8	47.8	91.8	66.8	30.8
interest arrears on long-term	5.0	5.0	0.8	0.8	0.8	0.8	0.8	0.8
Use of IMF credit	91.0	99.8	109.5	107.5	107.2	107.3	107.5	101.2
Long-term external debt								
Debt outstanding and disbursed	**2,188.2**	**911.0**	**477.2**	**366.8**	**299.3**	**309.8**	**328.6**	**309.3**
Public and publicly guaranteed	2,171.4	877.8	463.3	359.5	265.5	270.6	280.7	263.2
Official creditors	838.6	685.9	409.5	341.6	265.5	270.6	280.7	263.2
Private creditors	1,332.8	192.0	53.9	17.8	0.0	0.0	0.0	0.0
of which: Bonds	0.0	0.0	0.0	0.0	0.0	0.0	0.0	0.0
Private nonguaranteed	16.7	33.1	13.9	7.4	33.8	39.2	47.8	46.0
of which: Bonds	..	..	..	..	..	..	..	..
Disbursements	**430.1**	**89.0**	**35.2**	**25.5**	**44.4**	**54.7**	**58.0**	**43.8**
Public and publicly guaranteed	420.9	24.9	22.4	17.9	13.6	45.6	46.0	23.0
Official creditors	292.6	24.9	22.4	17.9	13.6	45.6	46.0	23.0
Private creditors	128.3	0.0	0.0	0.0	0.0	0.0	0.0	0.0
of which: Bonds	0.0	0.0	0.0	0.0	0.0	0.0	0.0	0.0
Private nonguaranteed	9.2	64.1	12.8	7.5	30.9	9.1	12.0	20.7
of which: Bonds	..	..	..	..	..	..	..	..
Principal repayments	**353.0**	**261.4**	**146.4**	**142.8**	**120.9**	**41.0**	**40.6**	**47.8**
Public and publicly guaranteed	347.4	189.1	146.4	129.8	118.4	37.1	35.3	33.8
Official creditors	44.0	112.6	112.4	96.7	100.0	37.1	35.3	33.8
Private creditors	303.4	76.5	34.0	33.1	18.4	0.0	0.0	0.0
of which: Bonds	0.0	0.0	0.0	0.0	0.0	0.0	0.0	0.0
Private nonguaranteed	5.5	72.3	..	13.0	2.5	3.9	5.3	14.1
of which: Bonds	..	..	..	..	..	..	..	..
Interest payments	**101.9**	**39.1**	**17.6**	**10.8**	**9.6**	**7.7**	**6.6**	**6.7**
Public and publicly guaranteed	101.2	37.3	17.1	10.3	9.0	7.1	6.2	6.0
Official creditors	27.8	23.9	14.3	9.6	8.7	7.1	6.2	6.0
Private creditors	73.4	13.4	2.8	0.8	0.3	0.0	0.0	0.0
of which: Bonds	0.0	0.0	0.0	0.0	0.0	0.0	0.0	0.0
Private nonguaranteed	0.7	1.8	0.4	0.4	0.6	0.6	0.4	0.7
of which: Bonds	..	..	..	..	..	..	..	..
Net financial flows								
Net debt inflows	-1.6	-280.4	-87.2	-137.3	-83.5	57.6	-7.6	-40.1
Official creditors (incl. IMF)	248.6	-87.7	-90.0	-78.7	-86.4	8.5	10.7	-10.7
Private creditors	-250.2	-192.7	2.8	-58.6	3.0	49.2	-18.3	-29.3
Long-term	-171.5	-84.7	-21.2	-38.6	10.0	5.2	6.7	6.7
Public and publicly guaranteed	-175.2	-76.5	-34.0	-33.1	-18.4	..	..	..
Private nonguaranteed	3.7	-8.1	12.8	-5.5	28.4	5.2	6.7	6.7
Short-term	-78.8	-108.0	24.0	-20.0	-7.0	44.0	-25.0	36.0
Net equity inflows								
Foreign direct investment	131.0	418.2	4,553.0	3,632.3	3,391.1	3,129.6	3,076.0	3,163.5
Portfolio equity	..	..	..	..	..	..	..	..
Major economic aggregates								
Gross national income (GNI)	2,727.4	7,541.4	18,957.5	20,254.0	25,874.7	30,628.4	38,094.0	44,982.9
Exports of goods, services & prim. income	..	..	..	..	..	..	..	..
Imports of goods, services & prim. income	..	..	..	..	..	..	..	..
Primary income on FDI	..	..	..	..	..	..	..	..
Personal transfers & comp. of employees	..	..	33.0	35.0	34.0	37.0	40.0	29.8
International reserves	..	..	..	..	..	..	..	..
Ratios								
External debt stocks to exports (%)	..	..	..	..	..	..	..	..
External debt stocks to GNI (%)	92.0	15.4	3.5	2.6	1.8	1.7	1.3	1.0
Debt service to exports (%)	..	..	..	..	..	..	..	..
Reserves to external debt stocks (%)	..	..	..	..	..	..	..	..

Notes:

Long-term public and publicly guaranteed debt from 2010 are World Bank staff estimates. Long-term private nonguaranteed debt data (excluding bonds) only cover European Bank for Reconstruction and Development lending.

UGANDA

(US$ million, unless otherwise indicated)

	2000	2005	2009	2010	2011	2012	2013	2014
Summary external debt data								
External debt stocks	**3,535**	**4,437**	**2,739**	**2,975**	**3,263**	**3,777**	**4,807**	**5,135**
Long-term external debt	3,051	4,184	2,223	2,673	2,963	3,479	4,067	4,217
Short-term external debt	129	79	235	26	26	26	469	666
interest arrears on long-term	58	29	26	26	26	26	27	26
Use of IMF credit	354	173	281	275	273	272	270	252
Long-term external debt								
Debt outstanding and disbursed	**3,051**	**4,184**	**2,223**	**2,673**	**2,963**	**3,479**	**4,067**	**4,217**
Public and publicly guaranteed	3,051	4,184	2,223	2,673	2,963	3,479	4,067	4,217
Official creditors	3,027	4,182	2,223	2,673	2,963	3,479	4,067	4,217
Private creditors	24	2	0	0	0	0	0	0
of which: Bonds	4	0	0	0	0	0	0	0
Private nonguaranteed	..	..	..	..	..	..	..	..
of which: Bonds	..	..	..	..	..	..	..	..
Disbursements	**219**	**224**	**494**	**486**	**335**	**560**	**632**	**465**
Public and publicly guaranteed	219	224	494	486	335	560	632	465
Official creditors	219	224	494	486	335	560	632	465
Private creditors	0	0	0	0	0	0	0	0
of which: Bonds	0	0	0	0	0	0	0	0
Private nonguaranteed	..	..	..	..	..	..	..	..
of which: Bonds	..	..	..	..	..	..	..	..
Principal repayments	**26**	**99**	**49**	**40**	**35**	**38**	**44**	**52**
Public and publicly guaranteed	26	99	49	40	35	38	44	52
Official creditors	25	98	49	40	35	38	44	52
Private creditors	1	1	0	0	0	0	0	0
of which: Bonds	0	0	0	0	0	0	0	0
Private nonguaranteed	..	..	..	..	..	..	..	..
of which: Bonds	..	..	..	..	..	..	..	..
Interest payments	**21**	**33**	**18**	**21**	**26**	**28**	**36**	**44**
Public and publicly guaranteed	21	33	18	21	26	28	36	44
Official creditors	20	32	18	21	26	28	36	44
Private creditors	0	0	0	0	0	0	0	0
of which: Bonds	0	0	0	0	0	0	0	0
Private nonguaranteed	..	..	..	..	..	..	..	..
of which: Bonds	..	..	..	..	..	..	..	..
Net financial flows								
Net debt inflows	177	85	222	237	298	521	1,029	608
Official creditors (incl. IMF)	184	95	445	447	298	521	586	411
Private creditors	-7	-10	-223	-209	..	..	443	197
Long-term	-1	-1	0	0	..	..	..	..
Public and publicly guaranteed	-1	-1	0	0	..	..	..	..
Private nonguaranteed	..	..	..	..	..	..	..	..
Short-term	-6	-10	-223	-209	..	..	443	197
Net equity inflows								
Foreign direct investment	161	381	771	248	573	922	826	970
Portfolio equity	..	..	131	-70	106	14	95	5
Major economic aggregates								
Gross national income (GNI)	6,086	8,748	16,702	18,472	18,343	23,281	24,042	25,898
Exports of goods, services & prim. income	716	1,592	3,398	3,491	4,324	5,022	5,222	4,752
Imports of goods, services & prim. income	1,574	2,641	5,638	6,500	7,855	8,255	8,438	8,653
Primary income on FDI	19	202	247	183	262	252	532	..
Personal transfers & comp. of employees	238	322	781	771	816	910	932	994
International reserves	808	1,344	2,994	2,706	2,617	3,167	3,338	3,316
Ratios								
External debt stocks to exports (%)	493.6	278.7	80.6	85.2	75.5	75.2	92.1	108.1
External debt stocks to GNI (%)	58.1	50.7	16.4	16.1	17.8	16.2	20.0	19.8
Debt service to exports (%)	10.6	10.8	2.1	1.8	1.5	1.4	1.6	2.1
Reserves to external debt stocks (%)	22.9	30.3	109.3	91.0	80.2	83.8	69.4	64.6

Notes:

Data include the effects of HIPC and MDRI debt relief.

UKRAINE

(US$ million, unless otherwise indicated)

	2000	2005	2009	2010	2011	2012	2013	2014
Summary external debt data								
External debt stocks	**13,890**	**33,706**	**104,327**	**125,083**	**135,396**	**130,842**	**147,156**	**130,686**
Long-term external debt	9,664	18,584	71,427	81,557	86,458	83,296	105,143	100,644
Short-term external debt	447	12,063	19,873	27,264	32,727	34,750	34,823	22,435
interest arrears on long-term	183	110	650	1,671	13	1,518	48	2,143
Use of IMF credit	3,779	3,059	13,027	16,262	16,212	12,795	7,190	7,608
Long-term external debt								
Debt outstanding and disbursed	**9,664**	**18,584**	**71,427**	**81,557**	**86,458**	**83,296**	**105,143**	**100,644**
Public and publicly guaranteed	8,123	9,054	18,032	24,877	25,368	27,051	32,303	34,549
Official creditors	5,000	5,021	11,093	14,731	12,528	11,797	11,656	13,483
Private creditors	3,123	4,033	6,939	10,146	12,840	15,254	20,647	21,065
of which: Bonds	2,366	2,835	5,832	9,058	11,768	14,197	20,607	21,043
Private nonguaranteed	1,541	9,530	53,395	56,681	61,090	56,245	72,840	66,095
of which: Bonds	..	550	5,114	5,319	5,794	5,294	9,269	7,614
Disbursements	**1,401**	**7,853**	**22,298**	**33,946**	**28,446**	**16,765**	**37,611**	**11,394**
Public and publicly guaranteed	173	1,411	5,581	7,944	3,352	4,163	11,566	4,744
Official creditors	141	563	5,581	4,259	600	560	3,116	3,744
Private creditors	32	847	0	3,685	2,753	3,603	8,450	1,000
of which: Bonds	0	747	0	3,685	2,750	3,600	8,450	1,000
Private nonguaranteed	1,228	6,442	16,717	26,002	25,094	12,602	26,046	6,650
of which: Bonds	..	450	846	1,730	1,550	..	3,975	..
Principal repayments	**2,114**	**4,033**	**17,870**	**23,073**	**24,069**	**21,614**	**26,430**	**8,753**
Public and publicly guaranteed	1,250	1,208	1,736	910	2,851	2,492	6,407	1,594
Official creditors	1,208	546	475	477	2,818	1,288	3,313	1,113
Private creditors	42	662	1,261	433	33	1,204	3,094	481
of which: Bonds	33	637	1,224	416	15	1,186	2,076	465
Private nonguaranteed	864	2,825	16,134	22,163	21,218	19,122	20,023	7,159
of which: Bonds	..	..	695	1,525	1,075	500	..	50
Interest payments	**447**	**894**	**4,171**	**3,494**	**4,302**	**4,472**	**5,315**	**5,163**
Public and publicly guaranteed	375	424	681	555	832	908	1,251	1,618
Official creditors	148	130	204	225	263	219	151	396
Private creditors	228	294	478	330	569	689	1,100	1,223
of which: Bonds	220	213	392	251	490	611	1,061	1,222
Private nonguaranteed	72	470	3,490	2,938	3,470	3,564	4,064	3,545
of which: Bonds	..	41	423	407	423	403	497	612
Net financial flows								
Net debt inflows	-1,285	5,219	9,431	20,676	11,498	-7,744	7,147	-10,957
Official creditors (incl. IMF)	-1,666	-283	11,187	7,215	-2,218	-4,142	-5,775	3,516
Private creditors	380	5,501	-1,756	13,461	13,716	-3,603	12,921	-14,473
Long-term	354	3,803	-678	7,091	6,595	-4,121	11,378	10
Public and publicly guaranteed	-10	186	-1,261	3,252	2,720	2,399	5,356	519
Private nonguaranteed	364	3,617	583	3,839	3,876	-6,519	6,022	-509
Short-term	26	1,698	-1,078	6,370	7,121	518	1,543	-14,483
Net equity inflows								
Foreign direct investment	595	7,493	4,456	5,550	6,121	6,248	3,668	712
Portfolio equity	146	82	105	290	519	516	1,180	-391
Major economic aggregates								
Gross national income (GNI)	30,320	85,157	114,788	134,410	159,364	172,813	178,236	130,247
Exports of goods, services & prim. income	19,665	43,384	56,704	70,341	89,137	93,598	89,486	70,835
Imports of goods, services & prim. income	19,032	43,695	61,101	76,332	103,078	110,909	108,153	77,708
Primary income on FDI	43	268	2,542	2,218	4,084	4,775	5,005	1,741
Personal transfers & comp. of employees	33	2,408	5,941	6,535	7,822	8,449	9,667	7,354
International reserves	1,353	18,988	25,557	33,327	30,409	22,656	18,776	6,622
Ratios								
External debt stocks to exports (%)	70.6	77.7	184.0	177.8	151.9	139.8	164.4	184.5
External debt stocks to GNI (%)	45.8	39.6	90.9	93.1	85.0	75.7	82.6	100.3
Debt service to exports (%)	18.4	13.2	39.7	38.6	32.7	31.8	42.3	25.2
Reserves to external debt stocks (%)	9.7	56.3	24.5	26.6	22.5	17.3	12.8	5.1

UZBEKISTAN

(US$ million, unless otherwise indicated)

	2000	2005	2009	2010	2011	2012	2013	2014
Summary external debt data								
External debt stocks	**4,980**	**4,656**	**6,962**	**7,796**	**8,435**	**8,849**	**10,681**	**13,389**
Long-term external debt	4,228	4,168	6,386	7,154	7,666	8,108	9,857	12,517
Short-term external debt	282	112	163	238	366	337	419	491
interest arrears on long-term	3	8	19	70	70	0	0	0
Use of IMF credit	469	376	412	405	403	404	405	381
Long-term external debt								
Debt outstanding and disbursed	**4,228**	**4,168**	**6,386**	**7,154**	**7,666**	**8,108**	**9,857**	**12,517**
Public and publicly guaranteed	3,762	3,626	3,269	3,423	3,756	3,983	4,379	5,653
Official creditors	2,117	2,451	2,934	3,197	3,529	3,821	4,254	5,468
Private creditors	1,645	1,175	335	226	227	163	125	185
of which: Bonds	0	0	0	0	0	0	0	0
Private nonguaranteed	467	542	3,117	3,730	3,910	4,125	5,478	6,864
of which: Bonds	..	..	..	..	..	..	..	..
Disbursements	**770**	**404**	**2,612**	**1,191**	**947**	**1,028**	**2,378**	**2,755**
Public and publicly guaranteed	713	262	475	455	603	587	780	1,002
Official creditors	409	200	466	440	528	577	770	883
Private creditors	304	62	8	15	75	10	10	119
of which: Bonds	0	0	0	0	0	0	0	0
Private nonguaranteed	57	142	2,138	736	344	441	1,598	1,753
of which: Bonds	..	..	..	..	..	..	..	..
Principal repayments	**584**	**620**	**713**	**493**	**460**	**516**	**528**	**675**
Public and publicly guaranteed	443	510	386	370	295	293	284	307
Official creditors	148	177	225	256	226	217	232	266
Private creditors	295	333	161	114	69	76	52	40
of which: Bonds	0	0	0	0	0	0	0	0
Private nonguaranteed	141	110	327	123	165	224	244	369
of which: Bonds	..	..	..	..	..	..	..	..
Interest payments	**206**	**140**	**120**	**118**	**158**	**173**	**163**	**206**
Public and publicly guaranteed	182	117	82	63	68	75	66	67
Official creditors	75	63	71	59	62	66	64	64
Private creditors	108	53	12	4	6	9	2	3
of which: Bonds	0	0	0	0	0	0	0	0
Private nonguaranteed	24	23	38	55	90	97	97	139
of which: Bonds	..	..	..	..	..	..	..	..
Net financial flows								
Net debt inflows	-223	-301	1,832	722	615	553	1,932	2,152
Official creditors (incl. IMF)	196	5	241	184	302	360	538	617
Private creditors	-419	-305	1,591	538	313	193	1,393	1,535
Long-term	-75	-239	1,658	514	185	152	1,311	1,463
Public and publicly guaranteed	9	-271	-153	-99	6	-66	-42	79
Private nonguaranteed	-84	32	1,811	613	179	218	1,353	1,384
Short-term	-344	-66	-67	24	128	41	82	72
Net equity inflows								
Foreign direct investment	75	192	842	1,636	1,635	563	686	751
Portfolio equity	..	..	..	..	..	..	..	..
Major economic aggregates								
Gross national income (GNI)	13,541	14,283	33,714	40,492	47,104	53,468	60,019	65,556
Exports of goods, services & prim. income	..	..	..	..	..	..	..	..
Imports of goods, services & prim. income	..	..	..	..	..	..	..	..
Primary income on FDI	..	..	..	..	..	..	..	..
Personal transfers & comp. of employees	..	..	2,052	2,845	4,262	5,668	6,633	5,588
International reserves	..	..	..	..	..	..	..	..
Ratios								
External debt stocks to exports (%)	..	..	..	..	..	..	..	..
External debt stocks to GNI (%)	36.8	32.6	20.6	19.3	17.9	16.6	17.8	20.4
Debt service to exports (%)	..	..	..	..	..	..	..	..
Reserves to external debt stocks (%)	..	..	..	..	..	..	..	..

VANUATU

(US$ million, unless otherwise indicated)

	2000	2005	2009	2010	2011	2012	2013	2014
Summary external debt data								
External debt stocks	**95.7**	**105.3**	**155.3**	**173.3**	**201.8**	**369.2**	**132.4**	**181.3**
Long-term external debt	73.1	71.9	98.8	99.3	98.8	92.2	84.3	76.7
Short-term external debt	1.4	10.2	31.0	49.0	78.0	252.0	23.0	81.0
interest arrears on long-term	0.0	0.2	0.0	0.0	0.0	0.0	0.0	0.0
Use of IMF credit	21.2	23.3	25.5	25.1	25.0	25.0	25.1	23.6
Long-term external debt								
Debt outstanding and disbursed	**73.1**	**71.9**	**98.8**	**99.3**	**98.8**	**92.2**	**84.3**	**76.7**
Public and publicly guaranteed	73.1	71.9	98.8	99.3	98.8	92.2	84.3	76.7
Official creditors	73.1	71.9	98.8	99.3	98.8	92.2	84.3	76.7
Private creditors	0.0	0.0	0.0	0.0	0.0	0.0	0.0	0.0
of which: Bonds	0.0	0.0	0.0	0.0	0.0	0.0	0.0	0.0
Private nonguaranteed	..	..	..	..	..	..	..	..
of which: Bonds	..	..	..	..	..	..	..	..
Disbursements	**14.2**	**0.0**	**11.7**	**0.0**	**0.0**	**0.0**	**0.0**	**0.0**
Public and publicly guaranteed	14.2	0.0	11.7	0.0	0.0	0.0	0.0	0.0
Official creditors	14.2	0.0	11.7	0.0	0.0	0.0	0.0	0.0
Private creditors	0.0	0.0	0.0	0.0	0.0	0.0	0.0	0.0
of which: Bonds	0.0	0.0	0.0	0.0	0.0	0.0	0.0	0.0
Private nonguaranteed	..	..	..	..	..	..	..	..
of which: Bonds	..	..	..	..	..	..	..	..
Principal repayments	**0.9**	**1.1**	**3.5**	**3.6**	**3.4**	**3.8**	**3.7**	**3.5**
Public and publicly guaranteed	0.9	1.1	3.5	3.6	3.4	3.8	3.7	3.5
Official creditors	0.9	1.1	3.5	3.6	3.4	3.8	3.7	3.5
Private creditors	0.0	0.0	0.0	0.0	0.0	0.0	0.0	0.0
of which: Bonds	0.0	0.0	0.0	0.0	0.0	0.0	0.0	0.0
Private nonguaranteed	..	..	..	..	..	..	..	..
of which: Bonds	..	..	..	..	..	..	..	..
Interest payments	**0.6**	**0.7**	**1.4**	**1.4**	**1.3**	**1.2**	**1.4**	**1.3**
Public and publicly guaranteed	0.6	0.7	1.4	1.4	1.3	1.2	1.4	1.3
Official creditors	0.6	0.7	1.4	1.4	1.3	1.2	1.4	1.3
Private creditors	0.0	0.0	0.0	0.0	0.0	0.0	0.0	0.0
of which: Bonds	0.0	0.0	0.0	0.0	0.0	0.0	0.0	0.0
Private nonguaranteed	..	..	..	..	..	..	..	..
of which: Bonds	..	..	..	..	..	..	..	..
Net financial flows								
Net debt inflows	13.6	-28.1	3.1	14.4	25.6	170.2	-232.7	54.5
Official creditors (incl. IMF)	13.4	-1.1	8.1	-3.6	-3.4	-3.8	-3.7	-3.5
Private creditors	0.3	-27.0	-5.0	18.0	29.0	174.0	-229.0	58.0
Long-term		..	..	..	..	..	..	..
Public and publicly guaranteed	..	..	..	..	..	..	..	..
Private nonguaranteed	..	..	..	..	..	..	..	..
Short-term	0.3	-27.0	-5.0	18.0	29.0	174.0	-229.0	58.0
Net equity inflows								
Foreign direct investment	20.3	13.5	23.8	40.6	57.8	37.2	31.9	-22.3
Portfolio equity	..	..	..	..	..	..	..	..
Major economic aggregates								
Gross national income (GNI)	259.0	369.0	586.8	679.1	765.7	746.6	768.6	..
Exports of goods, services & prim. income	175.7	204.6	330.9	365.5	395.7	413.8	408.6	..
Imports of goods, services & prim. income	178.8	258.6	345.5	422.7	465.8	480.9	457.7	..
Primary income on FDI	21.9	35.3	41.7	48.0	52.7	76.8	40.2	..
Personal transfers & comp. of employees	34.7	5.1	11.5	11.8	21.8	22.0	23.7	24.1
International reserves	38.9	67.2	148.6	161.4	173.8	182.2	179.2	184.0
Ratios								
External debt stocks to exports (%)	54.4	51.5	46.9	47.4	51.0	89.2	32.4	..
External debt stocks to GNI (%)	36.9	28.5	26.5	25.5	26.4	49.5	17.2	..
Debt service to exports (%)	1.6	1.6	1.7	1.6	1.6	2.1	1.9	..
Reserves to external debt stocks (%)	40.7	63.8	95.7	93.1	86.1	49.4	135.4	101.5

Notes:

Long-term public and publicly guaranteed debt data from 2010 are World Bank staff estimates. Short-term debt is based on data from the BIS.

VIETNAM

(US$ million, unless otherwise indicated)

	2000	2005	2009	2010	2011	2012	2013	2014
Summary external debt data								
External debt stocks	**12,859**	**19,039**	**33,084**	**44,923**	**53,072**	**59,119**	**65,491**	**71,890**
Long-term external debt	11,558	16,193	27,320	37,444	42,612	48,746	52,801	58,377
Short-term external debt	923	2,574	5,186	6,949	9,964	9,889	12,205	13,057
interest arrears on long-term	78	74	0	0	0	0	0	0
Use of IMF credit	378	272	578	529	496	484	485	456
Long-term external debt								
Debt outstanding and disbursed	**11,558**	**16,193**	**27,320**	**37,444**	**42,612**	**48,746**	**52,801**	**58,377**
Public and publicly guaranteed	11,558	16,193	27,320	32,764	36,750	39,940	42,940	44,818
Official creditors	8,680	14,259	23,938	27,435	31,077	33,465	34,770	35,915
Private creditors	2,878	1,934	3,382	5,329	5,673	6,475	8,170	8,903
of which: Bonds	534	1,145	1,301	2,020	2,001	1,982	2,586	1,900
Private nonguaranteed	..	..	..	4,680	5,862	8,806	9,861	13,559
of which: Bonds	..	..	..	..	90	90	290	290
Disbursements	**1,272**	**2,047**	**4,730**	**6,878**	**6,968**	**8,727**	**9,465**	**13,847**
Public and publicly guaranteed	1,272	2,047	4,730	5,593	4,751	5,958	7,033	7,530
Official creditors	1,176	1,261	4,104	3,675	4,001	4,711	4,821	5,384
Private creditors	96	786	627	1,918	750	1,247	2,212	2,147
of which: Bonds	0	750	0	1,000	0	0	627	0
Private nonguaranteed	..	..	..	1,285	2,217	2,769	2,433	6,316
of which: Bonds	..	..	..	..	90	..	200	..
Principal repayments	**937**	**480**	**915**	**1,048**	**3,082**	**3,276**	**3,274**	**5,303**
Public and publicly guaranteed	937	480	915	1,048	1,201	1,473	1,896	2,685
Official creditors	134	303	687	735	823	1,024	1,361	1,383
Private creditors	802	177	228	313	378	449	534	1,302
of which: Bonds	0	41	39	19	19	19	23	685
Private nonguaranteed	..	..	..	..	1,881	1,803	1,378	2,618
of which: Bonds	..	..	..	..	..	..	..	..
Interest payments	**296**	**317**	**476**	**707**	**902**	**1,012**	**1,074**	**1,239**
Public and publicly guaranteed	296	317	476	563	689	744	763	810
Official creditors	77	256	344	398	457	494	514	509
Private creditors	218	61	132	165	232	250	249	301
of which: Bonds	21	21	74	93	126	126	126	140
Private nonguaranteed	..	..	..	144	213	268	311	429
of which: Bonds	..	..	..	..	4	9	9	32
Net financial flows								
Net debt inflows	472	1,926	4,685	7,554	6,868	5,364	8,508	9,396
Official creditors (incl. IMF)	1,020	904	3,378	2,902	3,145	3,675	3,459	4,001
Private creditors	-548	1,022	1,307	4,652	3,722	1,689	5,049	5,395
Long-term	-706	609	399	2,889	707	1,764	2,733	4,543
Public and publicly guaranteed	-706	609	399	1,605	371	798	1,678	845
Private nonguaranteed	..	..	..	1,285	336	966	1,055	3,699
Short-term	158	413	908	1,763	3,015	-75	2,316	852
Net equity inflows								
Foreign direct investment	1,298	1,204	6,369	7,101	5,941	6,943	6,202	9,200
Portfolio equity	..	115	128	2,383	1,064	1,887	1,389	..
Major economic aggregates								
Gross national income (GNI)	33,194	56,575	101,448	111,513	129,698	149,569	164,021	176,894
Exports of goods, services & prim. income	17,481	36,987	63,615	80,153	106,180	124,468	142,916	161,510
Imports of goods, services & prim. income	18,107	40,927	76,671	92,314	114,629	123,618	142,922	161,976
Primary income on FDI	..	..	..	..	..	..	..	..
Personal transfers & comp. of employees	..	3,150	6,020	8,260	8,600	10,000	11,000	12,000
International reserves	3,417	9,051	16,447	12,467	13,539	25,573	25,893	34,189
Ratios								
External debt stocks to exports (%)	73.6	51.5	52.0	56.0	50.0	47.5	45.8	44.5
External debt stocks to GNI (%)	38.7	33.7	32.6	40.3	40.9	39.5	39.9	40.6
Debt service to exports (%)	7.5	2.6	2.3	2.3	3.9	3.6	3.2	4.2
Reserves to external debt stocks (%)	26.6	47.5	49.7	27.8	25.5	43.3	39.5	47.6

Notes:

Short-term debt is based on data from the BIS.

YEMEN, REPUBLIC OF

(US$ million, unless otherwise indicated)

	2000	2005	2009	2010	2011	2012	2013	2014
Summary external debt data								
External debt stocks	**5,162**	**5,501**	**6,734**	**6,682**	**6,418**	**7,556**	**7,647**	**7,710**
Long-term external debt	4,109	4,814	5,875	5,933	5,876	6,912	6,884	6,859
Short-term external debt	699	353	442	313	131	140	258	306
interest arrears on long-term	27	94	117	124	131	140	147	145
Use of IMF credit	355	333	417	436	410	504	505	546
Long-term external debt								
Debt outstanding and disbursed	**4,109**	**4,814**	**5,875**	**5,933**	**5,876**	**6,912**	**6,884**	**6,859**
Public and publicly guaranteed	4,109	4,814	5,875	5,933	5,876	6,912	6,884	6,859
Official creditors	4,046	4,807	5,871	5,930	5,874	6,911	6,883	6,859
Private creditors	63	7	5	3	2	1	1	0
of which: Bonds	0	0	0	0	0	0	0	0
Private nonguaranteed	..	..	..	..	..	..	..	..
of which: Bonds	..	..	..	..	..	..	..	..
Disbursements	**137**	**265**	**332**	**287**	**101**	**1,251**	**203**	**404**
Public and publicly guaranteed	137	265	332	287	101	1,251	203	404
Official creditors	137	265	332	287	101	1,251	203	404
Private creditors	0	0	0	0	0	0	0	0
of which: Bonds	0	0	0	0	0	0	0	0
Private nonguaranteed	..	..	..	..	..	..	..	..
of which: Bonds	..	..	..	..	..	..	..	..
Principal repayments	**81**	**94**	**140**	**155**	**175**	**181**	**194**	**216**
Public and publicly guaranteed	81	94	140	155	175	181	194	216
Official creditors	81	94	139	154	174	180	193	215
Private creditors	0	0	1	1	1	1	1	0
of which: Bonds	0	0	0	0	0	0	0	0
Private nonguaranteed	..	..	..	..	..	..	..	..
of which: Bonds	..	..	..	..	..	..	..	..
Interest payments	**45**	**55**	**72**	**74**	**75**	**73**	**75**	**87**
Public and publicly guaranteed	45	55	72	74	75	73	75	87
Official creditors	45	55	72	74	74	73	75	87
Private creditors	0	0	0	0	0	0	0	0
of which: Bonds	0	0	0	0	0	0	0	0
Private nonguaranteed	..	..	..	..	..	..	..	..
of which: Bonds	..	..	..	..	..	..	..	..
Net financial flows								
Net debt inflows	270	176	102	22	-288	1,163	213	312
Official creditors (incl. IMF)	-15	116	149	159	-98	1,164	103	263
Private creditors	285	61	-47	-137	-190	-1	110	50
Long-term	0	0	-1	-1	-1	-1	-1	0
Public and publicly guaranteed	0	0	-1	-1	-1	-1	-1	0
Private nonguaranteed	..	..	..	..	..	..	..	..
Short-term	285	61	-46	-136	-189	..	111	50
Net equity inflows								
Foreign direct investment	6	-302	129	43	44	30	-134	-578
Portfolio equity	..	..	..	..	..	..	..	..
Major economic aggregates								
Gross national income (GNI)	8,863	15,139	27,378	29,194	28,848	30,894	34,721	..
Exports of goods, services & prim. income	4,158	6,963	7,233	9,325	10,437	9,415	9,592	..
Imports of goods, services & prim. income	4,221	7,745	11,276	12,503	13,099	15,207	14,747	..
Primary income on FDI	855	1,603	927	1,510	2,025	1,145	1,352	..
Personal transfers & comp. of employees	1,288	1,283	1,160	1,526	1,404	3,351	3,343	3,455
International reserves	2,900	6,115	6,936	5,868	4,449	6,068	5,284	..
Ratios								
External debt stocks to exports (%)	124.2	79.0	93.1	71.7	61.5	80.3	79.7	..
External debt stocks to GNI (%)	58.2	36.3	24.6	22.9	22.2	24.5	22.0	..
Debt service to exports (%)	5.9	3.1	3.6	2.8	2.6	2.7	2.8	..
Reserves to external debt stocks (%)	56.2	111.2	103.0	87.8	69.3	80.3	69.1	..

Notes:

Long-term public and publicly guaranteed debt data for 2014 are World Bank staff estimates. Short-term debt is based on data from the BIS.

ZAMBIA

(US$ million, unless otherwise indicated)

	2000	2005	2009	2010	2011	2012	2013	2014
Summary external debt data								
External debt stocks	**5,811**	**5,459**	**3,774**	**4,419**	**5,188**	**5,935**	**6,061**	**7,373**
Long-term external debt	4,508	4,536	2,220	2,111	3,482	3,944	4,154	5,485
Short-term external debt	76	234	474	1,191	569	864	796	876
interest arrears on long-term	33	90	154	167	167	171	173	175
Use of IMF credit	1,227	689	1,080	1,117	1,137	1,126	1,110	1,011
Long-term external debt								
Debt outstanding and disbursed	**4,508**	**4,536**	**2,220**	**2,111**	**3,482**	**3,944**	**4,154**	**5,485**
Public and publicly guaranteed	4,444	3,940	1,200	1,317	1,964	3,182	3,392	4,484
Official creditors	4,412	3,644	1,158	1,284	1,857	2,347	2,579	2,688
Private creditors	31	295	42	33	108	835	813	1,796
of which: Bonds	0	0	0	0	0	750	750	1,750
Private nonguaranteed	65	596	1,020	794	1,517	763	763	1,002
of which: Bonds	..	..	..	..	..	..	..	..
Disbursements	**261**	**218**	**126**	**203**	**789**	**1,349**	**374**	**1,638**
Public and publicly guaranteed	251	114	91	176	696	1,316	341	1,258
Official creditors	251	114	91	176	605	566	341	258
Private creditors	0	0	0	0	91	750	0	1,000
of which: Bonds	0	0	0	0	0	750	0	1,000
Private nonguaranteed	10	105	35	27	93	33	33	380
of which: Bonds	..	..	..	..	..	..	..	..
Principal repayments	**98**	**136**	**122**	**86**	**139**	**143**	**192**	**224**
Public and publicly guaranteed	79	71	59	47	56	101	150	83
Official creditors	79	59	52	38	40	78	127	66
Private creditors	1	12	7	8	16	23	23	17
of which: Bonds	0	0	0	0	0	0	0	0
Private nonguaranteed	18	66	63	40	82	42	42	141
of which: Bonds	..	..	..	..	..	..	..	..
Interest payments	**80**	**58**	**36**	**29**	**48**	**59**	**99**	**131**
Public and publicly guaranteed	76	29	13	11	13	41	82	98
Official creditors	76	29	13	11	13	41	42	37
Private creditors	0	0	0	0	0	0	40	60
of which: Bonds	0	0	0	0	0	0	40	60
Private nonguaranteed	4	28	24	18	35	18	18	33
of which: Bonds	..	..	..	..	..	..	..	..
Net financial flows								
Net debt inflows	159	88	45	876	52	1,485	94	1,457
Official creditors (incl. IMF)	198	-8	283	193	589	476	197	156
Private creditors	-39	96	-238	683	-537	1,009	-102	1,300
Long-term	-9	27	-36	-21	85	718	-32	1,222
Public and publicly guaranteed	-1	-12	-7	-8	75	727	-23	983
Private nonguaranteed	-8	39	-29	-13	10	-9	-9	239
Short-term	-30	69	-202	704	-622	291	-70	78
Net equity inflows								
Foreign direct investment	122	329	472	1,228	942	-25	370	727
Portfolio equity	6	5	-13	101	25	-7	5	6
Major economic aggregates								
Gross national income (GNI)	3,445	7,700	14,910	18,903	22,576	24,606	25,668	25,550
Exports of goods, services & prim. income	891	2,842	4,906	8,063	9,430	10,521	11,607	11,077
Imports of goods, services & prim. income	1,567	3,181	4,509	6,969	8,715	9,603	12,170	11,762
Primary income on FDI	71	461	265	1,303	1,093	239	1,020	1,322
Personal transfers & comp. of employees	..	53	41	44	46	73	54	58
International reserves	245	560	1,892	2,094	2,324	3,042	2,684	3,078
Ratios								
External debt stocks to exports (%)	652.0	192.1	76.9	54.8	55.0	56.4	52.2	66.6
External debt stocks to GNI (%)	168.7	70.9	25.3	23.4	23.0	24.1	23.6	28.9
Debt service to exports (%)	21.2	10.0	3.5	1.9	2.3	2.2	2.8	3.7
Reserves to external debt stocks (%)	4.2	10.3	50.1	47.4	44.8	51.3	44.3	41.8

Notes:

Long-term private nonguaranteed before 2011 are World Bank staff estimates based on reports provided by the country. Short-term debt data are from the BIS reports. Data include the effects of HIPC and MDRI debt relief.

ZIMBABWE

(US$ million, unless otherwise indicated)

	2000	2005	2009	2010	2011	2012	2013	2014
Summary external debt data								
External debt stocks	**3,832**	**4,445**	**6,000**	**6,605**	**7,311**	**8,655**	**8,196**	**10,570**
Long-term external debt	2,970	3,209	3,824	4,259	4,724	5,715	4,952	7,776
Short-term external debt	568	1,111	1,634	1,817	2,061	2,420	2,724	2,307
interest arrears on long-term	55	534	915	938	1,054	1,144	1,236	908
Use of IMF credit	294	125	542	529	527	520	519	487
Long-term external debt								
Debt outstanding and disbursed	**2,970**	**3,209**	**3,824**	**4,259**	**4,724**	**5,715**	**4,952**	**7,776**
Public and publicly guaranteed	2,765	3,177	3,734	3,663	3,820	3,884	3,951	3,706
Official creditors	2,428	2,771	3,287	3,230	3,389	3,447	3,506	3,295
Private creditors	337	406	448	433	431	437	445	412
of which: Bonds	0	0	0	0	0	0	0	0
Private nonguaranteed	205	32	89	596	904	1,831	1,001	4,070
of which: Bonds	..	..	..	..	..	..	..	..
Disbursements	**185**	**25**	**79**	**847**	**1,584**	**1,433**	**1,710**	**6,237**
Public and publicly guaranteed	139	24	13	4	186	70	58	73
Official creditors	125	16	13	4	181	70	58	73
Private creditors	15	8	0	0	5	0	0	0
of which: Bonds	0	0	0	0	0	0	0	0
Private nonguaranteed	46	0	66	843	1,398	1,363	1,652	6,165
of which: Bonds	..	..	..	..	..	..	..	..
Principal repayments	**211**	**45**	**66**	**337**	**1,096**	**440**	**2,494**	**3,165**
Public and publicly guaranteed	146	31	0	1	6	5	12	68
Official creditors	113	21	0	1	6	5	8	68
Private creditors	33	10	0	0	0	0	4	0
of which: Bonds	0	0	0	0	0	0	0	0
Private nonguaranteed	65	14	66	336	1,091	435	2,482	3,096
of which: Bonds	..	..	..	..	..	..	..	..
Interest payments	**81**	**7**	**30**	**31**	**43**	**273**	**133**	**122**
Public and publicly guaranteed	64	3	14	13	14	14	6	21
Official creditors	50	2	14	13	14	14	6	21
Private creditors	13	1	0	0	0	0	0	0
of which: Bonds	0	0	0	0	0	0	0	0
Private nonguaranteed	17	4	16	18	29	259	127	101
of which: Bonds	..	..	..	..	..	..	..	..
Net financial flows								
Net debt inflows	-329	-180	-299	666	616	1,254	-574	2,983
Official creditors (incl. IMF)	-58	-169	13	-1	175	57	48	2
Private creditors	-271	-11	-312	667	441	1,196	-622	2,980
Long-term	-37	-16	0	507	313	927	-834	3,068
Public and publicly guaranteed	-19	2	..	0	5	..	-4	..
Private nonguaranteed	-19	-14	0	507	308	927	-830	3,068
Short-term	-233	5	-312	160	128	269	212	-88
Net equity inflows								
Foreign direct investment	23	103	105	166	387	400	400	545
Portfolio equity	..	..	..	..	..	..	..	..
Major economic aggregates								
Gross national income (GNI)	6,329	5,481	8,617	9,264	10,049	11,513	12,472	12,547
Exports of goods, services & prim. income	..	..	..	..	..	..	..	..
Imports of goods, services & prim. income	..	..	..	..	..	..	..	..
Primary income on FDI	..	..	..	..	..	..	..	..
Personal transfers & comp. of employees	..	..	..	..	..	..	..	..
International reserves	193	97	822	732	659	574	474	363
Ratios								
External debt stocks to exports (%)	..	..	..	..	..	..	..	..
External debt stocks to GNI (%)	60.5	81.1	69.6	71.3	72.8	75.2	65.7	84.2
Debt service to exports (%)	..	..	..	..	..	..	..	..
Reserves to external debt stocks (%)	5.0	2.2	13.7	11.1	9.0	6.6	5.8	3.4

Notes:

Data from 2001 include late interest fee owed to Paris Club and Commercial Creditors. Short-term debt is based on data from the BIS.

APPENDIX

About the Data

Data Sources and Methodology

Data Sources

Debtor Reporting System

The principal sources of information for the tables in *International Debt Statistics 2016* are reports to the World Bank through the World Bank's Debtor Reporting System (DRS) from member countries that have received either International Bank for Reconstruction and Development (IBRD) loans or International Development Association (IDA) credits. The DRS has its origin in the World Bank's need to monitor and assess the financial position of its borrowers. Since 1951, borrowers have been required to provide statistics on their public external debt and private sector debt that benefit from a public guarantee. In its design, consistency, and continuity of coverage, the DRS is a unique resource. Reporting countries submit detailed reports on the annual status, transactions, and terms of the long-term external debt of public agencies and that of private ones guaranteed by a public agency in the debtor country. The DRS maintains these records on a loan-by-loan basis. In 1973, coverage of the DRS was expanded to include private sector nonguaranteed borrowing, but for this category of debt, data are provided by borrowers in aggregate rather than loan by loan.

Data submitted to the DRS are processed in the World Bank External Debt (WBXD) system, along with additional information received from the files of the African Development Bank, the Asian Development Bank, the Inter-American Development Bank (IDB), the International Monetary Fund (IMF), institutions of the World Bank Group (IBRD and IDA), and the European Bank for Reconstruction and Development (EBRD). The WBXD is an internal system of the World Bank. Among its outputs is the International Debt Statistics (IDS) database, from which the tables in this publication and online database are produced.

Data on exports and imports (on a balance of payments basis), international reserves, current account balances, foreign direct investment (FDI) on equity, portfolio equity flows, and primary income of FDI are drawn mainly from the files of the IMF, supplemented by United Nations Conference on Trade and Development (UNCTAD) reports and country data. Balance of payments data are presented according to the sixth edition of the IMF's *Balance of Payments Manual* (BPM6). Official aid flows come from data collected and published by the Development Assistance Committee (DAC) of the Organisation for Economic Co-operation and Development (OECD). Short-term external debt data are as reported by debtor countries or are estimates based on the Bank for International Settlements (BIS) quarterly series of commercial banks' claims on low- and middle income countries. For some countries, estimates were prepared by pooling creditor and debtor information. Data on the gross national income of most low- and middle income countries are collected from national statistical organizations or central banks by visiting and resident World Bank missions.

Every effort has been made to ensure the accuracy and completeness of the external debt statistics. Coverage has been improved through the efforts of the reporting agencies and close collaboration between the Bank and our partners, Commonwealth Secretariat (COMSEC) and UNCTAD, which provide debt recording and reporting systems across the globe, as well as through the work of the World Bank missions, which visit member countries to gather data and to provide technical assistance on debt issues. Nevertheless, quality and coverage vary among debtors and may also vary for the same debtor from year to year. Data on long-term external debt reported by member countries are checked against, and supplemented by, data from several other sources. Among these sources are the statements and reports of several regional development banks, government lending agencies, and official government Web sites.

Quarterly External Debt Statistics

The Quarterly External Debt Statistics (QEDS) database, jointly developed by the World Bank and the IMF, brings together detailed external debt data of countries that subscribe to the IMF's Special Data Dissemination Standard (SDDS) and a selected number of countries that participate in the IMF's General Data Dissemination System (GDDS).

In October 2014, the World Bank, in collaboration with the IMF, launched the new QEDS database in line with the classifications and definitions of the 2013 External Debt Statistics: Guide for Compilers and Users (*2013 EDS Guide*) and sixth edition of the Balance of Payments and International Investment Position Manual (*BPM6*). The QEDS database reflects new concepts and definitions, classifications of external debt data, as well as expanded coverage that enhances the analytical use of the data. The database provides quarterly information on the stock of outstanding external debt, categorized by maturity as well as by borrowing entity and debt instrument. Reporting is voluntary but as of end 2014, 72 countries plus the Euro Area reported under the SDDS, and 47 countries reported under GDDS. The benefit of bringing together comparable external debt data is to facilitate macroeconomic analysis and cross-country data comparison.

The Quarterly External Debt Database, which is maintained by the World Bank, can be accessed via the Bank's web site through the World Bank Open Data at www.databank.worldbank.org.

Quarterly Public Sector Debt

As part of the World Bank Open Data Initiative, in December 2010, the World Bank launched for the first time an online, quarterly, Public Sector Debt (PSD) database (www.worldbank.org/qpsd), developed in partnership with the IMF, which allows researchers and policy makers to explore questions about recent developments in public sector debt. The PSD database, with the endorsement of the Inter-Agency Task Force on Finance Statistics (TFFS), initially focused only on low- and middle-income, and emerging market countries; now in partnership with the OECD and Eurostat, the PSD database has been expanded to include the advanced economies. The launch of the database is one of the recommendations in the G-20 Data Gaps Initiative.[1] The PSD database facilitates timely dissemination in standard formats of external debt data. By bringing such data and metadata together in one central location, the database supports macroeconomic analysis and cross-country comparison.

The database is organized into five sets of tables on the following sectors: General government; o/w central government; o/w budgetary central government; nonfinancial public corporations; and financial public corporations. The database is structured by instruments, maturity, and by creditors as the presentation format articulated in the table 4.3 in the IMF Public Sector Debt Guide. While central government is identified as having the most important key of macroeconomic analysis, the PSD database provides data on other levels of public sector, valuation methods, and debt instruments, and clearly defined tiers of debt where appropriate for central, state, and local governments, as well as extra-budgetary agencies and funds.

As of end 2014, 75 countries participated in the Quarterly Public Sector Debt Database, which is maintained by the World Bank; it can be accessed through the Bank's web site through the World Bank Open Data at www.databank.worldbank.org.

Methodology

Aggregations

Total debt stock and other aggregate measures are derived from the summation of loan-level data on stocks and flows after conversion to a common currency. Other tabulations are compiled using terms and conditions reported in the loan-level data, such as currency composition, cancellations, rescheduling of other liabilities into long-term public and publicly guaranteed external debt, and debt buybacks.

1. Please see http://www.imf.org/external/np/g20/pdf/102909.pdf. The Public Sector Debt Database is recommendation number 18 in the Data Gaps Initiative Report.

Aggregates for regional and income groups are based on the World Bank's operational classifications, which may differ from common geographic usage or income groups used by other organizations. Country classifications of DRS reporting countries in 2014 are shown in country groups in the back of the publication. The same classification is used for all historical data shown in *International Debt Statistics* and the online tables and online database.

Currency Conversion

Data on external obligations are normally reported to the World Bank in the currency of repayment and are converted into a common currency (U.S. dollars) using official exchange rates published by the IMF.

Commitments, disbursements, and debt service payments (flows) are converted to U.S. dollars at the annual average exchange rate for the year. Debt outstanding (disbursed and undisbursed) at the end of a given year (stock) is converted at the exchange rate in effect at the end of the relevant year. Consequently, year-to-year changes in debt outstanding and disbursed may not be equal to net flows (disbursements less principal repayments); similarly, changes in debt outstanding (including undisbursed debt) may not equal commitments less repayments. Discrepancies will be particularly significant when exchange rates have moved sharply during the year. Projected debt service is converted to U.S. dollars at rates in effect at the end of December 2014.

Beginning with 1991, all ruble debt owed to the former Soviet Union has been converted at a rate of US$1 = 0.6 ruble, except in cases where a bilateral agreement specifying a different conversion rate is in place. Adoption of this methodology does not constitute an endorsement by the World Bank staff of the appropriateness or validity of the exchange rate used. That matter must be resolved bilaterally between the Russian Federation and its debtor countries.

Starting with the 1988–89 edition of *World Debt Tables* (a predecessor of IDS), all data pertaining to IBRD loans from 1985 onward are recorded at their current market value. Starting with the 1991–92 edition, all data pertaining to Asian Development Bank loans from 1989 onward are recorded at their current market value. Starting with the 1998 edition, all data pertaining to African Development Bank and African Development Fund loans from 1997 onward are recorded at their current market value.

Debt Stock and Flow Reconciliation

Because of currency conversions and the timing of transactions, there may be differences between the change in aggregate stocks from one period to the next and flows during the relevant period; changes in debt outstanding, including undisbursed amounts, will therefore differ from commitments less repayments.

Changes in the stock of debt from one period to the next can be attributed to five factors: the net flow of debt, the net change in interest arrears, the capitalization of interest, a reduction in debt resulting from debt forgiveness or other debt reduction mechanisms, and cross-currency valuation effects. Any residual difference in the change in stock not explained by one of those five factors may indicate inconsistencies in the reported data or specific phenomena prevailing in an individual country (for example, an incomplete historical series for all categories of debt). Starting in 1989, the IDS includes the debt stock reconciliation, but not all components are shown in the IDS print edition and online tables.

External Debt Restructuring

Starting in 1985, the WBXD includes information on the restructuring of debt by official creditors in the context of the Paris Club, restructuring by commercial creditors, debt swap operations, buybacks, and bond exchanges. It attempts to capture accurately the effect of debt restructuring on both external debt stocks and external debt flows, consistent with the terms on which the restructuring takes place. In the compilation and presentation of external debt data, a distinction is made between cash flows and imputed flows. According to this criterion, restructured service payments and the shift in liabilities from one financial instrument to another as a result of debt restructuring are considered to be imputed flows. Both cash flows and imputed flows are recorded separately in WBXD.

The imputed flows and stock changes associated with debt restructuring are included in the IDS tables and online database to complement the cash-basis transactions recorded in the main body of the data. Such data encompass information on the debt stock and debt flows restructured each year, the amount of principal forgiven (interest forgiven is shown as a memorandum item), and the amount of external debt stock reduced either by forgiveness or by a debt buyback operation. Changes in creditors and debtors that result from debt restructuring are also reflected. For example, when insured commercial credits are rescheduled, the creditor classification shifts from private to official (bilateral), reflecting the assumption of the assets by the official credit insurance agencies in the creditor country. The IDS data will show a reduction in the external debt owed to the original private creditors equal or similar to the amount of debt restructured and a corresponding increase in the debt owed to the new official creditor. Similarly on the debtor side, when a government accepts responsibility for the payment of restructured debt previously owed by a private enterprise, the relevant change in the debtor category will be reflected. Likewise, if short-term external debt is restructured into a long-term obligation, the stock of short-term external debt will decline and the stock of long-term external debt will rise by the amount of short-term debt restructured. In the event of a debt swap of long-term external debt (external debt to equity, external debt for nature, or external debt for development), the face value of the external debt swapped will be recorded as a decline in long-term external debt stock, but no flow transaction (principal repayment) will be recorded.

Projections of Future Disbursements and Debt Service Payments

The WBXD system projects future disbursements and future debt service payments on the assumption that every existing loan commitment will be fully used and repaid in full.

Future Disbursements

Disbursement projections are made using one of the following methods:

- *Specific schedules.* Debtor countries are requested to submit a schedule of future disbursements, if available, at the time each new loan is first reported.
- *Standard schedules.* In the absence of specific schedules, the WBXD system projects the future disbursement schedule according to the undisbursed balance of each loan at the end of the most recent reporting period.

These projected schedules are based on profiles derived from the disbursement pattern of comparable loans that fully disbursed. Thirty different profiles have been compiled corresponding to each category of creditor and, in the case of official creditors, for concessional and nonconcessional loans. Each profile is derived by applying regression analysis techniques to a body of data on actual disbursements for each fully disbursed loan in the WBXD database. The profiles are periodically updated to take into account the evolving pattern of disbursements observed for fully disbursed loans.

Future principal payments are generated by the WBXD system according to the repayment terms of each loan. Principal repayments (amortization) are based on the amount of the loan commitment. If the amortization schedule follows a set pattern (for example, equal semiannual payments), the WBXD system calculates repayments automatically using the loan commitment amount, the first and final payment dates, and the frequency of the payments. If future payments are irregular, the WBXD system requires a schedule.

Future interest payments are generated by the WBXD system according to the disbursed and outstanding balance of the loan at the beginning of the period. Using the interest rate specified in the loan contract, the first and final interest payment dates, and the frequency of payments, the WBXD system calculates the stream of future interest payments due. If interest payments are irregular, the WBXD system requires a schedule.

Future debt service payments are the sum of future principal and interest payments due on existing commitments, including the undisbursed portion. They do not include debt service payments that may become due as a result of new loans contracted in subsequent years, nor do they take into account the effect of any change to future debt service obligations resulting from actions such as prepayment or rescheduling or from cancellations that occurred after the most recent year-end data reported to the DRS.

Both projected disbursements and future debt service payments are converted into U.S. dollars using end-December 2014 exchange rates. Likewise, future interest payments on loans with a variable interest rate (for example, loans from commercial banks tied to the London Interbank Offered Rate [LIBOR]) are based on the interest rate prevailing at end-December 2014.

Treatment of Arrears

The DRS collects information on arrears of both principal and interest. Principal in arrears is included in the amount of long-term external debt outstanding and is shown separately. Interest in arrears on long-term external debt and interest in arrears on the use of IMF credit are included as part of short-term external debt outstanding and are shown separately. Clearance of interest in arrears by repayment will be recorded as an interest payment in the relevant creditor category of the loan (or loans) on which the arrears were incurred, as a corresponding reduction in the level of short-term debt outstanding, and as a net reduction in interest arrears. Clearance of interest arrears through debt restructuring or forgiveness will be recorded as a reduction in the level of short-term debt outstanding and a net reduction in interest arrears. When interests are rescheduled, they will be capitalized: This change will be recorded as an increase in long-term debt outstanding equal to the amount of interest capitalized and the reduction in short-term debt outstanding noted previously.

External Debt and Its Components

This section describes the compilation of the major components of external debt included in the IDS tables and database and the relationship between them, as shown in figure A.1 on the next page. Information about general methods of compiling external debt data is discussed in the

Figure A.1. External Debt and Its Components

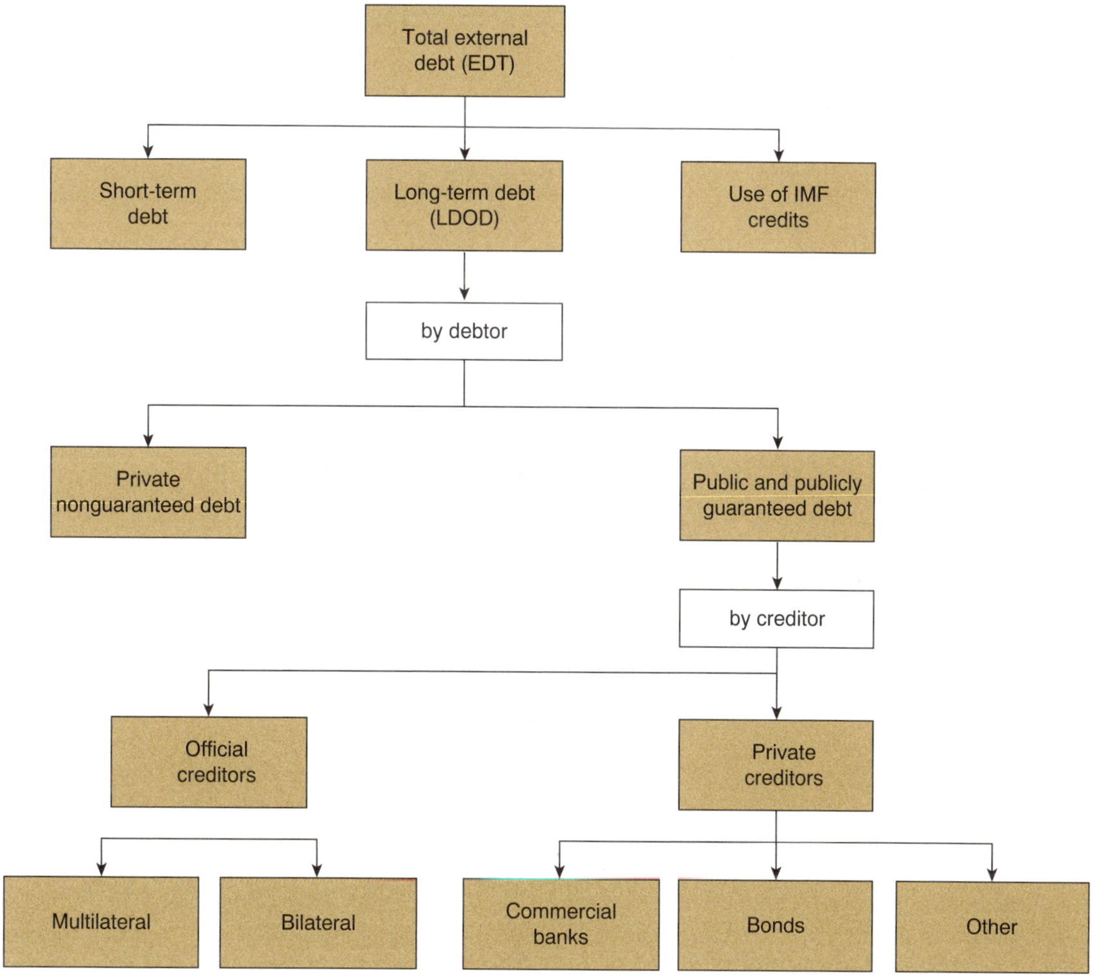

previous section titled "Methodology." For concise definitions, see the glossary.

Total External Debt

Total external debt shown in the IDS is the sum of long-term external debt, short-term debt, and IMF credit. It represents the total debt owed to nonresident creditors and is repayable in both foreign and domestic currency.

Short-Term Debt

Short-term debt is defined as external debt with an original maturity of one year or less. The DRS requires debtor countries to report only on their long-term external debt. However, to gain a comprehensive picture of total external obligations, the World Bank encourages debtor countries to voluntarily provide information on their short-term external obligations.

By its nature, short-term external debt is difficult to monitor: Loan-by-loan registration is normally impractical, and monitoring systems typically rely on information requested periodically by the central bank from the banking sector. The World Bank regards the debtor country as the authoritative source of information on its short-term debt. Unless otherwise specified in the country tables, the data for short-term debt are derived from the data provided by the quarterly external debt statistics database (see QEDS). BIS data on international bank lending is the second source of the short-term debt. These data are reported on the basis of residual maturity, but an estimate of short-term external liabilities by original maturity can be derived by deducting from claims due in one year those that, 12 months earlier, had a maturity of between one and two years. However, not all commercial banks report to the BIS in a way that allows the full maturity distribution to be determined, and the BIS data include liabilities only to banks within the BIS reporting area. Consequently, the results should be interpreted with caution.

The flow of short-term debt may be derived from the change in claims (stock) data in the BIS quarterly series over consecutive periods, but valuation adjustments resulting from exchange rate movements will affect the calculations, as will prepayment and refinancing of long-term maturities falling due. When short-term external debt has been rescheduled, lags in reporting and differences in the treatment of the rescheduled external debt by debtors and creditors may result in double counting.

Interest in arrears on long-term external debt and interest in arrears on the use of IMF credit are added to short-term debt and are separately identified.

Use of IMF Credit

Data related to the operations of the IMF are provided by the IMF Treasurer's Department. They are converted from special drawing rights (SDR) into dollars using end-of-period exchange rates for stocks and average-over-the-period exchange rates for flows. IMF trust fund operations under the Enhanced Structural Adjustment Facility, Extended Fund Facility, Poverty Reduction and Growth Facility, and Structural Adjustment Facility (Enhanced Structural Adjustment Facility in 1999) are presented together with all of the IMF's special facilities (buffer stock, supplemental reserve, compensatory and contingency facilities, oil facilities, and other facilities). SDR allocations are also included in this category. According to the BPM6, SDR allocations are recorded as the incurrence of a debt liability of the member receiving them (because of a requirement to repay the allocation in certain circumstances, and also because interest accrues). This debt item was introduced for the first time in IDS 2013 with historical data starting in 1999.

Long-Term Debt

Long-term debt has an original maturity of more than one year. It comprises the obligations of both public and private debtors. Private nonguaranteed debt comprises the external obligations of private debtors that are not guaranteed for repayment by a public entity in the debtor country.

Public and publicly guaranteed debt comprises the external obligations of public debtors and has two components: (a) public debt, which is borrowing by the national government or agency, by a political subdivision or agency, or by autonomous public bodies, and (b) publicly guaranteed debt, which is borrowing by a private agency that is guaranteed for repayment by a public entity.

Private Nonguaranteed Debt

The DRS reporting requirements were expanded in 1973 to include long-term private nonguaranteed debt. Data are reported annually on an aggregate basis and include, for the reporting year, the total amount of disbursed and outstanding debt; the amount of disbursements, principal repayments, and interest payments; the principal and interest rescheduled; and the projected principal and interest payments for future years. The aggregate data are usually reported in U.S. dollars, and no information on the underlying currency composition is given.

DRS reporting countries recognize the importance of monitoring borrowing by their private sector, particularly when it constitutes a significant portion of total external debt, but many countries acknowledge the difficulty of this process. Detailed data are available only when countries have registration requirements for private nonguaranteed debt in place, most commonly in connection with exchange controls. When formal registration of private nonguaranteed debt is not mandatory, compilers must rely on balance of payments data and financial surveys.

The data on private nonguaranteed debt in this publication is as reported or as estimated for countries where this type of external debt is known to be significant. The estimation of private nonguaranteed debt is based on the national data on quarterly external debt statistics (QEDS) or IMF data. Flows are derived from the change in stock over consecutive periods and are adjusted for the effects of exchange rate movements (assuming the currency composition mirrors that of public and publicly guaranteed debt) and for any known debt restructuring. Principal repayments are estimated on the basis of the average maturity observed for loans to private sector borrowers in countries reporting to the DRS and on the basis of the stock of debt outstanding. Interest payments are estimated on the basis of the stock of debt outstanding and interest rates prevailing in international capital markets.

Balance of payments data provide a useful guideline in the estimation process: private nonguaranteed external debt may be derived as a residual between net long-term external borrowing recorded in the balance of payments and net long-term public and publicly guaranteed external debt reported to the DRS.

Public and Publicly Guaranteed Debt

Data related to public and publicly guaranteed debt are reported to the DRS on a loan-by-loan basis. The data provide annual information on the disbursed and outstanding balance and the undisbursed balance of each loan, the cumulative disbursements, the principal and interest paid and principal and interest restructured in the reporting year, and the stock of any outstanding payment's arrears of principal and interest. Detailed information on the terms and conditions of each loan is also reported. Public debt and publicly guaranteed debt are shown as a single line in this publication and then further disaggregated by creditor type and, in the case of private creditors, by type of credit instrument.

Official Creditors

Official creditors include multilateral and bilateral lenders. In general, official creditors provide loans (and, in some cases, provide grants) to public bodies, although in some cases they may lend to other entities with a public guarantee.

Multilateral creditors are international financial institutions such as the World Bank, regional development banks, and other multilateral and intergovernmental agencies whose lending is administered on a multilateral basis. Funds administered by an international financial organization on behalf of a single donor government constitute bilateral loans (or grants). For lending by a number of multilateral creditors, the data presented in this publication are taken from the creditors' records. Such creditors include the African Development Bank, the Asian Development Bank, the IDB, IBRD, and IDA. (IBRD and IDA are institutions of the World Bank.)

Bilateral creditors are governments and their agencies, including central banks, aid agencies, official export credit agencies, and autonomous agencies such as the U.S. Department of Agriculture or the Federal Home Loan Bank. Member countries of the OECD Development Assistance Committee (DAC) and some other countries also report information on loans extended bilaterally or officially guaranteed to the Creditor Reporting System of the OECD.

Private Creditors

Private creditors include commercial banks, bondholders, and other private creditors. This line includes only publicly guaranteed creditors. Nonguaranteed private creditors are shown separately.

Bonds include publicly issued or privately placed bonds.

Commercial bank loans are loans from private banks and other private financial institutions.

Credits of other private creditors include credits from manufacturers, exporters, and other suppliers of goods, plus bank credits covered by a guarantee of an export credit agency. This line is included in the online database but is not shown in the published tables. It can be obtained as the difference between (a) credits of total private creditors and (b) bonds and commercial bank loans.

Sources of the Macroeconomic Indicators

The macroeconomic data are prepared by The World Bank from a variety of sources. Data on Personal Transfers and Compensation of Employees are prepared by World Bank staff based on IMF balance of payments statistics. Data on foreign direct investments are prepared by World Bank staff based on IMF balance of payments statistics and UNCTAD publication. Other macroeconomic data are from IMF balance of payments statistics.

Data on exports of goods, services, and primary income are gap-filled with countries' balance of payments statistics for the following countries:

Algeria (2014)
Angola (2014)
Benin (2013)
Burkina Faso (from 2011)
Cambodia (2014)
China (2014)
Comoros (from 2005)
Côte d'Ivoire (2014)
Djibouti (2014)
Dominica (2014)
Ecuador (2014)
Ghana (2014)
Grenada (2014)
Guinea-Bissau (2013)
Indonesia (2013)
Iran (2011–14)
Jordan (2014)
Kazakhstan (2014)
Lebanon (2014)
Malawi (from 2013)
Mauritania (from 2006–11)
Mongolia (2014)
Morocco (2014)
Nigeria (from 2013)
Peru (2014)
Samoa (2014)
São Tomé and Príncipe (2013)
Senegal (2013)
Serbia (2014)
Solomon Islands (2014)
Togo (2013)
Uganda (2014)

Data on imports of goods, services, and primary income are gap-filled with countries' balance of payments statistics for the following countries:

Algeria (2014)
Angola (2014)
Benin (2013)
Burkina Faso (from 2011)
Cambodia (2014)
China (2014)
Comoros (from 2005)
Côte d'Ivoire (2014)
Djibouti (2014)
Dominica (2014)
Ecuador (2014)
Ghana (2014)
Grenada (2014)
Guinea-Bissau (2013)
Indonesia (2013)
Iran (2011–14)
Jordan (2014)
Kazakhstan (2014)
Lebanon (2014)
Malawi (from 2013)
Mauritania (2006–2011)
Mongolia (2014)
Morocco (2014)
Nigeria (from 2013)
Peru (2014)
Samoa (2014)
São Tomé and Príncipe (2013)
Senegal (2013)
Serbia (2014)
Solomon Islands (2014)
Tanzania (2013)
Togo (2013)
Uganda (2014)

Data on current account balance are based on countries' balance of payments statistics for the following countries:

Algeria (2014)
Benin (from 2013)
Burkina Faso (from 2011)
Cambodia (2014)
Central African Republic (from 2005)
Chad (from 2005)
China (2014)
Comoros (from 2005)
Congo, Rep. (from 2010)
Côte d'Ivoire (2014)
Ecuador (2014)
Fiji (2014)
Gabon (from 2006)
Ghana (2014)
Guinea-Bissau (from 2013)
Indonesia (2014)
Jordan (2014)
Kazakhstan (2014)
Malawi (from 2013)
Malaysia (2014)
Mali (2014)
Mauritania (2007–2011)
Mongolia (2014)
Niger (2014)
Nigeria (from 2013)
Papua New Guinea (from 2013)
Peru (2014)
Samoa (2014)
Senegal (from 2012)
Serbia (2014)
Solomon Islands (2014)
St. Lucia (2014)
St. Vincent (2014)
Tanzania (2014)
Togo (from 2012)
Uganda (2014)
Vietnam (2014)
Zimbabwe (from 2005)

Data on personal transfers and compensation of employees are based on countries' balance of payments statistics for the following countries:

Honduras (2014)
Mongolia (2014)
Nigeria (from 2013)
Solomon Islands (2014)

Data on portfolio equity are based on countries' balance of payments statistics for the following countries:

Burkina Faso (from 2011)
China (2014)
Ecuador (2014)
Malawi (from 2013)
Mongolia (2014)
Nigeria (from 2013)
Uganda (2014)

Data on foreign direct investment are based on countries' balance of payments statistics for the following countries:

China (2014)
Dominica (2014)
Kazakhstan (2014)
Malaysia (from 2010)
Mongolia (2014)
Samoa (2014)
Solomon Islands (2014)
Tanzania (2014)
Uganda (2014)
Vietnam (2014)

Country Groups

Regional Groups

East Asia and Pacific

Cambodia (A)
China (P)
Fiji (A)
Indonesia (A)
Lao PDR (A)
Malaysia (E)
Mongolia (A)
Myanmar (E)
Papua New Guinea (A)
Philippines (A)
Samoa (A)
Solomon Islands (E)
Thailand (A)
Tonga (A)
Vanuatu (E)
Vietnam (A)

Europe and Central Asia

Albania (A)
Armenia (A)
Azerbaijan (A)
Belarus (A)
Bosnia and Herzegovina[a] (A)
Bulgaria (A)
Georgia (A)
Kazakhstan (A)
Kosovo (A)
Kyrgyz Republic (A)
Macedonia, FYR (A)
Moldova (A)
Montenegro (A)
Romania (A)
Serbia[a,b] (A)
Tajikistan (A)
Turkey (A)
Turkmenistan (E)
Ukraine (A)
Uzbekistan (A)

Latin America and the Caribbean

Belize (A)
Bolivia (A)
Brazil (A)
Colombia (A)
Costa Rica (A)
Dominica (A)
Dominican Republic (A)
Ecuador (A)
El Salvador (A)
Grenada (A)
Guatemala (A)
Guyana (A)
Haiti (A)
Honduras (A)
Jamaica (A)
Mexico (A)
Nicaragua (A)
Panama (A)
Paraguay (A)
Peru (A)
St. Lucia (A)
St. Vincent and the Grenadines (A)

Middle East and North Africa

Algeria (A)
Djibouti (A)
Egypt, Arab Rep. (A)
Iran, Islamic Rep. (A)
Jordan (A)
Lebanon (A)
Morocco (A)
Syrian Arab Republic (E)
Tunisia (A)
Yemen, Rep. (E)

South Asia

Afghanistan (A)
Bangladesh (P)
Bhutan (A)
India (A)
Maldives (A)
Nepal (A)
Pakistan (A)
Sri Lanka (A)

Sub-Saharan Africa

Angola (A)
Benin (A)
Botswana (E)
Burkina Faso (A)
Burundi (A)
Cabo Verde (A)
Cameroon (A)
Central African Republic (A)
Chad (E)
Comoros (A)
Congo, Dem. Rep. (P)
Congo, Rep. (A)
Côte d'Ivoire (A)
Eritrea (E)
Ethiopia (A)
Gabon (E)
Gambia, The (A)
Ghana (A)
Guinea (A)
Guinea-Bissau (E)
Kenya (A)
Lesotho (A)
Liberia (A)
Madagascar (A)
Malawi (A)
Mali (A)
Mauritania (A)
Mauritius (A)
Mozambique (A)
Niger (A)
Nigeria (A)
Rwanda (A)
São Tomé and Príncipe (A)
Senegal (A)
Sierra Leone (A)
Somalia (E)
South Africa (P)
Sudan[c] (P)
Swaziland (A)
Tanzania (A)
Togo (A)
Uganda (A)
Zambia (A)
Zimbabwe (A)

Note: Letters in parenthesis indicate DRS reporters' status: (A) as reported, (P) preliminary, and (E) estimated. The status "as reported" indicates that the country was fully current in its reporting under the DRS and that World Bank staff are satisfied that the reported data give an adequate and fair representation of the country's total public debt. "Preliminary" data are based on reported or collected information, but because of incompleteness or other reasons, an element of staff estimation is included. "Estimated" data indicate that countries are not current in their reporting and that a significant element of staff estimation has been necessary in producing the data tables.

a. For Bosnia and Herzegovina, total debt before 1999, excluding IBRD and IMF obligations and short-term debt, is included under Serbia.
b. Data prior to 2006 include Montenegro.
c. Data include South Sudan.

Income Groups

Low-income countries

Afghanistan
Benin
Burkina Faso
Burundi
Cambodia
Central African Republic
Chad
Comoros
Congo, Dem. Rep.
Eritrea
Ethiopia
Gambia, The
Guinea
Guinea-Bissau
Haiti
Liberia
Madagascar
Malawi
Mali
Mozambique
Nepal
Niger
Rwanda
Sierra Leone
Somalia
Tanzania
Togo
Uganda
Zimbabwe

Middle-income countries

Albania
Algeria
Angola
Armenia
Azerbaijan
Bangladesh
Belarus
Belize
Bhutan
Bolivia
Bosnia and Herzegovina
Botswana
Brazil
Bulgaria
Cabo Verde
Cameroon
China
Colombia
Congo, Rep.
Costa Rica
Côte d'Ivoire
Djibouti
Dominica
Dominican Republic
Ecuador
Egypt, Arab Rep.
El Salvador
Fiji
Gabon
Georgia
Ghana
Grenada
Guatemala
Guyana
Honduras
India
Indonesia
Iran, Islamic Rep.
Jamaica
Jordan
Kazakhstan
Kenya
Kosovo
Kyrgyz Republic
Lao PDR
Lebanon
Lesotho
Macedonia, FYR
Malaysia
Maldives
Mauritania
Mauritius
Mexico
Moldova
Mongolia
Montenegro
Morocco
Myanmar
Nicaragua
Nigeria
Pakistan
Panama
Papua New Guinea
Paraguay
Peru
Philippines
Romania
Samoa
São Tomé and Príncipe
Senegal
Serbia
Solomon Islands
South Africa
Sri Lanka
St. Lucia
St. Vincent and the Grenadines
Sudan
Swaziland
Syrian Arab Republic
Tajikistan
Thailand
Tonga
Tunisia
Turkey
Turkmenistan
Ukraine
Uzbekistan
Vanuatu
Vietnam
Yemen, Rep.
Zambia

Note: Low-income countries are those with a GNI per capita of $1,045 or less in 2014. Middle-income countries are those with a GNI per capita of more than $1,046 but less than $12,736. Italicized countries are IDA-only countries as of July 1, 2015; IDA-only excludes blend and IBRD countries.

Glossary

Debt Reporting System (DRS)

Average terms of new commitments provide information on the interest rate, maturity, and grace period of new commitments on public and publicly guaranteed external debt contracted with public and private creditors. Averages are weighted by the amounts of the loans.

Bilateral official creditors are official agencies that make loans on behalf of one government to another government or to public (and, in some cases, private) borrowers in another country.

Bonds are debt instruments issued by public and publicly guaranteed or private debtors with durations of one year or longer. Bonds usually give the holder the unconditional right to fixed money income or contractually determined, variable money income.

Commercial banks are private banks that provide loans and other financial services.

Commitments of public and publicly guaranteed debt constitute the total amount of new long-term loans to public sector borrowers or borrowers with a public sector guarantee extended by official and private lenders and for which contracts were signed in the year specified.

Concessional debt conveys information about the borrower's receipt of aid from official lenders at concessional terms as defined by the DAC, that is, loans with an original grant element of 25 percent or more. Loans from major regional development banks—African Development Bank, Asian Development Bank, and the Inter-American Development Bank—and from the World Bank are classified as concessional according to each institution's classification and not according to the DAC definition, as was the practice in earlier reports.

Contractual obligations on outstanding long-term external debt are the anticipated debt service payments on long-term external debt contracted up to December 31 of the reporting year.

Currency composition of public and publicly guaranteed debt provides information on the share of loans outstanding and disbursed by currency of repayment. For major multilateral creditors, the currency composition of the relevant unit of account is also taken into account. The principal currencies in which the external debt of low- and middle-income countries is contracted (the euro, Japanese yen, U.S. dollar, SDR, and all other currencies) are separately identified. Beginning in 2001, debt denominated in the currencies of the members in the Euro Area is included under the euro rather than the national currencies that previously prevailed.

Current account balance shows the difference between the sum of exports and income receivable and the sum of imports and income payable (exports and imports refer to both goods and services, while income refers to both primary and secondary income).

Debt buyback is the repurchase by a debtor of its own debt, either at a discount price or at par value. In the event of a buyback of long-term debt, the face value of the debt bought back will be recorded as a decline in stock outstanding of long-term debt, and the cash amount received by creditors will be recorded as a principal repayment. For example, if a country buys back long-term external debt of face value B at a price P, then long-term external debt will decline by B, and principal repayment will increase by P. The difference between the price at which the debt was bought back and the face value is recorded as a debt stock write-off (the related transactions are not separately identified in the International Debt Statistics [IDS] publication but are available in the online database).

Debt forgiveness grants include both debts canceled by agreement between debtor and creditor and reductions in the net present value of official nonconcessional loans resulting from concessional rescheduling or refinancing. Data are recorded on a disbursement basis and include debt forgiveness from bilateral and multilateral creditors.

Debt outstanding and disbursed is the value at year's end of long-term external debt owed by public and publicly guaranteed debtors and private nonguaranteed debtors.

Debt restructurings are revisions to debt service obligations agreed on by creditors and debtors. Such agreements change the amount and timing of future principal and interest payments.

Debt service to exports is the ratio of the sum of principal repayments and interest paid on total long-term debt (public and publicly guaranteed debt and private nonguaranteed debt) to the value of exports of goods and services and receipts of primary income from abroad.

Debt stock-flow reconciliation shows the indicators that affect the change in debt stocks from one period to the next.

Disbursements are drawings during the year specified on loan commitments contracted by the borrower.

Exports of goods, services, and primary income constitute the total value of exports of goods and services, receipts of compensation of nonresident workers, and investment income from abroad.

External debt flows are debt-related transactions during the year specified. They include disbursements, principal repayments, and interest payments.

External debt stocks comprise public and publicly guaranteed long-term external debt, private nonguaranteed long-term external debt, use of IMF credit, and short-term external debt, including interest arrears on long-term debt. The relation between external debt stock and its components is illustrated on page 159 (figure A.1).

External debt stocks to exports is the ratio of outstanding external debt to the value of exports of goods and services and receipts of primary income from abroad.

External debt stocks to GNI is the ratio of outstanding external debt to gross national income.

Foreign direct investment refers to direct investment equity flows in the reporting economy. It is the sum of equity capital, reinvestment earnings, and other capital. Direct investment is a category of cross-border investment associated with a resident in one economy having control or a significant degree of influence on the management of an enterprise that is resident in another economy. Ownership of 10 percent or more of the ordinary shares or voting stock is the criterion for determining the existence of a direct investment relationship.

Grace period is the time between the date on which a loan is committed and the date on which the first principal payment is due. The information presented in International Debt Statistics is the average grace period on all public and publicly guaranteed debt committed during the specified period.

Grants are legally binding commitments that obligate a specific value of funds available for disbursement for which there is no payment requirement. They include debt forgiveness grants and grants from bilateral and multilateral agencies (such as the International Development Association).

Gross national income (GNI) is the sum of value added by all resident producers, plus any product taxes (less subsidies) not included in the valuation of output, plus net receipts of primary income compensation of employees and property income from abroad. Yearly average exchange rates are used to convert GNI from local currency to U.S. dollars.

Heavily Indebted Poor Country (HIPC) Initiative is a program of the World Bank and the International Monetary Fund (IMF) to provide debt relief to qualifying countries with unsustainable debt burdens.

Imports of goods, services, and primary income constitute the total value of goods and services imported and income payable to nonresidents. Interest arrears on long-term debt are interest payments due but not paid, shown on a cumulative basis.

Interest arrears are due and payable immediately and are therefore regarded as short-term obligations. Thus, an increase in interest arrears on long-term debt will be recorded as an increase in short-term debt. Interest in arrears on the use of IMF credit is also considered to be part of short-term external debt.

Interest payments are the amounts of interest paid in foreign currency, goods, or services in the year specified.

Interest rate is the interest rate applicable to a loan commitment as specified in the loan contract. The information presented in International Debt Statistics is the average interest on all public and publicly guaranteed debt committed during the specified period.

International Bank for Reconstruction and Development (IBRD) is a multilateral official creditor. IBRD is the nonconcessional lending arm of the World Bank Group.

International Development Association (IDA) is a multilateral official creditor. It is the concessional financing arm of the World Bank Group. IDA also provides grant financing to qualified borrowers.

IMF charges are the amounts of interest paid in foreign currency in the year specified for transactions with the IMF.

IMF purchases are the total drawings on the general resources account of the IMF during the year specified, excluding drawings in the reserve tranche.

IMF repurchases are the amounts of principal (amortization) paid in foreign currency in the year specified for transactions with the IMF.

International reserves constitute the sum of a country's monetary authority's holdings of special drawing rights, its reserve position in the IMF, its holdings of foreign exchange, and its holdings of gold (valued at year-end London prices).

Long-term external debt is debt that has an original or extended maturity of more than one year and that is owed to nonresidents by residents of an economy and is repayable in foreign currency, goods, or services.

Long-term private sector debt is long-term debt owed by the private sector, whether publicly guaranteed or not.

Long-term public sector debt is long-term external debt owed by the public sector.

Maturity is the date on which the final principal repayment on a loan is due. It is the sum of the grace and repayment periods. The information presented in International Debt Statistics is the average maturity on all public and publicly guaranteed debt committed during the specified period.

Multilateral Debt Relief Initiative (MDRI) is a program of the World Bank, the IMF, the Inter-American Development Bank, and the African Development Bank that provides additional debt relief to countries that have completed the HIPC process.

Multilateral official creditors are official agencies owned or governed by more than one country that provide loan financing. They include international financial institutions such as the World Bank, regional development banks, and other intergovernmental agencies.

Multilateral to external debt stocks is the ratio of the stock of debt owed to multilateral creditors to total external debt.

Net flows on external debt are disbursements on long-term external debt and IMF purchases minus principal repayments on long-term external debt and IMF repurchases. Up to 1984, this calculation included only long-term external debt and IMF flows. Since 1985, the calculation includes the change in stock of short-term debt (excluding interest arrears on long-term external debt).

Official creditors are governments or other bilateral public entities, such as export-import agencies, development agencies, and multilateral financial institutions, such as the World Bank and regional development banks.

Personal transfers and compensation of employees is the sum of personal transfers and compensation of employees. Personal transfers consist of all current transfers in cash or in kind made or received by resident households to or from nonresident households. Personal transfers thus include all current transfers between resident and nonresident individuals. Compensation of employees refers to the income of border, seasonal, and other short-term workers who are employed in an economy where they are not resident and of residents employed by nonresident entities.

Portfolio equity is the category of international investment that covers investment in equity securities. Equity securities include shares, stocks, participation, or similar documents (such as American Depositary Receipts) that usually denote ownership of equity.

Present value of debt outstanding is the nominal value of all future debt service obligations on existing debt discounted at prevailing market rates of interest. The interest rates used in this calculation are the Commercial Interest Reference Rates (CIRR) for each relevant currency compiled and published by the Organisation for Economic Cooperation and Development.

Primary income on FDI are payments of direct investment income (debit side), which consist of income on equity (dividends, branch profits, and reinvested earnings) and income on the intercompany debt (interest).

Principal arrears on long-term debt are principal repayments due but not paid on long-term external debt, shown on a cumulative basis.

Principal repayments are the amounts of principal (amortization) paid in foreign currency, goods, or services in the year specified with respect to long-term external debt.

Private creditors are bondholders, commercial banks, and other trade-related lenders.

Private nonguaranteed debt is debt owed by private sector borrowers to external creditors on loans that do not benefit from a public sector guarantee by the debtor country.

Public and publicly guaranteed debt outstanding and disbursed is the value of debt at year's end of public sector borrowers, or borrowers with a public sector guarantee, owed to official and private lenders.

Public and publicly guaranteed external debt comprises public debt (an external obligation of a public debtor, such as the national government or agency, a political subdivision or agency, or an autonomous public body) and publicly guaranteed external debt (an external obligation of a private debtor that is guaranteed for repayment by a public entity).

Public debt is an external obligation of a public debtor, including the national government, a political subdivision (or an agency of either), and autonomous public bodies.

Publicly guaranteed debt is an external obligation of a private debtor that is guaranteed for repayment by a public entity.

Reserves to external debt stocks is the ratio of international reserves to outstanding external debt.

Reserves to imports (months) is the ratio of international reserves to the value of imports of goods, services, and primary income in the year shown and is expressed in months:

$$\frac{\text{Reserves}}{\text{Imports/12}}$$

Short-term external debt has an original maturity of one year or less. Available data permit no distinction among public, publicly guaranteed, and private nonguaranteed short-term external debt.

Short-term to external debt stock ratio is the ratio of short-term external debt to total outstanding external debt.

Special Drawing Rights (SDRs) refer to an international reserve asset that was created by the IMF in 1969 to supplement its member countries' official reserves. The value of SDRs is based on a basket of four key international currencies: the U.S. dollar, the pound sterling, the Japanese yen, and the euro. In addition to playing a role as a supplementary reserve asset, SDRs serve as the unit of account for the IMF and some other international organizations.

Technical cooperation grants include (a) free-standing technical cooperation grants, which are intended to finance the transfer of technical and managerial skills or of technology for the purpose of building up general national capacity without reference to any specific investment projects, and (b) investment-related technical cooperation grants, which are aimed at strengthening the capacity to execute specific investment projects.

Total amount forgiven is the total amount of principal and interest due, principal and interest in arrears, and debt stock forgiven in the year specified.

Total amount rescheduled is the total amount of external debt rescheduled, including principal and interest due, principal and interest in arrears, charges, penalties, and debt stock in the year specified.

Total change in external debt stocks is the difference in the external debt stock between two consecutive years.

Use of IMF credit denotes members' drawings on the IMF other than amounts drawn against the country's reserve tranche position. Use of IMF credit includes purchases and drawings under Stand-By, Extended, Structural Adjustment, Enhanced Structural Adjustment, and Systemic Transformation Facility Arrangements as well as trust fund loans. SDR allocations are also included in this category.

Quarterly Debt Statistics

Central bank sector is identical to the definition of that subsector in the 2008 System of National Accounts (SNA). The central bank is the financial institution (or institutions) that exercises control over key aspects of the financial system. It carries out such activities as issuing currency, managing international reserves, transacting with the IMF, and providing credit to deposit-taking corporations.

Central government subsector consists of the institutional unit(s) of the central government plus those nonmarket Non-profit institutions that are controlled by the central government. The political authority of the central government extends over the entire territory of the country.

Currency and deposits consist of notes and coins and deposits (both transferable and other). Notes and coins represent claims of a fixed nominal value usually on a central bank or government; commemorative coins are excluded. Deposits include all claims that are (a) on the central bank, deposit-taking corporations other than the central bank, and, in some cases, other institutional units; and (b) represented by evidence of deposit.

Debt liabilities owed by residents to residents of the same economy are classified as *domestic debt*, and debt liabilities owed by residents to nonresidents are classified as *external debt*. The definition of residence follows the current international standards (the System of National Accounts 2008 [2008 SNA] and the *Balance of Payments and International Investment Position Manual*, Sixth Edition [BPM6]).

Debt securities are negotiable financial instruments serving as evidence of a debt. The security normally specifies a schedule for interest payments and principal repayments. Examples of debt securities are bills, bonds, and debentures, including bonds that are convertible into shares, commercial paper, negotiable certificates of deposit, loans that have become negotiable from one holder to another, nonparticipating preferred stocks or shares, asset-backed securities and collateralized debt obligations, banker's acceptances, and similar instruments normally traded in the financial markets.

Deposit-taking corporations, except the central bank sector is identical with the corresponding subsector in the 2008 SNA. It includes commercial banks, institutions such as savings banks, savings and loan associations, credit unions or cooperatives, traveler's check companies, and specialized banks or other financial institutions if they take deposits or issue close substitutes for deposits Post office savings banks or other government-controlled savings banks are also included if they are institutional units separate from the government. Deposit-taking corporations that engage exclusively (or almost exclusively) with nonresidents, often called offshore banks or offshore banking units, are included in the deposit-taking corporations sector, but they may be excluded from the money-issuing sector because their liabilities are not included in broad money.

General government sector is identical with the definition of that sector in the 2008 SNA. The government units of a country consist of those authorities and their agencies that are units established by political processes and exercise legislative, judicial, and executive authority over other institutional units within a given territorial area. General government agencies that are residents of an economy include all departments, establishments, and bodies located in the economic territory of an economy's central, state, and local governments and all embassies, consulates, military establishments, and other entities, which are located elsewhere, of an economy's general government.

Insurance, pension, and standardized guarantee schemes comprise (a) nonlife insurance technical reserves, (b) life insurance and annuity entitlements, (c) pension entitlements, claims of pension funds on pension managers, and entitlements to nonpension funds, and (d) provisions for calls under standardized guarantees.

Loans include those financial assets created through the direct lending of funds by a creditor (lender) to a debtor (borrower) through an arrangement in which the lender either receives no security evidencing the transactions or receives a nonnegotiable document or instrument.

Other accounts receivable/payable covers items other than equity; currency and deposits; loans; insurance, pension, and standardized guarantee schemes; trade credit and advances; and SDRs.

Other sectors comprises other financial corporations (i.e., other than deposit-taking corporations), nonfinancial corporations, and households and nonprofit institutions serving households (NPISHs) subsectors.

SDR allocations are recorded as the incurrence of a debt liability of the member receiving them (because of a requirement to repay the allocation in certain circumstances, and also because of interest accrues).

Trade credit and advances consist of liabilities arising from the direct extension of credit by suppliers for transactions in goods and services, and advance payments by buyers for goods and services and for work in progress (or to be undertaken).

ECO-AUDIT

Environmental Benefits Statement

The World Bank Group is committed to reducing its environmental footprint. In support of this commitment, the Publishing and Knowledge Division leverages electronic publishing options and print-on-demand technology, which is located in regional hubs worldwide. Together, these initiatives enable print runs to be lowered and shipping distances decreased, resulting in reduced paper consumption, chemical use, greenhouse gas emissions, and waste.

The Publishing and Knowledge Division follows the recommended standards for paper use set by the Green Press Initiative. The majority of our books are printed on Forest Stewardship Council (FSC)–certified paper, with nearly all containing 50–100 percent recycled content. The recycled fiber in our book paper is either unbleached or bleached using totally chlorine free (TCF), processed chlorine free (PCF), or enhanced elemental chlorine free (EECF) processes.

More information about the Bank's environmental philosophy can be found at http://crinfo.worldbank.org/wbcrinfo/node/4.

green press INITIATIVE